A HISTORY OF FEMINIST LITER

Feminism has transformed the academic study of literature, fundamentally altering the canon of what is taught and setting new agendas for literary analysis. In this authoritative history of feminist literary criticism, leading scholars chart the development of the practice from the Middle Ages to the present. The first section of the book explores protofeminist thought from the Middle Ages onwards, and analyses the work of pioneers such as Wollstonecraft and Woolf. The second section examines the rise of second-wave feminism and maps its interventions across the twentieth century. A final section examines the impact of postmodernism on feminist thought and practice. This book offers a comprehensive guide to the history and development of feminist literary criticism and a lively reassessment of the main issues and authors in the field. It is essential reading for all students and scholars of feminist writing and literary criticism.

GILL PLAIN is Professor of English at the University of St Andrews, Scotland.

SUSAN SELLERS is Professor of English at the University of St Andrews, Scotland.

A HISTORY OF FEMINIST LITERARY CRITICISM

EDITED BY
GILL PLAIN
AND
SUSAN SELLERS

CAMBRIDGE
UNIVERSITY PRESS

CAMBRIDGE UNIVERSITY PRESS
Cambridge, New York, Melbourne, Madrid, Cape Town,
Singapore, São Paulo, Delhi, Mexico City

Cambridge University Press
32 Avenue of the Americas, New York, NY 10013-2473, USA

www.cambridge.org
Information on this title: www.cambridge.org/9781107609471

First published 2007
Fourth printing 2009
First paperback edition 2012

A catalogue record for this publication is available from the British Library.

ISBN 978-0-521-85255-5 Hardback
ISBN 978-1-107-60947-1 Paperback

Contents

v

Acknowledgements

Our thanks are due to the School of English at the University of St Andrews for the research funding, leave and support that have helped us to complete this project. Hope Jennings provided invaluable help with the compilation of the book – we could not have done this without her – and a number of people in St Andrews were generous in the provision of practical support. In particular we should like to thank the secretaries in the School of English: Jill Gamble, Jane Sommerville, Sandra McDevitt and Frances Mullan.

Susan Sellers would like to thank the Leverhulme Trust for the funding of a period of leave during which this project was first conceived, and we should both like to thank Ray Ryan and Maartje Scheltens at Cambridge University Press. Ray commissioned the book and supported it throughout its development, while Maartje carefully guided the book and us through the production process.

An enormous number of people helped in the preparation of the project, offering vital suggestions as we progressed. Inadequate records were kept of our many debts, but amongst those giving welcome advice were Sara Ahmed, Isobel Armstrong, Kate Chedgzoy, Priyamvada Gopal, Mary Jacobus, Jackie Jones, Judith Halberstam, Berthold Schoene, Elaine Showalter and Frances Spalding. Above all we would like to thank our contributors for their unstinting professionalism and enthusiasm for the project. We feel privileged to have had such an excellent group of critics devoting their time to the book.

Finally, we would like to dedicate this book to Jo Campling and to the many other feminist critics who have helped and inspired us over the years.

Contributors

LINDA ANDERSON is Professor of Modern English and American Literature at the University of Newcastle Upon Tyne. Her publications include *Women and Autobiography in the Twentieth Century* (1997), *Territories of Desire in Queer Culture* (with David Alderson, 2000), *Autobiography* (2001) and *Elizabeth Bishop: Poet of the Periphery* (with Jo Shapcott, 2002).

HELEN CARR is Professor in the Department of English and Comparative Literature at Goldsmiths College, University of London. She is the editor of *From My Guy to Sci-Fi: Women's Writing and Genre in the Postmodern World* (1989), and author of *Inventing the American Primitive* (1996) and *Jean Rhys* (1996). She was a co-founder and co-editor of *Women's Review* and is a co-founder and co-editor of *Women: A Cultural Review*.

CLAIRE COLEBROOK is Professor of English Literature at the University of Edinburgh and is the author of a number of books on Deleuze, literary criticism and literary theory. Her publications include *Ethics and Representation* (1999), *Gilles Deleuze* (2002) and *Gender* (2004).

CAROLYN DINSHAW is Professor of English and Social and Cultural Analysis at New York University, where she founded the Center for the Study of Gender and Sexuality. She is the author of *Chaucer's Sexual Poetics* (1989) and *Getting Medieval: Sexualities and Communities, Pre- and Postmodern* (1999), co-editor of *The Cambridge Companion to Medieval Women's Writing* (2003) and founding co-editor of *GLQ: A Journal of Lesbian and Gay Studies*.

MARY EAGLETON is Reader in the School of Cultural Studies at Leeds Metropolitan University. Her research interests focus on feminist literary history and theory, and contemporary women's writing. She has published widely in both areas. Recent publications include *A Concise Companion to Feminist Thought* (2003) and *Figuring the Woman Author in Contemporary Fiction* (2005).

ELIZABETH FALLAIZE is Professor of French Literature at the University of Oxford, and a Fellow of St John's College. Her books include *The Novels of Simone de Beauvoir* (1988), *French Women's Writing: Recent Fiction* (1993), *Simone de Beauvoir: A Critical Reader* (1998) and *French Fiction in the Mitterrand Years* (with C. Davis, 2000).

STACY GILLIS is Lecturer in Modern and Contemporary Literature at the University of Newcastle. She has published widely on cybertheory, cyberpunk and feminist theory. The co-editor of *Third Wave Feminism* (2004) and editor of *The Matrix Trilogy: Cyberpunk Reloaded* (2005), she is currently working on a monograph about British detective fiction.

JANE GOLDMAN is Reader in English at the University of Glasgow and General Editor, with Susan Sellers, of the Cambridge University Press Edition of the Writings of Virginia Woolf. She is the author of *Modernism, 1910–1945: Image to Apocalypse* (2004), *The Cambridge Introduction to Virginia Woolf* (2006) and *The Feminist Aesthetics of Virginia Woolf: Modernism, Post-Impressionism, and the Politics of the Visual* (1998).

CAROLINE GONDA is a Fellow and Director of Studies in English at St Catharine's College, Cambridge. She is the author of *Reading Daughters' Fictions 1709–1834: Novels and Society from Manley to Edgeworth* (1996) and editor of *Tea and Leg-Irons: New Feminist Readings from Scotland* (1992). She is the co-editor with Chris Mounsey of *Queer People: Negotiations and Expressions of Homosexuality 1700–1800* (2007). She has also written on British eighteenth-century and Romantic literature, on lesbian theory, children's literature and contemporary Scottish lesbian writing.

SUSAN GUBAR, Distinguished Professor of English at Indiana University, is the co-author with Sandra M. Gilbert of *The Madwoman in the Attic* (1979) and its three-volume sequel *No Man's Land* (1988). Besides co-editing the *Norton Anthology of Literature by Women* (1996), she has published a number of books including *Racechanges: White Skin, Black Face in American Culture* (1997), *Critical Condition: Feminism at the Turn of the Century* (2000) and *Poetry after Auschwitz* (2003).

ARLENE R. KEIZER is Associate Professor of English and American Civilization at Brown University. She is the author of *Black Subjects: Identity Formation in the Contemporary Narrative of Slavery* (2004), as well as articles and poems in *African American Review, American*

Literature, Kenyon Review and other journals. She is currently at work on a book on African-diaspora intellectuals and psychoanalysis.

HEATHER LOVE is Assistant Professor of Twentieth-Century Literature and Gender Studies in the English Department at the University of Pennsylvania. She has published articles on topics in modernism and queer theory in *GLQ, New Literary History, Feminist Theory, Postmodern Culture* and *Transition*. Her first book, *Feeling Backward: Loss and the Politics of Queer History* (2007), is published by Harvard University Press.

SUSAN MANLY is Lecturer in English at the University of St Andrews. She is the editor of Maria Edgeworth's *Harrington* and *Practical Education*, and the co-editor of *Helen* and *Leonora*, all in the twelve-volume *Novels and Selected Works of Maria Edgeworth* (1999/2003). She is also the editor of a paperback edition of *Harrington* (2004), and the author of *Language, Custom and Nation in the 1790s* (2007).

GILL PLAIN is Professor of English Literature and Popular Culture in the School of English at the University of St Andrews. Her publications include: *Women's Fiction of the Second World War* (1996), *Twentieth-Century Crime Fiction: Gender, Sexuality and the Body* (2001) and *John Mills and British Cinema: Masculinity, Identity and Nation* (2006). She is currently working on a literary history of the 1940s.

MADELON SPRENGNETHER is Professor of English at the University of Minnesota, where she teaches literature and creative writing. She has edited several books of feminist criticism, including *The (M)other Tongue: Essays in Feminist Psychoanalytic Interpretation* (1985), *Revising the Word and the World* (1993) and *Shakespearean Tragedy and Gender* (1996). She is also the author of *The Spectral Mother: Freud, Feminism and Psychoanalysis* (1990).

SUSAN SELLERS is Professor of English and Related Literature at the University of St Andrews. Her publications include *Myth and Fairy Tale in Contemporary Women's Fiction* (2001), *Hélène Cixous* (1996), *Language and Sexual Difference* (1995) and *Feminist Criticism* (1991). She is currently working on a scholarly edition of the writings of Virginia Woolf.

JUDITH STILL is Professor of French and Critical Theory at the University of Nottingham. Her books include *Justice and Difference in the Work of Rousseau* (1993) and *Feminine Economies: Thinking Against the Market in the Enlightenment and the Late Twentieth Century* (1997). She is the editor of *Men's Bodies* (2003) and also co-editor of *Textuality and Sexuality* (1993),

Women and Representation (1995) and *Brazilian Feminisms* (1999). She is currently researching theories and representations of hospitality.

CALVIN THOMAS is Associate Professor of English at Georgia State University. He is the author of *Male Matters: Masculinity, Anxiety, and the Male Body on the Line* (1996) and the editor of *Straight with a Twist: Queer Theory and the Subject of Heterosexuality* (2000). He is currently working on a book to be called *Adventures in Abjection*.

CHRIS WEEDON is Professor and Chair of the Centre for Critical and Cultural Theory at Cardiff University. She has published widely on feminism, cultural theory and women's writing. Her books include *Feminist Practice and Poststructuralist Theory* (1987), *Cultural Politics: Class, Gender, Race and the Postmodern World* (1995), *Feminism, Theory and the Politics of Difference* (1999), *Identity and Culture* (2004) and *Gender, Feminism and Fiction in Germany 1840–1914* (2007).

HELEN WILCOX is Professor of English at the University of Wales, Bangor. Her interests are in early modern literature, particularly devotional poetry, Shakespeare, women's writing, feminist criticism and the relationship of literature to music. Her publications include *Women and Literature in Britain, 1500–1700* (1996) and the co-edited collections *Her Own Life: Autobiographical Writings by Seventeenth-Century Englishwomen* (1989) and *Betraying Our Selves: Forms of Self-Representation in Early Modern English Texts* (2000).

Introduction

Gill Plain and Susan Sellers

The impact of feminism on literary criticism over the past thirty-five years has been profound and wide-ranging. It has transformed the academic study of literary texts, fundamentally altering the canon of what is taught and setting a new agenda for analysis, as well as radically influencing the parallel processes of publishing, reviewing and literary reception. A host of related disciplines have been affected by feminist literary enquiry, including linguistics, philosophy, history, religious studies, sociology, anthropology, film and media studies, cultural studies, musicology, geography, economics and law.

Why is it, then, that the term feminist continues to provoke such ambivalent responses? It is as if the very success of the feminist project has resulted in a curious case of amnesia, as women within and without the academy forget the debt they owe to a critical and political project that undid the hegemony of universal man. The result of this amnesia is a tension in contemporary criticism between the power of feminism and its increasing spectrality. Journalists and commentators write of 'post-feminism', as if to suggest that the need to challenge patriarchal power or to analyse the complexities of gendered subjectivities had suddenly gone away, and as if texts were no longer the products of material realities in which bodies are shaped and categorised not only by gender, but by class, race, religion and sexuality. This is not a 'post-feminist' history that marks the passing of an era, but rather a 'still-feminist' one that aims to explore exactly what feminist criticism has done and is doing from the medieval era to the present. It is a history that both records and appraises, examining the impact of ideas in their original contexts and their ongoing significance for a new generation of students and researchers. Above all, *A History of Feminist Literary Criticism* regards the feminist critical project as a vital

dimension of literary studies, and it aims to provide an accessible introduction to this vast and vibrant field.

DEFINING FEMINIST LITERARY CRITICISM

Feminist literary criticism properly begins in the aftermath of 'second-
wave' feminism, the term usually given to the emergence of women's
movements in the United States and Europe during the Civil Rights
campaigns of the 1960s. Clearly, though, a feminist literary criticism did
not emerge fully formed from this moment. Rather, its eventual self-
conscious expression was the culmination of centuries of women's writing,
of women writing about women writing, and of women – and men –
writing about women's minds, bodies, art and ideas. Woman, as Virginia
Woolf observes in *A Room of One's Own*, her formative text of feminist
literary criticism, is 'the most discussed animal in the universe' (1929/1977:
27).[1] Whether misogynist or emancipatory, the speculation excited by the
concept of woman, let alone by actual women and their desires, created a
rich history upon which second-wave feminism could be built. From the
beginning feminist literary criticism was keen to uncover its own origins,
seeking to establish traditions of women's writing and early 'feminist'
thought to counter the unquestioning acceptance of 'man' and male genius
as the norm. *A History of Feminist Literary Criticism* thus begins by
illustrating the remarkable 'protofeminist' writing that would eventually
form the basis of modern feminist thought.

As the title of the book indicates, in this history of feminism our
principal emphasis is on *literary* criticism and textuality. However, as the
reader progresses through the volume, it will become clear that the boundaries between literature and politics, activism and the academy, are fluid
and, consequently, can be difficult to determine. Although these blurred
boundaries are frequently productive, we would argue that feminist literary
criticism can be distinguished from feminist political activism and social
theory. Most obviously, the difference lies in the dimension of textuality.
From Carolyn Dinshaw's account of medieval symbolism, to Mary
Eagleton's consideration of patriarchal critique, to Heather Love's analysis
of queer bodies, debates around representation underpin all the chapters in
this book. Across the centuries woman has been the subject of innumerable
reconfigurations, and with every reinscription comes the necessity of re-
reading. In the space of the text woman can be both defamed and defended,
and it is here that the most persuasive possibilities can be found for
imagining the future of the female subject.

USING *A HISTORY OF FEMINIST LITERARY CRITICISM*

The book is divided into three parts, each of which is prefaced by an introduction explaining the rationale behind the territory covered. The chapters themselves have been produced by experts in the diverse fields of feminist literary criticism, and have been written in an accessible manner to provide orientation in the subject area for the beginner. However, because each chapter has been freshly commissioned for this project, and the contributors asked to return to the original sources, the resulting essays do more than provide an overview – they also offer new insights into the material, its history, reception and ongoing relevance, and these new readings will be of interest to scholars working in all areas of literary practice. Feminist literary criticism is a field characterised by the extensive cross-fertilisation of ideas. A number of key thinkers and their essays will appear in different contexts, and it is important to acknowledge these productive overlaps. Texts such as Adrienne Rich's 'Compulsory Heterosexuality and Lesbian Existence', Hélène Cixous' 'The Laugh of the Medusa' and Judith Butler's *Gender Trouble* did not simply influence one school of feminist thought, but rather resonated across the entire spectrum of critical activity. The index will guide readers to the multiple locations in which discussions of key thinkers, essays, articles and books can be found. We recommend reading 'across' the book as well as through it in order to experience the divergent, dissonant and challenging encounters that characterise the feminist enterprise.

Despite the battles and the bad press, feminist literary criticism is a source of pleasure, stimulation, confirmation, insight, self-affirmation, doubt, questioning and reappraisal: it has the potential to alter the way we see ourselves, others and the world. *A History of Feminist Literary Criticism* is indebted to the many wonderful studies of women, gender and writing that have enriched our understanding of the potentialities of feminist enquiry. In looking afresh at this material we are both taking stock and embracing the emergence of new critical possibilities. Feminist literary criticism is a subject with a future and it deserves the considered reflection of a substantial history. We hope this volume will contribute to that process.

NOTE

1. Virginia Woolf (1929/1977), *A Room of One's Own*, London: Grafton.

PART I

Pioneers and protofeminism

Introduction to Part I

Gill Plain

The history of feminist literary criticism properly begins some forty or fifty years ago with the emergence of what is commonly termed second-wave feminism. The history of this critical movement and its impact on culture and society will be charted in the second and third parts of this volume, but it is important to recognise that this story has a prequel. To write of pioneers and protofeminism is to explore the diverse texts, voices and lives that articulated feminist ideas and feminist critical positions before such categories existed. Medieval women were not 'feminists' and they had few opportunities to be critics, but as Carolyn Dinshaw observes in the opening essay, 'texts affect lived lives, and . . . if women had relatively little opportunity to author texts, they nonetheless felt their effects' (Dinshaw, 15). The history of women's engagement with texts and textuality far exceeds the parameters of second-wave feminism, and this history is integral to contemporary understandings of feminist practice.

Yet the history of the representation of women, their writing, their reading and their literary critical acts would in total need not a single volume but a library of texts, and in consequence Part I of this book sets out a combination of overview and example that indicates the complexity of feminism's origins without attempting an exhaustive survey. The overview begins with the first two chapters, Carolyn Dinshaw's 'Medieval Feminist Criticism' and Helen Wilcox's 'Feminist Criticism in the Renaissance and Seventeenth Century', which together establish the conditions of pre-Enlightenment female subjectivity. These chapters illustrate that 'woman' was a site of intense literary and critical activity that examined the power of the feminine as symbol even as it worked to contain and constrain women in practice. For Dinshaw, the tension between literary embodiments and lived reality is at the heart of the often fraught debates that surrounded narrative practice. These debates in many cases prefigured the concerns of contemporary feminist enquiry, but ultimately Dinshaw concludes that 'medieval critical gestures' cannot straightforwardly be regarded as 'protofeminism'. Nonetheless, there are important historical continuities that need to be acknowledged, and a recognition of the relationship between gender and textuality is integral to understanding the literature and culture of the medieval period, from Chaucer's iconic Wife of Bath to Margery Kempe's autobiographical acts of self-construction.

By the early modern period, however, it is possible to trace a significant shift in women's relationship to textual culture. Helen Wilcox observes that it is now possible to describe women as 'feminists', and to define a range of 'phenomena' that might be termed feminist literary criticism. Indeed, she argues that a woman writer could 'play the part of a protofeminist simply by virtue of her decision to write' (Wilcox, 31). This was a period in which 'continuing constraints as well as new freedoms' provoked 'an outburst of writing by women' (37), and although in general women's literacy levels remained low, they nonetheless acquired far greater visibility as both producers and consumers of texts. From pamphlets to poetry and from devotional literature to advice books, women became active participants in literary culture. Their position, however, was not uncontested, and Wilcox traces the dominant debates that circulated around women's character, her writing, her place in society and her relationship to the legacy of Eve. Drawing on a remarkable range of often anonymous publications, Wilcox finds a dynamic political engagement taking shape in women's licensed and unlicensed engagement with the practices of reading and writing.

Dinshaw and Wilcox together provide a crucial mapping of the often evasive and unexpected territory of women's textual encounters, and their work gives a clear indication of the historical embeddedness of literary critical practice. The remaining chapters of Part I, however, adopt a contrasting but supplementary approach. Across the historical expanse of the eighteenth, nineteenth and early twentieth centuries many women could have stood as pioneers of 'protofeminism': writers and activists whose thinking, writing and 'living' challenged the tenets of patriarchal social organisation and questioned the prescriptive norms of gender. In Britain writers such as Mary Shelley, Maria Edgeworth, Charlotte Brontë, Mrs Gaskell and George Eliot produced unconventional texts – and in some cases lived unconventional lives – which have long since been recognised as prefiguring the concerns of later feminist enquiry. Similarly political 'feminist' activists from Frances Power Cobbe to Millicent Garrett Fawcett produced groundbreaking journalism, polemics and cultural criticism. Much of this work has slipped from view, but it stands as a pertinent reminder of the symbiotic relationship between feminist politics and textual practice.[1] Even the seemingly conventional Jane Austen can be seen as a contributor to a history of pre-feminist writing, producing in *Northanger Abbey* (1803/1818) both a witty demonstration of the value of women's education and a powerful defence of that most 'female' of literary forms, the novel.

Fiction, then, was a crucial means through which women engaged with politics in the eighteenth and nineteenth centuries, and in America too the literary and the political were inescapably intertwined. As Elaine Showalter has observed, 'there were few novels by English women in the nineteenth century as radical or outspoken with regard to the woman question as those by their American counterparts' (1991: 3): from Harriet Beecher Stowe to Louisa May Alcott, from Margaret Fuller to Sojourner Truth, American women wrote, articulated and embodied a discourse that acknowledged the agency and independence of the female subject. The plenitude of pioneers around the world continues into the *fin de siècle* and the early twentieth century. Charlotte Perkins Gilman, Olive Schreiner and Winifred Holtby were just some of the influential writers whose textual practice was profoundly political and whose fictions constituted vital acts of cultural criticism, women who left a legacy of argument and ideas that would enrich the later practice of feminist literary criticism. Yet, from this wealth of women writers and early feminist activists, one woman stands out as exemplary. The influence of Mary Wollstonecraft on over two hundred years of feminist enquiry cannot be overstated, and Susan Manly's chapter offers a detailed analysis of Wollstonecraft as a literary critic and advocate of reason, who eloquently anticipated the concerns of second-wave feminism. At the heart of Wollstonecraft's work is an attack on the authority of Edmund Burke, John Milton and Jean-Jacques Rousseau, 'fellow authors of a fictitious femininity, and patriarchal enemies in league against female emancipation' (Manly, 49). Manly demonstrates the critical strategies through which Wollstonecraft exposed Burke's sentimental 'aestheticisation of beauty', Rousseau's construction of an ideal, objectified woman, and the flawed misogynistic construction of Milton's Eve. In her detailed readings of these texts, Wollstonecraft reveals herself adept at the deployment of what would later be termed feminist critique. But this is not the limit of her achievement. As Manly illustrates, Wollstonecraft also struggled to escape the confines of gendered subjectivity by exposing 'the fictionality of both femininity and masculinity' (50). Wollstonecraft's argument for the constructed nature of gender was a strategic one: if writing and thinking could demonstrably be seen to transcend the body, then there would be no argument for excluding women from the public sphere. Yet her eloquent exposure of gendered textuality makes more than a transient political point: it also makes explicit the extent to which textual constructions shape subjectivities. Wollstonecraft viewed the woman writer as rational, ethical and humane, the antithesis of 'false sensibility' (49), an achievement which, over a century later, would see her *Vindication of the Rights of Woman* acclaimed by Winifred Holtby as 'the bible of the women's movement in Great Britain' (1934: 41).

Manly's chapter traces the legacy of Wollstonecraft across the nineteenth century, exploring her often unacknowledged influence on writers from Maria Edgeworth to George Eliot. But it would not be until the twentieth century that another writer would leave a legacy of feminist thought and critical enquiry to rival that of Wollstonecraft. Our second 'pioneer', then, is Virginia Woolf, 'the founder of modern feminist literary criticism' (Goldman, 66). As Jane Goldman demonstrates, Woolf's groundbreaking essay *A Room of One's Own* constitutes a 'modern primer' for feminist criticism, and her influence on later generations of feminist thought has been immense. Woolf matters to feminist literary criticism not simply as a writer and critic, but also as a subject of critical enquiry. The rescuing of Woolf from the apolitical prisons of Bloomsbury and madness was one of the formative projects of second-wave feminist literary criticism (see Carr, Chapter 7), giving rise to a constructive relationship between the writer, her criticism and her critics. It is Woolf we must thank for the provocative concepts of thinking back through our mothers, the woman's sentence and the androgynous mind. It is Woolf who wrote of killing the angel in the house and demanded the adaptation of the book to the body. Goldman's chapter illustrates how, in Woolf's creative contradictions and her disruptive boundary-crossing imagination, we find sources for the many, often conflicting, theoretical positions of contemporary feminist thought.

Finally, Part I of this book examines the legacy of Simone de Beauvoir. Like Woolf, Beauvoir has left feminism with a rich lexicon of images and ideas, not least of which is her definitive assertion that 'one is not born a woman'. This concept is implicit in the work and debates surrounding all our protofeminists and pioneers, but in Beauvoir's *The Second Sex* this fundamental idea receives explicit articulation. As discussed in the general introduction, the recognition of the social construction of gender and the coercive nature of gendered subjectivities has been at the centre of feminist literary criticism, enabling it as a discourse to challenge humanist assumptions about identity, nature and progress, and to scrutinise the potent mythical formations of femininity and masculinity. From Kate Millett to Judith Butler, feminist critics have been inspired by Beauvoir, but, as Elizabeth Fallaize argues, the full substance of her monumental work is hardly known. Since the 1990s, a new generation of feminist literary critics have been working to revise the limited perceptions of Beauvoir's work, and Fallaize contributes to this vital process through a study of Beauvoir's analysis of myth. Myth, claimed Beauvoir, was instrumental in 'persuading women of the *naturalness* of their fate', and Fallaize traces her examination of feminine archetypes from Stendhal to Sade, in the process finding an ecumenical methodology that anticipates later literary-critical movements from Marxism to structuralism to psychoanalysis. *The Second Sex* prefaces the point at which *A History of Feminist Literary Criticism* more obviously begins and, as with Wollstonecraft and Woolf, the echoes of Beauvoir's influence will resonate throughout its pages.

NOTE

1. See Barbara Caine (1997), *English Feminism 1780–1980*, Oxford: Oxford University Press.

BIBLIOGRAPHY

Holtby, Winifred (1934), *Women and a Changing Civilization*, London: John Lane.
Showalter, Elaine (1991), *Sister's Choice: Tradition and Change in American Women's Writing*, Oxford: Oxford University Press.

CHAPTER I

Medieval feminist criticism

Carolyn Dinshaw

MEDIEVAL FEMINIST LITERARY CRITICISM?

Was there such a thing as feminist literary criticism in the Middle Ages? Given that 'feminism' is the ideology of a modern social movement for the advancement of women, taking shape (in its Western European and US forms) in the eighteenth century and based on principles of equality and emancipation in secular societies, it could not have been known in, say, late fourteenth-century England in the forms in which it is known in the United States or Britain today – to say the very least. Moreover, given that 'literary criticism' is as well a modern invention, in English dating back to perhaps Alexander Pope, perhaps John Dryden, perhaps Sir Philip Sidney, it is hard to say what relation 'medieval critical attitudes' (Copeland, 1994: 500) might have to literary criticism – especially in its postmodern, feminist form in which the modernist pretence of analytical objectivity is abandoned for an ideologically based and politically committed project.

Yet writers in the late Middle Ages did reflect on the activities of reading, interpreting and writing, in a vigorous commentary tradition in Latin and a vibrant vernacular literary practice as well as in the prescriptive tradition of Latin rhetorical *artes*.[1] Since originality was not the sine qua non of literature that it later became – a main priority of medieval thought was to articulate a tradition – a great deal of late medieval writing can be seen in fact to be rewriting. As Chaucer retells the *Aeneid*, for example, in his *House of Fame* and *Legend of Good Women*, or translates Boccaccio's *Filostrato* in *Troilus and Criseyde*, his literary acts are first and foremost literary critical acts. Criticism here is not separate from creation, but is rather built into the creative process; in this way, medieval writing has much in common with postmodern notions of writing and criticism (Allen and Axiotis, 1997). Moreover, the fact that postmodern literary practices like feminist critique are ideologically based does not only distance them from medieval ones but joins them as well (Minnis and Scott, 1988: ix): if writers of the Christian

Middle Ages presumed that reading should ultimately lead to greater understanding of God's plan, feminist critics of the late twentieth and early twenty-first centuries presume that reading can lead to an enlightened, progressive politics or, indeed, a world view.

Clearly in the late medieval period there was some awareness of texts' potential to harm women, harm that should be avoided. Why else would the translator of the late fifteenth-century *Spektakle of Luf* (*Spectacle of Love*) back away from responsibility for the 'displeasure' his text might cause to 'all ladies and gentlewomen' offended by its representation of women (Wogan-Browne et al., 1999: 207)? If we strip down the term 'feminist literary criticism' to some basic elements, then, and allow for historical change therein, we can build up a concept and explore its usefulness for the late medieval period in England – a period without a concept of civil rights as understood today, a period in which the victim's consent in rape law was 'irrelevant', a period in which sexual activity was seen in terms less of reciprocal relations than of acts done by one person to another (Cannon, 2000: 76; Karras, 2005). We shall see that medieval feminist analysis not only engages the category of 'woman' but also traces its relations to a range of intersecting concepts including gender, empire and embodiment, and we can begin to envision a genealogy of the modern phenomenon of feminist literary criticism.

Let us start with an infamous medieval literary episode involving a woman and a book: a woman is tormented night and day by her husband's gleeful reading aloud from an anthology of stories of horrible wives. Finally, in desperation, she tears pages out of the book as he reads it, then slugs him in the face with her fist. This little episode is, of course, part of the denouement of the Wife of Bath's Prologue, the long autobiographical introduction to her tale on the road to Canterbury. Written by Geoffrey Chaucer, an English civil servant, around the years 1390–5, it is a fiction, but while the Wife of Bath never existed as a living being, she is larger than her framing in the *Canterbury Tales*. What concept of 'medieval feminist literary criticism' might we develop if we take this gesture of defacing a hateful text as our starting point? This chapter will first explore the paradigmatic facets of this episode and will then extend its view to further acts of literary criticism by male and female authors.

For starters, then, this fictional figure was created by a male writer. Higher education and official (Latin) culture were closed to women, but women, both lay and religious, did read and write in the vernacular languages (English and French in later medieval England), and a very few may have gained sufficient learning to make them *litteratus* – literate in

Latin. Women in England in fact were intimately and pervasively involved with textual culture, as readers and owners of books, which they circulated amongst their acquaintances; as writers and addressees of letters; as audiences of sermons, romances, and devotional and liturgical literature; and as patrons of writers or manuscripts, to name a few textual possibilities. Women formed 'textual communities' through dense networks of personal relations, wherein textuality was 'of the spoken as well as the written word', as Felicity Riddy demonstrates: 'it begins in the book, which may have been read aloud by a clerk, but is then transmitted among the women by word of mouth'. Such active reading exerted a profound influence on what was written: the devout hermit Richard Rolle, for example, shifted from an exclusive and 'fantastical' Latin to straightforward English as his female friends' spiritual needs and desires obliged 'the elusive and eccentric solitary to discover his own capacity for teaching in English on the contemplative life' (Riddy, 1993: 111, 107). Gender differences were at times explicitly responsible for differences among the intentions of various readers: in a brief literary critical reflection on its potentially diverse audiences, for example, the translator of *The Knowing of Woman's Kind in Childing* (*Knowledge of the Nature of Woman in Childbirth*) acknowledges that English women know English best of any language and can thus read to and counsel unlettered women about their maladies; men are advised not to read the treatise in the spirit of malice or in order to slander women (Wogan-Browne et al., 1999: 157–8). If the vernacular is feminised here and in this way doubts about its authority vis-à-vis Latin registered, it is nonetheless the linguistic basis of these potentially powerful social groupings and cultural innovations; indeed, 'the vernacular may have the potential to feminize its male audience by aligning them with non-Latin-literate women' (Wogan-Browne et al., 1999: 121–2).

So women were textually engaged, but they were still in the minority: late medieval English literary culture was certainly dominated by men. This is reflected in the paucity of extant works by women: Julian of Norwich's *Revelation of Love* (Short Text, c. 1382–8) is 'the earliest work in English we are sure is by a woman' (Watson, 2003: 210), while even the women's names that appear to be signatures in the Findern Manuscript (late fifteenth to early sixteenth century) cannot be definitively assigned to the anonymous lyrics therein (Summit, 2003: 94; McNamer, 2003: 197). More profoundly, gender hierarchy was expressed in the very structure of literary activity: drawing on long traditions in classical and biblical discourses, medieval literary creation was figured as a masculine act performed on a surface gendered feminine – writing, for example, with pen on parchment

(Dinshaw, 1989: 3–27). The Bible enjoined women to keep silent, and medical writings confirmed women's secondary, derivative and frail nature; presumptions of feminine weakness and inferiority were widespread, expressed by women authors (sometimes quite cleverly: see Julian of Norwich's protestation that 'I am a woman, unlearned, feeble and frail', a commonplace that perhaps allowed her to spread her vision more persuasively) and assumed to be shared by women readers (Wogan-Browne et al., 1999: 18). And most generally, the broad and unremitting tradition of medieval anti-feminist writing performs, as it were, feminine subordination in the literary as well as in every other realm. Chaucer, as a man writing in the voice of a woman opposing this tradition, explores the impact of writing in creating gender itself.

The anthology defaced by the Wife of Bath is in fact a knowing compilation of anti-feminist literature, and the Wife's gesture is feminist insofar as it opposes this entrenched discourse of anti-feminism. Her husband Jankin's 'book of wicked wives' consists of the classics of this long and ungenerous tradition, and in its movement from the Bible (the Parables of Solomon, Proverbs 10:1–22:16 [Vulgate]) to antiquity (Ovid's *Art of Love*) to the Patristic era (the writings of Tertullian and Saint Jerome) to the later Middle Ages (Trotula, the woman who allegedly authored medical texts; Heloise, ill-fated lover of Abelard), it shows the chronological range of this discourse of woman-hating. It exemplifies, too, its intensely textual nature: Jerome in his treatise against the married monk Jovinian quoted a book by the classical philosopher Theophrastus, but the Theophrastus work is not extant and perhaps never existed at all; Jerome's immediate source may have been Seneca or Tertullian, but whatever the reality, this putative work, precisely because it was thought to be a written authority, was endlessly cited or quoted by just about everyone from Abelard onward – including Heloise (Blamires, 1992: 64; Mann, 2002: 39–45).

Abelard's exegesis of famous verses of the Canticles ('I am black but [*var.* and] beautiful, daughters of Jerusalem . . .') in his second letter to Heloise demonstrates a corollary to this discourse of misogyny. Intimately intertwined with the discursive 'othering' of women are other varieties of discursive othering – all available for social use and each depending on particular circumstances for deployment; women, blacks, Jews, Muslims, heretics, sodomites and 'the East', these categories emerge in relation to one another, creating a white male Christianity purged of any and all dangerous threats.[2] As David Wallace keenly analyses the letter, Abelard likens Heloise and her nuns to the black woman, then passes 'from one racialized discourse to another' in a reflection on his fellow monks behaving exhibitionistically, as 'Jews' (Wallace, 2004: 245–8). A dense mesh of misogyny and orientalism can be seen in the representation of the vile Syrian mother-in-law in Chaucer's *Man of Law's Tale* as well as in the courtly representations in his *Squire's Tale*, and we will see orientalising tropes in the thorough gendering of empire, including the politics of linguistic translation from Latin to the vernacular, in Chaucer's treatment of the *Aeneid*.

The fact that both Abelard and Heloise position themselves within misogynistic discourse suggests not only that gender is a system of hierarchised positions (which, like the racial and religious differences noted above, can be occupied by anybody, but with widely varying stakes, costs and effects) but also that there is a critical or dialectical element built into such discourse. Writers who penned works brutally abusive of women turned around and defended women from those self-same attacks: Jehan Le Fèvre, for example, in the late fourteenth century translated the bitter *Lamentations of Matheolus* and then wrote the *Livre de Leesce* (*The Book of Joy*), in which 'dame Leesce' responds one by one to Matheolus' sorry theses. Andreas Capellanus' late twelfth-century treatise *De Amore* (*On Love*) contains within it both gestures: in a work that might join these others as medieval *anti-feminist* literary criticism, the first two sections are a guide to courting women, the final section a ruthless deterrent from associating with them (Blamires, 1992). Indeed, scholars have not missed the ludic aspect of these exercises, the way in which 'woman' seems at times merely to provide writers with a site of philosophical abstraction, a rhetorical topic to be treated either positively or negatively (or both), or a locus for more complex othering.[3]

Yet the Wife of Bath's gesture indicates that women are not just rhetorical playthings in schoolmen's or clerics' discursive games. 'Now who could imagine, or could suppose,/ The grief and torment in my heart, the pain?' (1992: 221), the Wife seethes as she is subjected to this hatred. As we shall see, Christine de Pizan suffers from her own reading of Matheolus, and she reports that another woman has suffered as a consequence of the *Romance of the Rose*. Texts affect lived lives, and the Wife's feminist criticism demonstrates this: if women had relatively little opportunity to author texts, they nonetheless felt their effects. However, the Wife not only shows that texts have effects on lives; as a fiction she herself is made up of texts. She is in fact the anti-feminist stereotype of a nightmare wife come to life: she says to her husbands, for example, exactly what Theophrastus said bad wives say to their husbands. But even as she thus confirms the stereotype, the Wife in her mimesis takes a stand in subversion of it: she repeats the anti-feminist discourse with a difference, finally seizing that book and ripping it up.

Chaucer's creation of her is an act of feminist literary criticism. It is a deep and complex critical gesture indeed: her very life, constituted as it is by texts, is itself represented as a feminist literary critical act (cf. Dinshaw, 1989: 113–31).

Acts of medieval feminist literary criticism, then, consist of several intertwined characteristics. They are embedded in masculine literary culture and may respond explicitly to that condition. They focus on the estate of women or the nature of gender systems without in the first instance seeking to vilify women or femininity; they may, further, oppose anti-feminist writings outright – they may be *anti*-anti-feminist, that is – and they may be interrelated with other 'othering' discourses as well.[4] They may highlight the effects of texts on women's lives, and they often consist of women's engaging texts in their lives, living their responses even in the fashioning of their very selves.

CHAUCER AS FEMINIST LITERARY CRITIC

The Wife of Bath is but one of Chaucer's feminist literary critical creations: in his representation of her as well as of other characters, he manipulates the gendered structure of literary activity in order to critique that structure. This is not to say that his representations are somehow out of his time, an era characterised by the official subordination, not liberation, of women and the feminine; rather he sees the costs to both women and men of anti-feminism, imagining reform of patriarchal structures, not revolution. The characterisations are powerfully effective toward this reformist end: the Wife of Bath is figured as knowing in her bones that literary history exhibits a male bias – 'My God, had women written histories/ Like cloistered scholars in oratories/ They'd have set down more of men's wickedness/ Than all the sons of Adam could redress' (Blamires, 1992: 218) – and that clerks write against women once their own manly powers have failed. Proserpina in the *Merchant's Tale*, like the Wife of Bath, detests the oppressive use of textual authority by men, and her actions within the tale reverse the conventionally gendered structure of masculine interpretation of feminine matter: as David Wallace puts it, 'men will see, but women will explain what men see' (Wallace, 1997: 294). Chaucer's creation of Griselda in the *Clerk's Tale* brings the gender politics of vernacular translation to the fore and explores, moreover, what it feels like to a woman to be allegorised as matter to be interpreted. And in the Pardoner, Chaucer created a character who is patently and frighteningly outside of this gendered structure of literary activity altogether; neither fully masculine nor feminine, he threatens the possibility of interpretation itself.

Criseyde, a woman traded between groups of men at war in *Troilus and Criseyde*, is well aware that subsequent literary criticism will not be kind to her. Chaucer's representation of her reveals that literary history – like war – is a man-to-man affair, and women readers are without any other narrative or interpretive resources. 'Alas', wails Criseyde at the end of her sad story:

> of me, until the end of the world,
> No good word will be written or sung,
> For these books will disgrace me.
> O, rolled shall I be on many a tongue!
> Throughout the world, my bell shall be rung!
> And women will hate me most of all.　　　　(1987: 1058–63)

Robert Henryson, one of the so-called Scottish Chaucerians who followed the poet in the fifteenth century, obligingly enacted the patriarchal literary critical gesture so dreaded by Criseyde: in a broad gesture of anti-feminist literary criticism, in his *Testament of Cresseid* he created a Criseyde so corroded by shame that she is figured as a leper.

Gavin Douglas, another of the Scottish Chaucerians and first translator of the *Aeneid* into English, remarked famously in the first preface to his *Eneados* that Chaucer was 'evir, God wait, wemenis frend [always, God knows, a friend of women]'. This is not the feminist literary critical comment it is often presumed to be, however. As Jennifer Summit has astutely observed, Douglas considered Chaucer's rendition of the *Aeneid* (in his *Legend of Good Women*) unVirgilian and unheroic. Chaucer's narrator focuses not on Aeneas but rather on the pathetic and abandoned Dido; by so doing, writes Douglas, 'my master Chaucer greatly Virgil offended'. Heroic masculinity is key to the establishment of vernacular authority as well as to the stability and continuity of the literary canon, but Dido's story interrupts all that; Chaucer through his representation of Dido explores 'literary tradition's limits', particularly the margins whence the female is forced to act (Summit, 2000: 23–6). The imperial project of cultural transmission, particularly the translation of the artefacts of empire – here, Chaucer's Englishing of this literary epic – is enacted via the sad romance of Aeneas and Dido. The 'oriental' woman is left behind while Aeneas moves westward to fulfil his imperial destiny, and gender is implicated in the ideological problematics of empire (Wogan-Browne et al., 1999: 366–70).

Although there thus seems to be evidence both internal and external that Chaucer's various representations were indeed feminist literary critical gestures, there is as well a sense that they were controversial. The morality of his poetry may have been up for discussion at court, if protestations (in the voice of the Man of Law in the *Canterbury Tales*) of the uprightness of Chaucer's narratives are any indication. An explicit response to accusations of harm to women is found in the *Prologue* to the *Legend of Good Women*, a dream-vision poem begun by Chaucer in the mid-1380s and revised (perhaps because its self-defence was important) after a number of years.

In this dream-vision confrontation with his reading public, the narrator of the *Prologue* – a fictionalised image of Chaucer – is chastised by the mythological God of Love and Alceste, themselves fictionalised (if exaggerated) images of Chaucer's audience (Dinshaw, 1989: 65–74). Cupid has two objections: first, by translating the *Romance of the Rose*, a 'heresy' against Cupid's law, the poet-narrator has made 'wise folk from me withdraw' (*Riverside Chaucer*, 1987: G.257), and that by writing *Troilus and Criseyde* he has been intent on 'showing how women have done wrong' (G.266). The poet-narrator should have concentrated on stories of good women, of which there is a whole world of authors (G.280–310). To defend the poet-narrator, Alceste intervenes, finally ordering him to dedicate his writing only to positive images of women. The resultant *Legend of Good Women* is a study of misogyny intertwined with orientalism (cf. Delany, 1994); in it the poet-narrator depicts a string of women (including Dido) so passive and distanced in their victimisation by perfidious men that he himself becomes too bored to finish his task. The work is unfinished, but may nonetheless be complete in its representation of the silencing effects of such orientalising anti-feminism: constraining women, it limits men as well and ultimately strangles literary activity altogether.

CHRISTINE DE PIZAN AND THE QUARREL OVER THE *ROSE*

Even if the poet-narrator of the *Prologue* to the *Legend of Good Women* had convincingly defended himself against the charges – instead of sputtering ineffectively about his intentions – and even if he had made a decent start on his penance in the ensuing legends, the problems with the *Rose* would not go away. It was, after all, one of the most influential works of the Middle Ages: well over two hundred manuscripts circulated in and beyond France. At the turn of the fifteenth century this famous work and its famous author (Jean de Meun, who developed the poem in the late thirteenth century after its first author, Guillaume de Lorris, died) were made the objects of critique in the first literary debate in France, a debate pursued with urgency among some of the most powerful intellects in the country.

The *Rose* is a gargantuan allegorical poem with a simple narrative premise (a lover falls in love and pursues a beloved, figured as a rosebud)

forming the basis of a stream of advice and commentary on an encyclopaedic range of topics by personifications such as Reason, Nature, the
Jealous Husband, the Old Woman and the Friend. The speech of the
Jealous Husband tends toward the violently woman-hating; the Old
Woman, too, gives advice that is deeply unflattering to women; the figures·
of Nature and Genius (Nature's viceroy) speak of generation and the act of
procreation in baldly explicit terms; and the final sexual consummation is
only thinly veiled by allegorical figuration. As John V. Fleming succinctly
puts it, 'the objections to the *Roman de la Rose* are two: it is anti-feminist,
and it is filthy' (Fleming, 1971: 28).

Christine de Pizan, an established writer born in Italy but living in
France and writing in French, took exception to the poem and was joined
in her opposition by Jean Gerson, a powerful theologian and Chancellor of
the University of Paris. The debate apparently started in conversations
between Christine and Jean de Montreuil (Provost of Lille and sometime
Secretary to dukes, dauphin and king), who defended this esteemed and
beloved work. He was joined enthusiastically by the brothers Pierre Col
(Canon of Paris and Tournay) and Gontier Col (First Secretary and Notary
to the king) (Baird and Kane, 1978).

These initial conversations may have concerned some brief remarks
Christine had written in the voice of Cupid in her courtly poem *L'Epistre
au dieu d'Amours* (*The Letter of the God of Love*, 1399), a complaint by
Cupid that women are being unfairly defamed and abused by male writers.
In his letter Cupid cannily makes some feminist literary critical observations. The patriarchal, anti-feminist structure of education is clearly
indicted, as is the personal animus of the clerks who write against
women: misogynist scholars of the anti-feminist tradition base their
works on books that lie, Cupid asserts, and indoctrinate young boys early
in school. Echoing the Wife of Bath, Cupid assures his readers that if
women had written the books they would be mighty different. Ovid's
Remedies of Love gets special censure, as does the *Rose*. Jean de Meun's work
is criticised for being bombastic ('So many people called upon, implored,/
So many efforts made and ruses found/To trick a virgin – that, and nothing
more!' (Fenster and Erler, 1990: 53)) and illogical: if so much guile is
needed, Cupid avers, then women obviously cannot be as fickle or incon-
sistent as reputed.

Cupid would seem to have a point – well over 21,000 lines are needed to
'pluck' a 'rosebud' – but Christine de Pizan's boldness in presuming to
criticise 'that profound book' by that 'true Catholic, worthy master, and . . .
doctor of holy theology' may have been itself a shocking offence to some

of its readers (Baird and Kane, 1978: 42, 57). In the ensuing debate she saw herself as defending the 'feminine cause' (1978: 66), as she put it when addressing a dossier of debate documents to the Queen of France herself. Dedicated to the polemic, she refused to be intimidated by 'anti-feminist attacks' (63), and she aggressively revised the traditional feminine humility topos at the end of her letter to Jean de Montreuil:

> May it not be imputed to me as folly, arrogance, or presumption, that I, a woman, should dare to reproach and call into question so subtle an author, and to diminish the stature of his work, when he alone, a man, has dared to undertake to defame and blame without exception an entire sex. (56)

Though Christine acknowledges that there is some good in the work, she maintains that 'therein lies the greater peril, for the more authentic the good the more faith one puts in the evil' (54). She argues that the poem's defamation is contrary to fact – she knows via her own experience that women are not like this (though she maintains at other points that no experience is necessary when dealing with the truth) – and wonders just how much men really have suffered from the evils of women. When Pierre Col adduces an anecdote about a man saved by the *Rose*, she counters with a story of a woman whose husband – shades of the Wife of Bath's Jankin – reads it and feels justified in beating her. Books do have an effect on lived lives, Christine points out in her feminist literary critique:

> Not long ago, I heard one of your familiar companions and colleagues . . . say that he knew a married man who believed in the *Roman de la Rose* as in the gospel. This was an extremely jealous man, who, whenever in the grip of passion, would go and find the book and read it to his wife; then he would become violent and strike her and say such horrible things as, 'These are the kinds of tricks you pull on me. This good, wise man Master Jean de Meun knew well what women are capable of'. And at every word he finds appropriate, he gives her a couple of kicks or slaps. Thus it seems clear to me that whatever other people think of this book, this poor woman pays too high a price for it. (136)

Numerous literary critical principles are at stake in this debate. First, theories of language are debated: picking up from the *Rose* itself, in which the Lover berates Reason for uttering the word 'coilles' (testicles), Christine and Pierre Col argue about the relationship between words and things. The thing makes the word shameful, not vice versa, Christine maintains, despite what Pierre Col says, and so it is not possible to name dishonourable things (like testicles, originally beautiful but now shameful after the Fall) without shame. Second, dramatic characterisation is examined: all parties agree that a writer may create characters who express ideas that may not be the writer's own. Thus Jean de Meun creates the viciously miso-gynist Jealous Husband, and, according to Pierre Col, cannot be held responsible for this character's heinous opinions. But Jean de Meun is not consistent in his characterisations, Christine observes pointedly (130); moreover, under the logic of authorial irresponsibility, Meun cannot then be defended when a character says something morally praiseworthy. As Baird and Kane put it, Christine and Gerson 'are simply unwilling to allow that such a principle [of dramatic characterisation] gives absolute licence to a writer' (1978: 20). Similarly, a writer may disclaim responsibility if he is just repeating what other authorities say in their texts; thus the defenders of the poem argue. But Gerson states, 'we censure not characters but writings (whoever made them), since one who gives a poisoned drink, even if it is mixed by someone else, must not be judged free of guilt on that account' (150). There is a sense among the poem's detractors that hateful speech simply cannot be uttered without harm, no matter what the context. Third, the effects of other poetic devices are discussed. The final allegorical representation of the sex act, maintains Christine, is 'explicit' despite the elaborate figure (124), and more seductive than a literal representation would be. Christine declares to Pierre Col flatly that satirical methods are not effective: praising evil in order to teach that it should be avoided is counterproductive.

Issues of authorial intent and responsibility were indeed crucial in Chaucer's *Prologue* to the *Legend of Good Women*: there the poet-narrator pleads 'whatever my author meant,/God knows, it was entirely my intent/To further truth in love and cherish it,/And to beware of falseness and vice/By such example' (1987: G.460–4). It is no surprise, then, that the *Legend of Good Women* should appear in the midst of this *Rose* quarrel: at the height of the debate (1402), Thomas Hoccleve, civil servant and poetic disciple of Chaucer, adapted Christine's poem into English as *Letter of Cupid*, inter-polating into the text a stanza of praise for Chaucer's representation of faithless men (Fenster and Erler, 1990: 192). Here, Hoccleve seems to be saying what Gavin Douglas later said – Chaucer was ever women's friend – with perhaps (given Hoccleve's other changes to Christine's poem and his later worries about his representations of women) an ultimately similar view of masculine literary history (Fenster and Erler, 1990: 165–7; Chance, 1998).

Though no winners of the *Rose* debate were ever proclaimed, and though it would be a mistake to conclude that specific literary techniques were feminist or anti-feminist (Christine of course uses dramatic characterisa-tions and poetic figures herself), the quarrel brought the gender politics of literature into public discussion at a very high level. Interest in it was not confined to a coterie of elite intellectuals in France, either; the quarrel made its way into French sermons and into Middle English poetry as well (Baird and Kane, 1978: 11–12).

Her polemical energies undaunted, Christine continued her analysis of the effects of misogynist literature in *Le Livre de la Cité des Dames* (*The Book of the City of Ladies*), written three years later. The tone is decidedly personal as Christine introduces the project by recounting her depression and self-hatred resulting from her absorption of the misogyny – unavoidable, pervasive and therefore persuasive – of traditional moral writers. She has picked up a volume by one of them (none other than the egregious Matheolus) but, as she remarks, philosophers, poets, orators, 'they all speak from one and the same mouth' about the evils of women (Richards, 1982: 4). At the sudden appearance of three ladies in a vision (Reason, Rectitude and Justice), Christine receives consolation and encouragement: 'Come back to yourself', they urge her (1982: 6–8). To counter this insidious anti-feminist literary tradition (including its geographical othering, its racialising and orientalising), Christine has been chosen to 'establish and build the City of Ladies' (11); taking inspiration from Boccaccio and adding many more tales of illustrious women, she constructs in this narrative a fictional city whose foundation, walls, roofs and towers are made of good women – Christian and pagan, past and present – in which honourable women of the past, present and future may take refuge. Christine's conviction that books affect lived lives led her to try to arrest negative consequences and provide relief from the alienating wounds inflicted by traditional moral authorities – not a revolution, to be sure, given the reductive exemplary narratives and the final admonitions about wifely subordination and obedience, but a reformation keenly to be desired.

MARGERY KEMPE AS LITERARY CRITICISM

Women's lives take shape in relation to texts and thus they may themselves be performances of literary criticism. Texts and life interrelate in the *Book of Margery Kempe* so intimately that it is impossible to disentangle the one from the other. The *Book* is the first autobiography in English, written in the 1430s; the very process of writing it down demonstrates the intricate interaction of living, narrating, reading and writing. Since Margery could not read or write, she had to find a scribe for the narrative of her life, visions and revelations; the first man for this task (perhaps her son) used language and a script that were almost completely indecipherable, then died; the second, a priest, after hesitating for years (such was the controversy that surrounded this woman of extravagant devotional practices), finally was able with God's grace to read the nearly illegible book and convert it into readable prose. The process of producing the final English text was intensely collaborative: the priest read back to Margery every word of the book of her life that she had composed, and she helped him when difficulty arose. In the writing of her life Margery reacts to the text of her life.

Textual modelling is integral to the production of Margery's life in her *Book*. Another priest reads aloud to her from devotional works and lives of saints; she hears these lives and in so doing understands her own devotion and lives her life in relation to these narratives. Her priest-scribe at one point (chapter 62) records his misgivings about the source of Margery's inspiration, but notes that when he then read about the abundant tears and crying of the blessed Marie of Oignies and of other holy people (Richard Rolle and Saint Elizabeth of Hungary) he was convinced of the truth of Margery's devotional experiences: these written works shape his understanding – and thus his version – of her.

Of the saints whose lives inform Margery's, Saint Bridget of Sweden is the most explicit in the *Book*. Margery indeed seems to pit herself against Bridget in a sort of mystical competition: according to her own account she not only experiences better visions but also in fact incarnates the veracity of Bridget's own book. Jesus assures Margery, 'I tell you truly it is true every word that is written in Bridget's book and by you it shall be known for actual truth [be the it schal be knowyn for very trewth]' (Staley, 1996: 58). Margery is an advocate for Bridget, the authenticity of whose revelations was contested by Jean Gerson (with a scepticism tinged with misogyny, despite his teaming up with Christine in the *Rose* debate); indeed, through Margery's very life, 'Bridget's book' will be proven. In this structure of saintly fulfilment, Margery is a textual creature, indeed, many texts come to life.

In contrast, Mary Carruthers observes, 'A modern woman would be very uncomfortable to think that she was facing the world with a "self" constructed out of bits and pieces of great authors of the past, yet I think in large part that is exactly what a medieval self or "character" was' (Carruthers, 1990: 180). Carruthers makes this point vis-à-vis Heloise here; Margery's self is constructed similarly, through texts in memory, and (as does Heloise) she has some awareness of this very condition: indeed, Margery almost boasts about it in relation to Bridget. Lives and texts are merged in medieval selves both masculine and feminine, as Carruthers compellingly demonstrates, yet the significance of this condition may differ for men and for women. In a world in which reading and writing were in large measure controlled by men, women's textual access

was limited; as we see with Margery, of necessity women developed different modes of textual engagement. Feeling the power of literature to destroy
as well as to create and wanting engagement with it, these women might
have understood their own lived lives as part of this culture from which
they were in other ways excluded – indeed, as literary critical acts.

CONCLUSION

What does all this mean for a history of feminist literary criticism? It is crucial
not to regard these medieval critical gestures as 'protofeminism', because
such a view narrows the medieval instances to mere prefigurations of what we
now appreciate as the robust feminism of modernity. In the late medieval
period there was keen awareness of the masculine domination of textual
tradition and, concomitantly, a vibrant concern about the effects of the anti-
feminist literary tradition, though there was no consensus on how to correct
that tradition: what worked for Christine de Pizan in her *Book of the City of
Ladies* (unvarying portraits of good women) was seen as a punishment that
ironically backfires in the *Legend of Good Women* (cf. Delany, 1986). But in
such representations as Chaucer's powerful characters, Christine's polemics
and recuperative work and Margery Kempe's critical self, we may indeed
find works that have informed modern and postmodern feminist preoccupations with gender, empire, translation, textuality and embodiment. When
Virginia Woolf writes of Chaucer's language that 'There is . . . a stately and
memorable beauty in the undraped sentences which follow each other like
women so slightly veiled that you see the lines of their bodies as they go'
(Woolf, 1925: 34) the metaphor is no coincidence but marks the gendered
textuality that such medieval texts help us see and see beyond.

NOTES

All references to Chaucer's texts are to *The Riverside Chaucer*, and all translations,
except where otherwise noted, are my own.

1. Recent scholarship has argued that Latin and vernacular traditions deserve to be
   reckoned equally in histories of literary criticism, though earlier scholarship
   insisted that a history of medieval literary criticism would be a history of
   criticism written only in Latin. See Wogan-Browne et al. (1999).
2. Schibanoff (1996) focuses on internal threats such as heresy and femininity.
   Lampert (2004) documents 'gender and Jewish difference' within Christianity,
   and suggests how these differences emerge in relation to each other; Kruger
   (1997) and Heng (2000) develop intersectional analyses of gender and other
   categories. See also Wogan-Browne et al. (1999: 370).

3. Blamires (1992: 12–13) notes the playful quality of the rhetorical topos. For the effects of the abstraction of 'woman' see Bloch (1991) and Cannon (2004: 132).
4. The term 'anti-anti-feminism' is from Fleming (1971), though he distinguishes feminism from 'anti-anti-feminism' – chiefly, I think, because of the 'modern' associations of the former.

BIBLIOGRAPHY

Allen, Valerie and Ares Axiotis (1997), 'Introduction: Postmodern Chaucer', in *Chaucer, New Casebooks*, ed. V. Allen and A. Axiotis, London: Macmillan.
Baird, Joseph L. and John R. Kane (eds) (1978), *La Querelle de la Rose: Letters and Documents*, Chapel Hill: University of North Carolina Department of Romance Languages.
Blamires, Alcuin (ed.) (1992), *Woman Defamed and Woman Defended: An Anthology of Medieval Texts*, Oxford: Clarendon.
Bloch, R. Howard (1991), *Medieval Misogyny and the Invention of Western Romantic Love*, Chicago: University of Chicago Press.
Cannon, Christopher (2000), 'Chaucer and Rape: Uncertainty's Certainties', in *Studies in the Age of Chaucer* 22.
(2004), *The Grounds of English Literature*, Oxford: Oxford University Press.
Carruthers, Mary (1990), *The Book of Memory: A Study of Memory in Medieval Culture*, Cambridge: Cambridge University Press.
Chance, Jane (1998), 'Gender Subversion and Linguistic Castration in Fifteenth-Century English Translations of Christine de Pizan', in *Violence against Women in Medieval Texts*, ed. Anna Roberts, Gainesville: University Press of Florida.
Copeland, Rita (1994), 'Medieval Theory and Criticism', in *The Johns Hopkins Guide to Literary Theory and Criticism*, ed. Michael Groden and Martin Kreiswirth, Baltimore: Johns Hopkins University Press.
Delany, Sheila (1986), 'Rewriting Women Good: Gender and the Anxiety of Influence in Two Late Medieval Texts', in *Chaucer in the Eighties*, ed. Julian N. Wasserman and Robert J. Blanch, Syracuse, NY: Syracuse University Press.
(1994), *The Naked Text: Chaucer's 'Legend of Good Women'*, Berkeley: University of California Press.
Dinshaw, Carolyn (1989), *Chaucer's Sexual Poetics*, Madison: University of Wisconsin Press.
Dinshaw, Carolyn and David Wallace (eds) (2003), *Cambridge Companion to Medieval Women's Writing*, Cambridge: Cambridge University Press.
Fenster, Thelma S. and Mary Carpenter Erler (eds) (1990), *Poems of Cupid, God of Love*, Leiden: Brill.
Fleming, John V. (1971), 'Hoccleve's "Letter of Cupid" and the "Quarrel" over the *Roman de la Rose*', in *Medium Aevum* 40.
Heng, Geraldine (2000), 'The Romance of England: *Richard Coer de Lyon*, Saracens, Jews, and the Politics of Race and Nation', in *The Postcolonial Middle Ages*, ed. Jeffrey Jerome Cohen, New York: St Martin's.

Henryson, Robert (c. 1500/1997), *The Poems of Robert Henryson*, ed. Robert L. Kindrick, Kalamazoo, MI: Medieval Institute Publications.

Karras, Ruth Mazo (2005), *Sexuality in Medieval Europe: Doing unto Others*, New York: Routledge.

Kruger, Steven F. (1997), 'Conversion and Medieval Sexual, Religious, and Racial Categories', in *Constructing Medieval Sexuality*, ed. Karma Lochrie, Peggy McCracken and James A. Schultz, Minneapolis: University of Minnesota Press.

Lampert, Lisa (2004), *Gender and Jewish Difference from Paul to Shakespeare*, Philadelphia: University of Pennsylvania Press.

Mann, Jill (2002), *Feminizing Chaucer*, new edition, Cambridge: D. S. Brewer.

McNamer, Sarah (2003), 'Lyrics and Romances', in Dinshaw and Wallace (2003).

Minnis, A. J. and A. B. Scott, with David Wallace (eds) (1988), *Medieval Literary Theory and Criticism c. 1100–c. 1375: The Commentary Tradition*, Oxford: Clarendon Press.

Richards, Earl Jeffrey (ed. and trans.) (1982), *The Book of the City of Ladies*, by Christine de Pizan, New York: Persea.

Riddy, Felicity (1993), '"Women Talking about the Things of God": A Late Medieval Sub-culture', in *Women and Literature in Britain, 1150–1500*, ed. Carol M. Meale, Cambridge: Cambridge University Press.

The Riverside Chaucer (1987), gen. ed. Larry D. Benson, Boston: Houghton Mifflin.

Schibanoff, Susan (1996), 'Worlds Apart: Orientalism, Antifeminism, and Heresy in Chaucer's *Man of Law's Tale*', in *Exemplaria* 8.

Staley, Lynn (ed.) (1996), *The Book of Margery Kempe*, Kalamazoo, MI: Medieval Institute Publications.

Summit, Jennifer (2000), *Lost Property: The Woman Writer and English Literary History, 1380–1589*, Chicago: University of Chicago Press.

(2003), 'Women and Authorship', in Dinshaw and Wallace (2003).

Wallace, David (1997), *Chaucerian Polity: Absolutist Lineages and Associational Forms in England and Italy*, Stanford, CA: Stanford University Press.

(2004), *Premodern Places: Calais to Surinam, Chaucer to Aphra Behn*, Malden, MA: Blackwell.

Watson, Nicholas (2003), 'Julian of Norwich', in Dinshaw and Wallace (2003).

Wogan-Browne, Jocelyn, Nicholas Watson, Andrew Taylor and Ruth Evans (eds) (1999), *The Idea of the Vernacular: An Anthology of Middle English Literary Theory, 1280–1520*, University Park, PA: Pennsylvania State University Press.

Woolf, Virginia (1925), 'The Pastons and Chaucer', in *The Common Reader*, New York: Harcourt Brace.

CHAPTER 2

Feminist criticism in the Renaissance and seventeenth century

Helen Wilcox

EARLY MODERN WOMEN: COURAGEOUS OR SILENT?

The period under discussion in this chapter, approximately 1550 to 1700, was an immensely exciting time in terms of the history of women and literature in England. Female writers were beginning to publish their works, both through manuscript circulation and in printed books, in an enormous variety of genres including poems, plays, conversion narratives, advice books, translations, letters, devotional texts, prophecies, pamphlets, memoirs and works of philosophy and fiction.[1] In social and political terms, too, this was an era when female rulers – seen by John Knox and no doubt other contemporaries as a 'monstrous regiment' – came to prominence. When Mary Tudor became queen in 1553, she was England's first Queen Regnant since the disputed rule of Matilda in the twelfth century. The iconic female image of Elizabeth I, Mary's half-sister who succeeded her on the throne, is a symbol of the political and cultural dominance of the 'Virgin Queen' during the second half of the sixteenth century. Though Elizabeth felt the need to represent herself as possessing the 'heart and stomach of a king' in spite of having the body of a 'weak and feeble woman', she was in this way – paradoxically – not afraid to draw attention to her gendered identity (Elizabeth I, 2000: 326).

Spurred on by her example, as well as by frustration with prevailing patriarchal values, Elizabeth's female subjects began to publish defences of their own sex, even though they often did so under the protection of a pseudonym.[2] 'Jane Anger', for example, proclaimed the grace, wisdom and wit of women in 1589:

There is no wisdom but it comes by grace . . . But grace was first given to a woman, because to our lady: which premises conclude that women are wise. Now 'Primum est optimum' [the first is the best], and therefore women are wiser than men. That we are more witty, which comes by nature, it cannot better be proven than that by our answers men are often driven to Nonplus. (Anger, 1589/1985: 182)[3]

The terms of Anger's argument assume religious and classical frames of reference, but use them defiantly to demonstrate female superiority and women's capacity to reduce men to silence. In 1617, a pamphleteer who called herself 'Esther Sowernam' firmly reminded her female readers of their dignity: 'You are women: in Creation, noble; in Redemption, gracious; in use, most blessed' (Sowernam, 1617/1985: 220). In the early seventeenth century there was considerable controversy over the number of women who were dressing and behaving like men,[4] and in one of the anonymous written responses to this situation the author asserts the equality of women, who are 'as freeborn as Men, have as free election and as free spirits' (Anon., 1620/1985: 284). By 1660, women were able to wear their breeches on the public stage, and had come to increasing prominence in political and religious debates as a result of the social shockwaves of the English Revolution.[5] As the seventeenth century ended and the eighteenth began, the country again had females on the throne, the last two Stuart monarchs being Mary II (until 1694) and Anne (from 1702).

It would be totally misleading, however, to paint a picture of the early modern period simply as a time of protofeminist gains. After all, why was the pseudonymous Jane Anger so angry in the 1580s, and why did 'Mary Tattlewell and Joan Hit-him-home, Spinsters' feel moved to write and publish *The Women's Sharp Revenge* in 1640 (Tattlewell, 1640/1985: 306)? These women and their contemporaries suffered physically, socially and psychologically as a result of what was considered the inheritance of Eve. John Donne summed up the problem succinctly in two lines of his 'First Anniversarie: An Anatomy of the World', written in 1611:

> One woman at one blow, then kill'd us all,
> And singly, one by one, they kill us now.   (Donne, 1985: 331)

According to this dramatically uncompromising view, all women spend their lives repeating Eve's actions, interpreted here as the betrayal and murder of men. Countless widely read early modern texts, from the Bible newly translated into the vernacular (the Authorised Version of 1611) to pamphlets such as Joseph Swetnam's *The Arraignment of Lewd, Idle, Froward, and Unconstant Women* (1615), preached misogynous opinions or urged constraints on women, particularly through marriage. The words of St Paul were frequently cited: 'Wives, submit yourselves unto your own husbands, as unto the Lord' (Ephes. 5:22). Women had no legal independence and rarely any social identity in this period without reference to their fathers or husbands. The 'marryd state' afforded 'but little Ease', according to the poet Katherine Philips in the 1640s; she suggested that the distresses of marriage could be discerned in the care-worn faces of wives, even though they had learned to 'desemble their misfortunes well' (Philips, 1988: 188–9). If women were the daughters of Eve, they were certainly bearing her punishment in the early modern period: 'Unto the woman [God] said ... in sorrow shalt thou bring forth children; and thy desire shall be to thy husband, and he shall rule over thee' (Genesis 3:16).

In keeping with this perception of womanhood, female education was extremely limited in early modern England, confined mainly to useful domestic and devotional skills. As *The Women's Sharp Revenge* claimed in 1640, women:

have not that generous and liberal Education, lest we should be able to vindicate our own injuries, we are set only to the Needle, to prick our fingers, or else to the Wheel to spin ... If we be taught to read, they then confine us within the compass of our Mother Tongue ... or if ... we be brought up to Music, to singing, and to dancing, it is not for any benefit that thereby we can engross unto ourselves, but for their own particular ends, the better to please and content their licentious appetites when we come to our maturity and ripeness. (Tattlewell, 1640/1985: 313–14)

Even the restricted education described here was only available to a small proportion of the female population: literacy rates for women in London at the beginning of the seventeenth century have been estimated at no more than 10 per cent (Cressy, 1977: 147–8). For the 90 per cent of women who were unable to write, speaking was still a significant option, though this form of self-expression or intervention was seen by the patriarchal authorities as particularly threatening to religious and social order. Thomas Becon, echoing St Paul (1 Timothy 2:11–12), urged young women to 'keep silence. For there is nothing that doth so much commend, advance, set forth, adorn, deck, trim, and garnish a maid, as silence' (Becon, 1560/1844: 369). Once she had been 'trimmed' and 'garnished' for the marriage market, a young woman continued to be expected to remain silent in marriage. 'Husbands must hold their hands [not beat their wives] and wives their tongues', advised Henry Smith in *A Preparative for Marriage* (Smith, 1591: 58). Jane Anger's vision of women's wit driving men into silence[6] was probably the very opposite of many women's actual experience.

Given these contradictory impressions of the Renaissance and seventeenth century when it comes to the position of women and their activities as speakers and writers, is it really feasible to speak of any kind of protofeminism in this period, let alone feminist literary criticism? I would firmly suggest that it is possible to discover both, and my purpose in this chapter is to support this claim. The first, and most fundamental, sign of both feminism and feminist literary awareness in this period is the very fact that women wrote at all since, as 'Constantia Munda' lamented in 1617, 'feminine modesty hath confined our rarest and ripest wits to silence' (Munda, 1617/1985: 249). When a female 'wit' gave written expression to her insights, whether in manuscript or in print, the action in itself was a statement of independence and a belief in herself as a writer, even if hedged around with apologies and provisos. As Anne Finch pointed out in 'The Introduction' to her poems:

> Alas! a woman that attempts the Pen,
> Such an intruder on the rights of men,
> Such a presumptuous Creature, is esteem'd,
> The fault, can by no vertue be redeem'd.
>
> (Finch, c. 1690/2001: 459)

This boldness – or, from another perspective, lack of 'vertue' – in an early modern woman writer is precisely what we might term feminist initiative.

The presumption of her committing pen to paper in a creative manner was deeply felt by virtually every early modern woman writer, even when, as in the case of Elizabeth Jocelin, she was addressing her text to a private audience of one, her own as yet unborn child. Fearing her approaching childbed and wishing to undertake 'some good office' for her 'little one', she 'thought of writing, but then mine own weakness appeared so manifestly that I was ashamed, and durst not undertake it'. In the end this self-doubting author wrote her advice for the child, since she 'could find no other means to express my motherly zeal' (Jocelin, 1624/1994: 267), and it was printed posthumously as *The Mothers Legacie* (1624). Here authorship is justified on the grounds of a strong maternal desire to express her care for her offspring.[7] At the other extreme, some women felt that they were so much under attack *as women* that they had no choice but to write, since misogyny could not be allowed to go unanswered. Esther Sowernam published her pamphlet *Esther hath Hanged Haman* (1617) in defiantly public exasperation at Joseph Swetnam's *Arraignment of . . . Women*; as her parodying fictional surname demonstrates, she refuted the false 'sweet' with 'sour'. But even Sowernam felt the need to explain that, because Swetnam's book was 'so commonly brought up, which argueth a general applause, we are therefore enforced to make answer in defense of ourselves, who are by such an author so extremely wronged in public view' (Sowernam, 1617/1985: 235). If women are attacked in 'public view', she asserts, then they deserve the right to defend themselves equally publicly.

Writing could itself very easily make a woman into a target for scorn, particularly if the chosen subject was deemed inappropriate. Mary Wroth was ridiculed by Lord Denny for writing a secular romance, *Urania* – 'so many ill spent years of so vain a book' – and was urged to 'redeem the time with writing as large a volume of heavenly lays and holy love as you have of lascivious tales and amorous toys' (Wroth, 1983: 34). Denny went on to compare Wroth adversely with her 'virtuous and learned aunt', Mary Sidney, who had confined her literary skills largely to the translation of the Psalms. Interestingly, by condemning one female for her literary efforts, Denny was in fact cornered into indicating that some writing by women could be acceptable. The climate for female authors was certainly beginning to change, and the issue of the 'woman that attempts the Pen' became not only the subject of censure but also a topic of attention and debate. In her *Sociable Letters* (1664), Margaret Cavendish was able to write (perhaps with an element of wishful thinking) that she had given women 'Courage and Confidence to Write, and to Divulge what they had Writ in Print'. But, lest we get carried away with Cavendish in her undoubted sense of female confidence-building, we should not forget that she herself – like so many of her contemporaries – continued to reveal ambivalence about women authors. She goes on: 'give me leave humbly to tell you, that it is no Commendation to give [women writers] Courage and Confidence, if I cannot give them Wit' (Cavendish, 1664/1997: 120). In this sharp and (ironically) witty observation, protofeminist pride goes hand in hand with an edgy disparagement of other writers of 'our Sex'.

WOMEN AS WRITERS, SUBJECTS AND READERS

The early modern period was, thus, a time of transition for the position of women in general. During this era, a woman writer – though mirroring the anxieties of the age in her often ambivalent or defensive attitude to her role – could indeed play the part of a protofeminist simply by virtue of her decision to write.[8] But to what extent were there further features of early feminist criticism in how these women wrote or read? In this section we will look more closely into the early modern phenomena that might specifically be termed feminist literary criticism, focusing on the three main strands of a feminist critical approach: attention to women as writers, as subjects and as readers.

As we have seen, it was technically possible for a small percentage of early modern Englishwomen to function as writers. A basic female education did include learning to write, even if only in English. Elizabeth Jocelin requested that, if her child were a daughter, she should be brought up with 'learning the Bible, as my sisters do, good housewifery, *writing*, and good works' (Jocelin, 1624/1994: 183, my italics). The writing to be taught to young women had a specific moral purpose, too, as outlined by the humanist Juan Luis Vives:

And when she shall learn to write, let not her examples be void verses, nor wanton or trifling songs, but some sad sentences prudent and chaste, taken out of holy Scripture, or the sayings of philosophers . . . (Vives, 1529/1912: 55)

The 'sad sentences' copied out in their lessons led many female pupils to try something more ambitious – experimenting with writing of their own – and in due course they began to make observations on the phenomenon of the woman writer to whose formation they were actively contributing. For instance, by claiming the title 'author' in their prefatory poems, writers such as Isabella Whitney (1573), An Collins (1653) and Anne Bradstreet (c. 1666; see Bradstreet, 1981: 178) were offering a protofeminist challenge to the traditional idea of the 'author' as male, modelled on a masculine God, 'that Author from whom you receive all' (Sowernam, 1617/1985: 220). The title of Whitney's introductory poem, 'A Communication Which the Author Had to London Before She Made Her Will', explicitly gives the 'Author' the female personal pronoun, offering a regendering of authorship, in addition to claiming a kind of legal status for this function by writing a metaphoric 'Will' (Whitney, 1573/1998: 1).

Thus women writers of the early modern period were acting as feminist critics themselves in their self-conscious discourses on the nature of their work. These observations are frequently to be found in the prefatory material preceding female-authored texts, including dedicatory poems and epistles, apologias and letters to their readers.[9] The clearest case of an individual woman's feminist critical reflection on the issues of women and writing is that of Aemilia Lanyer, who published a volume of her own verse, *Salve Deus Rex Judaeorum*, in 1611. More than a third of the book is taken up with dedicatory material which is almost entirely addressed to women, as though she were assembling a cast of virtuous females as both advocates on her behalf and examples for her other readers. In the course of the dedications Lanyer presents her own writings to these female patrons and readers, characterising her poetry as a 'Mirrour of a worthy Mind' and the 'first fruits of a womans wit' (Lanyer, 1611/1993: 5, 11). The identification of text, author and gender is striking here, as is the boldness of her self-presentation. On the other hand, however, she does confess to considering her work to be mere 'rude unpollisht lines', though these can yet form a 'worke of Grace' since they were written through 'Gods powre' (Lanyer, 1611/1993: 4, 41, 36). This might not be termed a conventional feminist critical strategy of the modern era, but the reliance of early modern female authors on divine power could have the feminist consequence of licensing the act of writing by a woman. As the anonymous seventeenth-century poet 'Eliza' commented, in justification of her devotional verse:

if any shall say, others may be as thankefull as shee, though they talk not so much of it; Let them know that if they did rightly apprehend the infinite mercies of God to them, they could not be silent. (Eliza, 1652/2001: 9)

This is a clear example of the woman writer seizing the opportunity of going directly against that silence which was deemed to be women's 'greatest ornament' (Munda, 1617/1985: 249), in order to praise the God under whose very authority women were enjoined to silence.[10] Paradoxically, religious devotion proved for some women writers the ultimate source of liberation.

The implied or actual feminist commentary found in the dedications, justifications and marginal notes of early modern women writers' work must always be read against the backdrop of the prevailing masculinist criticism in the era. As Anne Bradstreet wrote in 'The Prologue' to her volume of poetry *The Tenth Muse* (1650),

> If what I doe prove well, it wo'nt advance,
> They'l say it's stolne, or else, it was by chance.
>
> (Bradstreet, 1650/1981: 7)

Before her book even went into circulation, Bradstreet was fully aware of the double bind which a female poet faced: do badly and you will be mocked, but do well and your authorship will be denied. Her recognition of this trap is indeed a feminist critical consciousness, though felt as experience rather than perceived as theory. The context for the reception of women's writing was uncompromising: as Rochester bluntly asserted in the Restoration period, 'Whore is scarce a more reproachful name,/Then Poetesse' (Rochester 1984: 83). Women writers knew that their work would be read in an oppositional spirit, typified at its most excessive in the rhetoric of the pamphlet wars (Sowernam, 1617/1985: 242). Implicit in the feminist political and social debates about women's strengths and rights, therefore, were assumptions about modes of speaking and writing – in other words, issues at the heart of feminist *literary* criticism. When we come across protofeminism in the early modern period, we are never far from specifically linguistic consequences, since women's access to language (discernible in the range of stereotypes from the silent virgin to the monstrous nagging wife) was always fundamental to the gender norms of the age.

Alongside its concern with women as users of language and creators of texts, feminist literary criticism has always had as one of its central tasks the interrogation of representations of women within texts. In the early modern period this activity took two main forms: female condemnation of male authors for their inadequate images of women, and the creation of alternative female character types. The former involved critical attacks on the harsh early modern stereotypes of women: the inconstant lover, the nagging wife, the shrewish spinster, the disdainful mistress or the seducing whore. Male authors were taken to task, through the dynamic medium of controversial pamphlets, for their incessant use of these limiting characterisations. Even in the knock-about context of the pamphlets, however, the women's arguments frequently had a consciously literary aspect, revealing an astute sense of the way in which feminine images in texts could prolong discrimination. In *The Women's Sharp Revenge*, Tattlewell and Hit-him-home are especially critical of the conventional male poets who wrote about their discontented relationships with a 'coy or disdainful Mistress'. The feminist pamphlet focuses its attack on the inaccurate and damaging fictions of the sort of love poet who does 'nothing but rail at us, thinking he hath done his Mistress praise, when it may be he hath no Mistress at all but only feigns to himself some counterfeit Phyllis or Amaryllis, such as had never any person but a mere airy name' (Tattlewell, 1640/1985: 313). The evident frustration in this passage is directed towards the dangerous falsification of women in male-authored works, and the references to 'Phyllis or Amaryllis', generic shepherdesses of Renaissance pastoral love poetry, make this attack specifically literary as well as social and educational. As a subsequent comment demonstrates, Tattlewell and Hit-him-home are sensitive to the damage that literary attitudes and the over-reliance on stereotypes can cause, for the 'vain enthusiasms and Raptures' of such poets result in 'the disgrace and Prejudice of our whole Sex' (313).

Many early modern women writers, discontented with the representation of women in imaginative texts by men, adopted a creative alternative to a negative attack on the stereotypes of men's writing: they formed new female character types of their own. Mary Wroth, for example, conscious of the constricting passivity and misrepresentation of the female object addressed by the typical sonnet sequence, turned the tables and wrote her own sonnets from the woman's perspective. *Pamphilia to Amphilanthus* (1621) gives voice and interiority to the female subject, and represents the male as the cruel and inconstant partner, or 'lover of two' as his name specifies. The situation of the female poet, speaker and lover is not a joyous one – her sonnets talk of 'grief' and she vividly reconstructs the 'labyrinth' of the lover's experience (Wroth, 1983: 123, 127) – but the project has the hallmarks of a feminist rethinking and rewriting, configuring anew the fundamental literary assumptions of the sonnet-writing era. Katherine Philips, too, intervened notably in the history of love poetry by reworking the conventions of the romantic lyric. In her mid-seventeenth century poems such as 'Friendship's Mysterys', she presents female friendship as a higher alternative to the 'captivity' of marriage – indeed, as a life of holiness, since 'There's a religion in our Love' (Philips, 1988: 193). Philips' poems were put to music by Henry Lawes, one of the leading composers of word-settings in the period. Thus even an inability to read was not an obstacle to the transfer of feminist re-appropriations of amorous stereotypes – for in a culture of performance, ideas were seen and heard in drama and music, as well as received through private reading.

This brings us to the third strand of feminist literary criticism, focusing on women as recipients of texts, and in particular as readers – an important and largely new phenomenon in the early modern period.[11] Though their numbers may have been small, women readers became significant consumers of literature during this era: as Margaret Cavendish wrote, 'our Sex is more apt to Read than to Write' (Cavendish, 1664/1997: 120). Male writers at the time predicated their hopes of success on the responsiveness of the woman reader. As Philip Sidney wittily demonstrated in sonnet 45 of *Astrophil and Stella* (c. 1582), the emotional reaction of Stella to a 'fable' or 'some thrice-sad tragedy' gave Astrophil some hope that she might, in turn, have pity on 'the tale' of his devotion to her (Sidney, 1973: 139). However, the scenario did not always work in the way the men intended, as Tattlewell and Hit-him-home humorously indicate in *The Women's Sharp Revenge*:

Captain Compliment ... would sometimes salute me with most delicious Sentences, which he always kept in syrup, and he never came to me empty mouthed or handed, for he was never unprovided of stewed Anagrams, baked Epigrams, soused Madrigals, pickled Rondelets, broiled Sonnets, par-boiled Elegies, perfumed poesies for Rings, and a thousand other such foolish flatteries and knavish devices which I suspected. (Tattlewell, 1640/1985: 315–16)

With this delightful application of a series of culinary adjectives to the popular poetic forms of the day, Tattlewell and Hit-him-home underline the importance of women as the intended audience of literary efforts. The female recipient of a literary text has significant power if she exercises her freedom to reject the rhetoric applied to her.

The prefaces addressed to female readers and patrons by Renaissance and seventeenth-century women writers form a fascinating body of

information about the prevalence of feminist literary concerns in the early
modern period. In 1589, Jane Anger praises 'the Gentlewomen of England'
for their high quality as readers: 'your wits are sharp and will soon conceive
my meaning' (Anger, 1589/1985: 173). A remarkable degree of partnership
between female writers and readers was envisaged by the authors. Anger,
doing her utmost to 'stretch the veins of her brains' in defence of women,
urged her readers to 'aid and assist' her in this action (174), while Aemilia
Lanyer even goes so far as to ask the Queen to check her work for her:

> Behold, great Queene, faire *Eves* Apologie,
> Which I have writ in honour of your sexe,
> And doe referre unto your Majestie,
> To judge if it agree not with the Text:
> And if it doe, why are poore Women blam'd,
> Or by more faultie Men so much defam'd?
>
> (Lanyer, 1611/1993: 6)

In this stanza addressed to Anne of Denmark (wife of James I), Lanyer
condenses and brings together all three central aspects of feminist literary
criticism. First, as a writer, Lanyer is drawing attention to her own text –
'Behold' – and highlighting its radical purpose as a book of poems written
'in honour' of women. Second, her subject is the world's mistakenly
negative estimation of women as daughters of Eve, whose reputation
Lanyer's work, particularly the section referred to as 'fair *Eves* Apologie',
seeks to reassess by shifting the blame for the fall to 'more faultie Men'.
And third, her intended reader is the highest woman in the land, the Queen
of England, from whom Lanyer confidently expects patronage. This is
likely to take the form not only of (she would hope) financial support but
also of careful reading of Lanyer's poem to check the accuracy of her
reinterpretation against 'the Text', Genesis, upon which the Western
world's prejudice against women was founded.

There is widespread evidence that women were active and highly critical
readers in the early modern period. Women writers certainly could not
count on the sympathy of their female readers, as comments in the letters of
Dorothy Osborne make uncomfortably clear. Writing to William Temple
in 1653 about the published literary work of her contemporary, Margaret
Cavendish (Duchess of Newcastle), Osborne asserts harshly that 'there are
many soberer People in Bedlam' (Osborne, 1987: 79). In an earlier letter
she reveals the assumptions underlying this judgement:

And first let me ask you if you have seen a book of poems newly come out, made by
my lady New Castle for God sake if you meet with it send it mee, they say it is ten

times more Extravagant then her dresse. Sure the poore woman is a litle distracted, she could never be soe rediculous else as to venture at writeing book's and in verse too. (Osborne, 1987: 75)

Osborne's preconceptions are made all too clear in these comments: though the Duchess might be an extreme case, any woman who writes and publishes books, particularly of poetry, must be mad. However, the 'distracted' Cavendish herself also demonstrates that women were responsive critical readers of a wide range of texts by men and women. In her own *Sociable Letters* – which, unlike Osborne's, were specifically intended for publication – Cavendish wrote the earliest known critical essay on the works of Shakespeare from the point of view of a reader rather than spectator of his plays:

I wonder how that Person you mention in your Letter, could either have the Conscience, or Confidence to Dispraise Shakespear's Playes ... one would think that he had been Metamorphosed from a Man to a Woman, for who could Describe Cleopatra Better than he hath done, and many other Females of his own Creating, as Nan Page, Mrs Page, Mrs Ford, the Doctors Maid, Bettrice, Mrs Quickly, Doll Tearsheet, and others, too many to Relate? (Cavendish, 1664/1997: 130)

With these remarks on the women in the plays and her fascinating suggestion of Shakespeare's creative androgyny, we may safely claim that Cavendish's account includes the first feminist commentary on Shakespeare. Feminist literary criticism was indeed alive and well in seventeenth-century England.

FEMINIST LITERARY CRITICISM IN THE MAKING

So far we have seen how the complex gender politics of the early modern period gave rise, through continued constraints as well as new freedoms, to an outburst of writing by women. In their texts, the three fundamental aspects of feminist literary criticism – concern with women as writers, subjects and readers of literature – may all be discerned. The final section of this chapter will highlight some of the ways in which Renaissance and seventeenth-century feminist critical responses to literature also foreshadowed the questions and anxieties of later feminist criticism.

It is noteworthy, for instance, that early modern women writers were concerned with fundamental issues of access to the conventions and culture of the literary world, rather as Virginia Woolf was when excluded from the library of a Cambridge college (Woolf, 1929). As Martha Moulsworth asks with startling simplicity in her autobiographical 'Memorandum' of 1632, when noting that her father taught her some Latin:

> And why not so? The muses females are
> And therefore of us females take some care.
> Two universities we have of men;
> Oh that we had but one of women then!
>
> (Moulsworth, 1632/1996: 12)

Moulsworth perceived that to be prevented from gaining classical learning, and denied access to the centres of higher education, was in direct contradiction to the assumed femininity of the muses, the sources of literary inspiration. Nevertheless, middle-class women like Moulsworth wrote creatively in this period, giving expression to their own muses in whatever vernacular forms or personally devised genres they felt appropriate; the 'Memorandum', for example, matches its number of couplets to the number of years in Martha's life at the point of writing. Indeed, the individualised experience of writing is a phenomenon most fully recorded in this period by women, anticipating the autobiographical turn of much modern feminist criticism. 'Constantia Munda', addressing Joseph Swetnam in 1617, gives an impression of herself as a writer at work: 'I would give a *supersedeas* [the command to forbear] to my quill, but there is a most pregnant place in your book which is worthy the laughter that comes in my mind' (Munda, 1617/1985: 261). The mingling of the physical and mental aspects of writing (the quill, pregnancy, laughter, the mind), as well as the close interaction of reading and writing, gives a sense of the immediacy of authorship and links writing to the body and personality of the writer. A similar effect was created some thirty years later in Margaret Cavendish's description of the writing process, included in her autobiographical memoir 'A True Relation'. Despite referring to her art as more 'scribbling than writing', she gives a remarkable account of how, when 'thoughts are sent out in words', they cease to draw back but tumble out like a 'ragged rout' too quickly for her pen to keep up (Cavendish, 1656/1989: 93–4). In their attentive awareness of the moment of writing, early modern women writers prefigured the continuing feminist critical desire to understand the process of writing by women.

The gendering of literature, from authorship and readership to the forms and genres of texts themselves, was also very much a concern of early modern women. To what extent could they break through the conventional associations of masculinity with literary creativity and femininity with textuality? Towards the end of the seventeenth century,

Aphra Behn still experienced the 'poet' within her as her 'masculine part' (Behn, 1994: xxii), even though her works were among the most pioneering of the period in their treatment of the roles and rights of women. Literary genres, as well as authorship, were understood in gendered terms in the early modern period. Translating texts was a mode of literary activity much favoured by (and for) women, and according to John Florio 'all translations are reputed femalls', on the grounds that they are 'defective' works, secondary by nature (Florio, 1603: A2r). In slightly more flattering terms, Cornelius Agrippa called history-writing 'the Mistresse of life' (Agrippa, 1575: E1v), not by association with women writers but metaphorically implying the relationship between living in the present (male action) and considering the past (female accompaniment). However, certain kinds of texts were particularly associated with female authors in practice, through accessibility or apparent appropriateness.[12] In her *Sociable Letters* Cavendish listed the genres most commonly written by women as including not only letters themselves but also 'Devotions', 'Romances', 'Receits [recipes] of Medicines, for Cookery or Confectioners' and 'Verses'. Ironically for such a prolific writer, Cavendish pointed out that the works which 'our Sex do Write . . . seems rather as Briefs than Volumes', whereby women express their 'Brief Wit' in 'Short Works' (Cavendish, 1664/1997: 120–1). The very idea of wit was itself gendered: Lanyer was not alone in the period in defiantly referring to her poetry as the fruit or offspring of her 'womans wit' (Lanyer, 1611/1993: 11), and Cavendish used revealingly gendered – largely feminine – metaphors in a survey of varieties of wit, which included 'Gossiping Wit, as Midwife and Nurse Wit, also Wafer and Hippocras Wit, Ale and Cake Wit, as in Christning, Churching, Lying in . . .' (Cavendish, 1664/1997: 57).[13] The focus of recent feminist criticism on the gendered nature of the literary process has its forerunner in these Renaissance and seventeenth-century observations.

Intimations of some of the fundamental clashes within recent feminist thinking are also to be detected in the poetic and critical works of early modern women writers. Should women emulate men as they attempt to make the world a fairer place, or is it better to focus on the different strengths that women can offer to society? Can strident intervention be counter-productive? Is a desire for modest change an admission of failure? These issues inform the works of many Renaissance women writers, and are often given expression in explicitly literary ways. Elizabeth Cary's early seventeenth-century drama, *The Tragedy of Mariam*, for example, offers several alternative models of female heroism as the embodiment of these very dilemmas. Mariam, the tragic heroine, is shown to be at her strongest and yet her most vulnerable through her eloquent use of language: her opening line, 'How oft have I with public voice run on' (Cary, 1613/1994: 69, I.1), is an immediate sign of both danger and inspiration. In the end she dies a victim of Herod and his patriarchal world, despite her perceived chastity and the 'sweet tune' of her final speech like that of a 'fair dying swan' (1613/1994: 141, V.65). Mariam's sister-in-law, Salome, by contrast, asks passionately why men should have the 'privilege' of being able to divorce an unworthy partner, while that right is 'barr'd from women' (80, I.305–6). Her question, 'Are men than we in greater grace with Heaven?', sounds sympathetically egalitarian, but the line which follows, 'Or cannot women hate as well as men?', strikes a more aggressive tone (80, I.307–8). The full range of possible female – or feminist – reactions to the masculine world order is sketched in Cary's tragic drama.[14]

The feminist vision of the early modern period was not restricted to tragedy, however. As we have discovered, works from this era were equally capable of celebrating women's initiatives, praising good men and women, envisioning unfettered female friendship and enjoying a comic or satiric response to the strangeness of women's position in the world. Importantly, they were also able to look forward, imagining new worlds and setting them ablaze with their imaginations.[15] The existing world around them was not getting any friendlier towards women – indeed, at the beginning of the eighteenth century Mary Chudleigh complained that women were still 'Debarred from knowledge' and told they were 'incapable of wit' (Chudleigh, 1701/1994: 283), while Mary Astell observed that 'The world will hardly allow a Woman to say anything well, unless as she borrow it from Men, or is assisted by them' (Astell, 1706). The opportunities for women as writers, speakers or readers were not necessarily improving at the end of the seventeenth century, but the central issues of what we would term feminist literary criticism had undoubtedly entered the literary and social consciousness during the early modern period. Through their increased literary production in private and public, and their active participation as consumers as well as creators of texts, early modern women gave shape to the prevailing questions of subsequent feminist literary criticism. Virginia Woolf, so important a figure in that later movement, may have thought that not a word of the 'extraordinary literature' of the Renaissance period had been written by a woman, even though 'every other man, it seemed, was capable of a song or sonnet' (Woolf, 1929: 41). Fortunately, however, the quarrelsome, expressive and witty works of those once-hidden women writers are now available to be acknowledged, read and enjoyed – and not least for their contribution to the history of feminist literary criticism.

NOTES

1. For useful surveys of the work of early modern women writing in these genres in English, see Beilin (1987), Hobby (1988), Krontiris (1992), Lewalski (1993), Schleiner (1994), Wilcox (1996) and Wray (2004). For an example of a female-authored conversion narrative (an autobiographical confession of sinfulness followed by an account of religious conversion), see Hannah Allen, *Satan his Methods and Malice Baffled* (1683), in Graham et al. (1989: 197–210).

2. For an excellent defence of these women writers against the claim that their pseudonyms masked male authors, see Henderson and McManus (1985: 20–4).

3. This quotation is taken from Anger's text as anthologised by Henderson and McManus, a principle which is followed as far as possible throughout this chapter in order to enable non-specialist readers further to explore this remarkable body of work. Among the most useful modern anthologies of early modern texts by or about women are Aughterson (1995), Ceresano and Wynne-Davies (1996), Graham et al. (1989), Greer et al. (1988), Henderson and McManus (1985), Keeble (1994), Stevenson and Davidson (2001), Trill et al. (1997) and Wynne-Davies (1998).

4. This was such a trend in the early seventeenth century that a number of pamphlets were published on the subject (including *Hic Mulier; or, The Man-Woman*, and *Haec Vir; or, The Womanish Man*, 1620) and King James I made a royal pronouncement against women wearing men's apparel (Henderson and McManus, 1985: 17–18, 264–89).

5. For the work of women writers during the turbulent years of the mid-seventeenth century, see Davies (1641/1995) and Trapnel (1654/2000); for discussions of them and their contemporaries, see Davies (1998), Chalmers (2005) and Hinds (1996).

6. Anger claimed that women's clever answers often led men to 'Nonplus' – that is, to admit that they could say nothing more in response; see above.

7. For a fuller account of mothers' advice books, see Wayne (1996).

8. It has certainly been considered possible to describe women from this period as feminists; see Smith (1982) and Ferguson (1985).

9. See Wilcox (2001).

10. See Luckyj (2002) and Hannay (1985).

11. See Hull (1982) and Pearson (1996).

12. Women writers and readers were, for example, especially associated with the romance (Hackett, 2000; Lucas, 1989).

13. These women were, like all feminist critics, working against the grain of accepted convention; Donne's poetic skill, for example, was praised by Thomas Carew for its 'masculine expression' (Donne, 1985: 497).

14. For a fuller discussion of female roles in *The Tragedy of Mariam*, see Ferguson (1996) and Beilin (1987).

15. For instance, Margaret Cavendish's *Blazing World* (1666), in Cavendish (1992).

BIBLIOGRAPHY

Agrippa, Henrie Cornelius (1575), *Of the Vanitie and Uncertaintie of Artes and Sciences*, trans. Ia. San. Gent., London: Henrie Bynneman.

Anger, Jane (1589/1985), *Her Protection for Women*, in Henderson and McManus (1985).

Anon. (1620/1985), *Hic Mulier; or, The Man-Woman* and *Haec Vir; or, The Womanish Man*, in Henderson and McManus (1985).

Astell, Mary (1706), *Some Reflections upon Marriage*, 3rd edition, London.

Aughterson, Kate (ed.) (1995), *Renaissance Woman: A Sourcebook*, London: Routledge.

Becon, Thomas (1560/1844), *A New Catechism*, ed. John Ayre, Cambridge: Cambridge University Press.

Behn, Aphra (1994), *The Poems of Aphra Behn: A Selection*, ed. Janet Todd, London: William Pickering.

Beilin, Elaine V. (1987), *Women Writers of the English Renaissance*, Princeton, NJ: Princeton University Press.

The Bible: Authorised King James Version (1611/1997), ed. Robert Carroll and Stephen Prickett, Oxford: Oxford University Press.

Bradstreet, Anne (1650/1981), *The Tenth Muse Lately Sprung Up in America*, in Bradstreet (1981).

—— (1981), *The Complete Works*, ed. Joseph R. McElrath and Allan P. Robb, Boston: Twayne.

Cary, Elizabeth (1613/1994), *The Tragedy of Mariam*, ed. Barry Weller and Margaret W. Ferguson, Berkeley: University of California Press.

Cavendish, Margaret, Duchess of Newcastle (1656/1989), 'A True Relation of My Birth, Breeding and Life', in Graham et al. (1989).

—— (1664/1997), *Sociable Letters*, ed. James Fitzmaurice, New York: Garland.

—— (1992), *'The Blazing World' and Other Writings*, ed. Kate Lilley, Harmondsworth: Penguin.

Ceresano, S. P. and Marion Wynne-Davies (eds) (1996), *Renaissance Drama by Women: Texts and Documents*, London: Routledge.

Chalmers, Hero (2005), *Royalist Women Writers, 1650–1689*, London: Oxford University Press.

Chudleigh, Lady Mary (1701/1994), *The Ladies Defence*, in Keeble (1994).

Collins, Ann (1653/1996), *Divine Songs and Meditacions*, ed. Sidney Gottlieb, Tempe: Medieval and Renaissance Texts and Studies.

Cressy, David (1977), 'Literacy in Seventeenth-Century England: More Evidence', in *Journal of Interdisciplinary History* 8.

Davies, Lady Eleanor (1641/1995), *Her Appeale to the High Court of Parliament*, in *Prophetic Writings*, ed. Esther E. Cope, New York: Oxford University Press.

Davies, Stevie (1998), *Unbridled Spirits: Women of the English Revolution, 1640–1660*, London: Women's Press.

Donne, John (1985), *Complete English Poems*, ed. C. A. Patrides, London: Dent.

Eliza (1652/2001), *Eliza's Babes: Or the Virgin's Offering*, ed. L. E. Semler, Madison: Fairleigh Dickinson University Press.

Elizabeth I (2000), *Collected Works*, ed. Leah S. Marcus, Janel Mueller and Mary Beth Rose, Chicago: University of Chicago Press.

Ferguson, Margaret W. (1996), 'Renaissance Concepts of the "Woman Writer"', in Wilcox (1996).

Ferguson, Moira (1985), *First Feminists: British Women Writers 1578–1799*, Urbana: University of Illinois Press.

Finch, Anne (c. 1690/2001), 'The Introduction', in Stevenson and Davidson (2001).

Florio, John (1603), Preface to Michel de Montaigne, *Essayes*, trans. John Florio, London.

Graham, Elspeth, Hilary Hinds, Elaine Hobby and Helen Wilcox (eds) (1989), *Her Own Life: Autobiographical Writings by Seventeenth-Century Englishwomen*, London: Routledge.

Greer, Germaine, Jeslyn Medoff, Melinda Sansone and Susan Hastings (eds) (1988), *Kissing the Rod: An Anthology of 17th Century Women's Verse*, London: Virago.

Hackett, Helen (2000), *Women and Romance Fiction in the English Renaissance*, Cambridge: Cambridge University Press.

Hannay, Margaret P. (ed.) (1985), *Silent but for the Word: Tudor Women as Patrons, Translators, and Writers of Religious Works*, Kent, Ohio: Kent State University Press.

Henderson, Katherine Usher and Barbara F. McManus (eds) (1985), *Half Humankind: Contexts and Texts of the Controversy about Women in England, 1540–1640*, Urbana: University of Illinois Press.

Hinds, Hilary (1996), *God's Englishwomen: Seventeenth-Century Radical Sectarian Writing and Feminist Criticism*, Manchester and New York: Manchester University Press.

Hobby, Elaine (1988), *Virtue of Necessity: English Women's Writing 1649–88*, London: Virago.

Hull, Suzanne W. (1982), *Chaste, Silent, and Obedient: English Books for Women, 1475–1640*, San Marino, CA: Huntington Library.

Jocelin, Elizabeth (1624/1994), *The Mothers Legacie to her Unborn Childe*, in Keeble (1994).

Keeble, N. H. (ed.) (1994), *The Cultural Identity of Seventeenth-Century Woman: A Reader*, London: Routledge.

Knox, John (1558), *The First Blast of the Trumpet against the Monstrous Regiment of Women*, Geneva.

Krontiris, Tina (1992), *Oppositional Voices: Women as Writers and Translators of Literature in the English Renaissance*, London: Routledge.

Lanyer, Aemilia (1611/1993), *The Poems of Aemilia Lanyer: Salve Deus Rex Judaeorum*, ed. Susanne Woods, New York: Oxford University Press.

Leigh, Dorothy (1616/1994), *The Mothers Blessing*, in Keeble (1994).

Lewalski, Barbara Kiefer (1993), *Writing Women in Jacobean England*, Cambridge, MA: Harvard University Press.

Lucas, Caroline (1989), *Writing for Women: The Example of Woman as Reader in Elizabethan Romance*, Milton Keynes: Open University Press.

Luckyj, Christina (2002), 'A Moving Rhetoricke': Gender and Silence in Early Modern England, Manchester: Manchester University Press.

Moulsworth, Martha (1632/1996), 'The Memorandum of Martha Moulsworth, Widow', in 'The Birthday of My Self': Martha Moulsworth, Renaissance Poet, ed. Ann Depas-Orange and Robert C. Evans, Princeton, NJ: Critical Matrix.

Munda, Constantia (1617/1985), The Worming of a Mad Dog, in Henderson and McManus (1985).

Osborne, Dorothy (1987), Letters to Sir William Temple, ed. Kenneth Parker, London: Penguin.

Pearson, Jacqueline (1996), 'Women Reading, Reading Women', in Wilcox (1996).

Philips, Katherine (1988), 'A Marryd State' and 'Friendship's Mysterys', in Greer et al. (1988).

Rochester, John Wilmot, Earl of (1984), 'A Letter from Artemiza in the Towne to Chloe in the Countrey', in Poems, ed. Keith Walker, Oxford: Basil Blackwell.

Schleiner, Louise (1994), Tudor and Stuart Women Writers, Bloomington: Indiana University Press.

Sidney, Sir Philip (1973), Selected Poems, ed. Katherine Duncan-Jones, Oxford: Clarendon Press.

Smith, Barbara and Ursula Appelt (eds) (2001), Write or Be Written: Early Modern Women Poets and Cultural Constraints, Aldershot: Ashgate.

Smith, Henry (1591), A Preparative for Marriage, London.

Smith, Hilda L. (1982), Reason's Disciples: Seventeenth-Century English Feminists, Urbana: University of Illinois Press.

Sowernam, Esther (1617/1985), Esther hath Hanged Haman, in Henderson and McManus (1985).

Stevenson, Jane and Peter Davidson (eds) (2001), Early Modern Women Poets: An Anthology, Oxford: Oxford University Press.

Tattlewell, Mary and Joan Hit-him-home (1640/1985), The Women's Sharp Revenge, in Henderson and McManus (1985).

Trapnel, Anna (1654/2000), The Cry of a Stone, ed. Hilary Hinds, Tempe: Medieval and Renaissance Texts and Studies.

Trill, Suzanne, Kate Chedgzoy and Melanie Osborne (eds) (1997), Lay by Your Needles Ladies, Take the Pen, London: Edward Arnold.

Vives, Juan Luis (1529/1912), The Instruction of a Christian Woman, trans. Richard Hyrde, in Vives and the Renascence Education of Women, ed. Foster Watson, New York: Longmans Green.

Wayne, Valerie (1996), 'Advice for Women from Mothers and Patriarchs', in Wilcox (1996).

Whitney, Isabella (1573/1998), 'Her Will to London', in Wynne-Davies (1998).

Wilcox, Helen (ed.) (1996), Women and Literature in Britain, 1500–1700, Cambridge: Cambridge University Press.

(2001), '"First Fruits of a Woman's Wit": Authorial Self-Construction of English Renaissance Women Poets', in Smith and Appelt (2001).

Woolf, Virginia (1929/1977), A Room of One's Own, London: Grafton.

Wray, Ramona (2004), *Women Writers of the Seventeenth Century*, Tavistock: Northcote House.

Wroth, Lady Mary (1983), *Poems*, ed. Josephine A. Roberts, Baton Rouge: Louisiana State University Press.

Wynne-Davies, Marion (ed.) (1998), *Women Poets of the Renaissance*, London: Dent.

CHAPTER 3

Mary Wollstonecraft and her legacy

Susan Manly

INTRODUCTION

Although she is generally regarded as a writer of great influence for the
development of feminist political thought and the feminist analysis of
literary representations of women, Mary Wollstonecraft's work remains
controversial. Particular attention has been paid to her alleged rejection or
suspicion of sexuality, imagination and emotional expression. Cora Kaplan
summarises the divergence of modern critical opinion on Wollstonecraft's
life and work thus:

Was the erotic and affective imagination, gendered or universal, a blessing or a
curse for women? Was it indispensable to radical consciousness, irrefutably a part
of human psychic life, or was it something that could and should be jettisoned
or retrained? If gendered identity was largely a matter of social construction . . .
then could a brave new world reconstruct its unconscious as well as its conscious
wishes? (Kaplan, 2002: 259)[1]

Wollstonecraft struggled with these questions of identity, fantasy and
desire, and her work shows the fierceness of the contest. Emerging in the
shadow of the momentous changes in society and destruction of old
and powerful institutions that the French Revolution represented,
Wollstonecraft's writings reflected the urgency and excitement, and eventually the crushing despair, felt by all those who wished for, and acted to
bring about, a 'brave new world'. The Revolution, asserted Virginia Woolf,
'was not merely an event that had happened outside her; it was an active
agent in her own blood', with all the contentions, contradictions and
contesting for dominance that the metaphor suggests (Woolf, 1932/1986:
158). It prompted Wollstonecraft to experiments in her own life – her love
affairs, her illegitimate child, her friendships with men and her determination to live independently – as well as giving impetus to her ideas about
female sexuality and sensibility, and women's status as writers, intellectuals, mothers and citizens. These ideas were not only played out in her

46

own lived experience (which many subsequent feminists, including Woolf and Emma Goldman, have found as compelling as, or even more compelling than, her work); they also found public expression in her two *Vindications* and in her last novel, *The Wrongs of Woman* (1798).[2] This chapter will focus on Wollstonecraft's writing, showing how the issues she raised were taken up in the 1790s and into the nineteenth century by other writers, including Maria Edgeworth, Mary Robinson, Harriet Martineau, Harriet Taylor, John Stuart Mill and George Eliot.[3]

Elaine Showalter has defined late twentieth-century feminist literary criticism as developing out of two kinds of writing. In the first place, she suggests, there is feminist critique, which focuses on the analysis of women as readers and as textual subjects, both of male- and female-authored works. In other words, feminist critique is concerned with woman as 'the consumer of male-produced literature', with what happens when we consciously reflect on what it means to read as a woman, and to become aware of the significance of the sexual codes and stereotypes embedded within a given text. Showalter identifies a different kind of feminist critique in 'gyno-critics', which focuses on the theory and practice of women as writers – on 'woman as the producer of textual meaning' (Showalter, 1979: 25). Yet in her *Vindications*, Wollstonecraft was already combining both of these: she attacks the false sensibility that she labels as corrupt and artificial in Edmund Burke's work, and she rewrites her own authorial femininity as a regenerated natural discourse of rational, humane feeling and ethical imagination. In so doing, she constructs an idea of the woman writer as the antithesis of artifice and corruption, and as a being essentially without gender, in contrast with Burke, whom she identifies as himself embodying the inauthentic femininity that is the byproduct of an unprincipled society and aesthetic. For Wollstonecraft, Burke's aesthetic ideas, together with his sexual politics and political conservatism, perpetuate a degenerate old order undeserving of preservation. Through her allusions to Burke's aesthetic theory, the influential *Philosophical Enquiry into the Origin of Our Ideas of the Sublime and Beautiful*, and her analysis of his *Reflections on the Revolution in France*, Wollstonecraft begins the critique of textual femininity that she continues two years later in *A Vindication of the Rights of Woman*.[4]

WOLLSTONECRAFT AND FEMINIST CRITIQUE

In his *Philosophical Enquiry*, Burke had identified the sublime with power, masculinity and the experience of pain, while the beautiful was associated with weakness, femininity and the experience of pleasure: 'Those virtues which cause admiration, and are of the sublimer kind, produce terror rather than love' (Burke, 1757/1990: 100). Whereas the sublime was powerfully affecting, fearful in its ability to rob the mind of thought, beauty had, Burke argued, a very different effect on feeling and intellect: rather than being 'hurried out of itself' (1757/1990: 57), the mind was soothed and flattered. Throughout the *Enquiry*, Burke assumes that his reader, and the mind he describes, are male, and repeatedly refers to the emotions aroused in heterosexual men by the female body and 'feminine' behaviour to explain the affective character of beauty. 'By beauty I mean, that quality or those qualities in bodies by which they cause love', he elaborates, and goes on:

this quality, where it is highest in the female sex, always carries with it an idea of weakness and imperfection. Women are very sensible of this; for which reason, they learn to lisp, to totter in their walk, to counterfeit weakness, and even sickness. In all this, they are guided by nature ... The sublime ... always dwells on great objects, and terrible; the [beautiful] on small ones, and pleasing; we submit to what we admire, but we love what submits to us; in one case we are forced, on the other we are flattered into compliance. (1757/1990: 83, 103)

As Wollstonecraft herself suggests, Burke's aesthetic categories, already implicitly justifying and naturalising the hierarchy of the powerful over the powerless, become explicitly political in his *Reflections on the Revolution in France*. In particular, she notices how Burke uses 'courtly insincerity' and 'unrestrained feelings' to arouse a strong response in his reader and compares him to a 'celebrated beauty' who is 'anxious ... to raise admiration on every occasion, and excite emotion' rather than 'the calm reciprocation of mutual esteem and unimpassioned respect' (Wollstonecraft, 1790/1995: 6). In contrast with this, Wollstonecraft represents herself as speaking 'with manly plainness', offering a 'manly definition' of 'the rights of humanity' and 'the liberty of reason' (1790/1995: 36, 5). It is the inauthenticity of Burke's representation of gender and his unconvincing 'parade of sensibility' which disturbs Wollstonecraft; as Stephen Cox points out, she sees both as socially conservative because they replace 'truly spontaneous and individual consciousness with externally imposed imitations of feeling' (Cox, 1990: 66). Thus her critique of the artificiality of gender constructions merges with and is mediated through her critique of artificial feeling, as we see when she suggests that Burke's imaginings of the sufferings of the French king and queen at the hands of the revolutionary mob are 'pretty flights' arising from his 'pampered sensibility'. When Burke argues, she asserts, 'you become impassioned, and ... reflection inflames your imagination, instead of enlightening your understanding' (Wollstonecraft, 1790/1995: 6, 7). Indeed, for Wollstonecraft, Burke is a stereotypically 'feminine' Eve-figure. She summarises Burke's anti-revolutionary rhetoric as a ploy to tempt his readers into regarding 'unnatural customs' as 'the sage fruit of experience' (1790/1995: 8), the language here suggesting that this is in fact a fatal fruit, which leads to expulsion from the site of real naturalness: 'numberless vices, forced in the hot-bed of wealth, assume a sightly form to dazzle the senses and cloud the understanding', 'stifl[ing] the natural affections on which human contentment ought to be built' (1790/1995: 24). Rather than resisting these temptations and refusing to offer them to others, Burke has, she contends, allowed himself to be seduced, becoming 'the adorer of the golden image which power has set up' (1790/1995: 12).[5]

Wollstonecraft thus exposes the 'romantic spirit' in Burke's panegyric, which she associates with 'the *pretended* effusions of the heart' and a 'sentimental jargon' devoid of the only kind of sovereignty she thinks legitimate: 'the regal stamp of reason' (1790/1995: 29, 30). She shows that Burke is at once feminised and feminising: he displays the false sensibility, the 'dry raptures' and absence of principle of artificial femininity (1790/1995: 29), but he also uses a discourse of beauty to attach his readers to the idea of aristocracy and monarchy, in short, to induce them to love the idea of inequality, as women are supposed to do. Both false sensibility and the importance attached to beauty are, for Wollstonecraft, corrupt and inauthentic: to her mind, they suggest the supposed 'dignity' and 'infallibility of sensibility' in the wives of plantation-owners, who 'compose their ruffled spirits and exercise their tender feelings by the perusal of the last imported novel' to recover themselves after having dreamt up new tortures and punishments for slaves (1790/1995: 46).

Wollstonecraft rejects Burke's 'feminine' submission to artificial sentiment, then, in favour of 'the feelings of *humanity*', which involve 'active exertions of virtue' (1790/1995: 56; her italics). The corrupt imagination and aestheticisation of inequality demonstrated in Burke's discourse of beauty is, Wollstonecraft declares, inimical to the virtuous state: this could only arise 'if man was contented to be the friend of man, and did not seek to bury the sympathies of humanity in the servile appellation of master' (1790/1995: 61). Her critique of artificiality and inequality, and the way this is propagated through literature, is continued in the more famous *Vindication of the Rights of Woman*: again, her target is Burke's *Philosophical Enquiry* and *Reflections*, but Burke is joined by Milton and Rousseau as fellow authors of a fictitious femininity, and patriarchal enemies in league against female emancipation.

In the *Vindication of the Rights of Men*, Wollstonecraft had suggested the power of textual representations of women, blaming Burke's theory of beauty and sublimity for the behaviour of ladies who 'have laboured to be pretty, by counterfeiting weakness', choosing 'not to cultivate the moral virtues that might chance to excite respect, and interfere with the pleasing sensations they were created to inspire' (1790/1995: 47). In her introduction to the *Vindication of the Rights of Woman*, she likewise alleges that women have been corrupted and stunted by their reading, which has 'enfeebled' their minds with notions of false refinement – a consequence not confined to those who read frivolous novels, but also communicated through 'books of instruction, written by men of genius' (Wollstonecraft, 1792/1995: 74). She therefore sets out to construct a model of non-gendered identity – one which will ultimately benefit men as well as women, since she sees both as degraded by sexualised and oppositional models of identity. Wollstonecraft is writing this time expressly as a woman, making her sex clear at the outset of the work, rather than implicitly assuming the masculine persona of the anonymously issued *Vindication of the Rights of Men*; but crucially, she represents writing and thinking as activities in which the body and its sex are transcended. For her, it seems necessary to assert this transcendence in order to reach beyond women's objectification and the idea that female subjectivity, conventionally defined by sexual submission, acceptance of intellectual inferiority and delicate sensibility, was distinct from male subjectivity, defined in diametrically opposed terms.

Such is the ferocity of Wollstonecraft's rejection of conventional femininity that it can seem as if she is suggesting that there is nothing to be valued about being a woman: as Barbara Taylor observes, 'the rhetorical weight of Wollstonecraft's attack falls so heavily on her own sex as to make a reader begin to wonder whether the aim is less to free women than to abolish them' (Taylor, 2003: 13). The point of Wollstonecraft's critique of women is that she is determined to reveal the fictionality of both femininity and masculinity; indeed, she calls the word 'masculine' a bugbear (Wollstonecraft, 1792/1995: 78), since the virtues it may denote are human virtues: reason, ambition, active self-determination, active and effective benevolence – not qualities which are gendered by nature. Gender, she argues, does not exist in the mind or the soul, only in the body, so that, unless we deny that women have intellect and an immortal soul, there is no sense in maintaining that gender difference is real. It is, she argues, the 'desire of being always women', rather than human beings first and foremost, that is the 'very consciousness that degrades the sex' (1792/1995: 181). As Janet Todd explains, quoting Denise Riley, Wollstonecraft is denying that there is any essential difference between the two sexes, and trying to point out that gender, if taken as definitive of personal and social identity, is a prison: 'Can anyone fully inhabit a gender without a degree of horror? How could someone "be a woman" through and through without suffering claustrophobia?' (Riley, 1988: 6; Todd, 2001: 186).

In the authorial identity she assumes, Wollstonecraft emphasises the sexlessness of the ennobled 'human character' she believes all men and women will achieve once gender stereotypes have been discarded (Wollstonecraft, 1792/1995: 75). Refusing to flatter women as creatures of '*fascinating* graces', she declares her intention of eschewing 'soft phrases', and disdains the idea that women must be treated with 'delicacy of senti-ment, and refinement of taste'. In so doing, she demonstrates the difference between a mode of authorial address that recognises the equality of female with male readers, and one that uses the 'epithets of weakness' to 'soften our slavish dependence'. The women that she addresses have a choice as readers and as citizens: they can either consent to be patronised as weak, inferior beings, and eventually to 'become objects of contempt', or they can regard themselves as 'rational creatures', who have no need of flattery (1792/1995: 76). The artificial weakness and inferiority usually associated with women has been communicated, Wollstonecraft argues, through literature: women have been taught through their reading to use 'cunning, softness of temper, *outward* obedience, and . . . a puerile kind of propriety' to obtain male protection (1792/1995: 87; her italics).

The first literary exemplar of this propagation of artificial femininity is Milton's Eve, and it is through an interrogation of the descriptions of Eve in *Paradise Lost* that Wollstonecraft focuses her critique of sexualised and gendered identity. As her first *Vindication* had argued, true virtue, true self-realisation (the terms are synonymous for Wollstonecraft), was only to be achieved through active, independent thought; it was not to be attained through indulging sensibility and emotion at the expense of rational enquiry and endeavour. Therefore, if women were to fulfil their moral and spiritual potential as human beings, and to achieve an 'inner mirroring of God's sublimity' (Taylor, 2003: 105), they would need to reject self-abnegation and self-objectification, and the pursuit of merely physical beauty, in favour of an 'enlightened self-love', generating self-respect out of reverence for the reason bestowed by God on all human beings for their use in 'communicating good' (Wollstonecraft, 1790/1995: 34). Wollstonecraft repeats the idea in her second *Vindication*, asserting: 'it is a farce to call any being virtuous whose virtues do not result from the exercise of its own reason. This was Rousseau's opinion respecting men: I extend it to women' (1792/1995: 90).

This is why, in Chapter 2 of *A Vindication of the Rights of Woman*, Wollstonecraft criticises Milton's characterisation of the first woman as a being 'formed for softness and sweet attractive grace', made 'to gratify the senses of man when he can no longer soar on the wing of contemplation' (1792/1995: 87). In particular, she rejects Milton's description of Eve as 'adorn'd' with *'perfect beauty'*, obeying Adam unquestioningly (*'unargued'*) as her 'Author and Disposer', and attacks the way in which Eve is used to ventriloquise Milton's misogyny: 'God is *thy law, thou mine*: to know no more/Is Woman's *happiest* knowledge and her *praise*' (1792/1995: 87, 88; her italics).[6] Such imperfect cultivation of the mind as is permitted to women, she argues, places constraints on women's intellectual and spiritual advancement and in effect constitutes a deliberate corruption on the part of men: 'Weakness may excite tenderness, and gratify the arrogant pride of man; but the lordly caresses of a protector will not gratify a noble mind that pants for, and deserves to be respected' (1792/1995: 98). As Wollstonecraft points out, Milton's emphasis on Eve's beauty, unquestioning obedience and lack of independent knowledge is at odds with his own representation of Adam's original request for a companion who is his equal: 'Among *unequals* what society/Can sort, what harmony or true delight?/... of *fellowship* I speak/Such as I seek, fit to participate/All rational delight ...' (1792/1995: 89; her italics).[7] But what exercises her most is Milton's insistence, despite this speech, on Eve's inferiority to Adam, an inferiority closely identified with her beauty. When, for instance, Eve recalls their first meeting, her alarm at Adam's appearance, 'Less winning soft, less amiably mild' than the 'smooth watery image' of her own reflection, is quickly quelled, and her 'submissive charms' are displayed in her 'meek surrender' to his claims on her as 'His flesh, his bone'. Again, Milton ventriloquises, presenting Eve as the justifier of her own subjection: 'I yielded, and from that time see/How beauty is excelled by manly grace/And wisdom, which alone is truly fair'. Milton so describes this willing subordination of Eve as to suggest that it is the necessary precondition for the 'bliss on bliss' of the pair, 'Imparadised in one another's arms'.[8] He emphasises Eve's self-surrender, submission and self-objectification, her renunciation of sublime 'manly grace/And wisdom, which alone is truly fair', and her recognition that her beauty and 'sweet attractive grace' is what dictates her 'meek surrender' to Adam. Although Wollstonecraft does not specify the passage in *Paradise Lost* to which she is responding, when she describes her lack of envy of the 'paradisiacal happiness' of Adam and Eve, it is reasonable to suppose that these are the lines which prompt her extreme reaction: rather than identifying with Eve's subjection, Wollstonecraft declares that she has 'with conscious dignity, or Satanic pride, turned to hell for sublimer objects' (1792/1995: 94).⁹

Wollstonecraft's critique of Rousseau is similar; indeed, she summarises his ideal woman, as outlined in the fifth book of *Emile* (1762), in terms which echo those applied to Milton's Eve. The first four books of *Emile* had dwelt upon the education of a boy brought up to be independent, a self-reliant, free-thinking 'natural man' not governed by the 'slavish prejudice' or the 'control, constraint [and] compulsion' that Rousseau finds so offensive in civilised society (Rousseau, 1762/1911: 7, 10). In the fifth book, however, realising that his fictional Emile would soon need a wife, Rousseau outlines the education of a girl, Sophie, who is to have the opposite upbringing. Indeed, he urges, as Wollstonecraft notes, that this education should be designed to bring home to Sophie her destiny as a subordinate being: 'a woman should never . . . feel herself independent, . . . she should be governed by fear . . . and made a coquettish slave in order to render her a more alluring object of desire, a *sweeter* companion to man, whenever he chooses to relax himself'. Just as Milton's Eve is meant to understand that she is Adam's object rather than governing her own desires and aspirations, Rousseau's Sophie is to be educated in obedience 'with unrelenting rigour'. Worst of all, in Wollstonecraft's eyes, is Rousseau's idea that this control and constraint of women's freedom will bring out their '*natural* cunning' – that it will, in short, be an education conformable to their nature (Wollstonecraft, 1792/1995: 94; her italics). In Rousseau's view, cunning is what enables women to achieve the only kind of power possible for them: by exploiting tears and caresses, displaying their tender sensibility, offering or withholding sexual favours, Rousseau suggests, women can obtain some influence over men.

For Wollstonecraft, this is an 'illegitimate power' because it involves self-degradation: 'to their senses, are women made slaves, because it is by their sensibility that they obtain present power'; '[t]aught from their infancy that beauty is woman's sceptre, the mind shapes itself to the body, and, roaming round its gilt cage, only seeks to adorn its prison' (1792/1995: 90, 116). Instead of striving for power over men by using their bodies and 'sweet attractive grace', she urges, women 'must return to nature and equality', and labour 'by reforming themselves to reform the world' (1792/1995: 87, 90, 117). She takes Rousseau's dictum about female cunning and uses it to redefine what she means by 'power': ' "Educate women like men," says Rousseau, "and the more they resemble our sex the less power will they have over us." This is the very point I aim at. I do not wish them to have power over men; but over themselves' (1792/1995: 138). Wollstonecraft does not mean to eliminate sexual attraction altogether; she does wish, however, to open out the feelings through the development of the understanding, so that women have 'a chance to become intelligent; and let love to man be only a part of that glowing flame of universal love, which, after encircling humanity, mounts in grateful incense to God' (1792/1995: 144). Instead of being in subjection to men – as Eve is made subordinate to Adam: 'God is thy law, thou mine' – Wollstonecraft wants women to be released from the slavery of beauty into the sublime realm of reason and active participation in public life.

A similar motivation lies behind Wollstonecraft's book reviews, often scornful responses to romantic fiction, published in the *Analytical Review* between 1788 and 1797.[10] As Mitzi Myers points out, 'Wollstonecraft as critic assumes a maternal stance toward the imagined girl readers of the fiction she considers, her textual self-constitution offering an educative example of the integration [of sense and sensibility] she desires'; the reviews reveal 'a woman writer's struggle to define her "difference of view", to evade the "already-written"' (Myers, 1990: 121, 120). In her *Vindication of the Rights of Woman*, Wollstonecraft argued that romantic novels were among the causes of women's subordination, since they encouraged their readers to view sentiments as events, confirming women as 'creatures of sensation' (Wollstonecraft, 1792/1995: 282), rather than of real intellect and authentic feeling. Her reviews expand on this idea: she writes, for instance, of young women being 'termed romantic, when they are under the direction of artificial feelings; when they boast of being tremblingly alive all o'er, and faint and sigh as the novelist informs them they should'; and she suggests that this has a detrimental effect on women's power to think for themselves: 'the imagination, suffered to stray beyond the utmost verge of probability, where no vestige of nature appears, soon shuts out reason, and the dormant faculties languish for want of cultivation; as rational books are neglected, because they do not throw the mind into an *exquisite* tumult'. Moral degradation follows: 'false sentiment leads to sensuality, and vague fabricated feelings supply the place of principles'. These kinds of fiction, Wollstonecraft warns, 'poison the minds of our young females, by fostering vanity, and teaching affectation' (Wollstonecraft, 1788–97/1989: 19, 20).

By contrast, those works which Wollstonecraft judges to combine reason with genuine feeling can influence their readers to positive effect: they may 'awaken the opening mind to a sense of *real* woe', which, she suggests, is a source of 'public benefit, as a seed of active virtue . . . may extend its benign branches and shade many a wretch from misery' (1788–97/1989: 96). Richard Price's pro-revolutionary *Discourse on the Love of Our Country*, for example, is praised for 'breath[ing] the animated sentiments of ardent virtue in a simple, unaffected ... style; ... the heart speaks to the heart in an unequivocal language, and the understanding, not bewildered by sophisticated arguments, assents, without an effort, to such obvious truths' (1788–97/1989: 185). As Myers notes, Wollstonecraft's reviews 'both discuss and stylistically enact a politics of change, an attempt to unite a spontaneity of affect with a morality of reason', proposing a non-gendered human subject who integrates emotional and intellectual faculties, and whose reading is vitally connected to action. Feminist literary criticism is thus presented as a 'liberating intellectual perspective – a *political* act, aimed not just at interpreting the world but at changing it through changing the consciousness of readers' (Myers, 1990: 123).[11]

WOLLSTONECRAFT'S CONTEMPORARIES

After Wollstonecraft's death, the emergence of scandalous details about her private life in 1797–8 and the increased ferocity of anti-revolutionary propaganda in government publications, such as the *Anti-Jacobin Review*, made it risky for women writers to name her, even when constructing their own critiques of literary femininity and women's intellectual subordination. This did not, however, deter them from propagating her ideas. Maria Edgeworth's *Letters for Literary Ladies*, for instance – in which Wollstonecraft's work is a clear but unspoken influence – first appeared in 1795, but was revised and reissued in 1798, with changes which effectively, as its author noted, 'assert[ed] more strongly the female right to literature', to independent thought, and to participation in the public sphere (1798/1993: xxvii). Another of Edgeworth's 1798 publications – *Practical Education* – similarly declines to name Wollstonecraft, but prominently praises her anti-Rousseauvian stance in its first chapter, on toys. This is an important allusion, since in the Wollstonecraft passage that Edgeworth closely paraphrases, from the *Vindication of the Rights of Woman*, the critique focuses on dolls, recommended by Rousseau for instructing girls in 'their life's work', '[t]he art of pleasing ... in due time [the child] will be her own doll' (Edgeworth, 1798/2003: 12; fn.3, 449). Edgeworth's *Letters for Literary Ladies* casts the argument about women's place as writers and subjects as an exchange of letters between two gentlemen who disagree about the way in which a daughter should be educated, and both in its emphasis on education, and in its defence of women as writers, thinkers and citizens, Edgeworth follows Wollstonecraft closely. She rejects, for instance, the idea that women's reading should properly be

confined to 'romance, poetry, and all the lighter parts of literature', as well
as the idea that women should play no part in the public realm of
intellectual debate or political action (Edgeworth, 1798/1993: 2).

Edgeworth also echoes Wollstonecraft in her critique of Burke's sexual
politics. The first gentleman in *Letters for Literary Ladies* regards educated
women as 'monsters' who exhibit their 'mental deformities'; in particular,
women who seek to exert public influence, either through direct involvement in government, or through publication, are represented by him as
depraved: 'the influence, the liberty, and the *power* of women have been
constant concomitants of the moral and political decline of empires' (1798/
1993: [1], 2, 4). Women, he suggests, must 'preserve inviolate the purity of
their manners'; it is a mistake to talk 'in loud strains to the sex of the noble
contempt of prejudice. You would look with horror at one who should go
to sap the foundations of the building; beware then how you venture to tear
away the ivy which clings to the walls, and braces the loose stones together'
(1798/1993: 5). Here, female purity and dependence on established conventional structures is represented as integral to the stability of the state, just as
the fantasy of Marie Antoinette's beauty and decorative presence is, for
Burke, emblematic of the dignity and grace of the *ancien régime*, and of the
'sentiments which beautify and soften' society (Burke, 1790/1986: 171). The
second gentleman – the father of the new-born daughter – rejects this
identification of innocence with dependence, pointing out the 'wide difference between innocence and ignorance' (a very Wollstonecraftian preoc-
cupation), and sees women's involvement in writing as a sign of social and
political advancement (Edgeworth, 1798/1993: 25).

The first gentleman is not to be dissuaded and again suggests that women
should, Eve-like, 'see things through a veil, or cease to be women', that only
men can 'see things as they are', and that 'silent happiness' and a modest
avoidance of the 'public eye' are their proper treasures; they should cultivate beauty, since this makes them conscious that they 'depend upon
the world for their immediate gratification' – that they are in fact, as
Wollstonecraft puts it, 'the *modest* slaves of opinion' (1798/1993: 3, 7–9;
Wollstonecraft, 1792/1995: 124). Such women, he maintains, 'are sensible of
their dependence; they listen with deference to the maxims, and attend to
the opinions of those from whom they expect their reward and their daily
amusements. In their subjection consists their safety' (Edgeworth, 1798/
1993: 9). The second gentleman invokes and inverts this use of the figure of
Eve, declaring: 'Women have not erred from having knowledge, but from
not having had experience'; engaging in publication is potentially a way of
gaining this valuable experience, and has radically changed women's place in

the world: 'their eyes are opened, – the classic page is unrolled, they *will* read', and they will gain access to, and contribute to, the 'rapid and universal circulation of knowledge' (1798/1993: 34; Edgeworth, 1795: 56, 47).[12]

Edgeworth further echoes Wollstonecraft in her epistolary fiction the *Letters of Julia and Caroline* (published as part of *Letters for Literary Ladies*); this time the exchange is between two women as they debate the relative merits of sense and sensibility. Julia's opening words are: 'In vain, dear Caroline, you urge me to *think*; I profess only to *feel*'; throughout the exchange, she is depicted as a kind of Rousseauvian woman, a Sophie, who believes that 'a woman's part in life is to please' (1798/1993: 39, 40). By contrast, Caroline, the Wollstonecraftian woman, urges her to seek self-esteem and the respect of her husband. Real feeling, she argues, is nothing like the sentimentality of the romantic fiction on which Julia models her persona: idealising imaginary distresses is detrimental to real sympathy, since 'pity should . . . always be associated with the active desire to relieve. If it be suffered to become a *passive sensation*, it is a *useless weakness*, not a virtue' (1798/1993: 45).

Here, the critique of the training in artificial femininity and false sensibility which Wollstonecraft saw as the most poisonous aspect of romantic fiction is echoed by Edgeworth's female thinker. Yet Edgeworth clearly felt compelled in *Letters for Literary Ladies* to present her Wollstonecraftian arguments under the cover of fictional characters, and in part to have them voiced by 'a gentleman', rather than owning them herself. Mary Robinson likewise published her *Letter to the Women of England, on the Injustice of Mental Subordination* (1799) under a pseudonym – 'Anne Frances Randall' – although she had no qualms about declaring the need for 'a *legion of Wollstonecrafts*' to undermine the poisons of prejudice and malevolence' and ensure women's emancipation. Again, Robinson follows Wollstonecraft, using language which is 'undecorated', and denouncing the textual representation of women as 'a lovely and fascinating part of the creation' (Robinson, 1799/2003: 41). Rejecting women's confinement to the cultivation of physical attractions as a means of finding their own identity, Robinson urges women to think and write – to disobey the male edict that 'you shall not evince your knowledge, or employ your thoughts, beyond the boundaries which we have set up around you'. She further calls on them to participate, and encourage their daughters to participate, in enlightenment: 'Shake off the trifling, glittering shackles, which debase you . . . Let your daughters be liberally, classically, philosophically, and usefully educated; let them speak and write their opinions freely . . . [teach] them to feel their mental equality with their imperious rulers' (1799/2003: 78, 83).

WOLLSTONECRAFT AND THE VICTORIANS

As Barbara Caine has noted, Wollstonecraft's name is rarely mentioned by Victorian feminists, although her ideas are recognisably present in writings by John Stuart Mill, Harriet Taylor and others (Caine, 1997: 261–2; Mill, 1869; Taylor, 1850). Harriet Taylor had noted that '[t]he literary class of women, especially in England, are ostentatious in disclaiming the desire for equality or citizenship, and proclaiming their complete satisfaction with the place that society assigns to them'. They were, she thought, 'anxious to earn pardon and toleration' for the strengths displayed in their published work 'by a studied display of submission . . . that they may give no occasion for vulgar men to say . . . that learning makes women unfeminine, and that literary ladies are likely to be bad wives' (Taylor, 1850/1995: 34–5). With this anxiety about adverse male opinion, the reluctance to claim Wollstonecraft as an influence or source is understandable: for Victorian feminists, as Caine suggests, 'connection with Wollstonecraft suggested only moral laxity' (Caine, 1997: 262). Harriet Martineau, for instance, considered Wollstonecraft, 'with all her powers, a poor victim of passion' (1877/1983: 1.400): an impression instituted early on in Wollstonecraft's posthumous reputation, partly as a result of William Godwin's 1798 selection of her unpublished works, which included many of her love letters to Gilbert Imlay, the faithless father of her illegitimate child, in addition to Godwin's unwisely frank biography of his late wife, also published in 1798.[13]

Yet Martineau's 1832 essay on women in Scott's novels again clearly reveals the impact of Wollstonecraft's ideas about literature and liberation. She takes four of Scott's female characters, among them Rebecca from *Ivanhoe*, as examples of women who have 'escaped from the management of man'. In creating such characters, Martineau argues, Scott has (whether he intended to or not) contributed to women's emancipation, 'by supplying a principle of renovation to the enslaved, as well as by exposing their condition; by pointing out the ends for which freedom and power are desirable, as well as the disastrous effects of withholding them'. He has thus, she continues, 'taught us the power of fiction as an agent of morals and philosophy' (Martineau, 1832/2003: 39, 40). In particular, the expulsion of Rebecca at the close of *Ivanhoe* is interpreted by Martineau as revealing the waste of talent involved in excluding women from active, equal citizenship. As readers, she explains, we are made to ask

how she should possibly remain or re-appear in a society which alike denies the discipline by which her high powers and sensibilities might be matured, and the objects on which they might be worthily employed? As a woman, no less than as a

Jewess, she is the representative of the wrongs of a degraded and despised class: there is no abiding-place for her among foes to her caste; she wanders unemployed … through the world; and when she dies, there has been, not only a deep injury inflicted, but a waste made of the resources of human greatness and happiness. (1832/2003: 39–40)

There are strong echoes here of Wollstonecraft's final work, her novel *The Wrongs of Woman* (1798), which its author intended as a 'history … of woman' (Wollstonecraft, 1798/1989: 73); like Scott's *Ivanhoe* as interpreted by Martineau, this shows the way in which a talented and spirited woman is expelled from polite society and made into an outcast; but the sentiments are equally evocative of the arguments made in the *Vindication of the Rights of Woman* in favour of women's equal participation in the necessary reformation of society.

It was George Eliot – one of those who dared to assert women's sexual freedom in her life, if not in her work – who broke the silence about Wollstonecraft's feminist legacy in her 1855 essay, 'Margaret Fuller and Mary Wollstonecraft', although as Caine comments, Wollstonecraft was only fully rehabilitated as a feminist forerunner in the 1890s.[14] Eliot notes the 'vague prejudice' against Wollstonecraft's *Vindication of the Rights of Woman* as a 'reprehensible book', and points out that in fact it is 'eminently serious' and 'severely moral'; she praises Wollstonecraft for 'seeing and painting women as they are', and echoes her call for intellectual emancipation for both sexes: 'we want freedom and culture for woman, because subjection and ignorance have debased her, and with her Man; for – "If she be small, slight-natured, miserable,/How shall men grow?" ' (Eliot, 1855/ 1963: 201, 205).[15] Eliot's essay, 'Silly Novels by Lady Novelists', also shows the influence of Wollstonecraft in its analysis of the impact of fiction on the status of women. She deplores the effect of 'silly novels', not only on their female readers, but also on men hostile to women's emancipation, who can point to 'lady novelists' as evidence of the folly of educating women. This hostility is, she contends, 'unconsciously encouraged by many women who have volunteered themselves as representatives of the feminine intellect', whom she characterises as keeping 'a sort of mental pocket-mirror', 'continually looking in it at [their] own "intellectuality" ', as opposed to those women writers of 'true culture', who make their knowledge 'a point of observation from which to form a right estimate' of themselves (Eliot, 1856/1963: 316, 317). In other words, like Wollstonecraft, and Edgeworth in the *Letters of Julia and Caroline*, Eliot wants women to think, rather than simply to feel; to see themselves and others clearly, rather than to become fixated on a false image of themselves.

Whereas Wollstonecraft sees the destabilisation of gendered identity as
the precondition for women's self-realisation as writers and as citizens,
however, Eliot, though insistent that the best women writers can 'fully
equal men', also argues that women 'have a precious speciality, lying quite
apart from masculine aptitudes and experience' (1856/1963: 324). This argument is to some extent anticipated in her 1854 essay, 'Woman in France:
Madame de Sablé', in which she compares the French literary canon to the
British, concluding that French literature is more 'feminine', and therefore
superior. Women's writing in English is, she asserts, 'usually an absurd
exaggeration of the masculine style, like the swaggering of a bad actress in
male attire'. Such masquerade is designed to prove that there is 'no sex in
literature'; French women's writing, by contrast, recognises that women
'have something specific to contribute', and that the psychological and
physical differences between men and women can be used creatively: this
difference, Eliot argues, 'instead of being destined to vanish before a
complete development of woman's intellectual and moral nature, will be
a permanent source of variety and beauty' in women's literature. French
women writers have, she maintains, freely displayed 'the feminine character of their minds'; thinking 'little, in many cases not at all, of the public',
they have instead written 'what they saw, thought, and felt, in their
habitual language, without proposing any model to themselves, without
any intention to prove that women could write as well as men, without
affecting manly views or suppressing womanly ones'. The sources of this
confident, unconstrained self-presentation are somewhat contradictorily
identified by Eliot: on the one hand, she argues that women are naturally
'intense and rapid rather than conservative', and that this mode of intellect
is prevalent among male as well as female writers in France; but she also
ascribes French women writers' superior literary standing to the lower
cultural status of marriage there, a much more political, and more
Wollstonecraftian, argument. In France, she explains, marriage, as a
union 'formed in the maturity of thought and feeling, and grounded
only on inherent fitness and mutual attraction, tended to bring women
into more intelligent sympathy with men, and heighten and complicate
their share in the political drama' (Eliot, 1854/1963: 53, 54, 56).[16]

John Stuart Mill, writing fifteen years later, is more sceptical about the
natural difference which Eliot cites as a source of strength in women's
writing: for those hostile to women's advancement, he notes, '[w]omen
who read, much more women who write, are, in the existing constitution
of things, a contradiction and a disturbing element' (Mill, 1869/1985: 245);
but 'a literature of their own', if such a thing really existed, was some way in

the future, 'subdued by the influence of precedent and example ... it will require generations more, before [women's] individuality is sufficiently developed to make head against that influence' (287, 288). Compared with Eliot and Mill, Wollstonecraft's vision of women as creative, thinking, aspirant beings emerges as much more optimistic, even utopian, depending as it does on a conviction that sexual distinction is 'arbitrary', that this difference is eradicable, and that 'the most salutary effects tending to improve mankind might be expected from a revolution in female manners' (Wollstonecraft, 1792/1995: 292). Yet despite her misgivings about the abuse of imagination and fantasy as conservative discourses tending to inhibit the progress of women, Wollstonecraft too gestured towards a different kind of writing, a different kind of self-imagining, able to invent and encompass a future state beyond the prison of sex: a 'precious speciality' which still remains to be expressed.

NOTES

1. For more on Wollstonecraft, sexuality, emotion and imagination, see Kaplan (1987), Kaplan (1990), Kelly (1992 and 1997), Barker-Benfield (1992), Johnson (1995) and Taylor (2003).
2. Testament to the enduring fascination of Wollstonecraft's life, there have been at least six recent biographies, not counting William St Clair's *The Godwins and the Shelleys* (1989), which considers Wollstonecraft's life alongside those of William Godwin, Mary Shelley and Percy Bysshe Shelley: see Tomalin (1974), Sunstein (1974), Tims (1976), Todd (2001), Jacobs (2001) and Gordon (2005).
3. Maria Edgeworth, writer of fiction for adults and children and educational thinker (1768–1849); Mary 'Perdita' Robinson, actress, novelist and poet (1758–1800); Harriet Martineau, writer (1802–76); Harriet Taylor (1807–58), wife of and intellectual collaborator with John Stuart Mill, philosopher and social reformer (1806–73); George Eliot (Mary Ann/Marian Evans), novelist and translator of Feuerbach (1819–80).
4. The concept of the sublime, often contrasted with the beautiful, was widely discussed in eighteenth-century literature on aesthetics: Addison, Baillie, Burke, Gerard and Hume were particularly interested in the natural sublime, although Burke anticipates the Romantic sublime as discussed by Kant in his *Critique of Judgement* (1790). Whereas the natural sublime was provoked by great and terrible objects, such as mountains and abysses, which stunned the mind into inertia and then transport, the Romantic sublime had its source in, and revealed, the individual's own powers, and was often identified with emotion, genius and the liberated imagination. For more detail, see Peter Otto's summary in McCalman (1999: 723); M. H. Abrams' account of the sublime in relation to Wordsworth in *Natural Supernaturalism* (1971); and Ronald Paulson's account of the theories of the sublime and beautiful in relation to

revolutionary politics in *Representations of Revolution* (1983). For a full-length study of the sublime, see Weiskel (1976).

5. For more on Wollstonecraft's representation of Burke as a 'feminised' man, see Claudia L. Johnson (1995).

6. Milton, *Paradise Lost*, IV, 634–8.

7. Ibid., VIII, 383–4, 389–91.

8. Ibid., IV, 479–80, 483, 498, 494, 489–91, 508, 506. Wollstonecraft herself does not quote these lines.

9. For a reading of Milton's Eve which runs counter to Wollstonecraft's, see Newlyn (1993/2004).

10. A radical journal, owned and edited by the Unitarian bookseller Joseph Johnson. Wollstonecraft contributed reviews from 1788 until she went to France in 1792, and then again in 1796–7.

11. For more on Wollstonecraft's reviews, see Wardle (1947), Roper (1958), Stewart (1984) and Myers (1986, 1987 and 2002).

12. Interestingly, this Wollstonecraftian point about women erring because of being denied the experience which would instruct them otherwise (see 1792/1995: 193) is one of the casualties of the revisions for the generally more Wollstonecraftian second edition of 1798; as is the assertion of women's contribution to the 'rapid and universal circulation of knowledge'.

13. Godwin's *Memoirs of the Author of 'The Rights of Woman'* scandalised contemporary readers with its candid accounts of her love affairs and her religious heterodoxy: see, for example, the review of the *Memoirs* in the *Monthly Review* 27 (November 1798). The *Anti-Jacobin Review* of July 1798 referred to Wollstonecraft in its index under 'P' for 'Prostitution', adding, '*See* Mary Wollstonecraft', and published a vicious poem satirising Wollstonecraft and Godwin, 'The Vision of Liberty', in 1801. Interestingly, as Caine (1997) notes, it was a new edition of Wollstonecraft's *Letters to Imlay*, published by Kegan Paul in 1879, which marked the revival of Wollstonecraft's reputation.

14. Eliot's essay on Wollstonecraft and Fuller was published the year after she had moved in with her lover, G. H. Lewes. Margaret Fuller (1810–50), was an American feminist thinker and writer, Transcendentalist and author of *Woman in the Nineteenth Century* (1845).

15. Eliot's quotation is from Tennyson, *The Princess*, VII, 249–50.

16. Eliot's essay was prompted principally by Victor Cousin's book, *Madame de Sablé: études sur les femmes illustres et la société du XVIIe siècle* (1854), to which Elizabeth Gaskell also responded in her 'Company Manners' (1854): see Jenny Uglow's comparison of the two essays in *Elizabeth Gaskell: A Habit of Stories* (1993/1999). The French women writers discussed by Eliot are mainly of the seventeenth, eighteenth and very early nineteenth centuries, such as de Sévigné, de Staël, Roland and d'Epinay; Eliot also mentions a contemporary French woman writer, the nineteenth-century novelist George Sand (Amandine Aurore Lucile Dupin), for whom she had a profound respect.

BIBLIOGRAPHY

Abrams, M. H. (1971), *Natural Supernaturalism*, New York: Norton.

Barbauld, Anna Letitia (2002), *Selected Poetry and Prose*, ed. William McCarthy and Elizabeth Kraft, Peterborough, Ontario: Broadview Press.

Barker-Benfield, G. J. (1992), *The Culture of Sensibility: Sex and Society in Eighteenth-Century Britain*, Chicago: University of Chicago Press.

Burke, Edmund (1757/1990), *A Philosophical Enquiry into the Origin of Our Ideas of the Sublime and Beautiful*, ed. Adam Phillips, Oxford: World's Classics.

(1790/1986), *Reflections on the Revolution in France*, ed. Conor Cruise O'Brien, London: Penguin Books.

Caine, Barbara (1997), 'Victorian Feminism and the Ghost of Mary Wollstonecraft', in *Women's Writing* 4: 2.

Conger, Syndy McMillen (ed.) (1990), *Sensibility in Transformation: Creative Resistance to Sentiment from the Augustans to the Romantics: Essays in Honour of Jean H. Hagstrum*, London: Associated University Presses.

Cox, Stephen (1990), 'Sensibility as Argument', in Conger (1990).

Edgeworth, Maria (1795), *Letters for Literary Ladies*, London: Joseph Johnson.

(1798/1993), *Letters for Literary Ladies*, ed. Claire Connolly, London: J. M. Dent.

(1798/2003), *Practical Education*, ed. Susan Manly, in *Novels and Selected Works of Maria Edgeworth*, vol. XI, ed. Marilyn Butler and Mitzi Myers, consulting ed. W. J. McCormack, 12 vols, London: Pickering and Chatto (1999/2003).

Eliot, George (1855/1963), 'Margaret Fuller and Mary Wollstonecraft', in *The Leader* 6 (October 1855), reproduced in Pinney (1963).

(1856/1963), 'Silly Novels by Lady Novelists', in *Westminster Review* 66 (October 1856), reproduced in Pinney (1963).

(1854/1963), 'Woman in France: Madame de Sablé', in *Westminster Review* 62 (October 1854), reproduced in Pinney (1963).

Gordon, Lyndall (2005), *Vindication: A Life of Mary Wollstonecraft*, London: Little, Brown.

Jacobs, Diane (2001), *Her Own Woman: The Life of Mary Wollstonecraft*, London: Abacus.

Jacobus, Mary (ed.) (1979), *Women Writing and Writing about Women*, London: Croom Helm.

Johnson, Claudia L. (1995), *Equivocal Beings: Politics, Gender, and Sentimentality in the 1790s – Wollstonecraft, Radcliffe, Burney, Austen*, Chicago: University of Chicago Press.

(ed.) (2002), *The Cambridge Companion to Mary Wollstonecraft*, Cambridge: Cambridge University Press.

Kaplan, Cora (1987), 'Wild Nights: Pleasure/Sexuality/Feminism', in *The Ideology of Conduct: Essays on Literature and the History of Sexuality*, ed. Nancy Armstrong and Leonard Tennenhouse, New York and London: Methuen.

(1990), 'Pandora's Box: Subjectivity, Class, and Sexuality in Socialist-Feminist Criticism', in *British Feminist Thought: A Reader*, ed. Terry Lovell, Oxford: Blackwell.

(2002), 'Mary Wollstonecraft's Reception and Legacies', in Johnson (2002).

Kelly, Gary (1992), *Revolutionary Feminism: The Mind and Career of Mary Wollstonecraft*, Basingstoke: Macmillan.

(1997), '(Female) Philosophy in the Bedroom: Mary Wollstonecraft and Female Sexuality', in *Women's Writing* 4: 2 (July).

McCalman, Iain (ed.) (1999), *An Oxford Companion to the Romantic Age*, Oxford: Oxford University Press.

Martineau, Harriet (1832/2003), 'Achievements of the Genius of Scott', in *Tait's Magazine* 2 (December 1832), reproduced in Solveig Robinson (2003).

(1877/1983), *Autobiography*, 2 vols, London: Virago Press.

Mill, John Stuart (1869/1985), *The Subjection of Women*, with Mary Wollstonecraft, *A Vindication of the Rights of Woman* (1792), ed. Mary Warnock, London and Melbourne: J. M. Dent.

Myers, Mitzi (1986), 'Impeccable Governesses, Rational Dames, and Moral Mothers: Mary Wollstonecraft and the Female Tradition in Georgian Children's Books', in *Children's Literature* 14 (ed. Margaret Higonnet and Barbara Rosen).

(1987), '"A Taste for Truth and Realities": Early Advice to Mothers on Books for Girls', *Children's Literature Association Quarterly* 12: 3 (Fall 1987).

(1990), 'Sensibility and the "Walk of Reason": Mary Wollstonecraft's Literary Reviews as Cultural Critique', in Conger (1990).

(2002), 'Mary Wollstonecraft's Literary Reviews', in Johnson (2002).

Newlyn, Lucy (1993/2004), *'Paradise Lost' and the Romantic Reader*, Oxford: Oxford University Press.

Paulson, Ronald (1983), *Representations of Revolution, 1789–1820*, New Haven and London: Yale University Press.

Pinney, Thomas (ed.) (1963), *Essays of George Eliot*, London: Routledge and Kegan Paul.

Pyle, Andrew (ed.) (1995), *The Subjection of Women: Contemporary Responses to John Stuart Mill*, Bristol: Thoemmes Press.

Riley, Denise (1988), *'Am I That Name?': Feminism and the Category of 'Women' in History*, London: Macmillan.

Robinson, Mary (1799/2003), *'A Letter to the Women of England' and 'The Natural Daughter'*, ed. Sharon M. Setzer, Peterborough, Ontario: Broadview Press.

Robinson, Solveig (ed.) (2003), *A Serious Occupation: Literary Criticism by Victorian Women Writers*, Peterborough, Ontario: Broadview Press.

Roper, Derek (1958), 'Mary Wollstonecraft's Reviews', in *Notes and Queries* 203.

Rousseau, Jean-Jacques (1762/1911), *Emile, or Education*, trans. Barbara Foxley, London and Toronto: Dent.

St Clair, William (1989), *The Godwins and the Shelleys: The Biography of a Family*, London: Faber and Faber.

Showalter, Elaine (1979), 'Towards a Feminist Poetics', in *Women Writing and Writing about Women*, ed. Mary Jacobus, London: Croom Helm.

Stewart, Sally (1984), 'Mary Wollstonecraft's Contributions to the *Analytical Review*', in *Essays in Literature* 11: 2 (Fall 1984).

Sunstein, Emily (1974), *A Different Face: The Life of Mary Wollstonecraft*, New York: Harper and Row.

Taylor, Barbara (2003), *Mary Wollstonecraft and the Feminist Imagination*, Cambridge: Cambridge University Press.

Taylor, Harriet (1850/1995), 'The Enfranchisement of Women', in *The New York Tribune for Europe* (29 October 1850), reproduced in Pyle (1995).

Tims, Margaret (1976), *Mary Wollstonecraft: A Social Pioneer*, London: Millington.

Todd, Janet (2001), *Mary Wollstonecraft: A Revolutionary Life*, London: Phoenix Press.

Tomalin, Claire (1974), *The Life and Death of Mary Wollstonecraft*, London: Weidenfeld and Nicolson.

Uglow, Jenny (1993/1999), *Elizabeth Gaskell: A Habit of Stories*, London: Faber.

Wardle, Ralph M. (1947), 'Mary Wollstonecraft, *Analytical* Reviewer', in *PMLA* 62.

Weiskel, Thomas (1976), *The Romantic Sublime*, Baltimore: Johns Hopkins University Press.

Wollstonecraft, Mary (1798/1989), *'The Wrongs of Woman', with 'Mary'*, ed. Gary Kelly, Oxford: World's Classics.

(1798), *Posthumous Works of the Author of a 'Vindication of the Rights of Woman'*, 4 vols, ed. William Godwin, London: Joseph Johnson.

(1790/1995, 1792/1995), *'A Vindication of the Rights of Men' with 'A Vindication of the Rights of Woman' and 'Hints'*, ed. Sylvana Tomaselli, Cambridge: Cambridge University Press.

(1788–97/1989), *Works*, ed. Janet Todd and Marilyn Butler, asst. Emma Rees-Mogg, 7 vols: vol. VII, *On Poetry* (1791) and *Contributions to the Analytical Review* (1788–97), London: William Pickering.

Woolf, Virginia (1925/1984; 1932/1986), *The Common Reader*, 2 vols, ed. Andrew McNeillie, London: Vintage.

CHAPTER 4

The feminist criticism of Virginia Woolf

Jane Goldman

FEMINIST LITERARY CRITICISM BEFORE WOOLF AND IN WOOLF'S ERA

Virginia Woolf is rightly considered the founder of modern feminist literary criticism. Prior to her landmark contributions to the field, in particular her feminist manifesto of literary criticism, *A Room of One's Own* (1929), very few works register in historical accounts of its genesis. Catherine Belsey and Jane Moore, in their account of 'The Story So Far', point to Esther Sowernam and Bathsua Makin, in the seventeenth century, who identified the presence of powerful female deities and muses in classical literature, and to Mary Wollstonecraft at the end of the eighteenth century, who argued against the infantilising effects on women of sentimental novels, and who also 'contributed to a feminist anthology of sorts called *The Female Reader*' (Belsey and Moore, 1997: 1). As in many received accounts of feminist literary history, anxious to press on to the heady modern period of its flourishing, Belsey and Moore list no one else between Wollstonecraft and Woolf, no one at all alongside Woolf, and no one after Woolf until Simone de Beauvoir (1997: 1). Glenda Norquay's *Voices and Votes: A Literary Anthology of the Women's Suffrage Campaign* (1995) redresses the critically neglected area of early feminist literature, introducing novels, short stories and poems of the suffrage era (until 1930), an era that spans much of the period of Woolf's formative literary career and closes as *A Room of One's Own* makes its first impact. But Norquay points to no significant feminist literary criticism aside from Woolf's (and this in passing). She does, however, demonstrate that the novel and the short story were often the preferred genres of feminist writers arguing for 'the cause'; and this hinterland of feminist fiction, mapped by Norquay, may well provide some interesting antecedents to Woolf's *A Room of One's Own*, especially in its narrative tendencies towards fiction (discussed below).

In Woolf's era there were numerous literary magazines with a feminist slant, and feminist magazines with a literary slant, where one might chart the interpenetration of feminist and literary politics: for example, *The Englishwoman*, Dora Marsden's and Mary Gawthorpes' *The Freewoman*, Marsden's and Harriet Shaw Weaver's *The New Freewoman*, which became Weaver's and Ezra Pound's *The Egoist*, Margaret Anderson's and Jane Heap's *Little Review*, and Margaret Haig Thomas (Lady Rhondda)'s *Time and Tide*.[1] Woolf herself published pieces in *Time and Tide*, including extracts from *A Room of One's Own*. Among Woolf's contemporaries there are many modernist writers (men and women) who are now recognised for their contributions to the cultural and political debates on gender (Scott, 1990). There are, of course, many women writers among her contemporaries whom we may regard as feminist. Some wrote manifestos on (feminist/socialist/pacifist) politics (Alexandra Kollontai, Emma Goldman, Mina Loy, Storm Jameson, Rebecca West, Christina Stead) or on literary aesthetics (Amy Lowell, Gertrude Stein, May Sinclair, Marianne Moore), but Woolf stands out for her sustained attempts to combine both. Her work was nevertheless influenced by feminist intellectuals in other disciplines, not least by the Cambridge classical anthropologist Jane Harrison (1850–1928), who was a mentor to Woolf, and also by the feminist writer and activist Ray Strachey (1887–1940), a member of Woolf's Bloomsbury circle and author of *The Cause* (1928), a history of the modern British feminist movement. Woolf published under Strachey's editorship 'The Plumage Bill', in the *Woman's Leader* (23 July 1920: 559–60). At the Hogarth Press, the progressive publishing house Woolf founded with her husband Leonard Woolf, she published Strachey's work, along with other key works by feminists, including Harrison.[2]

Woolf's feminist literary criticism is not, then, *sui generis*, as further evidenced by her large body of writings on her feminist antecedents and contemporaries; nor is it safe to assume that her arguments are entirely original. Woolf's interests, set out in *A Room of One's Own*, in the gender politics of literary production and consumption, and the impact on fiction of the rise of women, for example, are to some extent anticipated in 'Men and Art', a chapter in the now almost forgotten *The Man-Made World or Our Androcentric Culture* (1911), by the feminist writer Charlotte Perkins Gilman. Yet it is Woolf's *A Room of One's Own* that has come to be canonised as the first modern work of feminist literary criticism.

Writing her memoir, 'A Sketch of the Past' (1939–40), during the German air raids on the English coast, Virginia Woolf came to encapsulate her 'philosophy' (Woolf, 1985: 72) in a now much-cited passage:

that behind the cotton wool is hidden a pattern; that we – I mean all human beings – are connected with this; that the whole world is a work of art; that we are parts of the work of art. *Hamlet* or a Beethoven quartet is the truth about this vast mass that we call the world. But there is no Shakespeare, there is no Beethoven; certainly and emphatically there is no God; we are the words; we are the music; we are the thing itself. (1985: 72)

Woolf's 'philosophy' here clearly anticipates later literary critical and theoretical declarations of the death of the author by Roland Barthes and Michel Foucault, but its feminist import is perhaps less obvious. Her understanding of the world as a text in which we all – 'all human beings' – participate is only implicitly feminist in its rejection of the authority of Shakespeare, Beethoven and God. Would her explanation make similar sense were she to choose female instances of supreme authorship? Why not, instead of Shakespeare, Woolf herself, who, in her feminist manifesto, *A Room of One's Own* (1929), speculates on the coming of a woman to rival the bard, the phantom of 'Shakespeare's sister'? Why not, instead of Beethoven, Woolf's close companion, Ethel Smyth, the feminist composer of the suffragette anthem, 'The March of the Women' (1911)? Why not, instead of God, some mythical mother Goddess, such as Isis or Gaia, allusions to whom pepper Woolf's work?

To declare 'there is no Woolf, there is no Smyth; certainly and emphatically there is no Goddess', would certainly alter Woolf's semantics. Not least it would undo the last six decades of feminist scholarship, following Woolf, that has insisted on the inclusion of women writers, artists and composers in previously almost exclusively male canons. It would also subvert feminist accounts of experience and knowledge that insist on the acknowledgement of how universals are expressed through the metaphor of gender, given that the generalisations we make about common human existence and experience may still be accorded masculine attributes more often than not. What is at stake here is how we interpret the goals of feminist literary criticism and theory. Woolf's declaration of the death of the author brings with it an alternative, collective, model of authorship, a questioning of canonicity and a revision of our metaphors of gender. As well as encouraging us to read the works of male authors with a different attention to authority and gender, Woolf also prompts us to consider the nature of a literary canon that includes women authors, and the nature and form of literary texts written by and about women. In doing so, she also simultaneously revises and opens up the very nature and form of literary criticism and theory, forging a new feminist literary critical language, a new feminist agenda.

Defining Woolf's contribution to feminist literary criticism and theory, however, is difficult partly because it is so enormous and so multi-faceted, and partly because of her own suspicion of the term feminism itself. Woolf did not so much come up with one approach or theory as frame and ask several important questions for feminist criticism, not all of which she answered or even attempted to answer definitively. Indeed, in her essay 'Why?' (1934), Woolf stages a number of unanswered questions concerning the definition of feminism and the efficacy of the academic study of English literature. Woolf was far from consistent in her use of the term feminism. In 1916 she privately declared: 'I become steadily more feminist' (Woolf, 1975–80: II. 76), and at this time she was active in feminist and suffragist politics as organiser of her local Women's Co-Operative Guild at Richmond, and had been involved in suffragist activities as early as 1910. In so far as she was active in such politics, she participated in the constitutional methods of the suffragists, rather than in the extra-legal tactics of the suffragettes, in militating for reform. The vote itself was hardly the main goal of Woolf's feminism, and having run hot and cold with suffragist politics, when the Suffrage Bill was finally passed in 1918 she could only record her indifference: 'I dont feel much more important – perhaps slightly so. Its like a knighthood; might be useful to impress people one despises' (Woolf, 1977–84: I. 104). But by 1924 she was saying 'If I were still a feminist' (1977–84: III. 318), perhaps acknowledging that the achievement of suffrage rendered the cause redundant or perhaps that she herself had moved beyond feminism; by the time *A Room of One's Own* was published in 1929 she was nevertheless glumly forecasting being 'attacked for a feminist and hinted at for a Sapphist' (1977–84: III. 262), and by 1931 was again hesitating over the term (1975–80: IV. 312). In *Three Guineas* (1938), Woolf famously declares 'feminist' a 'vicious', 'corrupt' and 'obsolete' term, which:

according to the dictionary, means 'one who champions the rights of women.' Since the only right, the right to earn a living, has been won, the word no longer has a meaning. And a word without a meaning is a dead word . . . Let us therefore celebrate this occasion by cremating the corpse. Let us write that word in large black letters on a sheet of foolscap; then solemnly apply a match to the paper. Look, how it burns! (1938: 184)

Given that even some seven decades later women still do not actually enjoy equal representation in most professions in Britain (as well as in most of the world's other nations and cultures), Woolf's observations on the achievement of the right to work remain ironical, to say the least. After the partial enfranchisement of British women in 1918, and their full enfranchisement in 1928, Woolf nevertheless celebrates the destruction of 'the word "feminist"', metaphorically burning it as women were once burned for witches, after which 'the air is cleared; and in that clearer air what do we see? Men and women working together for the same cause.' The cause in the late 1930s is anti-fascism, and Woolf proposes that the 'feminists' of earlier generations 'were in fact the advance guard' of the present anti-fascist movement (1938: 185). Woolf was a politically active anti-fascist, and a member of a number of different organisations and committees (Bradshaw, 1997 and 1998), and, as she makes clear in *Three Guineas*, anti-fascism and feminism are for her inextricably linked. Addressing her fellow anti-fascists, she acknowledges that earlier feminists, including suffragists and suffragettes, 'were fighting the tyranny of the patriarchal state as you are fighting the tyranny of the Fascist state. Thus we are merely carrying on the same fight that our mothers and grandmothers fought; their words prove it; your words prove it' (Woolf, 1938: 186). Suffragism and feminism, then, have not disappeared or been eclipsed, according to Woolf's argument, but have provided the vital political foundations of anti-fascism. Just as Woolf's engagement with suffragist aesthetics in much of her fiction and non-fiction, and her fictional representations of suffragists and suffragettes (in *Night and Day* and *The Years*), may be understood in relation to, and as underpinning, a broader continuum of feminist aesthetics (Goldman, 1998: 208) and a spectrum of fictional representations of feminist women, so her feminism may be understood in relation to, and as underpinning, her broader and increasingly more urgent pacifist and anti-fascist thinking.

Unlike *A Room of One's Own*, which primarily addresses the topic of 'women and fiction', *Three Guineas* is not centred in literary criticism, although it does address the position of women in the cultural sphere and in education. It focuses on the political and social institutions of patriarchy and connects the politics of the rising fascism in Europe with the politics of the personal and domestic sphere at home. Woolf declares women to have 'outsider status', and she radically separates off the category of women as, paradoxically, transcending all boundaries, including national ones: 'As a woman, I have no country. As a woman I want no country. As a woman my country is the whole world' (Woolf, 1938: 313). *Three Guineas* is in three chapters, and each chapter spends a guinea on a different cause. In the first, Woolf begins to answer the book's central question 'How are we to prevent war?' (1938: 4), a question that leads her directly to the politics of gender, and to the material basis for women's economic independence and education. Only by escaping domestic tyranny through the offices of formal education can women begin to prevent war. Chapter Two addresses the need for women to become economically independent, if they are to prevent war, and considers the contradictions inherent in women's entry into the professions. Chapter Three explores the irony of a woman's being asked to sign a manifesto to preserve 'culture and intellectual liberty', when women have been systematically denied access to both.

A ROOM OF ONE'S OWN

Woolf was already connecting feminism to anti-fascism in *A Room of One's Own* (1929), which addresses in some detail the relations between politics and aesthetics. The book is based on lectures Woolf gave to women students at Cambridge, but its innovatory style makes it read in places like a novel, blurring boundaries between criticism and fiction. It is regarded as the first modern primer for feminist literary criticism, not least because it is also a source of many, often conflicting, theoretical positions. The title alone has had enormous impact as cultural shorthand for a modern feminist agenda. Woolf's room metaphor not only signifies the declaration of political and cultural space for women, private and public, but the intrusion of women into spaces previously considered the spheres of men. *A Room of One's Own* is not so much about retreating into a private feminine space as about inter-ruptions, trespassing and the breaching of boundaries (Kamuf, 1982: 17). It oscillates on many thresholds, performing numerous contradictory turns of argument (Allen, 1999). But it remains a readable and accessible work, partly because of its playful fictional style: the narrator adopts a number of fictional personae and sets out her argument as if it were a story. In this reader-friendly manner some complicated critical and theoretical issues are introduced. Many works of criticism, interpretation and theory have developed from Woolf's original points in *A Room of One's Own*, and many critics have pointed up the continuing relevance of the book, not least because of its open construction and resistance to intellectual closure (Stimpson, 1992: 164; Laura Marcus, 2000: 241). Its playful narrative strategies have divided feminist responses, most notably prompting Elaine Showalter's disapproval (Showalter, 1977: 282). Toril Moi's counter to Showalter's critique forms the basis of her classic introduction to French feminist theory, *Sexual/Textual Politics* (1985), in which Woolf's textual playfulness is shown to anticipate the deconstructive and post-Lacanian theories of Hélène Cixous, Julia Kristeva and Luce Irigaray.

Although much revised and expanded, the final version of *A Room of One's Own* retains the original lectures' sense of a woman speaking to women.

A significant element of Woolf's experimental fictional narrative strategy is her use of shifting narrative personae to voice the argument. She anticipates recent theoretical concerns with the constitution of gender and subjectivity in language in her opening declaration that ' "I" is only a convenient term for somebody who has no real being . . . (call me Mary Beton, Mary Seton, Mary Carmichael or by any name you please – it is not a matter of any importance)' (Woolf, 1929: 5). And *A Room of One's Own* is written in the voice of at least one of these Mary figures, who are to be found in the Scottish ballad 'The Four Marys'. Much of the argument is ventriloquised through the voice of Woolf's own version of 'Mary Beton'. In the course of the book this Mary encounters new versions of the other Marys – Mary Seton has become a student at 'Fernham' college, and Mary Carmichael an aspiring novelist – and it has been suggested that Woolf's opening and closing remarks may be in the voice of Mary Hamilton (the narrator of the ballad).[3] The multi-vocal, citational *A Room of One's Own* is full of quotations from other texts too. The allusion to the Scottish ballad feeds a subtext in Woolf's argument concerning the suppression of the role of motherhood – Mary Hamilton sings the ballad from the gallows where she is to be hanged for infanticide. (Marie Carmichael, furthermore, is the *nom de plume* of contraceptive activist Marie Stopes who published a novel, *Love's Creation*, in 1928.)

The main argument of *A Room of One's Own*, which was entitled 'Women and Fiction' in earlier drafts, is that 'a woman must have money and a room of her own if she is to write fiction' (1929: 4). This is a materialist argument that, paradoxically, seems to differ from Woolf's apparent disdain for the 'materialism' of the Edwardian novelists recorded in her key essays on modernist aesthetics, 'Modern Fiction' (1919; 1925) and 'Mr Bennett and Mrs Brown' (1924). The narrator of *A Room of One's Own* begins by telling of her experience of visiting an Oxbridge college where she was refused access to the library because of her gender. She compares in some detail the splendid opulence of her lunch at a men's college with the austerity of her dinner at a more recently established women's college (Fernham).[4] This account is the foundation for the book's main, materialist, argument: 'intellectual freedom depends upon material things' (1929: 141). The categorisation of middle-class women like herself with the working classes may seem problematic, but in *A Room of One's Own* Woolf proposes that women be understood as a separate class altogether, equating their plight with the working classes because of their material poverty, even among the middle and upper classes (1929: 73–4).[5]

Woolf's image of the spider's web, which she uses as her simile for the material basis of literary production, has become known in literary criticism as 'Virginia's web'.[6] It is conceived in the passage where the narrator of *A Room of One's Own* begins to consider the apparent dearth of literature by women in the Elizabethan period:

fiction is like a spider's web, attached ever so lightly perhaps, but still attached to life at all four corners. Often the attachment is scarcely perceptible; Shakespeare's plays, for instance, seem to hang there complete by themselves. But when the web is pulled askew, hooked up at the edge, torn in the middle, one remembers that these webs are not spun in mid-air by incorporeal creatures, but are the work of suffering human beings, and are attached to grossly material things, like health and money and the houses we live in. (1929: 62–3)

According to this analysis, literary materialism may be understood in several different ways. To begin with, the materiality of writing itself is acknowledged: it is physically made, and not divinely given or unearthly and transcendent. Woolf seems to be attempting to demystify the solitary, romantic figure of the (male) poet or author as mystically singled out, or divinely elected. But the idea that a piece of writing is a material object is also connected to a strand of modernist aesthetics concerned with the text as self-reflexive object, and to a more general sense of the concreteness of words, spoken or printed. Woolf's spider's web also suggests, furthermore, that writing is a bodily process, physically produced. The observation that writing is 'the work of suffering human beings' suggests that literature is produced as compensation for, or in protest against, existential pain and material lack. Finally, in proposing writing as 'attached to grossly material things', Woolf is delineating a model of literature as grounded in the 'real world', that is in the realms of historical, political and social experience. Such a position has been interpreted as broadly Marxist, but although Woolf's historical materialism may 'gladden the heart of a contemporary Marxist feminist literary critic', as Michèle Barrett has noted, elsewhere Woolf, in typically contradictory fashion, 'retains the notion that in the correct conditions art may be totally divorced from economic, political or ideological constraints' (Barrett, 1979: 17, 23). Yet perhaps Woolf's feminist ideal is in fact for women's writing to attain, not total divorce from material constraints, but only the near-imperceptibility of the attachment of Shakespeare's plays to the material world, which 'seem to hang there complete by themselves' but are nevertheless 'still attached to life at all four corners'.

As well as underlining the material basis for women's achieving the status of writing subjects, *A Room of One's Own* also addresses the status of women as readers, and raises interesting questions about gender and subjectivity in connection with the gender semantics of the first person.

After looking at the difference between men's and women's experiences of University, the narrator of *A Room of One's Own* visits the British Museum where she researches 'Women and Poverty' under an edifice of patriarchal texts, concluding that women 'have served all these centuries as looking glasses ... reflecting the figure of man at twice his natural size' (Woolf, 1929: 45). Here Woolf touches upon the forced, subordinate complicity of women in the construction of the patriarchal subject. Later in the book, Woolf offers a more explicit model of this when she describes the difficulties for a woman reader encountering the first person pronoun in the novels of 'Mr A': 'a shadow seemed to lie across the page. It was a straight dark bar, a shadow shaped something like the letter 'I' ... Back one was always hailed to the letter 'I' ... In the shadow of the letter 'I' all is shapeless as mist. Is that a tree? No it is a woman' (1929: 130). For a man to write 'I' seems to involve the positioning of a woman in its shadow, as if women are not included as writers or users of the first person singular in language. This shadowing or eliding of the feminine in the representation and construction of subjectivity not only emphasises the alienation experienced by women readers of male-authored texts, but also suggests the linguistic difficulties for women writers in trying to express feminine subjectivity when the language they have to work with seems to have already excluded them. When the word 'I' appears, the argument goes, it is always and already signifying a masculine self.

The narrator of *A Room of One's Own* discovers that language, and specifically literary language, is not only capable of excluding women as its signified meaning, but also uses concepts of the feminine itself as signs. Considering both women in history and woman as sign, Woolf's narrator points out that there is a significant discrepancy between women in the real world and 'woman' in the symbolic order (that is, as part of the order of signs in the aesthetic realm):

Imaginatively she is of the highest importance; practically she is completely insignificant. She pervades poetry from cover to cover; she is all but absent from history. She dominates the lives of kings and conquerors in fiction; in fact she was the slave of any boy whose parents forced a ring upon her finger. Some of the most inspired words, some of the most profound thoughts in literature fall from her lips; in real life she could scarcely spell, and was the property of her husband. (1929: 56)

Woolf here emphasises not only the relatively sparse representation of women's experience in historical records, but also the more complicated business of how the feminine is already caught up in the conventions of representation itself. How is it possible for women to be represented at all when 'woman', in poetry and fiction, is already a sign for something else? In these terms, 'woman' is a signifier in patriarchal discourse, functioning as part of the symbolic order, and what is signified by such signs is certainly not the lived, historical and material experience of real women. Woolf understands that this 'odd monster' derived from history and poetry, this 'worm winged like an eagle; the spirit of life and beauty in a kitchen chopping suet', has 'no existence in fact' (1929: 56).

Woolf converts this dual image to a positive emblem for feminist writing, by thinking 'poetically and prosaically at one and the same moment, thus keeping in touch with fact – that she is Mrs Martin, aged thirty-six, dressed in blue, wearing a black hat and brown shoes; but not losing sight of fiction either – that she is a vessel in which all sorts of spirits and forces are coursing and flashing perpetually' (1929: 56–7). This dualistic model, combining prose and poetry, fact and imagination is also central to Woolf's modernist aesthetic, encapsulated in the term 'granite and rainbow',[7] which renders in narrative both the exterior, objective and factual ('granite'), and the interior, subjective experience and consciousness ('rainbow'). The modernist technique of 'Free Indirect Discourse' practised and developed by Woolf allows for this play between the objective and subjective, between third person and first person narrative.

A Room of One's Own can be confusing because it puts forward contradictory sets of arguments, not least Woolf's much-cited passage on androgyny, which has been influential on later deconstructive theories of gender. Her narrator declares: 'it is fatal for anyone who writes to think of their sex' (1929: 136) and a model of writerly androgyny is put forward, derived from Samuel Taylor Coleridge's work:

one must be woman-manly or man-womanly. It is fatal for a woman to lay the least stress on any grievance; to plead even with justice any cause; in any way to speak consciously as a woman ... Some collaboration has to take place in the mind between the woman and the man before the art of creation can be accomplished. Some marriage of opposites has to be accomplished. (1929: 136)

Shakespeare, the poet playwright, is Woolf's ideal androgynous writer. She lists others – all men – who have also achieved androgyny (Keats, Sterne, Cowper, Lamb, and Proust – the only contemporary). But if the ideal is for both women and men to achieve androgyny, elsewhere *A Room of One's Own* puts the case for finding a language that is gendered – one appropriate for women to use when writing about women.

One of the most controversial of Woolf's speculations in *A Room of One's Own* concerns the possibility of an inherent politics in aesthetic form, exemplified by the proposition that literary sentences are gendered. *A Room of One's Own* culminates in the prophecy of a woman poet to equal or rival Shakespeare: 'Shakespeare's sister'. But in collectively preparing for her appearance, women writers need to develop aesthetic form in several respects. In predicting that the aspiring novelist Mary Carmichael 'will be a poet ... in another hundred years' time' (1929: 123), Mary Beton seems to be suggesting that prose must be explored and exploited in certain ways by women writers before they can be poets. She also finds fault with contemporary male writers, such as Mr A who is 'protesting against the equality of the other sex by asserting his own superiority' (1929: 132). She sees this as the direct result of women's political agitation for equality: 'The Suffrage campaign was no doubt to blame' (1929: 129). She raises further concerns about politics and aesthetics when she comments on the aspirations of the Italian Fascists for a poet worthy of fascism: 'The Fascist poem, one may fear, will be a horrid little abortion such as one sees in a glass jar in the museum of some county town' (1929: 134). Yet if the extreme patriarchy of fascism cannot produce poetry because it denies a maternal line, Woolf argues that women cannot write poetry either until the historical canon of women's writing has been uncovered and acknowledged. Nineteenth-century women writers experienced great difficulty because they lacked a female tradition: 'For we think back through our mothers if we are women' (1929: 99). They therefore lacked literary tools suitable for expressing women's experience. The dominant sentence at the start of the nineteenth century was 'a man's sentence ... It was a sentence that was unsuited for women's use' (1929: 99–100).

Woolf's assertion here, through Mary Beton, that women must write in gendered sentence structure, that is develop a feminine syntax, and that 'the book has somehow to be adapted to the body' (1929: 101) seems to contradict the declaration that 'it is fatal for anyone who writes to think of their sex'. She identifies the novel as 'young enough' to be of use to the woman writer: 'No doubt we shall find her knocking that into shape for herself ... and providing some new vehicle, not necessarily in verse, for the poetry in her. For it is the poetry that is still denied outlet. And I went on to ponder how a woman nowadays would write a poetic tragedy in five acts' (1929: 116). Now the goal of *A Room of One's Own* has shifted from women's writing of fictional prose to poetry, the genre Woolf finds women least advanced in, while 'poetic tragedy' is Shakespeare's virtuoso form and therefore the form to which 'Shakespeare's sister' should aspire. Woolf's speculations on feminine syntax anticipate the more recent exploration of *écriture féminine* by French feminists such as Cixous. Woolf's interest in the body and bodies, in writing the body, and in the gender and positionality thereof, anticipates feminist investigations of the somatic, and has been understood as materialist, deconstructive and phenomenological (Doyle, 2001). Woolf's interest in matters of the body also fuels the sustained critique, in *A Room of One's Own*, of 'reason', or masculinist rationalism, as traditionally disembodied and antithetical to the (traditionally feminine) material and physical.

A Room of One's Own is concerned not only with what form of literary language women writers use, but also with what they write about. Inevitably women themselves constitute a vital subject matter for women writers. Women writers will need new tools to represent women properly. The assertion of woman as both the writing subject and the object of writing is reinforced in several places: 'above all, you must illumine your own soul' (Woolf, 1929: 117), Mary Beton advises. The 'obscure lives' (1929: 116) of women must be recorded by women. The example supplied is Mary Carmichael's novel which is described as exploring women's relationships with each other. *A Room of One's Own* was published shortly after the obscenity trial of Radclyffe Hall's *The Well of Loneliness* (1928),[8] and in the face of this Woolf flaunts a blatantly lesbian narrative: 'if Chloe likes Olivia and Mary Carmichael knows how to express it she will light a torch in that vast chamber where nobody has yet been' (1929: 109). Her refrain, 'Chloe likes Olivia', has become a critical slogan for lesbian writing. In *A Room of One's Own*, Woolf makes 'coded' references to lesbian sexuality in her account of Chloe and Olivia's shared 'laboratory' (Woolf, 1929: 109; Marcus, 1987: 152, 169), and she calls for women's writing to explore lesbianism more openly and for the narrative tools to make this possible.[9]

One of the most controversial and contradictory passages in *A Room of One's Own* concerns Woolf's positioning of black women. Commenting on the sexual and colonial appetites of men, the narrator concludes: 'It is one of the great advantages of being a woman that one can pass even a very fine negress without wishing to make an Englishwoman of her' (1929: 65). A number of feminist critics have questioned the relevance of Woolf's feminist manifesto for the experience of black women (Walker, 1985: 2377), and have scrutinised this sentence in particular (Marcus, 2004: 24–58). In seeking to distance women from imperialist and colonial practices, Woolf disturbingly excludes black women here from the very category of women. This has become the crux of much contemporary feminist debate concerning the politics of identity. The category of women both unites and divides feminists: white middle-class feminists, it has been shown, cannot speak for the experience of all women;[10] and reconciliation of universalism and difference remains a key issue. 'Women – but are you not sick to death of the word?' Woolf retorts in the closing pages of *A Room of One's Own*, 'I can assure you I am' (Woolf, 1929: 145). The category of women is not chosen by women, it represents the space in patriarchy from which women must speak and which they struggle to redefine.

Another contradictory concept in *A Room of One's Own* is 'Shakespeare's sister', a figure who represents the possibility that there will one day be a woman writer to match the status of Shakespeare, who has come to personify literature itself. 'Judith Shakespeare' stands for the silenced woman writer or artist. But to seek to mimic *the* model of the individual masculine writing subject may also be considered part of a conservative feminist agenda. On the other hand, Woolf seems to defer the arrival of Shakespeare's sister in a celebration of women's collective literary achievement – 'I am talking of the common life which is the real life and not of the little separate lives which we live as individuals' (1929 148–9). Shakespeare's sister is a messianic figure who 'lives in you and in me' (1929: 148) and who will draw 'her life from the lives of the unknown who were her forerunners' (1929: 149), but has yet to appear. She may be the common writer to Woolf's 'common reader' (a term she borrows from Samuel Johnson),[11] but she has yet to 'put on the body which she has so often laid down' (1929: 149). *A Room of One's Own* closes with this contradictory model of individual achievement and collective effort.

OTHER KEY FEMINIST ESSAYS BY WOOLF

A Room of One's Own is Woolf's richest manifesto for feminist literary criticism, but there are other essays by Woolf that have made important contributions to the field. For example, she puts forward a theory of gendered aesthetic form in 'Romance and the Heart' (1923), her review of Dorothy Richardson's novel *Revolving Lights* (1923). According to Woolf, Richardson 'has invented . . . a sentence which we might call the psychological sentence of the feminine gender. It is of a more elastic fibre than the old, capable of stretching to the extreme, of suspending the frailest particles, of enveloping the vaguest shapes' (Woolf, 1986–92: III. 367). But, acknowledging that men too have constructed similar sentences, she points out that the difference lies with content rather than form: 'It is a woman's sentence only in the sense that it is used to describe a woman's mind by a writer who is neither proud nor afraid of anything that she may discover in the psychology of her sex' (1986–92: III. 367). Woolf emphasises Richardson's achievement as mapping previously unrecorded experiences of women. She has constructed a sentence whose form enables this process of inscription.

In her pivotal feminist essay 'Professions for Women' (1931), a paper she read to the National Society for Women's Service, Woolf insists on the woman writer's necessary suppression of a traditionally submissive – and domestic – feminine role, encapsulated in Coventry Patmore's famous poem on Victorian domestic virtues, 'The Angel in the House' (1862). The 'Angel in the House' personifies the submissive patriarchal woman: 'she was so constituted that she never had a mind or a wish of her own, but preferred to sympathize always with the minds and wishes of others' (Woolf, 1966: II. 285). The angel renders writing and reviewing impossible: 'Had I not killed her she would have killed me. She would have plucked the heart out of my writing. For, as I found, directly I put pen to paper, you cannot review even a novel without a mind of your own' (1966: II. 286). The struggle to suppress this phantom is something every woman writer must endure: 'Killing the Angel in the House was part of the occupation of a woman writer' (1966: II. 286). The paper closes with Woolf's acknowledgement that women have made, by 1931, some significant material gains. She returns to her central feminist metaphor when she remarks that the women in her audience, 'have won rooms of your own in the house hitherto exclusively owned by men. You are able, though not without great labour and effort, to pay the rent. You are earning your five hundred pounds a year' (1966: II. 289). These are the material conditions Woolf puts forward, in *A Room of One's Own*, as necessary for women writers to flourish. But, she warns here, 'this freedom is only a beginning; the room is your own, but it is still bare. . . . How are you going to furnish it, how are you going to decorate it? With whom are you going to share it, and upon what terms?' (1966: II. 289). The material conditions for women writers extend to other professional women, and vice versa. As a writer Woolf is aligning herself with other women who work. The 'Angel in the House' represents those women who still endure the enforced and unpaid domestic servitude of wife and mother. She is a spectre that haunts all working women.

In 'Memories of a Working Women's Guild' (1931), Woolf explores the complexities of her position as an educated and privileged middle-class woman aligned with working-class women in organised suffragist and feminist politics. It was written as an introduction to *Life as We Have Known It*, a collection of pieces by former members of the Working Women's Guild (in which Woolf herself had been active). Woolf begins by recalling her initially private reservations about Margaret Llewelyn

Davies' request for the very article she now writes. Thinking back to a 1913 conference in Newcastle where in 'a public hall hung with banners and loud voices' (Woolf, 1931/1982: xxiii) she heard working-class women speakers demand 'divorce, education, the vote – all good things . . . higher wages and shorter hours' (1931/1982: xviii), she marks the difference in perspective she derives from the material benefits of class difference: 'If every reform they demand was granted this very instant it would not touch one hair of my comfortable capitalistic head' (1931/1982: xviii–xix). She also recalls her sense of futility since at the time 'among all those women who worked, who bore children, who scrubbed and cooked and bargained, there was not a single woman with a vote' (1931/1982: xix). The Women's Co-Operative Guild was a powerful force for working-class women, and Woolf goes on to explore the letters that comprise *Life as We Have Known It*, concluding: 'These pages are only fragments. These voices are beginning only now to emerge from silence into half articulate speech. These lives are still half hidden in profound obscurity' (1931/1982: xxxix). These women, it appears, have begun to fulfil Woolf's injunction, in *A Room of One's Own*, to 'illumine your own soul' (1931/1982: 135). Woolf closes with the example of the Guild's secretary, Miss Kidd, and quotes her 'fragment of a letter': 'When I was a girl of seventeen', she writes, 'my then employer, a gentleman of good position . . . sent me to his home one night, ostensibly to take a parcel of books, but really with a very different object. When I arrived at the house all the family were away, and before he would allow me to leave he forced me to yield to him. At eighteen I was a mother.' Woolf does not 'presume to say' whether such writing 'is literature or not literature . . . but that it explains much and reveals much is certain. Such then was the burden that rested on that sombre figure as she sat typing your letters, such were the memories she brooded as she guarded your door with her grim and indomitable fidelity' (1931/1982: xxxviii–xxxix). This essay shows Woolf's continuing interest in suffragist politics and aesthetics at a time when her pacifism and anti-fascism were becoming more prominent. It shows her awareness of the class issues that confront feminism, and it also puts into practice her espousal of a collective, multi-vocal women's writing, albeit framed by her own frank class self-consciousness and fraught by doubts over the project's cultural status. But more interesting than her own, much debated, self-critique here is the uncomfortable analogy that Woolf points up between Miss Kidd's two social and cultural roles, as the mother of a child conceived in rape at the hands of her first, patriarchal, employer, and as the secretary who loyally reproduces the writings of her current, feminist, employer. Davies' publication of Miss Kidd's own words is the first step towards her former amanuensis' claim on authorship and self-fashioning, and Woolf's own citation of those words as textual authority, in her introduction, is another; steps that also promise to unsettle our definitions of the literary, as Woolf indicates, and to question the gender and class politics of its (re)production.

In 'The Leaning Tower' (1940), a paper given to the Workers' Educational Association, Woolf points up the historical status of writers as upper and middle class, and looks forward to abolishing their now leaning literary tower altogether (Woolf, 1966: II. 177–8). She looks forward to the 'next generation' who will be, 'when peace comes, a post-war generation too. Must it too be a leaning-tower generation – an oblique, sidelong, squinting, self-conscious generation with a foot in two worlds? Or will there be no more towers and no more classes and shall we stand, without hedges between us, on the common ground?' (1966: II. 178). This common ground for literature, a post-war 'world without classes or towers', will be made possible by the prospect, profered by the politicians, of 'equal opportunities, equal chances of developing whatever gifts we may possess', and by the material underpinning of that prospect by 'income tax'. Woolf's feminist concerns are subsumed here into class ones; and her concept of the 'common ground' of literature marks out a future egalitarian, republican democracy of letters, which appears to be beyond gender concerns.

In 'Thoughts on Peace in an Air Raid' (1940), however, gender and feminism resurface as Woolf meditates, while German bombs drop on British civilian targets, on the 'queer experience, lying in the dark and listening to the zoom of a hornet which may at any moment sting you to death' (Woolf, 1966: IV. 173). She gives warning of the gender politics inherent in this horrific aspect of modern warfare which has young men bombing unarmed women and children: 'Unless we can think peace into existence we – not this one body in its one bed but millions of bodies yet to be born – will lie in the same darkness and hear the same death rattle overhead' (1966: IV. 173). The gender division of this situation has men at war with each other in the sky – 'the defenders are men, the attackers are men' – while women 'must lie weaponless to-night' listening for the bombs. But, citing William Blake's 'Jerusalem', Woolf urges women to 'fight with the mind', free the men 'from the machine' and 'compensate the man for the loss of his gun' (1966: IV. 174). One target is the 'subconscious Hitlerism' in men that turns them against women. In this poignant late essay, espousing feminist, anti-fascist culture and writing, Woolf defines the 'mental fight' we should muster in times of war as fierce, intellectual independence. She rallies us to think 'against the current, not with it' (1966: IV. 174).

This chapter's brief samplings of Woolf's feminist literary criticism can only begin to show the range, breadth and depth of Woolf's considerable contribution to the field. Her own writings have never been out of print since first publication, and there now exists a huge body of feminist literary criticism on Woolf and on the numerous debates concerning feminism and literature that her work has engendered. Her 'mental fight' continues.

NOTES

1. See Symons (1987) and Marek (1995).
2. See Strachey (1936) and Harrison (1925); other women writers published by Woolf at Hogarth include: Rose Macaulay, Gertrude Stein, Frances Cornford, Rosamond Lehmann, Rebecca West, Vita Sackville-West, E. M. Delafield, Edith Sitwell, Nancy Cunard, Melanie Klein, Naomi Mitchison, Anna Freud and Dorothy Wellesley.
3. For discussion of this ballad (variously known as 'The Four Marys' and 'Mary Hamilton'), see Jane Marcus, 'Sapphistry: Narration as Lesbian Seduction in *A Room of One's Own*', in Marcus (1987).
4. Fernham is a fictionalisation of Newnham College at the University of Cambridge. Founded in 1871, Newnham was the first college to admit women to the University.
5. *A Room of One's Own* was published in the year after the full enfranchisement of women, ten years after the enfranchisement of working-class men along with middle-class, propertied women over thirty years of age.
6. See Hartman (1970).
7. 'Granite and rainbow' are used by Woolf in her essay 'The New Biography' (1927) to describe the two different aspects of biography: the objective and factual and the spiritual, subjective and imaginary (1986–92: IV. 473).
8. See Jane Marcus (1992).
9. See Faderman (1994) and Zimmerman (1984); see also Barrett and Cramer (1997).
10. See Smith (1989/1997).
11. See her essay 'The Common Reader' (1925), reproduced in Woolf (1986–92: IV. 19).

BIBLIOGRAPHY

Allen, Judith (1999), 'The Rhetoric of Performance in *A Room of One's Own*', in *Virginia Woolf and Communities: Selected Papers from the Eighth Annual Conference on Virginia Woolf*, ed. Jeanette McVicker and Laura Davis, New York: Pace University Press.

Barrett, Michèle (1979), 'Introduction', in *Virginia Woolf on Women and Writing*, ed. Michèle Barrett, London: Women's Press.

——— (2001), 'Reason and Truth in *A Room of One's Own*: A Master in Lunacy', in *Virginia Woolf Out of Bounds: Selected Papers from the Tenth Annual Conference on Virginia Woolf*, ed. Jessica Berman and Jane Goldman, New York: Pace University Press.

Barrett, Eileen and Patricia Cramer (eds) (1997), *Virginia Woolf: Lesbian Readings*, New York: New York University Press.

Bradshaw, David (1997/1998), 'British Writers and Anti-Fascism in the 1930s, Part I: The Bray and Drone of Tortured Voices' and 'British Writers and Anti-Fascism in the 1930s, Part II: Under the Hawk's Wings', in *Woolf Studies Annual* 3 and 4.

Belsey, Catherine and Jane Moore (1997), 'Introduction: The Story So Far', in *The Feminist Reader*, ed. Catherine Belsey and Jane Moore, 2nd edn, London: Palgrave.

Doyle, Laura (2001), 'The Body Unbound: A Phenomenological Reading of the Political in *A Room of One's Own*', in *Virginia Woolf Out of Bounds: Selected Papers from the Tenth Annual Conference on Virginia Woolf*, ed. Jessica Berman and Jane Goldman, New York: Pace University Press.

Faderman, Lillian (ed.) (1994), *Chloe Plus Olivia: An Anthology of Lesbian Literature from the Seventeenth Century to the Present*, London: Viking.

Goldman, Jane (1998), *The Feminist Aesthetics of Virginia Woolf: Modernism, Post-Impressionism, and the Politics of the Visual*, Cambridge: Cambridge University Press.

Gruber, Ruth (2005), *Virginia Woolf: The Will to Create as a Woman*, New York: Carroll & Graf.

Harrison, Jane (1925), *Reminiscences of a Student Life*, London: Hogarth Press.

Hartman, Geoffrey (1970), 'Virginia's Web', in *Beyond Formalism: Literary Essays 1958–1970*, New Haven and London: Yale University Press, and Montreal: McGill-Queen's University Press.

Holtby, Winifred (1932), *Virginia Woolf*, London: Wishart.

Kamuf, Peggy (1982), 'Penelope at Work: Interruptions in *A Room of One's Own*', in *Novel* 16.

Marcus, Jane (1987), *Virginia Woolf and the Languages of Patriarchy*, Bloomington and Indianapolis: Indiana University Press.

——— (1992), 'Sapphistory: The Woolf and the Well', in *Lesbian Texts and Contexts: Radical Revisions*, ed. Karla Jay and Joanne Glasgow, London: Onlywomen Press.

——— (2004), *Hearts of Darkness: White Women Write Race*, New Brunswick, NJ: Rutgers University Press.

Marcus, Laura (2000), 'Woolf's Feminism and Feminism's Woolf', in *The Cambridge Companion to Virginia Woolf*, ed. Sue Roe and Susan Sellers, Cambridge: Cambridge University Press.

Marek, Jayne E. (1995), *Women Editing Modernism: 'Little' Magazines and Literary History*, Lexington: University Press of Kentucky.

Moi, Toril (1985), *Sexual/Textual Politics: Feminist Literary Theory*, London: Methuen.

Norquay, Glenda (1995), *Voices and Votes: A Literary Anthology of the Women's Suffrage Campaign*, Manchester: Manchester University Press.

Scott, Bonnie Kime (ed.) (1990), *The Gender of Modernism: A Critical Anthology*, Bloomington and Indianapolis: Indiana University Press.

Showalter, Elaine (1977), *A Literature of Their Own: British Women Novelists from Brontë to Lessing*, Princeton, NJ: Princeton University Press.

Smith, Valerie (1989/1997), 'Black Feminist Theory and the Representation of the "Other"', in *Feminisms: An Anthology of Literary Theory and Criticism*, ed. Robyn R. Warhol and Diane Price Herndl, Basingstoke: Macmillan (1997).

Stimpson, Catherine (1992), 'Woolf's Room, Our Project: The Building of Feminist Criticism', in *Virginia Woolf: Longman Critical Readers*, ed. Rachel Bowlby, London: Longman.

Strachey, Ray (ed.) (1936), *Our Freedom and Its Results*, London: Hogarth Press.

Symons, Julian (1987), *Makers of the New: The Revolution in Literature, 1912–1939*, New York and London: Random House.

Walker, Alice (1985), 'In Search of Our Mothers' Gardens', in *The Norton Anthology of Literature by Women: The Tradition in English*, ed. Sandra M. Gilbert and Susan Gubar, New York: Norton.

Woolf, Virginia (1929), *A Room of One's Own*, London: Hogarth.

— (1931/1982), 'Introductory Letter' ['Memories of a Working Women's Guild'], in *Life as We Have Known It by Co-Operative Working Women*, ed. Margaret Llewelyn Davies, London: Virago.

— (1938), *Three Guineas*, London: Hogarth.

— (1966), *Collected Essays*, 4 vols, ed. Leonard Woolf, London: Chatto.

— (1975–80), *The Letters of Virginia Woolf*, 6 vols, ed. Nigel Nicolson and Joanne Trautmann, London: Hogarth.

— (1977–84), *The Diary of Virginia Woolf*, 5 vols, ed. Anne Olivier Bell and Andrew McNeillie, London: Hogarth.

— (1985), *Moments of Being: Unpublished Autobiographical Writings*, 2nd edn, ed. Jeanne Schulkind, London: Hogarth.

— (1986–92), *The Essays of Virginia Woolf*, 4 of 6 vols, ed. Andrew McNeillie, London: Hogarth.

Zimmerman, Bonnie (1984), 'Is "Chloe Liked Olivia" a Lesbian Plot?', in *Women in Academe*, ed. Resa L. Dudovitz, Oxford: Pergamon.

CHAPTER 5

Simone de Beauvoir and the demystification of woman

Elizabeth Fallaize

Simone de Beauvoir's *The Second Sex* (1949) is one of the most famous and influential books of the twentieth century. It had a profound influence on the development of twentieth-century feminism, providing a key theoretical tool in the elaboration of the concept of the social construction of gender and offering a model of feminist enquiry for the theorists, literary critics, historians, philosophers, theologians and critics of scientific discourse who developed the new fields of study which her multidisciplinary essay opened up. Beauvoir's radical attack on the social institutions of motherhood and the family together with her frank discussion of female sexuality led to a public furore on the book's publication in France, a bare five years after De Gaulle at last conceded the right to vote to French women in 1944. The Pope put the book on the list of works which Roman Catholics are forbidden to read and François Mauriac, a leading French novelist and right-wing commentator, led a public campaign to have it banned. However, the media excitement also attracted the attention of the American publisher Knopf who, partly because of a misunderstanding about the book's actual content, commissioned an English translation from a zoologist, Howard Parshley. Parshley's work on the book was undoubtedly a labour of love, but he was obliged by the publisher to make very substantial cuts in the lengthy two-volume text, and was further hampered by the fact that he did not share Beauvoir's training in philosophy.[1]

Nevertheless, despite its inadequacies, the translation duly appeared in 1952 and it enabled a highly significant transmission of ideas to a generation of Anglophone women readers. They included Betty Friedan, Kate Millett, Shulamith Firestone, Juliet Mitchell, Ann Oakley and Germaine Greer, all of whom took up some of Beauvoir's lines of enquiry from the early 1960s onwards, often without realising the extent to which they had been influenced by their reading of *The Second Sex*, and almost always without acknowledging it. This was no doubt partly because Beauvoir's language and politics appeared impossibly exotic (especially as conveyed in some of the translator's more impenetrable sentences), but it was also, as Kate Millett was later to put it, because of the revelatory nature of Beauvoir's work. 'It was a revelation – how could it have been a source?' commented Millett at a 1999 conference on *The Second Sex* (Galster, 2004: 16). In the 1980s, both Monique Wittig and Judith Butler developed Beauvoir's famous distinction between sex and gender in radical new directions, with Butler reading Beauvoir's formulation 'One is not born but rather becomes a woman' as a programme for the daily interpretation of gender (Butler, 1986) and Wittig arguing in her essay 'One Is Not Born a Woman' that the categories 'man' and 'woman' are political categories which should be abolished (Wittig, 1981). The rise to prominence of the French feminist theorists of difference led to a temporary eclipse of *The Second Sex*. As feminist theory found itself faced with something of an impasse between essentialism and the postmodern dissolution of the subject, however, there was a renewed interest in Beauvoir's account of situated subjectivity which allows both for the possibility of political action and, simultaneously, for the constraints of oppression. In 1994 Toril Moi wrote: 'if we are to escape from current political and theoretical dead ends, feminism in the 1990s cannot afford to ignore Beauvoir's pioneering insights' (Moi, 1994: 185).

From the 1990s onwards, there has been a new wave of scholarship which has succeeded in removing long-held misapprehensions about Beauvoir's work: the originality of her philosophical method (long presumed simply to be borrowed from Sartre) has emerged; her use of a materialist and historical framework to support her ontological analysis of oppression has been underlined; her recognition of the embodied nature of consciousness and her concern with establishing a basis for co-operation between individual freedoms have become a focus of discussion.[2] It is in particular this emphasis on the potential for fruitful relations between people, together with her concern with ethics, that marks Beauvoir out from the intellectual shadow of her lifelong companion Jean-Paul Sartre, whose dominance of French intellectual life in the years immediately following the Second World War had an unfortunate effect on perceptions of Beauvoir's thought.

Much of this new work has taken place in the philosophical domain; however, there has been far less exploration of Beauvoir's highly original analysis of the networks of cultural myth operated by patriarchy across the centuries, and of the way in which her work on myth led her to develop a deconstructive method of reading myth in male writers. In this chapter, I shall therefore examine Beauvoir's general theorisation of myth, and the role it plays in the wider project of *The Second Sex*, before turning to an analysis of how her critical method works in the textual readings of five major male writers which she undertakes to illustrate the ways in which myth underpins cultural production. Beyond *The Second Sex* itself, she pursued her deconstructive readings in two particularly interesting essays, both on topics which at first sight look like surprising choices: the first, in 1952, on the writings of the Marquis de Sade and the second, in 1959, on the films of Brigitte Bardot. I shall look at how her method developed in those critical essays, and assess the potential which Beauvoir's approach offers feminist literary criticism today.

MYTH IN *THE SECOND SEX*

Although Simone de Beauvoir had trained and worked as a philosopher she considered herself primarily to be a writer. When she began work on *The Second Sex* in 1946 she was already the author of three novels and a play, and in 1954 she was to win the prestigious Goncourt prize for her fourth novel, *The Mandarins*. *The Second Sex* began life as a piece of autobiographical writing, for which she decided to consider the impact on her life of having been born female:

It was a revelation: this world was a masculine world, my childhood had been nourished by myths forged by men, and I hadn't reacted to them in at all the same way I should have done if I had been a boy. I was so interested in this discovery that I abandoned my project for a personal confession in order to give all my attention to finding out about the condition of women in its broadest terms. I went to the Bibliothèque Nationale to do some reading and what I studied were the myths of femininity. (Beauvoir, 1963: 103)

As this account shows, the analysis of myth provided the original intellectual impulse for the whole project of *The Second Sex*, and Beauvoir published it in *Les Temps Modernes* in 1948, whilst she was still working on finishing the book. In the final and complete French version, 'Myths' occupies nearly two hundred of the thousand or so pages of *The Second Sex*, and the thinking behind it often drives the argument in other sections, notably the chapters on biology, history, dress and, significantly, the important final chapter on 'The Independent Woman'. In this portrait of 'modern woman' Beauvoir underlines the extent to which myths continue to create problems for the woman who seeks to build an independent life in the late 1940s.

But what did Beauvoir understand by myth? The anthropologist Claude Lévi-Strauss allowed her to read the manuscript version of *The Elementary Structures of Kinship*, and she drew on his work quite extensively for *The*

Second Sex. Lévi-Strauss approached the study of myth as a study of deeply rooted patterns in cultural beliefs and, influenced by the linguist Roman Jakobson, Lévi-Strauss sought to reduce a wide diversity of apparently complex practices to a small number of structural affinities. The idea of individual myths as generators of universal patterns was grist to Beauvoir's mill in her attempt to identify the mechanisms of patriarchy. The sharp distinction which Lévi-Strauss appeared to be making between nature and culture supported her concept of femininity as cultural product, and the central role which he attributes to sexuality as a negotiation between nature and culture offers a theoretical justification for her concern with sexuality.[3] Psychoanalysis provided her with the notion of archetypes. Despite her vigorous rejection of Freud's thinking on women, Beauvoir nevertheless found that Jung's notion of archetypes – 'the truly amazing phenomenon that certain motifs from myths and legends repeat themselves the world over in identical forms' (Jung, 1943/1972: 65) – fitted her purpose. She cites not only Jung but also Gaston Bachelard, who uses archetypes to probe unconscious beliefs about nature. This approach is not incompatible with Lévi-Strauss, for whom myths become a collective creation and category of the unconscious. However, Beauvoir parts company with the anthropologist's approach in her adoption of the Marxist conception of myth as ideology, an important tool in her attack on myths as beliefs that work to sustain patriarchy. In her view, myths of 'Woman' have been invented by men for the specific purpose of keeping women in their place, and in her deconstruction of them she indicates clearly how cultural myth operates in conjunction with economic and social factors to reinforce the oppression of women as a group.

Beauvoir's choice of these major thinkers to help her forge a theory of myth was a prescient one, when one considers the impact on literary criticism all were to make in later decades. Lévi-Strauss was to become one of the founding fathers of structuralism, the key literary critical movement of the 1960s, whilst both psychoanalytic criticism and Marxist criticism went on to form important critical schools. However, despite the influence that these thinkers have on her approach, all three are essentially used to support Beauvoir's overarching theory, which is existentialist and ontological. Throughout the discussion, Beauvoir returns repeatedly to her central thesis that women are constrained to operate as man's other. Instead of acceding to the subjectivity which she considers to be the source of all freedom and value, women find themselves cast into the role of subservient object, cut off from an empowering autonomy and pressed into the role of supporting male subjectivity. Beauvoir discusses at length in *The Second Sex* how this has come about and brings into play a panoply of historical and social factors. Myth is seen as having a very particular part to play in persuading women of the *naturalness* of their fate. In the basic ontological paradigm which Beauvoir sees as underlying all human relations, every individual consciousness experiences a fundamental hostility towards other consciousnesses and tries to constitute the other as inessential, as object. At the same time, the other is necessary to us, since we require the other's recognition to fully exist as subject. We are thus caught in a double bind, which Hegel characterised as the master-slave dialectic. The master treats the slave as other but his need to gain recognition from the slave means that he also has to admit the slave's subjectivity, and thus the master is himself eventually reduced to the other by the slave.

Beauvoir (unlike Hegel and Sartre) argues that there is a way out of this dilemma, if each party offers full recognition of the other's subjectivity and a common agreement is made not to try to enslave the other. This state of reciprocal recognition requires considerable self-mastery and has a high moral status in Beauvoir's eyes: it is the state to which she hopes men and women will eventually work their way forward, and she tries to show it working in her first novel, *She Came to Stay* (1943).[4] However, in her discussion of myths, written almost ten years later, Beauvoir describes the master-slave dialectic as having so far worked almost universally to women's disadvantage. She opens her chapter on myths by explaining how women have been persuaded by a sleight of hand into adopting a position which allows men a double win. By identifying women with the inert world of the body and with nature, men are able to maintain themselves in the master/subject position; yet at the same time, women are just sufficiently proximate to subjectivity to offer men the recognition they need, which no other man would offer without challenge. Women have thus either occupied the slave position or, worse still, as Lundgren-Gothlin shows, they have remained outside the struggle for recognition altogether (Lundgren-Gothlin, 1991/1996: 99). Beauvoir writes that woman is man's metaphysical dream incarnate: neither offering the challenge that a man would, nor as passive as a pure object (Beauvoir, 1949: 172).

This then is the metaphysical bind which Beauvoir sets out at the beginning of her discussion of myth, and in which myth has such a crucial role to play. She then turns to the myths themselves. Amongst those she treats are creation myths, in which women are always subsidiary (Eve as Adam's rib and subordinate); fecundity myths which identify women with a passive body and with nature (woman as earth, man as the plough); virginity myths, in which virginity is prized in young women but feared as unmastered sexuality in older women; *femme fatale* myths, in which women are held responsible for the sins of the flesh and for tempting men (Eve; the figure of the mermaid; woman as vampire, symbolically castrating the male); myths of the Holy Mother (Mary, the inverse of Eve), in which Mary is apparently glorified but only in return for her role as servant of God, and myths of the evil mother, in which fear of mothers is channelled into stepmother stories (Snow White, the goddess Kali); the Pygmalion myth, expressing the male desire to model and educate his wife; the myth of feminine mystery (Freud's dark continent), which permits men to ignore women's real needs and what they have to say.

From this abundance of material, a number of important points about the general functioning of myths about women emerge. First, myths are characterised as inevitably indefinable and contradictory by nature. Woman is both Mary and Eve, man's salvation and his downfall: the purpose of myth is to represent woman according to patriarchy's needs, and in contradistinction to whatever man considers himself to be. The ambivalence of the myths is also identified by Beauvoir as reflecting man's fundamental ambivalence about nature: in women's bodies he both reveres nature and is at the same time reminded of his natural origins in a woman's body, and thus by association of his inevitable death. Beauvoir notes that this ambivalence is often expressed through binary opposites – a concept later developed by Hélène Cixous. A second characteristic of myth consists in its absolutism: myth is not open to challenge in the face of experience. Myth substitutes a timeless and absolute truth for the multiple and contingent experience of women. It fixes women into the position of absolute other.

A third feature of myth emerges particularly clearly from the myth of feminine mystery – one of the most advantageous to the ruling male caste, Beauvoir dryly notes. The myth of feminine mystery is an elaboration of the fact that other people are always a mystery, since we can never know how others experience their subjectivity. Between the sexes, Beauvoir believes this mystery to be deepened by the fact that each sex has no access to the other sex's subjective experience of sexuality (a concept which is returned to frequently in her literary readings). There is then a counterpart to 'female mystery' in the mystery that the subjective experience of male sexuality represents for women. But this is never described as a male mystery, not only, Beauvoir argues, because male conceptual categories are always constituted as universal and absolute, but also because there is an economic infrastructure to the notion of mystery. The economic equal or superior is never said to be a mystery – but the economic dependant who is kept on the margins *is* said to be a mystery. Perhaps the most important point which comes out of the discussion of feminine mystery, however, is the alienating effect it has on women. At its most effective, the myth of feminine mystery persuades women that they are a mystery to themselves, making any question of aspiring to recognition seem quite impossible.

Throughout her analysis Beauvoir stresses the widespread and pervasive nature of myth. Returning to it at many junctures in the essay as a whole, she shows how it impacts on even the 'Independent Woman', who has to try to cope with the pressures of the contradiction between her successes and the mythology of the feminine with which she is still associated. Through myth, she writes, patriarchal society imposes its laws on individuals in a particularly effective mode, working through the intermediary of 'religions, traditions, language, tales, songs, movies' to insinuate itself into everyone's consciousness (1949/1972: 290). It is clear that Beauvoir understands myth as operating at every level of culture, including the popular culture of song and cinema, and here she reads as a forerunner of Roland Barthes' *Mythologies* (Lavers, 2004: 265). However, it is to serious literature – to high culture in other words – that Beauvoir turns for her extended examples of how myths of Woman are circulated and customised, no doubt conscious that to have focused on popular culture would have risked not being taken seriously.

Her selection of authors is, revealingly, dominated by her own contemporaries. Her choice of Montherlant, D. H. Lawrence, Claudel and Breton allowed her to discuss the way contemporary writers represented social, sexual and amorous relations and provided a particularly significant reference point for her concern with the difficulties of 'the independent woman'. In different degrees, all four emerge as manipulators of patriarchal myth and Beauvoir's readings thus allow her to express her frustration with contemporary sexual mores. Stendhal, who wrote at the end of the eighteenth and beginning of the nineteenth century, serves as a strong foil and is praised for creating free and independent women characters and heterosexual couples who relate to each other authentically. Each of the authors allows her to focus on a different aspect of myth: thus Montherlant, the first author discussed, exemplifies a long tradition of misogyny which identifies Woman with weakness and the flesh, and converts her into a monstrous praying mantis (a myth which reverberates throughout *The Second Sex*). Beauvoir also uses his case to link misogyny to racism and fascism. D. H. Lawrence, her second author, is shown to equate Woman with nature; she is man's partner in a cosmic communion with the universe, but always subsidiary to the supreme power of the phallus. The Catholic writer Claudel, the third author, exalts Woman as divine (myth of

Mary); her very saintliness condemns her to the social role of man's vassal and servant. Breton, the fourth, equally idealises Woman, identifying her with Beauty, Poetry and Truth, but he simultaneously reduces her to the child-woman and never conceives of her as subject. Only Stendhal largely avoids the mythmaking process, though even he, in the end, assumes that the destiny of woman is man. Overall, Woman emerges as flesh, imma-nence, nature, poetry, man's means of communication with God or with the surreal, destined to serve man – and if she refuses these roles, she becomes monstrous. Beauvoir's readings supply an ample demonstration of the working out of the myths she had identified earlier.

POWER PLAY IN THE HETEROSEXUAL COUPLE

The demonstration of the myths at work is not however Beauvoir's only concern in her reading of authors who had personally marked her own trajectory as a woman. Again and again she returns to the issue of power play in the heterosexual couple, to the dynamics of sexuality itself and to an assessment of the potential of the couple to provide the breakthrough in the Hegelian double bind bedeviling all human relationships. Montherlant, her starting point, provides the worst-case scenario. The Montherlant hero is psychotic, in Beauvoir's view. His will to power has its roots in an inferiority complex which leads him to shore up his own virility by insist-ing that woman be strictly confined to the role of flesh. He condemns out of hand the female harpies 'who have the audacity to pose as autonomous subjects, to think, to act' (Beauvoir, 1949/1972: 233, translation adapted). The Montherlant hero's determination to dominate abolishes any hope of a reciprocal relationship, and, on the sexual front, interestingly, this domina-tion translates into a determination to give sexual pleasure to the woman and to take none himself. This idea of bringing the woman to orgasm as an act of mastery also feeds into the chapter on 'The Independent Woman', where Beauvoir speaks of the problem for women of being obliged to accept the gift of sexual pleasure actively brought about by a man, a gift which Beauvoir appears to think women cannot reciprocate.

D. H. Lawrence offers what at first sight seems to be a much more positive model of the couple in which both partners give body and soul. Not only though does Lawrence turn out to be a worshipper of the phallus, he is extremely dismissive of 'modern' women, 'creatures of celluloid and rubber laying claim to a consciousness' (1949/1972: 250–1). Beauvoir dis-cusses his portraits of independent women – Gudrun, Ursula, Miriam, Teresa – to show how they are rejected unless they consent to give up their autonomy and adopt the hero's values. And, on the level of sexual relations, his heroines fare worse than Montherlant's, since they are required to renounce orgasm altogether. Beauvoir concludes that Lawrence offers merely another version of the 'woman who unreservedly accepts being defined as the Other' (1949/1972: 254). In Claudel, the union between the couple is a sacred union, leading the partners to God, but his major female figures express their saintliness through renunciation and service, remaining a figure of the absolute other. In Breton, woman is again salvation but the figure pronounced by Breton to be the future of humanity is the child-woman, who in Breton's own words incarnates 'the *other* prism of vision' (1949/1972: 267). No equal partnership is envisaged.

The insufficiencies of these constructions of the couple spring into sharp relief when we turn to Beauvoir's reading of Stendhal. In pages of extraordinary lyricism, Beauvoir sings the praises of heroines who are 'free and authentic beings' (1949/1972: 271) casting aside conventions and laws, and breaking out of the prisons in which society has confined them. Beauvoir writes that their 'ardent quest for valid reasons for living', their search for 'the infinite risk of happiness' gives 'glory to these women's lives' (1949/1972: 275–6). She goes on to extol the relationships which the Stendhalian heroine constructs with the hero who admires her, who understands her, and who in understanding the heroine comes to a better understanding of himself. Here at last we have the breakthrough to reciprocal recognition:

It is through women, under their influence, in reaction to their behaviour, that Julien, Fabrice, Lucien learn about the world and about themselves. Test, reward, judge, friend, woman truly is in Stendhal what Hegel was for a moment tempted to make of her: that other consciousness which in reciprocal recognition gives to the other subject the same truth that she receives from him. The happy couple who recognize each other in love defy the universe and time; the couple is self-sufficient, it attains the absolute. (1949/1972: 277, translation adapted.)

In Stendhal, the heterosexual couple thus becomes a privileged locus of human relationships, a model for the resolution of the Hegelian conflict.[5] Yet this enthusiasm is not repeated later in *The Second Sex*. The dangers for women of falling in love are fully set out in the section entitled 'The Woman in Love', while in 'The Independent Woman' Beauvoir states that the numerous difficulties encountered by such women are nowhere more acute than in the sexual domain and goes on to catalogue all the barriers preventing women from leading a free sexual life. At the end of her catalogue, she does return to the idea that it is theoretically possible for the two partners to recognise each other as equals. But this time, she appears to find the chances of this happening slim and, referring back to her Stendhalian couples, she argues that if Julien had been a woman and Madame de Renâl a man, the couple could not have existed. The change in tone is remarkable:

We have seen that it is possible to avoid the temptations of sadism and masochism when the two partners recognize each other as equals; if both the man and the woman have a little modesty and some generosity, ideas of victory and defeat are abolished; the act of love becomes a free exchange. But paradoxically, it is much more difficult for the woman than for the man to recognize an individual of the other sex as an equal. (1949/1972: 701)

What has happened here to the lyrical version of the couple? No doubt a biographical explanation could be sought in the difficulties of Beauvoir's relationship with her American lover Nelson Algren, much more evident to her by the time she finished writing the book than at the time she began it. However, it is also plausible that her perspective had been changed by the very process of writing *The Second Sex*. In her chapter on Stendhal, written at the beginning of her work on the book, she explicitly identifies with Julien, the male lover. By the time she comes to her final chapter, she is able to imagine an independent woman in the dominant role, and she perceives all the difficulties inherent in that position.

Beauvoir's five literary case studies, then, not only serve to show how myths of Woman are disseminated by contemporary writers, but also tie the myths into an analysis of power relations within the couple, placing sexuality at the heart of the mystery of the other and trying to gauge the potential of the couple for the near-impossible state of reciprocity. Along the way she analyses contemporary masculinity to show that these writers are unable to imitate Stendhal in opening themselves up to an element of femininity and thus escape damaging models of virility. Turning now briefly to her essays on Sade and Bardot, we shall see how she went on to develop the dual focus of her method.

FROM SADE TO BARDOT

Beauvoir's essay on Sade, first published less than three years after her essay on myth, appears at first sight to have rather different preoccupations from her readings in *The Second Sex*. Myth has become a set of mystifications perpetrated specifically by a social class – the bourgeoisie – which, after the French Revolution of 1789, is said to have erected its own class interests into a set of 'universal' values. Beauvoir presents Sade as a demystifier of bourgeois values, and makes the claim that he uses sexuality to challenge bourgeois myths annihilating the individual. As Judith Butler puts it, in her reading of the essay, Beauvoir 'insists upon the counterintuitive claim that Sade is everywhere concerned with ethics' (Butler, 2003: 175). One might wonder how Beauvoir manages to argue this, when Sade's writings depict the sexual subjection of women and the deliberate infliction of pain upon them. She does not of course *approve* Sade's practices but neither does she spend much time denouncing them; what interests her in Sade's project is not the cruelty as such but the relation with the other which he constructs in sexual acts. According to Beauvoir, Sade suffered from a disabling sense of solitude and disempowerment, and tried to compensate for the loss of power of his generation of young aristocrats by trying to act out in the bedroom the feudal despotism and illusion of sovereignty which earlier generations enjoyed. He thus resorted to extreme means to receive confirmation of his own dominance, whilst remaining convinced that the self is always locked into subjectivity. Yet Beauvoir manages to detect cracks in his citadel of solitude. On the level of his sexual practice, she points out that Sade's very dependence on his victim's reactions involves a recognition of the other, whilst his penchant for collective debauchery achieves a communion with others which is mirrored in the process of writing.

Sade's attempt to build a sexual ethic denying the other is thus doomed to failure in Beauvoir's view, since it in fact depends on the other. From a wider perspective she also points out that he essentially attempts to re-enact a situation of social privilege and fails to see the possibility of human solidarity in action. Why does Beauvoir invest so much effort and sympathy in understanding Sade? What Sade's case allows Beauvoir to do is not only to extend her myth analysis to an analysis of social class, but to continue her investigation of the nature of sexual relations and of the power play at work in them.

Oddly, it is Brigitte Bardot who provides a breakthrough in those power stakes. Beauvoir's essay on Bardot, written in 1959 for an American audience, pursues the analysis of sexuality and power, conjoined this time with a dissection of the myths of femininity rather than of social class. On one level, Beauvoir sees the Bardot persona, created by husband and director Roger Vadim, as merely a modernised version of traditional myths of the eternal feminine, allying women and nature, and inviting the male spectator to see himself as the master and saviour of a weaker vessel. Bardot replaces the *femme fatale* model with a child-woman model, whose tousled hair, simple dress and petulant behaviour suggest an unsophisticated child of nature who requires male taming and protection. Beauvoir identifies the rising popularity of the child-woman as a direct response to the growing role of women in public life.

However, Beauvoir also perceives a more subversive element to the image as Bardot's 'naturalness' extends to sexuality. Demystifying sex and stripping it of social hypocrisy, Bardot operates as a sexual predator, on equal terms with men. She substitutes an assertive sexuality for the magic trap of the vamp. This, suggests Beauvoir, is the reason why Bardot is so unpopular in France. The average Frenchman is unable to cope with a woman operating sexually on equal terms. Picking up on a theme pursued in *The Second Sex* in 'The Independent Woman', Beauvoir underlines the difference between a liberated woman and an 'easy' woman; Bardot is the first but not the second, and thus presents a stumbling block to ribald male fantasies. It is difficult to resist Mandy Merck's claim (Merck, 1993: 73–5) that there is an identificatory process at work here; though the 51-year-old intellectual and the Bardot nymphet have obvious dissimilarities, the furious reception which had greeted Beauvoir's treatment of female sexuality in *The Second Sex* certainly suggests that the two women occupied similar ground. Merck also goes on to discuss Beauvoir's analysis of the spectator as voyeur, and credits Beauvoir with 'anticipating the feminist criticism which would come after her, particularly its interest in films which "foreground" relations of spectatorship' (Merck, 1993: 81–2).[6] In discussing Bardot, Beauvoir is thus extending her analysis of myth, engaging with popular culture and beginning to develop a theory of the gendered 'look' in the cinema, but she is also identifying the potentially positive charge of a cultural myth which might destabilise the balance of power inherent in sexual relations.

CONCLUSIONS

I began by saying that Beauvoir has not been very fully acknowledged by feminist theorists following in her wake, especially by Kate Millett, whose *Sexual Politics* (1971) contains four case studies of male writers and is generally credited with having launched deconstructive feminist criticism of male writing.[7] It is striking that Millett opens her first chapter with a reading of a scene from Henry Miller depicting power play in the sexual act. Like Beauvoir, she is interested in the politics of sexual relations, she discusses contemporary writers and she begins with examples of those she considers to be reactionary (of whom one is D. H. Lawrence), before concluding with one whom she sees as offering a way forward (Jean Genet). Millett's concepts of power and domination are drawn from Max Weber rather than from Hegel, and she deploys the vocabulary of politics rather than that of philosophy, but in her section on myth and religion she borrows the vocabulary of man as the norm and subject to which the female is 'the other'. Like Beauvoir, Millett does not include any women writers in her major case studies, but she does discuss the novels of Charlotte Brontë at some length. In *The Second Sex*, women writers are largely used to illuminate aspects of women's lives; though she draws on over sixty different women writers, Beauvoir makes it plain that she does not consider that women writers have as yet produced work of genius (despite her admiration for Colette and Woolf). She is of course firm that this is a result of women's current situation rather than indicative of their future capacity. Nevertheless, she would have been surprised by the turn to gynocriticism in feminist literary studies, from which she herself has benefited.

What does Beauvoir's theorisation of myth have to offer feminist literary criticism? In the first place, it identifies a set of archetypal myths of Woman, still actively at work in our culture, and it offers myriad examples of the diversity of ways in which those myths can be customised. Secondly, anticipating Cixous and Barthes, it offers some general principles about the functioning of myth – its fitness to purpose, representing whatever patriarchal society needs it to represent; its tendency to function through binary opposites; its substitution of an absolute 'truth' for the reality and contingency of experience; its relationship to economic infrastructures; its alienating effect on women themselves; and its penetration into every area of culture and existence. Beauvoir's creative borrowing of concepts drawn from anthropology (structuralism *avant la lettre*), Marxism and psychoanalysis enables her to bolster her fundamental analysis of woman as man's other. It emboldens her to pursue her task onto the terrain of sexuality itself, allying her deconstruction of myth to an analysis of the power struggle at work within the couple, and within sexual relations. Her analysis initially leads her to a dizzying moment of optimism in reading Stendhal that the heterosexual couple might break through the Hegelian double bind, but her contemporaries offer no light ahead and her note of optimism is fast cooling by the end of *The Second Sex*. She continues to seek glimpses of the holy grail of reciprocity in the highly improbable case of the Marquis de Sade. A decade after *The Second Sex* Beauvoir at last intuits a cultural shift in the sexual power stakes as Bardot is shown enjoying and taking charge of her own sexuality, moving on beyond the traps in which 'The Independent Woman' of 1949 is caught. At the end of her analysis of the way in which Bardot strips away the myths surrounding female sexuality Beauvoir remarks: 'The debunking of love and eroticism is an undertaking that has wider implications than one might think. As soon as a single myth is touched, all myths are in danger' (Beauvoir, 1959/1960: 58).

Beauvoir grasped the importance of this feminist task and forged an impressive set of tools to begin on a work of deconstruction that is far from complete. The decisive impact which her thinking had on the development of feminist literary and cultural criticism may not always have been fully recognised, but it deserves to be acknowledged as one of the many legacies of *The Second Sex.*

NOTES

1. For a discussion of the difficulties of the translation see Simons (1983) and Moi (2002).
2. See for example Moi (1994), Simons (1995), Lundgren-Gothlin (1996), O'Brien and Embree (2001), Bauer (2001), Delphy and Chaperon (2002).
3. Johnson describes Beauvoir's reading of Lévi-Strauss as 'a selective and partial one' and cites Lévi-Strauss' comments in an interview of 1972 that his book was generally wrongly supposed to be existentialist 'basically because of the sharp distinction which I made at the start of the book between the order of nature and the order of culture' (Johnson, 2003: 46). It is important to note that Beauvoir read the manuscript of his book only after the publication of her first version of 'Myths' in *Les Temps Modernes* (Beauvoir, 1963: 177).
4. The novel has an epigraph from Hegel, unfortunately missing from the English translation: 'Each consciousness pursues the death of the other.'
5. Beauvoir seems to be referring to Hegel's discussion of 'Man and Woman' in *Phenomenology of Spirit* (1807/1977: 266–93).
6. Beauvoir's name continued to be associated with that of Bardot: the Bardot heroine of *The Truth* (1960) is indicted for having read *The Mandarins.* Vincendeau (1992: 89) comments that Beauvoir's name is used in the film to connote the 'glamorous cultural myth' of St Germain. The demythologiser is thus mythologised herself.
7. See for example Mills et al. (1989), who state in the introduction that 'feminist literary criticism became a theoretical issue with the publication of Kate Millett's *Sexual Politics* in 1969' (1989: 5).

BIBLIOGRAPHY

Barthes, Roland (1957/1973), *Mythologies*, trans. Annette Lavers, London: Cape.
Bauer, Nancy (2001), *Simone de Beauvoir: Philosophy and Feminism*, New York: Columbia University Press.
Beauvoir, Simone de (1949/1972), *The Second Sex*, trans. Howard Parshley, Harmondsworth: Penguin.
    (1951/1953), 'Must We Burn Sade?', in *The Marquis de Sade: An Essay by Simone de Beauvoir*, trans. Annette Michelson, New York: Grove.
    (1960), *Brigitte Bardot and the Lolita Syndrome*, London: André Deutsch.
    (1963/1985), *Force of Circumstance*, trans. Richard Howard, Harmondsworth: Penguin.

Butler, Judith (1986), 'Sex and Gender in Simone de Beauvoir's *The Second Sex*', in *Yale French Studies* 72.

(2003), 'Beauvoir on Sade: Making Sexuality into an Ethic', in *The Cambridge Companion to Simone de Beauvoir*, ed. Claudia Card, Cambridge: Cambridge University Press.

Delphy, Christine and Sylvie Chaperon (eds) (2002), *Cinquantenaire du 'Deuxième Sexe'*, Paris: Editions Syllepse.

Fallaize, Elizabeth (1998), *Simone de Beauvoir: A Critical Reader*, London: Routledge.

(2004), 'Claudel et la servante du Seigneur', in Galster (2004).

Galster, Ingrid (ed.) (2004), *Simone de Beauvoir: 'Le Deuxième Sexe'*, Paris: Champion.

Hegel, Georg (1807/1977), *Phenomenology of Spirit*, trans. A. V. Miller, Oxford: Oxford University Press.

Johnson, Christopher (2003), *Claude Lévi-Strauss: The Formative Years*, Cambridge: Cambridge University Press.

Jung, Carl (1928 and 1943/1972), *Two Essays on Analytical Psychology*, Princeton, NJ: Princeton University Press.

Lavers, Annette (2004), 'Le mythe de la femme dans la vie quotidienne', in Galster (2004).

Lévi-Strauss, Claude (1949/1970), *The Elementary Structures of Kinship*, trans. James Harle Bell et al., London: Eyre and Spottiswoode.

Lundgren-Gothlin, Eva (1991/1996), *Sex and Existence: Simone de Beauvoir's 'The Second Sex'*, trans. Linda Schenck, London: Athlone.

Merck, Mandy (1993), *Perversions: Deviant Readings*, London: Virago.

Mills, Sara, Lynne Pearce, Sue Spaull and Elaine Millard (1989), *Feminist Readings/Feminists Reading*, New York: Harvester Wheatsheaf.

Moi, Toril (1994), *Simone de Beauvoir: The Making of an Intellectual Woman*, Oxford: Blackwell.

(2002), 'While We Wait: The English Translation of *The Second Sex*', in *Signs: Journal of Women in Culture and Society* 27.

O'Brien, Wendy and Lester Embree (eds) (2001), *The Existential Phenomenology of Simone de Beauvoir*, Dordrecht: Kluwer.

Sellers, Susan (2001), *Myth and Fairy Tale in Contemporary Women's Fiction*, Basingstoke: Palgrave.

Simons, Margaret (1983), 'The Silencing of Simone de Beauvoir: Guess What's Missing from *The Second Sex*', in *Women's Studies International Forum* 6.

(ed.) (1995), *Feminist Interpretations of Simone de Beauvoir*, University Park, PA: Pennsylvania State University Press.

Vincendeau, Ginette (1992), ' "The Old and the New": Brigitte Bardot in 1950s France', in *Paragraph: A Journal of Modern Critical Theory* 15.

Weiand, Christof (2004), 'Stendhal ou le romanesque du vrai', in Galster (2004).

Wittig, Monique (1981/1992), *The Straight Mind and Other Essays*, Hemel Hempstead: Harvester Wheatsheaf.

Creating a feminist literary criticism

Introduction to Part II

Gill Plain and Susan Sellers

This section will map the development and the central issues of feminist literary criticism, from the groundbreaking work of critics such as Germaine Greer, Kate Millett and Eva Figes, through the search for a women's tradition and the impact of autobiographical discourses, to the challenges posed by black, lesbian and male feminists and critics. This inaugural work is the product of a crucial period for feminist literary criticism, and from the mid-1960s to the early 1990s it is possible to trace the concept's gradual development from an initial revolt against the androcentrism that had dominated literary studies, to a complex and diverse set of discourses seeking to problematise the assumptions, not only of gender, but also of race, class and sexuality.

As a number of the chapters in this section observe, 'second-wave' feminism emerged in the aftermath of, and in conjunction with, a number of radical political movements. For many women – writers, critics, activists – the personal became the political in contexts as diverse as the American Civil Rights Movement and the British Campaign for Nuclear Disarmament (CND). The result of this activist parenting was a critical practice that was always already political, or rather, one that – in contradistinction to the assumptions of commonsense patriarchal humanism – always already knew itself to be political. Not surprisingly, the emergence of such a discourse was dramatic and at times confrontational, and Part II of this volume also seeks to illustrate the excitement that attended feminism's 'coming out'. Beginning with what have been termed the 'totalising studies' of patriarchal critique, Mary Eagleton's chapter coolly reappraises the often heated debates of the 1970s. Eagleton reminds us of the scope of feminist enquiry in these early years and notes the extent to which feminist ideas permeated contemporary literature and culture, concluding that the decade was 'more complex and more nuanced than later accounts have suggested' (111). This valuable work of feminist critique was accompanied by the search for lost women's voices – a project at the centre of Helen Carr's complementary chapter tracing feminist criticism's construction of a history of women's writing. It would be easy now to forget that university syllabuses once imagined whole centuries written exclusively by men, and Carr's chapter traces not only the process of correcting the historical record, but also the debates around canon formation such scholarship produced.

That the process of canon formation was a fraught one is evident from the chapters that follow this initial territorial mapping. Arlene Keizer and Caroline Gonda describe, respectively, the framing of black and lesbian approaches to literature and examine the exclusionary perspective of the predominantly white, heterosexual, middle-class academic feminist establishment. In these chapters a series of different but related stories are told: the recovery of lost and marginalised traditions of women's writing, the desire to articulate dissonant stories and experiences, the need to find a voice and position from which to speak. In Keizer and Gonda's analyses, as in Linda Anderson's account of the debates surrounding autobiography and personal criticism, crucial questions of self and subjectivity emerge. Implicit within these questions is the onset of uncertainty, a product, in part, of the diffuse and yet pervasive impact of poststructuralism on feminist criticism. What, ask these essays, are the appropriate subjects of feminist literary study? Should black feminist criticism confine itself to black texts? Can textuality embody desire, and if so what are the parameters of lesbian criticism? Is the admission of the personal into criticism an acknowledgement of the impossibility of objectivity, or an indulgence that ultimately serves only those critics with privileged access to the academy?

As these questions suggest, the essays in Part II of this volume both look forward to the challenges of poststructuralism, postcolonialism, psycho-analysis and queer theory, and back towards the groundbreaking work of the earlier pioneers. They delineate the variety and complexity of feminist literary critical discourses and offer fresh readings of some of the most influential work to emerge in these fields. The final chapter of Part II, however, considers not a form of feminist criticism, but a relationship. Men and feminism is, as Calvin Thomas acknowledges, an awkward conjunction, but it is a relationship that cannot be ignored. In a perverse sense, feminism is 'man-made' – the product of women's resistance to patriarchal oppression – but, more positively, the new discourse of mas-culinity studies is of woman born. The boundaries of feminism are per-meable, and the possibility of turning the critical gaze onto male bodies and the construction of masculinity is a product of what might be termed the feminist critical diaspora. Feminism's concern with questions of female subjectivity and representation has made it possible to interrogate how men have come to inhabit and replicate the destructive patterns of patriarchal masculinities. But, while men and feminism might be reimagined as a constructive cohabitation, Thomas' essay begins with a complication. Focusing on what he terms the 'linguistic turn' in literary critical history, Thomas exposes not only the radically constructed nature of the wor(l)ds we inhabit, but also the impossibility of escaping the 'socially devised meanings' of gender (188). The chapter thus anticipates the engagement with poststructuralist theory that will be central to the final section of this book. As Part III will illustrate, feminism's willingness to interrogate questions of increasing ontological and epistemological complexity made it open and receptive to work being undertaken in related disciplines. As the 1990s progressed, the insights emerging from poststructuralism, deconstruction, postcolonialism, psychoanalysis and queer theory were embraced by feminist critics seeking new ways of articulating the problems of human subjectivity. This process, and its literary repercussions, will be the subject of Part III.

CHAPTER 6

Literary representations of women

Mary Eagleton

'THE "TOTALIZING" STUDIES'

Eva Figes introduces her study, *Patriarchal Attitudes*, with some bemusement as if, inexplicably, the book has escaped her control: 'To begin with it was intended that this should be a book about women in relation to society as a whole, on the traditional role they have played for so long, the reasons for it, and the ways that I think this role should now change. It has turned out to be a book largely about men' (Figes, 1970/1987: 10). Kate Millett's opening to *Sexual Politics* is similarly less than encouraging to her reader:

Before the reader is shunted through the relatively uncharted, often even hypothetical territory which lies before him, it is perhaps only fair he be equipped with some general notion of the terrain. The first part of this essay is devoted to the proposition that sex has a frequently neglected political aspect. I have attempted to illustrate this first of all by giving attention to the role which concepts of power and domination play in some contemporary literary descriptions of sexual activity itself. (Millett, 1969/1972: xi)

Nonetheless, both these introductions tell us something significant about what Juliet Mitchell refers to as 'the "totalizing" studies of the oppression of women' (Mitchell, 1974/1975: 300–1) that were so important in the emergence of second-wave feminism in the late 1960s and early 1970s. Mitchell includes, alongside Figes and Millett, Betty Friedan's *The Feminine Mystique* (1963), Germaine Greer's *The Female Eunuch* (1970) and Shulamith Firestone's *The Dialectic of Sex* (1970).

Firstly, and paradoxically, it appears that some of these feminists are as guilty as the most misogynistic men of marginalising women and not representing them at all. Figes' admission about the male focus of the book and Millett's use of the generic 'he', normative at the time, give an indication. Yet to say this is to misjudge the context. As Figes intimates, she *wants* to get to women but feels obliged first to cut through a long history of laws, precepts, ideologies, institutional and cultural practices – all, she believes, created and sustained by men. Only when this excrescence is cleared away will the ground be set for women to reveal their full potential. In the meantime, as Virginia Woolf perceived in *A Room of One's Own*, there is a terrible 'straight dark bar, a shadow shaped something like the letter "I" ' which obliterates the insubstantial figure of the woman (Woolf, 1929/1993: 90). In these studies, therefore, literary representations of women come mostly from the pens of men and are nearly always critiqued for their inadequacy. In Chapter 1 of *Sexual Politics*, Millett discusses extracts from the work of Henry Miller, Norman Mailer and Jean Genet, while the whole third section of the text (124 pages) is concerned with an analysis of the same three writers alongside D. H. Lawrence. Apart from seven pages on Charlotte Brontë's *Villette*, women authors are barely mentioned and, where they are, it is usually in a footnote. Secondly, what is equally notable is the central place that these studies accord to literature. Millett innovatively linked the sexual or, as we would now say, 'gender', to questions of politics and power and, in so doing, coined a term, 'sexual politics', that became indispensable to future debates. She saw literature as a key location for the creation, expression and maintenance of a sexual politics that oppressed women and, hence, literary analysis became an essential part of her methodology.[1] 'Lib and Lit', the title of Greer's 1971 review of Millett's book, neatly encapsulates the relation; women's liberation was going to come, in some measure, through the analysis of literature.

The problem of tone evident in these introductions relates to the authors' difficult position within the academy; they are working with few resources, within a largely antagonistic field and without the benefit of antecedents. For example, Millett's extensive bibliography – the book came from her PhD thesis at Columbia University – contains only four titles that one could recognise as having relevance to feminist literary criticism: Woolf's *A Room of One's Own*, Simone de Beauvoir's *The Second Sex* (1949/1952), Katharine M. Rogers' *The Troublesome Helpmate* (1966) and Mary Ellmann's *Thinking about Women* (1968). Some years later, Patricia Meyer Spacks notes the same problem in *The Female Imagination* (1975). Remarking on the scarcity of theories by women about women, she quotes the same names as Millett – Woolf, de Beauvoir, Ellmann – and then substitutes Millett herself for Rogers. This is the problem of all pioneers: what they are trying to do is precisely that which has never been done. Women's literary history is seen as 'subterranean' or an 'undercurrent'. In both the titles and introductions to numerous texts at this time, a vocabulary of 'silence', 'absence' and 'hiding' vies with one of 'revelation', 'uncovering', 'discovery'. Thus, Carolyn Heilbrun describes the subject matter of her book *Toward a Recognition of Androgyny* as 'the hidden river of androgyny ... running silently and undetected beneath the earth, here or there emerged as a spring or well' (1973/1974: xx), while Tillie Olsen writes that 'literary history and the present are dark with silences', one of which is the writing of women (1978/1980: 6).

It is hard to exaggerate the enormity of the task these critics set themselves. Even when the topic is more restricted, the historical range is huge. In Heilbrun's study, we move from Ancient Greece to Virginia Woolf, in Rogers' history of misogyny in literature from the Garden of Eden to the twentieth century – all within seven chapters. In retrospect, we can see the undertaking as foolhardy, the impossible scope of these works inevitably opening the authors to critiques from every side, but it was also brave and audacious. If a sense of unease was betrayed in the style, there was too a refreshing, impassioned indignation. Feminist literary criticism, like Marxist literary criticism, was never disinterested but associated with polemic and advocacy. At odds with the cool formalism that was the dominant mode of literary criticism at this time, particularly in the US, feminist critics had to prove that what they were doing was not merely special pleading or social engineering or sociology in disguise – all accusations that were repeatedly levelled against feminist criticism – but a legitimate form of criticism that asked fundamental questions about literary history and literary production.

CHERCHEZ LA FEMME

Increasingly throughout the 1970s, the focus moved to literary representations of women, by women and for women. Judith Fetterley's *The Resisting Reader* and Elaine Showalter's 'Towards a Feminist Poetics' mark a turning point. Fetterley offers her reading of male-authored, canonical works in American literature as 'a self-defence survival manual' (Fetterley, 1978: viii). The sentiment is deliberately overdone and droll but does not hide the seriousness of her intent. To Fetterley, the American canon is largely unreadable for women since so many texts demonstrate man's power over women, while the narrative strategies of these texts oblige the woman reader to identify as male. The problem of American culture, says Fetterley, is not the emasculation of men but the 'immasculation of women' (1978: xx). The woman reader, then, should become conscious of these narrative strategies, 'make palpable their designs' (1978: xii). The word 'designs' suggests not only the text's form, but also 'designs upon' the female reader and, thus, she must be 'resisting'.

Showalter's essay is a plea to move on from this position. Though she does not mention Fetterley's study, she gives her own example of what she terms 'the feminist critique' of a canonical author in analysing the opening to Thomas Hardy's *The Mayor of Casterbridge*. The problem with this approach is that it is male-orientated: 'If we study stereotypes of women, the sexism of male critics, and the limited roles women play in literary history, we are not learning what women have felt and experienced, but only what men have thought women should be' (Showalter, 1979: 27). The danger of such work is in perpetuating a victimised view of women and a 'temporal and intellectual investment' (1979: 28) in the works of men. Showalter's advice to Fetterley and other feminist critics involved in reading the male canon is, basically, 'don't bother'. However, the names Showalter mentions in her essay are not the stars of either American or British literature but Louis Althusser, Roland Barthes, Pierre Macheray and Jacques Lacan. Her anxiety about that determining male presence had extended beyond the American and British literary canons to the male French philosophers and psychoanalysts who, at this time, were cutting a swathe through the US and UK academies. Showalter's shift of emphasis is from the female reader's estrangement from male-authored texts to the female reader's identification with female-authored texts. Reader, author and character come together in what Showalter sees as a shared 'female subculture' (1979: 28), in which the focus on women enables new methodologies. This perspective rescues women from being tokens or the derided 'also-rans' in a male literary culture. Showalter called the approach 'gynocriticism' and it became the leading feminist literary mode in the Anglophone academy.

Showalter's *A Literature of Their Own*, published two years before her essay, Sandra Gilbert and Susan Gubar's *The Madwoman in the Attic* (1979) and earlier texts such as Patricia Meyer Spacks' *The Female Imagination* (1975) and Ellen Moers' *Literary Women* (1976) are influential examples of a gynocritical approach. Simply asking the basic questions – where were the women writers, what did they write, how did they come to write – produced a mass of new material, complicated our understanding of literary history, impressed on critics the significance of gender in the production of writing and revitalised interest in more private literary forms such as letters, diaries and journals. None of this could have been achieved without the books themselves being in print. The establishment of feminist publishing companies enabled the retrieval of lost 'classics': for example, the publication in 1973 by the Feminist Press in New York of Charlotte Perkins Gilman's 'The Yellow Wallpaper' and in 1979 of

Florence Nightingale's *Cassandra*. In the UK, Virago was instrumental in bringing into focus the work of writers such as Antonia White, Rosamond Lehmann and Djuna Barnes as part of its Modern Classics series, launched in 1978. Other companies, such as the Women's Press or the Onlywomen Press, encouraged contemporary women authors, some of whom succeeded, as Woolf could not, in 'telling the truth about [their] own experiences as a body' (Woolf, 1942/1993: 105). Feminist book shops, reading groups, book festivals and conferences, adult education and extra-mural classes provided the infra-structure for an explosion in women's writing. The literary field that previously seemed to have contained little more than the 'famous five' of Jane Austen, George Eliot, Charlotte and Emily Brontë and Woolf began to be filled with an extensive and varied range of female authors.

Showalter's project, like that of the other gynocritical writers, was the creation of a female literary tradition which would offer new ways of understanding representations of women. By naming a literary tradition as 'female', as Showalter does in the first chapter of *A Literature of Their Own*, she exposes the exclusivity of the dominant tradition and raises questions about the construction of literary history and the aesthetic values that have always seemed to find women's writing lacking. But the phrase also suggests that there *is* a specificity and a commonality about women's writing and this proved difficult to establish without drifting into stereotypes about feminine sensibilities and values, which elsewhere feminism quite rightly questions, or claims about stylistic and thematic links which are hard to substantiate. One of the interesting aspects of Showalter's study is how she, at once, invokes and interrogates the existence of a female literary tradition or any female commonality. Thus, she is on guard against *ad feminam* arguments – '[t]here is clearly a difference between books that happen to have been written by women, and a "female literature"' (Showalter, 1977/1978: 4); she does not like the idea of women's writing as a 'movement' because she is so aware of the discontinuities, the 'holes and hiatuses' (1977/1978: 11); and she takes issue with Spacks' concept of a 'female imagination' because, in her view, it relies too much on a specious belief in a fundamental, unchanging difference between men and women. For Showalter, the female literary tradition comes not from innate writerly dispositions common to all women but from, on the one hand, a self-awareness on the part of the woman writer – this is an observation of Spacks' with which Showalter does agree – and, on the other, the critic's situating of the woman author within her period and the cultural formations of that period. Together the writer and the critic create this figure, 'the woman author'. Showalter is interested in the difference – not the utter separateness – of women's historical position, the consequences that might have for writing and how the difference changes over time.

Increasingly, then, other representations of women emerge. No longer 'silent' or 'hidden', women characters and authors take on life and energy and are conceived of as heroic, passionate, subversive. Moers' reluctant coinage is 'heroinism' – 'reluctant' since the term sounds 'more like an addiction to drugs than a seal on literary accomplishment' (Moers, 1976/ 1978: 147). She reads women's literature from Mary Wollstonecraft to Woolf for signs of the 'heroic structure [of] the female voice in literature' (1976/1978: 123) and finds evidence in the many women who *can* think, act, love or exert power. Showalter's three phases for women's literature – the feminine, the feminist and the female – may start with imitation and the internalisation of the established tradition but they move to responses of protest and demands for autonomy and then to a phase of self-discovery that breaks free from both acquiescence to and rebellion from the social norms. Above all, Gilbert and Gubar's monumental study of the nineteenth-century woman writer reveals a fundamental inversion of the given. They see the sexual, questioning, angry woman – of whom Bertha Mason in *Jane Eyre* is the prototype – as neither mad nor bad. Rather she is the dark 'other' of the Angel in the House, the figure of danger and disruptive desires who can tear down both the father's home and the Houses of Fiction. As Showalter perceived, new reading demands new methodologies and, as Fetterley illustrated, these are often readings against the grain. Thus, Gilbert and Gubar recast Harold Bloom's characterisation of literary history as an 'anxiety of influence' in which each generation battles with its 'precursor', the literary father, in an oedipal contest to the death. They see the woman author as restrained by an 'anxiety of authorship'. With few female precursors and pitted in an unequal struggle with a long-established male tradition, the woman author doubts her place in creativity. Not surprisingly, then, when she discovers her precursors, she does not want to 'kill' them but to sustain and learn from them. As Rita Felski astutely notes, the gynocritical writers create the precursors they need rather than the ones they have to dispose of: 'Their description of Victorian women struggling against a repressive society to find their true selves often made these women sound remarkably like American feminists of the 1970s' (Felski, 2003: 67).

In the event, gynocriticism never could square the circle because its position was inherently contradictory. It critiqued literary history and canonical thinking but wanted to be part of it; it looked for a commonality among women but was wary of imposing uniformity; it doubted traditional aesthetic values but used them to valorise women writers; it wanted to speak for all women yet invested in a particular raced and classed group, at a particular historical moment. But, in insisting on 'women writers' as a category, however problematic, in radically re-assessing the accepted view of literary history, in showing there was a whole other way – in fact, lots of other ways – to tell our literary history, in insisting on a link between aesthetics and politics, gynocriticism set an agenda that is still productive.

THE THEORETICAL TURN

History has not been kind to feminist literary criticism of the 1970s. The numerous theoretical positions that became current in the academy during the 1980s and beyond often looked back on 70s feminism as 'untheoretical', 'naïve', hopelessly tied to empiricism or unsophisticated notions of identity. This sniffy attitude ignores the political and intellectual context in which 70s feminism developed. It also ignores the existence within the period of both a self-critique and a wide range of theoretical positions with which feminism engaged. I want to give two examples of how the criticism of the period is more complex and more nuanced than later accounts have suggested. Firstly, if we return to Millett's work, we can see how its weaknesses as well as its strengths were remarked upon at the time. Greer in her review, Spacks in *The Female Imagination* and Cora Kaplan in her 1979 essay, 'Radical Feminism and Literature: Rethinking Millett's *Sexual Politics*' all notice how Millett's focus is fixed steadfastly on the most macho elements in her chosen texts which only serve to prove, time and again, her case concerning the patriarchal impetus of her male authors. Greer shows how this has consequences that are at once political – 'if, as Millett seems to argue, the fucked is always female and always inferior, the patterns of exploitation seem ineradicable' – and literary – '[t]he writer is identified with his persona and accused of the crimes of his characters although it is he who has exposed them' (Greer, 1971: 356). Millett's writing has a power but also a wilfulness in wrenching all material to fit her pre-ordained position. This results in misreadings of Charlotte Brontë, as Spacks shows, and of D. H. Lawrence, as Kaplan illustrates. Both Spacks and Kaplan agree that literary representations of women have to be largely excluded from Millett's work because she cannot count on women behaving how she would want them to behave. Thus, history and literature are equally flattened, devoid of ambiguity or contradiction. If Millett's prose has an authority, it comes, says Spacks, 'from the intensely focused vision of one wearing blinkers' (Spacks, 1975/1976: 30).

Juliet Mitchell's questioning of Millett and the other 'totalizing' authors she discusses is in the context of their response to Freud. Mitchell wants to rescue Freud for feminism, a position which, again, casts doubt on the received wisdom of the 70s as an anti-theoretical decade. Mitchell believes that Millett's error is in critiquing Freud's views on femininity without placing them in the context of psychoanalysis, particularly theories of the unconscious and infantile sexuality. Millett acknowledges the significance of Freud's part in the discovery of the unconscious but, then, in her writing denies the consequences so that Freud's work becomes a conspiracy to keep women in their place. Not only does Millett interpret Freud's concern with the unconscious as preventing him from recognising the history of social inequality but, claims Mitchell, she even proposes that Freud invented the unconscious for that purpose. Mitchell argues that the social realism of Millett cannot handle concepts of desire, fantasy and the unconscious. Thus, in representing women, Millett always insists on the pre-eminence of rationality and the evidence of social history.

However, Kaplan's re-reading of both Millett, and Mitchell on Millett, complicates the situation by finding an unexpected congruence between the two. In both authors, Kaplan sees a displacement of awkward questions about class and the sexual division of labour. For Millett, capitalism has been reduced to an effect of patriarchy, while Mitchell might recognise the unsettling potential in the gaps between patriarchal and capitalist ideologies but her emphasis is very much on the psychic rather than the materiality of women's work. The variety of theoretical perspectives in play is evident in Kaplan's description of Millett's position as 'radical feminist idealism' and Mitchell's as 'Marxist-feminist structuralism' (Kaplan, 1979/1986: 23). As if that were not enough, Mitchell's Marxist feminism is involved, like Kaplan's own, in a dialogue with psychoanalysis, but that too is a relationship in dispute. Kaplan, for instance, questions Mitchell's application of Louis Althusser's concept of ideology to the work of Freud and Lacan while still herself being interested in these theorists, for example in her 1976 essay, 'Language and Gender'. The more one looks, the more complex the relations become. We might remember that two of those names – Althusser and Lacan – were specifically mentioned by Showalter as enticing women away from a focus on women authors and theorists, while Janet Todd has pointed out how Marxism lost out in the battle with American empiricism and French theory; it was, she says, 'in the margin of the great Margin of feminist criticism' (Todd, 1993: 241). Far from being a monolithic entity, feminism emerges as both internally diverse and involved in complementary and competing relations with other theoretical positions.

As a second example, let us reconsider Showalter's important opposition in 'Towards a Feminist Poetics' of 'the feminist critique' and 'gynocriticism'. Her essay features in Mary Jacobus' edited collection, *Women Writing and Writing about Women* (1979), alongside Jacobus' own essay, 'The Difference of View'. The two essays make an interesting comparison, not least in that both look to Thomas Hardy for one of their textual illustrations. But they compare more profoundly in that Jacobus takes up a similar opposition to Showalter but does something different with it. Her title comes from Virginia Woolf's comment on George Eliot, whom Woolf saw as caught between a desire for a male-dominated culture (the one Showalter warns against in 'the feminist critique') and a valuing of women's separateness, 'the difference of view, the difference of standard' (the world of 'gynocriticism'). Jacobus is aware of the difficulties on both sides. Women's desire for access to the widest cultural realm is legitimate but demands conformity to the dominant order, while a position of difference risks another confinement, to marginality or the irrational. Jacobus' response is to opt for neither one nor the other but to deconstruct the opposition which, if left in place, will always restrict. (Mary Ellmann's witty deconstruction of feminine stereotypes in *Thinking about Women* constitutes an earlier example of this mode.) The vocabulary of Jacobus' essay, then, is one of 'boundary crossing', 'contradiction', 'instability', 'transgression', 'subversion'. Jacobus looks for those moments in writing when the centre *does not* hold, when what is silent becomes heard. Thus, representations of women are viewed as neither sexist travesties nor idealised paragons nor 'true' or 'untrue' images of women but are, as Jacobus says of Hardy's Tess, 'a rich source of mythic confusion, ideological contradiction, and erotic fascination' (Jacobus, 1979a: 13). One can read the end of Jacobus' essay as a polite response to Showalter. Jacobus asserts that a female tradition 'need not mean a return to specifically "female" (that is, potentially confining) domains'. Yet, the 'need not' seems to warn about the dangers of gynocriticism and that, without careful handling, it certainly could lead to essentialism. Secondly, Jacobus states that a 'feminist colonising' of critical theory (Marxist, psychoanalytic, poststructuralist are named) is perfectly possible. Unlike Showalter, she does not believe that an engagement with other theories will blunt feminism's critical edge. She writes optimistically of an alliance between feminism and the *avant-garde* that might, with revolutionary potential, call into question accepted ideas on language, psychoanalysis and literary criticism. What Jacobus insists on is the fictionality of discourse and the necessary re-visionings that make '"the difference of view" a question rather than an

answer, and a question to be asked not simply of women but of writing too'
(1979a: 21).

Jacobus footnotes in her essay references to the writings of Hélène
Cixous, Luce Irigaray, Julia Kristeva and Michèle Montrelay. These
names constitute examples of work on representation explored from psychoanalytic and structuralist perspectives; they also function as an interesting female counter to the names Showalter rejected in her essay, namely
Althusser, Barthes, Macheray and Lacan. Moreover, as we saw with respect
to the setting up of feminist publishing companies, the references remind
us of the importance of different publishing outlets in both creating and
responding to markets. In this case, we see the key role played by feminist
journals and magazines, alongside those in French studies and critical
theory, in introducing French intellectual thought into the Anglophone
academies. Jacobus mentions Cixous' 'The Laugh of the Medusa' in *Signs*
(Vol. 1, no. 4, 1976), Elaine Marks' 'Women and Literature in France'
in *Signs* (Vol. 3, no. 4, 1978) and Michèle Montrelay's 'Inquiry into
Femininity' in *m/f* (no. 1, 1978). She could also have included the English
translation of an extract from Kristeva's *Des Chinoises* in the first issue of
Signs in Autumn 1975; or the interview with Marguerite Duras in the
second issue (Winter 1975); or the interviews by Alice Schwartzer of
Simone de Beauvoir in the American magazine *Ms.* during July 1972 and
July 1977. At the same time as Jacobus' essay was published, Michèle
Barrett and Mary McIntosh published 'Christine Delphy: Towards a
Materialist Feminism?' in the first issue of *Feminist Review* in 1979, an
essay trenchantly responded to by Delphy herself in a 1980 issue, while in
the autumn of that year Irigaray's 'When Our Lips Speak Together'
appeared in *Signs* (Vol. 6, no. 1, 1980).

Signs, *Feminist Review* and *Ms.* continue to flourish. The journal *m/f*,
which ran from 1978 to 1986, was an intriguing attempt, as its enigmatic
title perhaps hints, to marry *M*arxism and *f*eminism, *M*arx and *F*reud. Its
first editorial questioned the sufficiency of a retrieval of women's history as
the prime feminist project and positioned itself against any 'essential
femininity' or any ultra-Marxism in terms of prioritising class or seeing
working-class women as the revolutionary vanguard. Its focus was not on
the representation of women as what they are or what they could be but
with 'how women are produced as a category' (*m/f*, no. 1, 1978: 5). As is the
case with Jacobus, it was the construction of the sign 'woman' that was of
interest. In this venture, the editorial group looked to psychoanalysis and,
though they were guarded about Marxism, embraced a social awareness
which they described as 'the particular historical moment, the institutions

and practices within which and through which the category of woman is produced' (1978: 5). In short, what these two examples show is not simply something of the range of responses to Millett or the similarities and differences between Showalter and Jacobus or a general burgeoning of feminist publishing but, more significantly, how feminist theoretical debates of the period were multi-faceted, in dialogue amongst themselves, conscious of debates elsewhere and, often, in dialogue with them too, and far more divergent than subsequent accounts might indicate.

THE CREATIVE TURN

If the feminist literary critic turned to women's writing as the place to find meaningful, if problematic, representations of women, it is equally true that women writers and popular feminist magazines embraced feminist literary criticism. Indeed, as the 'Lib and Lit' tag hints, distinctions between the analytical and the creative, the political and the aesthetic were constantly blurred. Thus the practice of consciousness-raising, which enabled groups of women to discuss the sexual politics of their lives with the aim of producing new knowledge and political strategies based on women's experience, found expression in what Lisa Maria Hogeland calls 'the consciousness-raising novel'. These bestselling novels, such as Marilyn French's *The Women's Room* (1977) or Erica Jong's *Fear of Flying* (1973), trace the raising of the heroine's consciousness and often have the effect of doing the same for their female reader, not in any programmatic way but, as Hogeland says, 'by personalizing and novelizing feminist social criticism' (Hogeland, 1998: ix). *Spare Rib*, the UK feminist magazine, and its American counterpart, *Ms.*, traversed a range of discourses around women in a way that now seems quite startling. The early issues of *Spare Rib* covered those staples of women's magazines in this period, recipes and knitting patterns, alongside politics, articles on Jean Rhys, Ursula LeGuin, Buchi Emecheta, Elizabeth Barrett Browning and Erica Jong, and short stories from Margaret Drabble, Fay Weldon and Edna O'Brien. The preview issue of *Ms.* in Spring 1972 juxtaposed an advert for mink coats and numerous adverts for cigarettes and alcohol with Cynthia Ozick's humorous account of sexism in education and literature, and Sylvia Plath's poem 'Three Women'. Later issues included poetry from Alice Walker, June Jordan and Adrienne Rich, review essays on contemporary fiction, a regular poetry and fiction section, an excerpt from Doris Lessing's new novel of 1973, *The Summer Before the Dark*, articles on Aphra Behn and Charlotte Perkins Gilman and an extract from Woolf's unpublished letters.

Contributors also crossed demarcations. Catharine Stimpson, who wrote regularly for *Ms.* in the early 1970s while teaching at Barnard, was, by the mid 1970s, editor of the academic journal *Signs*.

The literary form most suited to a mixing of modes – creative, political polemic, historical commentary, literary criticism, biography and auto-biography – is the essay, and the period produced some striking examples, amongst which are Adrienne Rich's 'When We Dead Awaken: Writing as Re-Vision' (1971), Alice Walker's 'In Search of Our Mothers' Gardens' (1974) and Hélène Cixous' 'The Laugh of the Medusa' (1976). Despite very different social backgrounds, both Walker and Rich draw on a political and historical awareness of civil rights and antiwar movements and particular cultural legacies.[2] Rich's careful thinking, reflectiveness and range of read-ing – all the hallmarks of the good student – are impregnated with urgency and ardour. A similar tone in Walker's work takes on a prophetic register as she draws on the discourses of black spirituality and creativity. Including elements from their own biographies, each shows the difficulty of repre-senting herself as 'a woman author'. Rich recognises her ambiguous rela-tion to poetry. Her early style was formed by poetic *masters* and, though she seeks out older women poets, it is to compare them to male poets. She recounts the struggle to be a wife, mother and, specifically, a *woman* poet, the effort it took to loosen her style and to stop looking to male authorities for approval. In Walker's case, the black woman author is represented in relation to canonical literature, white feminism – Walker 're-visions' Woolf's story of Judith Shakespeare to include the missing black women authors – and the aesthetics of the dispossessed in a legacy of singing, story-telling, quilting and gardening.[3]

The writing of Rich and Walker is not theoretically probing. Walker, in particular, has a transcendent view of the writer. 'Artists', 'Poets' and 'Creators' all warrant initial capital letters and she happily talks of 'genius' and 'the soul'. Cixous, in contrast, writes in the context of Lacanian psychoanalysis and Derridean deconstruction. She gestures towards the social and historical position of women that is so central to Rich and Walker, but her references are always generalised. In 'The Laugh of the Medusa', she is not interested in the thematics of women's writing or the retrieval of lost women authors; the work of both men and women 'either obscures women or reproduces the classic representations of women (as sensitive – intuitive – dreamy, etc.)' (Cixous, 1976/1981: 248). Her interest is in the relation between a feminine libidinal economy and feminine writing. 'A libidinal economy' refers to the body, desire, the sexual and the drives that impel us; 'the feminine' does not necessarily equate with 'the female' but suggests the potential of sexual difference. 'More body, hence more writing' is Cixous' cry (1976/1981: 257). The conjunction is explosive. The poetic, in particular, is the gateway to the unconscious and to unleashing the repressed woman who must, on the one hand, write herself and the sexuality which has been censored and, on the other, take her place in history, '[t]o become *at will* the taker and the initiator, for her own right, in every symbolic system, in every political process' (1976/1981: 250). What unites these three essays is a strong sense of women at a moment of change and the importance of seizing that moment. The sensibility is, at least, hopeful; in Cixous' essay it is utopian and, at times, ecstatic. The rapid moves of Cixous' argument, her allusions and neologisms create a style which is both expressive and consciously excessive. Rich asks women to 'move out', 'move forward', 'go through'; Cixous' exhortations are to break loose, to bite, to explode, to overflow. The woman who was represented as lost, hidden or victimised, the woman who was silent or who had to be kept silent until her consciousness was suitably raised, the woman who was angry and deranged bursts forth in Cixous' essay as an unstoppable, volcanic force.

Needless to say, this euphoric moment could not last. Equally, it is a long time since anyone has turned to literature for true, coherent representations of women. Now one is more likely to encounter a vocabulary of fragmentation and splitting or, in a more optimistic vein, metamorphosising or multiplicity. These changing representations have to be seen in an historical context. As Bharati Mukherjee's narrator warns: 'The past presents itself to us, always, somehow simplified. He wants to avoid that fatal unclutteredness, but knows he can't' (1994: 6). The 1970s has suffered from a 'fatal unclutteredness'. Recognising the context of the feminist literary debates of the 70s, the numerous theoretical positions, their links and differences, the growing points and the dead-ends should lead us to question the dismissiveness with which this period has sometimes been treated. Above all, for feminism as a politics, the retrospective look reminds us of the need to sustain the link between 'Lib and Lit'. We must continue to unpick the complex construction of women in history, in culture, in the psyche as a necessary part of envisaging a new politics.

NOTES

I should like to note my thanks to the British Academy for funding a Small Research Grant to assist with the writing of this chapter.

1. Millett is not alone here. The fact that several of these authors – not only Millett, but also Figes and Greer – were trained in literature is relevant.

2. Walker was born in Eatonton, Georgia into a poor, African American share-cropper family. Rich's origins are white, middle-class, educated and, through her father, Jewish.

3. In *A Room of One's Own* Virginia Woolf constructs a possible biography for Shakespeare's imaginary sister. Though just as talented as William, the circumstances of the time would probably have led Judith to a tragic end.

BIBLIOGRAPHY

Cixous, Hélène (1976/1981), 'The Laugh of the Medusa', in Marks and de Courtivron (1981).

Felski, Rita (2003), *Literature after Feminism*, Chicago and London: University of Chicago Press.

Fetterley, Judith (1978), *The Resisting Reader: A Feminist Approach to American Fiction*, Bloomington: Indiana University Press.

Figes, Eva (1970/1987), *Patriarchal Attitudes: Women in Society*, New York: Persea Books.

Gilbert, Sandra M. and Susan Gubar (1979), *The Madwoman in the Attic: The Woman Writer and the Nineteenth-Century Literary Imagination*, New Haven and London: Yale University Press.

Goodings, Lennie (4 June 1993), 'Cleaning the Office, Changing the World', in *The Bookseller*.

Greer, Germaine (25 March 1971), 'Lib and Lit', in *The Listener*.

Heilbrun, Carolyn (1973/1974), *Toward a Recognition of Androgyny*, New York: Harper Colophon Books.

Hogeland, Lisa Maria (1998), *Feminism and Its Fictions: The Consciousness-Raising Novel and the Women's Liberation Movement*, Philadelphia: University of Pennsylvania Press.

Jacobus, Mary (1979a), 'The Difference of View', in Jacobus (1979b).

    (ed.) (1979b), *Women Writing and Writing about Women*, London and Sydney: Croom Helm.

Kaplan, Cora (1976/1986), 'Language and Gender', in *Sea Changes: Culture and Feminism*, London: Verso.

    (1979/1986), 'Radical Feminism and Literature: Rethinking Millett's *Sexual Politics*', in *Sea Changes: Culture and Feminism*, London: Verso.

Marks, Elaine and Isabelle de Courtivron (eds) (1981), *New French Feminisms*, Brighton: Harvester Press.

Millett, Kate (1969/1972), *Sexual Politics*, London: Abacus.

Mitchell, Juliet (1974/1975), *Psychoanalysis and Feminism*, Harmondsworth: Penguin.

Moers, Ellen (1976/1978), *Literary Women*, London: The Women's Press.

Mukherjee, Bharati (1994), *The Holder of the World*, London: Virago.

Olsen, Tillie (1978/1980), *Silences*, London: Virago.

Rich, Adrienne (1971/1979), 'When We Dead Awaken: Writing as Re-Vision', in *On Lies, Secrets, and Silence: Selected Prose 1966–1978*, New York: Norton.

Showalter, Elaine (1977/1978), *A Literature of Their Own: British Women Novelists from Brontë to Lessing*, London: Virago.

(1979), 'Towards a Feminist Poetics', in Jacobus (1979b).

Spacks, Patricia Meyer (1975/1976), *The Female Imagination: A Literary and Psychological Investigation of Women's Writing*, London: Allen and Unwin.

Todd, Janet (1993), 'Anglo-American Difference: Some Thoughts of an Aging Feminist', in *Tulsa Studies in Women's Literature* 12: 2.

Walker, Alice (1974/1983), 'In Search of Our Mothers' Gardens', in *In Search of Our Mothers' Gardens: Womanist Prose*, New York: Harcourt Brace Jovanovich.

Woolf, Virginia (1929/1993), *A Room of One's Own*, ed. Michèle Barrett, Harmondsworth: Penguin.

(1942/1993), 'Professions for Women', in *The Crowded Dance of Modern Life*, ed. Rachel Bowlby, Harmondsworth: Penguin.

CHAPTER 7

A history of women's writing

Helen Carr

When feminist literary criticism began to emerge in the late sixties and early seventies, bursting into prominence with the publication of such provocative and influential texts as Kate Millett's *Sexual Politics* (1971), Germaine Greer's *The Female Eunuch* (1970) and Eva Figes' *Patriarchal Attitudes* (1970), these pioneering polemics gave surprisingly little attention to women's writing. Paradoxically, in spite of their vigorous attacks on the academic literary establishment, they shared one of its most striking characteristics: they were, as Mary Eagleton has pointed out in the previous chapter, almost solely concerned with men. At that period only a handful of women writers made it on to university English courses. Jane Austen and George Eliot had been placed by Leavis within the great tradition, and were allowed canonical status.[1] Emily Brontë's *Wuthering Heights* was judged to be a classic, though her sisters, Charlotte and Anne, had their writing dismissed as melodramatic, sentimental and lacking in form. Virginia Woolf was thought overly genteel, far too ladylike to be taken seriously, part of effete Bloomsbury, and even those who praised her, like David Daiches, agreed her art was 'limited' (Daiches, 1971: 561). Mary Shelley's *Frankenstein*, now it seems on virtually every university's first-year English course, was simply not regarded as literature. In Leavis' famous divide between 'mass civilisation' and 'minority culture', *Frankenstein* was undoubtedly, like so much women's writing, on the wrong side.

What I shall be concerned with in this chapter is feminist literary critics' gradual re-discovery and re-evaluation of women's writing during the two decades that followed that irruption of feminist protest. I first, however, want to look at the reasons why these pioneers' focus was elsewhere, in order to situate the political moment out of which that quest for re-discovery would come. What that incisive new wave of feminist critics had been concerned with was in fact summed up by Eva Figes' title: they were attacking patriarchal attitudes, cultural misogyny and the ingrained belittlement of women. Kate Millett, for example, who saw patriarchy as a universal social condition, offers critiques of Norman Mailer, Henry Miller, Jean Genet, D. H. Lawrence, Thomas Hardy and Freud. Her few remarks about women authors now seem astonishingly complicit with the dismissive misogynist views that she elsewhere attacks. Speaking of George Meredith, she calls his plots 'as slight and agreeable as any of Austen's'. Virginia Woolf, she says, 'glorified two housewives, Mrs Dalloway and Mrs Ramsay ... and was argumentative yet somehow unsuccessful, perhaps because unconvinced, in conveying the frustrations of the woman artist in Lily Briscoe'. Even in her eight-page discussion of Charlotte Brontë's *Villette*, by far the longest and the only appreciative treatment of a woman's novel in the book (though, as later feminist critics have pointed out, she misremembers the plot), Millett repeats the current male judgements, rebuking Brontë for 'the deviousness of her fictional devices, her continual flirtation with the bogs of sentimentality' and describes the book as 'occasionally flawed by mawkish nonsense', though she does conclude 'it is nevertheless one of the most interesting books of the period and, as an expression of revolutionary sensibility, a work of some importance' (Millett, 1971: 134, 139–140, 146, 147). *Sexual Politics* was a racy, broad-brush attack on contemporary attitudes to the relations between men and women, a vigorous diatribe that propelled Millett's arguments into leading newspapers on both sides of the Atlantic, something Germaine Greer also achieved, and their political impact – in the broader sense of the political that they did so much to foster – should not be underestimated. Figes' book was perhaps a more sober, though trenchantly written, analysis of Western attitudes to women over the centuries, but it too attracted a good deal of attention. To begin their campaign by attacking the oppressor was an understandable tactic, and one very much of the time.

Second-wave feminism came, it should not be forgotten, out of a period of social protest, and the women's movement was modelled on and aligned with other campaigning groups of the sixties. In the States, the Civil Rights Movement played a significant role in alerting those who emerged as feminists to their own lack of rights. Kate Millett makes this clear near the beginning of *Sexual Politics*:

In America, recent events have forced us to acknowledge at last that the relationship between the races is indeed a political one which involves the general control of one collectivity, defined by birth, over another collectivity, also defined by birth. Groups who rule by birthright are fast disappearing, yet there remains one ancient and universal scheme for the domination of one birth group by another – the scheme that prevails in the area of sex. The study of racism has convinced us that a truly political state of affairs operates between the races to perpetuate a series

of oppressive circumstances ... What goes largely unexamined, often even unacknowledged (yet is institutionalised nonetheless) in our social order, is the birthright priority whereby males rule females. (Millett, 1971: 24–5)

In Britain, it was also the refusal to accept white supremacy that acted as
model and instigation, though in a rather different context: the Women's
Liberation Movement quite consciously named itself by analogy with the
anti-colonial national liberation movements around the world. Juliet
Mitchell, for example, deeply involved in the New Left and its support for
these nationalistic, anti-imperialist struggles, has recalled how she gradually
became conscious that women experienced what appeared a comparable
even if very differently constituted oppression for which these movements
could serve as a model of resistance.[2] Her 1966 article 'Women: The Longest
Revolution', which was the opening salvo of the new British women's
movement, had appeared in the *New Left Review*, which did so much to
foster the cause of these anti-colonial movements, and on whose editorial
board she was the sole woman. It must swiftly be acknowledged that these
second-wave feminists were, on both sides of the Atlantic, at this stage
predominantly white and middle class, and the dubiousness of such comparisons with oppressed races would soon become an issue, but nonetheless it
was out of such revolutionary protest that second-wave feminism emerged.
The sixties was a decade in which traditional hierarchies were being challenged on a wide front: attitudes to class, race, social authority and colonial
dominance were all subject to critique and re-examination. In philosophy,
thinkers like Derrida, who questioned the whole foundation of Western
metaphysics, 'white mythology' as he would soon call it, were making their
first impact on the English-speaking world (Derrida, 1971/1982). By the end
of the decade, attention had turned to gender as well.

　　Germaine Greer sums up the new movement with her usual panache in
The Female Eunuch. Contrasting second-wave feminism with the suffragette movement, she writes:

Then genteel middle-class ladies clamoured for reform, now ungenteel middle-
class women are calling for revolution. For many of them the call for revolution
came before the call for the liberation of women. The New Left has been the
forcing house for most movements, and for many of them liberation is dependent
on the coming in of the classless society and the withering away of the state ... If
women liberate themselves, they will perforce liberate their oppressors. (Greer,
1970/1971: 11, 18)

Yet for all her fighting talk, Greer was, at this stage, as belittling of
women's work as Millett: 'most creative women', she pronounces, 'bear

the stamp of futility and confusion in their work' (77).[3] Mary Ellmann, whose elegant critique of misogynistic stereotypes is the only work of American feminist criticism to be praised by Toril Moi, writes more about women writers than the other three critics I have mentioned, but she too rebukes them for accepting and reproducing stereotypes of women much as male writers do, conniving in their own oppression. Feminists would soon, however, be finding other and more positive things to say about women writers.

THE TURN TO WOMEN'S WRITING

Ellmann, it should be pointed out, makes it clear that, even if she had criticisms to make, she was reading both earlier and contemporary women writers with some avidity, and she suggests that the dissipation of authoritative norms in literary form as in society as a whole was creating new possibilities for women's writing. The sixties had in fact seen an impressive wave of imaginative writing by women who were already questioning women's roles and the relationships between men and women. For example, Doris Lessing brought out her highly influential *The Golden Notebook* in 1962, and completed her autobiographical five-volume Martha Quest series, *Children of Violence*, in 1966; Sylvia Plath's novel *The Bell Jar* came out in 1963 and her posthumous volume of poetry, *Ariel*, in 1965; Jean Rhys' most famous book, her prequel to *Jane Eyre*, *Wide Sargasso Sea*, was published in 1966, and Angela Carter's first four novels, including *The Magic Toyshop* in 1967 and *Heroes and Villains* in 1969, had all appeared by the end of the decade. Not all of these writers would have categorised themselves as feminists, indeed only Angela Carter would have done so, and none of them was only concerned with the problems of women; they also explored issues such as colonialism, race, class, political oppression and mental illness. Besides these four writers, there was a range of other women publishing in the sixties: Margaret Drabble, A. S. Byatt and Edna O'Brien brought out their first novels, and Nadine Gordimer, Iris Murdoch and Muriel Spark, who had begun writing in the fifties, and Mary McCarthy, whose first book came out in the forties, were publishing regularly. As Margaret Drabble was to comment in 1973, 'the large amount of fiction written by women in the last decade ... bears witness that a lot of women started to worry about the same things at the same time, and turned to fiction to express their anxieties' (Drabble, 1973/1983: 76). Although the degree to which they were explicitly engaged in the questioning of gender varied, there is no doubt that these writers helped to make it possible for their women readers to recognise the dilemmas of their own lives and to make feminist theory thinkable.

As the women's movement developed in the seventies, and feminist focus moved from attacking patriarchy to the task that Greer had urged for them, liberating themselves, women's writing, both contemporary and from the past, would be increasingly drawn upon to interpret and articulate feminist women's concerns. Cora Kaplan has drawn attention to the 'triangular shape of the relationship [in those years] between the development of a feminist criticism, feminism as a social movement and women's writing; that is, the creative space and new renaissance of women writing ... [I]n the 1970s ... we *all* read poetry and novels as they came out ... those texts were part of the ongoing debate of the social movement of which we were part' (Kaplan, 1989: 17–18). Kaplan is referring particularly to books by those who wrote 'self-consciously as feminist writers', of whom there were a growing number in the seventies and eighties (Marge Piercy, Margaret Atwood, Michèle Roberts, Erica Jong, Marilyn French, Zoë Fairbairns, Valerie Miner, Pat Barker, to mention just a few), but, as she goes on to say, it also applied to the work of other women writers, including those from the past. In fact, when feminist literary critics first began to turn their attention to women's writing, they were in general as much or more concerned with the nineteenth-century novel as with more recent writing.

As early as 1973, in response to this new interest, the feminist publishing house Virago was founded in London, concentrating on republishing out-of-print women's writing; soon their dark green books with the bitten apple symbol were to be seen being read by young women on seemingly every bus and tube. The Women's Press would follow in 1978, and Pandora in 1983. In the States, the Feminist Press was launched in the early seventies, and there too other publishers specialising in women's writing followed. What Elaine Showalter would later call 'gynocriticism', criticism that focused on literature by women, emerged as a ground-up movement: the engagement with, and excitement over, women's writing was already there. As Cora Kaplan also points out, however, second-wave feminist thought had rather different locations in America and Britain. In the States, feminist theory found a much earlier place in academic institutions; after all, *Sexual Politics* had been the book of Kate Millett's PhD thesis. In Britain, where higher education remained more conservative, feminism took longer to enter the institutions, and in the seventies mainly flourished outside them, in women's groups which were closely associated with the left and involved in direct social and political action.[4] Such groups also began to study women's history; feminist historians like Sheila Rowbotham, Sally Alexander and Barbara Taylor taught in Extra-Mural classes (the adult education movement having a strong socialist tradition in Britain) putting on courses far more radical than anything happening within the universities. In 1972 Rowbotham published *Women, Resistance and Revolution* and in 1973 *Hidden from History: 300 Years of Women's Oppression and the Struggle against It*, bringing a different way of looking at women from that of Millett's and Greer's early work, and one that would migrate into feminist literary criticism. On the one hand, there was the recuperation of women omitted from standard male-dominated accounts, and on the other, a consciousness, not just of women's oppression, but also of the degree to which women resisted and challenged their position. Feminists were finding a new value and significance in women's work, as well as using it to understand their own dilemmas in the contemporary world.

A WOMEN'S LITERARY TRADITION?

None of those early feminist critics had implied women lacked the talent to write well, only the opportunity, given their lack of economic independence, lack of status and lack of time. Now, however, the emphasis moved from their difficulties to how much they had achieved in spite of these obstacles in their way. Feminist studies of women's writing gradually began to appear in the early seventies, to start with largely focusing on the nineteenth century.[5] One of the first book-length works to come out was Patricia Meyers Spacks' *The Female Imagination* (1975), which begins by evoking Virginia Woolf as one of the first of the few 'female theorists' to concern themselves 'with women's literary manifestations' (Spacks, 1975/1976: 9).[6] Spacks, like Ellmann, identifies 'a hidden level of female self-doubt' (1975/1976: 28) in her predecessors, and in particular rebukes Woolf for evading her own anger, but in other ways she is much more affirmative about the wide range of women writers she discusses, examining novels and memoirs for what they have to say about 'what it means, what it *can* mean, to be a girl, a woman' (1975/1976: 37).

The origin of Spacks' book is particularly significant for the way in which feminist literary criticism would develop. As she explains in her 'Prologue', it came out of teaching an undergraduate course called 'Woman Writers and Women's Problems' at Wellesley College, a prestigious women's college just outside Boston. Her students, she says, 'were looking for help, for models, ways of being, of coping with perplexing perceptions and feelings. For "liberation" ... They felt (although they suspected they weren't supposed to feel anything of the sort, it wasn't "intellectual") that to read books by women would have direct personal meaning for them' (1975/1976: 4). Spacks had tape-recorded her classes, and refers at intervals during the book to her students and their views, an engagingly fresh and open tactic, setting the very form of her work in opposition to the impersonal academic criticism of the day. Yet – and this would become a fiercely contested issue – she assumes that one can make generalisations about women as a whole. The book opens with the question, 'What are the ways of female feeling, the modes of responding, that persist in spite of social change?', and she goes on to assert that 'Changing social conditions increase or diminish the opportunities for women's action and expression, but a special female self-awareness emerges through literature in every period' (1975/1976: 3). This is in spite of the fact she goes on to acknowledge that virtually all the books she examines are by white middle-class women writing in the Anglo-American tradition, hardly the basis for such grand universalist claims.[7] However, Spacks' book is a lively, sympathetic and engaging discussion of women writers from Austen to Lessing, and signalled an unmistakeable new enthusiasm for these texts.

Spacks' book was followed the next year by Ellen Moers' *Literary Women*, which unambiguously proclaims the achievements of women writers: 'what does it matter', she asks in her first paragraph, 'that so many of the great writers of modern times have been women? . . . For this was something new, something distinctive of modernity itself, that the written word in its most memorable form, starting in the eighteenth century, became increasingly and steadily the work of women . . . Literature is the only intellectual field to which women, over a long stretch of time, have made an indispensable contribution' (Moers, 1976: xi). Moers ranges over English, American and French women writers from the eighteenth to the early twentieth century (Fanny Burney, Mary Brunton, Mme de Staël, Jane Austen, the Brontës, Elizabeth Barrett Browning, Emily Dickinson, George Sand, Harriet Beecher Stowe and many more), sometimes setting them in the context of, and contrasting them with, the practice of male authors, including Richardson, Rousseau and Ovid. It is a broad canvas, both erudite and meditative, suggestive and perceptive. The book contained an influential chapter on the then neglected field of the female Gothic, in which Moers wrote about Mary Shelley's *Frankenstein* as a 'birth myth', a 'myth of genuine originality', forged out of her responses to the 'hideously intermixed' experience of death and birth through which she was living at the time of its writing. In the same chapter she provocatively describes the critically respected *Wuthering Heights* as a perversely erotic Gothic tale, as she does Christina Rossetti's *Goblin Market*, then regarded as a 'faded Victorian classic' (Moers, 1976: 92, 93, 96, 100). Like Spacks, she sees these women writers as representing a shared tradition, 'a literary movement apart from but hardly subservient to the mainstream'; they formed an 'undercurrent, rapid and powerful', in the male-dominated world of literature (1976: 42). She makes this comment in a chapter entitled 'Women's Literary Traditions and the Individual Talent', a reference to Eliot's famous essay that reminds one that in the critical climate of the time, these early feminist critics believed that to demonstrate that women writers were significant entailed establishing a literary tradition for them, an alternative canon of great works. As with Spacks, this is a white, essentially bourgeois tradition, however bohemian these writers' lives may have been, and Moers is clearly writing for a similar audience.

The book with which *Literary Women* is often paired, Elaine Showalter's *A Literature of Their Own*, appeared in 1977, introducing a further range of forgotten or neglected writers, in particular the sensation novelists Mary Braddon and Mrs Henry Wood, and the 'New Women' Sarah Grand, Mona Caird and George Egerton. Showalter was less sanguine than Spacks or Moers about seeing women writers as any kind of 'movement'. Quoting Greer's comment on the 'phenomenon of the transience of female literary fame', Showalter argues that 'each generation of women writers has found itself, in a sense, without a history, forced to rediscover the past anew, forging again and again the consciousness of their sex'. Yet she nonetheless suggests that there is a 'female literary tradition' which follows the pattern of development of any literary subculture, a three-part trajectory beginning with imitation, moving to critique and finally reaching a phase of self-discovery (Showalter, 1977/1982: 11–12, 13). Showalter's book was the product of wide research, a cultural as well as a literary history, and along with Moers' book established the richness of women's writing to be mined; it was still within the same cultural hegemony as Spacks' book, in fact rather narrower as Showalter only deals with British writers (she would make up for her neglect of American women writers in her 1991 book, *Sister's Choice*), but that a feminist literary criticism existed that took the works of women writers seriously was now an undeniable feature of the critical scene. In the next fifteen years, the recuperation of women's texts would continue apace, moving back to the seventeenth century and earlier.[8]

TOWARDS A BLACK AND LESBIAN FEMINIST CRITICISM

In the aftermath of Spacks', Moers' and Showalter's groundbreaking work, however, dissent swiftly erupted. Even before Showalter's book had appeared, Barbara Smith, in an article entitled 'Towards a Black Feminist Criticism', had attacked Spacks and Moers, as well as a 1975 article by Showalter which had anticipated much of the argument of *A Literature of Their Own*. Why, Smith demanded, if they could uncover 'dozens of truly obscure white women writers', could they not take black women writers seriously? Spacks, she points out, was teaching at Wellesley at the same time as Alice Walker was there taking one of the first classes in the States on black women writers. Showalter, she writes,

> obviously thinks that the identities of being Black and female are mutually exclusive, as this statement illustrates. "Furthermore, there are other literary subcultures (black American novelists, for example) whose history offers a precedent for feminist scholarship to use." The idea of critics like Showalter *using* Black literature is chilling, a case of barely disguised cultural imperialism. (Smith, 1977/ 1985: 172)[9]

These charges against white feminists would be powerfully revisited in more general terms in bell hooks' *Ain't I a Woman* (1981), which again took issue with these critics' tendency to equate white women's oppression with that of the blacks, without thinking about the position in which that left black women; as the title of a collection of black feminist criticism published in 1982 wittily put it, *All the Women Are White, All the Blacks Are Men, But Some of Us Are Brave*. Millett in her 'Postscript' had used such comparisons as her final rallying cry in *Sexual Politics*:

> When one surveys the spontaneous mass movements taking place all over the world, one is led to hope that human understanding itself has grown ripe for change. In America one may expect the new women's movement to ally itself on an equal basis with blacks and students in a growing radical coalition ... As the largest alienated element in our society, and because of their numbers, passion, and length of oppression, its largest revolutionary base, women might come to play a leadership part in social revolution, quite unknown before in history. The changes in fundamental values such a coalition of expropriated groups – blacks, youth, women, the poor – would seek are especially towards freedom from rank or prescriptive role, sexual or otherwise. (1971: 363)

For Millett, this was a radical vision; for her black critics, it was ignoring the realities of their very different experiences of oppression as black women. By the late seventies, to neglect non-white women writers was undoubtedly to fail to respond to some of the most striking writing of the time, with, in the USA alone, books being brought out by Toni Morrison, Audre Lorde, Maya Angelou, Paule Marshall and Alice Walker among the African Americans, as well as the Asian American Maxine Hong Kingston and the Native American Leslie Marmon Silko. The repertoire of women writers considered by feminist critics would have to grow. The Women's Press in Britain, founded a year after Smith's article appeared, and built up by Ros de Lanerolle, a South African who had earlier been much involved in opposition to apartheid, from the beginning had a policy of publishing work by black and what were then referred to as Third World writers. By the time Alice Walker's *The Color Purple*, whose British publisher they were, won the Pulitzer Prize in 1983, the significant role of black women's writing in the new wave of female creativity was widely acknowledged.

A further extension of both the range of interest in women's writing and its interpretation came from lesbian critics, such as Bonnie Zimmerman, who critiqued the 'heterosexism' of what were already being seen as 'mainstream' feminist critics, drawing attention to the way that even when writers like Woolf or Stein were discussed, their lesbianism was passed over. Adrienne Rich, herself a fine poet as well as a gifted essayist, published her famous article 'Compulsory Heterosexuality and Lesbian Existence' in 1980, in which she talks of a 'lesbian continuum' of women who in one way or another want to define themselves without reference to men; she cites H. D., Woolf once more, Emily Dickinson and Charlotte Brontë, but also adds Lorraine Hansberry, Zora Neale Hurston and Toni Morrison's *Sula*. The mention of those three black writers is significant: as Zimmerman acknowledged in an article first published in 1981, American lesbian criticism, like American feminism in general, was often seen by black feminists as racist in its exclusively white interests, though it had in fact, she says, been much influenced by black lesbian critics. Rich's references make clear that she recognises the necessity of acknowledging the contribution of African American women writers; she wants to argue for the alliance of lesbian and feminist critical endeavours, and for the shared concerns of white and black women, but for all that Rich would be one of those attacked by hooks for her idealisation of white women's sympathy for blacks. There would be further stormy disagreements ahead.

SUBVERTING THE LAW OF THE FATHER

As the seventies drew to a close, the political climate was changing; the revolutionary fervour of the sixties mutated into the Reaganite and Thatcherite eighties, and the buoyant confidence of the 'ungenteel middle-class women' invoked by Greer that liberation would be swiftly achieved was now muted. In spite of the growth of the women's movement, resistance seemed if anything harder, though just as essential, and feminist discussions of women's writing would reflect that sense of struggle. Sandra Gilbert and Susan Gubar's *The Madwoman in the Attic* (1979), another book that came out of a college course in women's literature, has been seen in many ways as continuing the tradition of Spacks, Moers and Showalter in its impassioned and detailed reading of nineteenth-century women's texts, confining itself even more narrowly than they did to those who were rapidly becoming the feminist reader's established greats: Austen, Mary Shelley, the Brontës, George Eliot and Emily Dickinson, with briefer discussions of Elizabeth Barrett Browning and Christina Rossetti. It was a highly influential text, a good deal of its appeal lying in its repeated heroic tale of women writers' 'battle for self-creation' against an overwhelmingly powerful patriarchal authority; chapter after chapter traces their hard-won success against the odds. It was an exhilarating affirmation to its readers of their own possibilities of defying the patriarchal norms. Jane Eyre was Everywoman, according to Gilbert and Gubar, and their readers, they imply, can make a similar triumphant pilgrimage of 'escape-into-whole-ness' (Gilbert and Gubar, 1979: 49, 336).

For all that, however, there is an anxiety in *The Madwoman in the Attic* not present in the earlier seventies celebrations of women writers. Gilbert and Gubar had identified two dominant metaphors in their texts: escape and enclosure. There were those who pointed out, justly enough, that they paint such a nightmare scenario of homogeneous patriarchal dominance that it becomes amazing, if not incredible, that the subversive strategies of liberation they identify in these women writers were possible at all. That intensified sense of the woman writer's struggle would be part of other feminist theories in the eighties; if for Gilbert and Gubar it was with the oppressive phallic weight of a male literary tradition, for others, as Lacan's notion of the symbolic order as the Law of the Father grew in influence, it would be with language itself. This had been for some time the concern of French feminist theory, and in 1980 Elaine Marks and Isabelle de Courtivron brought out a collection entitled *New French Feminisms*, for many Anglophone feminists their first introduction to the work of such influential figures as Hélène Cixous and Julia Kristeva. In both Britain and the States interest in their ideas grew rapidly, particularly in their strategies for subversive writing (discussed in detail by Judith Still in Chapter 14).

For Cixous and Kristeva, Cixous' now famous notion of an *écriture féminine* is by no means confined to biological women; in fact they associated it most often with modernist male writers, an anti-essentialism which made their ideas particularly welcome to some feminists, but political anathema to others. Yet one important effect of these ideas was a new appreciation of and attention to the work of women modernists and *avant-garde* writers, and a new interest in textuality and in the operations of gender and desire within texts. Until the eighties, there had been little feminist engagement with modernism, or any challenge to the masculinist view that it had been dominated by men. Even Woolf was only gradually recuperated during the seventies, and then more often as a commentator on women's writing than as a writer herself; most feminist critics remained ambivalent about her novels, and, as Toril Moi was to argue with some passion, were on the whole much happier with realist women novelists than with her modernist and experimental writing. All this was now to change, and in addition, with the new interest in textuality, it became no longer necessary – as had sometimes been the case in the past – to ascertain if a woman writer's intentions had been feminist or at least women-centred to find value in their texts.

Feminist literary criticism in the eighties became more diverse, more sophisticated and more wide-ranging, but also more divided. In 1979, Mary Jacobus, herself already influenced by Kristeva and Cixous, had published a distinguished collection of essays entitled *Women Writing and Writing about Women*, pointing out in her introduction that the book 'contains many feminisms, many definitions of the relation between women and literature, between women and representation', and that the contributors included poets and translators as well as critics (Jacobus, 1979: 7). Such tolerant plurality was not necessarily to continue. The interest in French feminism was just one example of how the influence of Derridean deconstruction and other French versions of structuralism and poststructuralism had changed the critical landscape in the academy in both the States and Britain. With the importation of what traditional scholars saw as arcane and meretricious theories from the Continent, Anglo-American academia became the site of so-called 'theory wars', which exploded between young, left-wing critics, who took up the cause of theory, and the older, more conservative and established academics who, on the whole, opposed it vigorously. It was inevitable that feminists, very much aligned with the young and the left, would be drawn in. In 1985, Toril Moi, herself a Marxist-feminist poststructuralist, published what was to be another highly influential and cogently argued text, *Sexual/Textual Politics*, in which she was deeply critical of books like Showalter's, Moers' and Gilbert and Gubar's, though her denunciation was on quite different grounds from Barbara Smith's or Bonnie Zimmerman's. For Moi, traditional Anglo-American feminist criticism (and in this she includes black and lesbian critics) was fatally flawed by its naïve essentialism, although she

commends it for its feminist political consciousness. She contrasts it with
the French feminists, with their post-Derridean subtlety, though in their
case, she concludes, their work is unfortunately marred by the fact that it is,
as she says of Kristeva, 'politically unsatisfactory' (Moi, 1985: 170). (This
distinction has always reminded me of Sellar and Yeatman's description in
1066 and All That of the Cavaliers and the Roundheads, the former being
Wrong but Wromantic, while the latter were Right but Repulsive. I leave
my readers to decide how those descriptions map on to schools of feminist
criticism.) Anglo-American criticism, Moi argues, has not freed itself from
the patriarchal assumptions of humanism; in its search for unity and
wholeness, it remains ideologically part of traditional male-dominated
literary criticism. Whilst not necessarily disputing that, one might note
that such uncompromising certainty of judgement, characteristic of many
British poststructuralists of the period, had a good deal in common with
the very masculinist pronouncements of the Leavisite and New Critical
scholars of whom they so strongly disapproved, and sits uneasily with their
emphasis, so fruitful for feminist thought, on the provisionality and
fragmentation of identities and meaning. As Lisa Jardine was to suggest
provocatively the next year, left-wing 'theory' with its emphasis on rigour
and discipline had as part of its subtext the making of the potentially
effeminate study of English safe for men (Jardine, 1986: 208–17). But Moi's
book was a sign of the times; feminism, with its early utopian ideals of
sisterhood, was becoming a multifarious and dispersed project, perhaps not
an altogether negative thing. Early second-wave feminism had represented
a very limited social group of women, and it was a sign of its success that it
was acquiring so many forms.

The theorists that Moi commends most for their combination of political commitment and theoretical sophistication were the Marxist-Feminist
Literature Collective, which had come together in London in the second
half of the seventies, and produced some of the earliest academic feminist
literary criticism on this side of the Atlantic. The majority of British
feminists identified themselves as socialist feminists, or later as materialist
feminists, terms which covered both members of the Communist and the
Labour Parties; in addition, the Marxist-Feminist Literature Collective,
which included many who would later become well-known critics, such as
Cora Kaplan, Jean Radford, Maud Ellmann, Mary Jacobus, Helen Taylor
and Michèle Barratt, were also interested in Lacanian psychoanalysis and
French theorists such as Louis Althusser and Pierre Machery. (Lacan's work
was originally introduced to Britain through an article by Althusser in the
New Left Review in 1969, and had been brought into the feminist debate by

Juliet Mitchell's groundbreaking *Psychoanalysis and Feminism* in 1974.) The Marxist-Feminist Literature Collective wanted to explore issues of class and gender, and argued that 'because of the subordinated place of women within the ruling classes ... women's writing both articulates and challenges the dominant ideology from a decentered position within it' (Kaplan, 1986: 3). Although to a great extent operating as a reading and discussion group, the collective presented several joint papers, the most high-profile of which was a much discussed paper on the Brontës and Barrett Browning that ten members of the collective presented at the first University of Essex Sociology of Literature Conference in 1977, according to Cora Kaplan startling the male critics present with their departure from the time-honoured mode of the single critic presenting his (as it generally had been) individual, career-building and finely honed views. The collective included both students and teachers in higher education, thus also disrupting the academic hierarchal distinctions then generally strictly observed, even by those on the left (Kaplan, 1986: 61–4). The group disbanded in the late seventies, but as individuals many of them went on to contribute significantly to the development of feminist literary criticism in higher education in the eighties.

WOMEN'S WRITING AS A HISTORY; A HISTORY OF WOMEN'S WRITING

Yet the eighties also saw a continuing excitement about women's writing outside the academy. Readings by women writers proliferated, the International Feminist Book Fair was founded and conferences were organised on women's writing. Books in which contemporary women writers talked about their own experience of creating texts, such as *On Gender and Writing* (1983), edited by Michelene Wandor, or *Delighting the Heart: A Notebook by Women Writers* (1989), edited by Susan Sellers, became increasingly popular, and publishers' lists, like Penguin's Lives of Modern Women, and Virago's Pioneers, celebrated women writers' achievement in a range of fields. Feminist magazines of the period, on both sides of the Atlantic, like *Ms*, *Women's Review of Books*, *Spare Rib*, *Women's Review* and *Everywoman*, published interviews with women writers as well as reviews of their work, and books which collected interviews with women writers began to appear.

The range of writers that women were reading continued to grow. I have already mentioned the increasing interest in non-white writers, whether African American, British Caribbean, diasporic Asian, or, in a phrase which emerged among its own set of contentions in the second half of the eighties, the 'postcolonial' novel. It is not without significance that in 1978, one year after Showalter's book had established the unmistakeable arrival of feminist literary criticism, Edward Said's *Orientalism* indicated the opening up of this other revolutionary field of literary criticism. Described at first as the analysis of colonial discourse before being renamed, postcolonial theory, like feminist literary theory, began with the critique of the oppressors' texts before turning to the works of resistance. British feminists had realised increasingly in the seventies that it was not possible to consider gender in isolation from issues of class, but American feminists had perhaps become aware earlier that it was essential not to isolate issues of gender from race, and that lesson was now being learnt in Britain in the eighties, with some equally fiery eruptions. Yet from the early eighties, both feminist literary criticism and postcolonial theory were beginning to find their way into the literature departments of the more radical Higher Education institutions in Britain, as had already happened in the States, and were eagerly seized on by students. Writers like the South African Bessie Head, the Nigerian Buchi Emecheta, the Maori New Zealander Keri Hulme and the Caribbean Grace Nichols were read by young women, both black and white, within and without the academy.

The repertoire of women's writing of importance to feminists was expanding in other ways as well. A number of feminist critics, including some ex-members of the Marxist-Feminist Literature Collective, and others they influenced, such as Cora Kaplan's student Alison Light, were now engaging with more popular and until then despised forms of literature, such as the romance, fantasy, family sagas, detective fiction and the 'middlebrow' domestic novel. As Jean Radford suggested, in the introduction to *The Progress of Romance*, the rise of the populist right made it urgent for left-wing feminists to understand the appeal of the popular, but this was not in a spirit of what she describes as 'left moralism and puritanism' (Radford, 1986: 7).[10] Rather, as Alison Light suggests:

If we see women's writing as a history, then such texts show women to be a subject-in-process, always becoming, and the connections we choose to make between 'women' and 'writing' are enormously, and centrally, political ... [W]omen's writing reminds us of our proactive energy in the face of passivity, our demands for pleasure despite 'duty'. ... [A] feminist attention to women's writing is part of feminism's desire to achieve a more compassionate and generous understanding of human consciousness and its effects, of how political changes come about, and of the extent to which the resistance of all peoples, their capacity to represent themselves, is always possible. (Light, in Radford, 1986: 163)

Light here sums up imaginatively and humanely the sense that feminist readers had evolved of the productiveness, vitality and radical potential of women's writing, whatever its political or ideological constraints. By the end of the eighties, women's writing was a significant part of the publishing world, as well as a firmly established academic topic of study. As Nicci Gerrard argued in 1989, women's writing had entered the mainstream. There were those who feared political apostasy, others who welcomed the transformation. No one could deny that, although there was more to do, a history of women's writing had been uncovered and established.

NOTES

1. By most at any rate – as Mary Ellmann reminds us in *Thinking about Women*, Anthony Burgess, for one, deplored Jane Austen's lack of 'strong male thrust' (Ellmann, 1968/1979: 23).
2. Mitchell described this in 'Women: How Long is the Longest Revolution to Be?', a talk given at the South Bank Centre, 13 March 1997.
3. Later, these feminists developed a much more positive attitude to women's writing: Greer would edit a collection of seventeenth-century women writers, and Figes write a book on women writers before 1850.
4. See Sheila Rowbotham (1983: 32–44).
5. For example, Colby (1970), Heilbrun (1973) and Basch (1974).
6. Spacks regularly refers to her as 'Mrs Woolf' (she also writes about 'Mlle de Beauvoir', and even more incongruously, about 'Miss Millett'), a convention of the time in academic discussions of women writers that reads very oddly now, and one which feminist critics would soon abandon.
7. There are a few references to non-Anglo-American women writers, such as the Danish Isak Dinesen and the Russian Marie Bashkirtseff.
8. Spacks had made reference to the memoirs of the seventeenth-century Duchess of Newcastle and of the eighteenth-century Mrs Thrale, but on the whole the seventies critics did not go back before the nineteenth century.
9. Showalter admirably included Smith's article in her 1985 compilation of essays, *The New Feminist Criticism*.
10. Although I am illustrating this move through a British example, some of the first in this field were Americans: Tania Modleski (1982) and Janice Radway (1984).

BIBLIOGRAPHY

Althusser, Louis (1969), 'Freud and Lacan', in *New Left Review* 55.
Basch, Françoise (1974), *Relative Creatures: Victorian Women in Society and the Novel, 1837–1867*, trans. from the French ms, London: Allen Lane.
Colby, Vineta (1970), *The Singular Anomaly: Women Novelists of the Nineteenth Century*, New York: New York University Press.

Daiches, David (ed.) (1971), *The Penguin Companion to Literature*, vol. 1, *Britain and the Commonwealth*, Harmondsworth: Penguin.

Derrida, Jacques (1971/1982), 'White Mythology', in *Margins of Philosophy*, trans. Alan Bass, London and New York: Prentice Hall.

Drabble, Margaret (1973/1983), 'A Woman Writer', in Wandor (1983).

Ellmann, Mary (1968/1979), *Thinking about Women*, London: Virago.

Figes, Eva (1970), *Patriarchal Attitudes*, London: Granada.

Gerrard, Nicci (1989), *Into the Mainstream: How Feminism Has Changed Women's Writing*, London: Pandora.

Gilbert, Sandra and Susan Gubar (1979), *The Madwoman in the Attic: The Woman Writer and the Nineteenth-Century Literary Imagination*, New Haven: Yale University Press.

Greer, Germaine (1970/1971), *The Female Eunuch*, London: Paladin.

Heilbrun, Carolyn G. (1973), *Towards a Recognition of Androgyny: Aspects of Male and Female in Literature*, London: Gollancz.

hooks, bell (1981/1982), *Ain't I a Woman: Black Women and Feminism*, London: Pluto Press.

Hull, Gloria T., Patricia Bell Scott and Barbara Smith (1982), *All the Women Are White, All the Blacks Are Men, But Some of Us Are Brave*, Old Westbury, NY: Feminist Press.

Jacobus, Mary (1979), *Women Writing and Writing about Women*, London: Croom Helm.

Jardine, Lisa (1986), ' "Girl Talk" (for Boys on the Left)', in *Oxford Literary Review: Sexual Difference* 8, special issue 1 and 2.

Kaplan, Cora (1986), *Sea Changes: Culture and Feminism*, London: Verso.

(1989), 'Feminist Criticism Twenty Years On', in *From My Guy to Sci-Fi: Genre and Women's Writing in the Postmodern World*, ed. Helen Carr, London: Pandora.

Marks, Elaine and Isabelle de Courtivron (eds) (1980), *New French Feminisms*, Brighton: Harvester.

Millett, Kate (1971), *Sexual Politics*, London: Sphere Books.

Mitchell, Juliet (1966), 'Women: The Longest Revolution', in *New Left Review* 40.

(1974/1975), *Psychoanalysis and Feminism*, Harmondsworth: Penguin.

Modleski, Tania (1982), *Loving with a Vengeance: Mass-Produced Fantasies for Women*, Hamden: Archon.

Moers, Ellen (1976), *Literary Women*, New York: Doubleday.

Moi, Toril (1985), *Sexual/Textual Politics: Feminist Literary Theory*, London: Methuen.

Radford, Jean (ed.) (1986), *The Progress of Romance: The Politics of Popular Fiction*, London: Routledge and Kegan Paul.

Radway, Janice (1984), *Reading the Romance: Women, Patriarchy and Popular Literature*, Chapel Hill: University of North Carolina Press.

Rich, Adrienne (1980), 'Compulsory Heterosexuality and Lesbian Existence', in *Signs: Journal of Women in Culture and Society* 5:4.

Rowbotham, Sheila (1972), *Women, Resistance and Revolution*, London: Allen Lane.

(1973), *Hidden from History: 300 Years of Women's Oppression and the Struggle against It*, London: Pluto Press.

(1983), 'The Beginnings of Women's Liberation in Britain', in *Dreams and Dilemmas*, London: Virago.

Sellar, Walter Carruthers and Robert Julian Yeatman (1930/1990), *1066 and All That*, London: Folio Society.

Sellers, Susan (ed.) (1989), *Delighting the Heart: A Notebook by Women Writers*, London: The Women's Press.

Showalter, Elaine (1977/1982), *A Literature of Their Own: British Women Novelists from Brontë to Lessing*, London: Virago.

(1991), *Sister's Choice: Tradition and Change in American Women's Writing*, Oxford: Clarendon Press.

Smith, Barbara (1977/1986), 'Towards a Black Feminist Criticism', in *The New Feminist Criticism: Essays on Women, Literature and Theory*, ed. Elaine Showalter, London: Virago.

Spacks, Patricia Meyers (1975/1976), *The Female Imagination: A Literary and Psychological Investigation of Women's Writing*, London: Allen and Unwin.

Wandor, Michelene (ed.) (1983), *On Gender and Writing*, London: Pandora Press.

Zimmerman, Bonnie (1981/1986), 'What Has Never Been: An Overview of Lesbian Feminist Criticism', in *The New Feminist Criticism: Essays on Women, Literature and Theory*, ed. Elaine Showalter, London: Virago.

CHAPTER 8

Autobiography and personal criticism

Linda Anderson

INTIMACY AND THEORY

'Personal Criticism', the term Nancy Miller used in 1991 to refer to 'an explicitly autobiographical performance in the act of criticism' had, as she acknowledged, many disparate roots in feminist writing in the seventies and eighties (Miller, 1991: 1). There had been, for instance, such diverse but bold experiments as Adrienne Rich's turn to autobiography in 1979 in her influential essay 'When We Dead Awaken: Writing as Revision' (Rich, 1980), Rachel Blau du Plessis' montage of different discourses, including autobiographical asides, in 'For the Etruscans' in 1980, or Hélène Cixous' resounding 'concert of personalizations' in 'The Laugh of the Medusa' (Cixous and Clément, 1975/1986: 84). All these examples have in common an element of surprise for the reader (certainly reading them in the early 1980s) which comes from their deliberate challenge to the accepted norms of academic discourse; but there was also a way in which they awakened a sense of collusion with the woman reader as well. Here was a space, it seemed, where secrets could be shared, a common alienation acknowledged, a different intimacy entered into. Criticism could openly address those vulnerabilities and desires which it was usually forced to conceal; it could admit the ways the intellectual was necessarily joined to the social, domestic and physical life.

It is perhaps not surprising that *Between Women*, one of the earliest collections of essays to foreground the subjectivity and personal life of the critic, also cited Virginia Woolf as an influence. Its editors recall that it had originally been envisioned as a work in which women would 'tell personal stories about their reading and writing on Virginia Woolf' (Ascher et al., 1984: xiii). Though the scope of the collection broadened beyond this, its aim remained the same: to produce a book where women could tell the personal stories of their relation to the authors they studied, eschewing 'distance and impartiality' for personal narratives which valued

138

identification and process (1984: xxiii). Woolf's influence still figured strongly, though perhaps, for such a complex writer, in too simple a way: 'Woolf encouraged all women to speak in their own, not a borrowed voice', Sarah Ruddick claimed (1984: 145). However, Toril Moi's theoretical work *Sexual/Textual Politics*, which was published the next year, and which famously made Virginia Woolf's polemical essay, *A Room of One's Own*, a testing ground for different versions of feminist theory, also helps us to map out a different rationale for personal criticism. For Moi the 'I' which Woolf adopted in her essay was a pioneering experiment with language and form, a deconstructive strategy to undermine the assumed unity and confidence of the humanist subject. For Moi the 'I' was to be seen as a deliberate challenge and affront to the authority of a discourse which denied its own masculine bias, its subjective basis (Moi, 1985: 2–18). Her argument was pitted against Elaine Showalter's earlier criticism that Woolf avoided representing her own feminist views by using a series of personae in *A Room of One's Own* which are fictional and which conceal or parody her own experience: 'Despite its illusions of spontaneity and intimacy, *A Room of One's Own* is an extremely impersonal and defensive book' (Showalter, 1977: 282). Showalter's polemic is directed at Woolf, in particular, and is born out of a critical moment which assumed that to write about the self was a matter of simple volition. Debates about autobiography have tended since the 1980s to refute Showalter by seeing *all* attempts to write the subject as drawing on linguistic and narrative codes and as being, therefore, necessarily entangled with fiction. Nevertheless the political impetus for autobiography to have some purchase on 'real' lives or the desire, such as that experienced by the editors of *Between Women*, to find within writing an intimacy with a living presence has never really disappeared (Anderson, 2001: 90–1).

Personal criticism, as a self-conscious critical mode, could be said to have drawn on this dual inheritance: on the one hand, the need to deconstruct the unity and hegemony of the critical subject and its claims to objectivity, and attest to the variety of different points of view which have been overlooked or disenfranchised by the academy; on the other, an awareness that a theory of the subject in itself could not address sufficiently the particularity, even the 'humanity', of the subject and the social world they inhabit, or offer a style open enough to the unpredictable possibilities of 'truth'.[1] Personal criticism is thus boldly subversive *and* deliberately engaging, closely focused and intimate. For Nancy Miller it could precisely cross the (supposed) divide between the theoretical and the personal, revealing how far each is implicated in the other (Miller, 1991: 5).

The notion that *all* criticism is to a greater or lesser extent personal is the theme of many of the respondents to the *Modern Language Association*'s wide-ranging *Forum* on personal criticism published in 1996, which collects together many of the arguments for and against personal criticism to date. For many of the critics represented here, both male and female, the personal 'permeates' both scholarship and the critical; criticism is redolent of the critic's place and standing within the academy, and inevitably revealing of secret motivations and drives (*Forum*, 1996: 1146–50). Jane Gallop points out how prefaces, acknowledgements, dedications and footnotes can provide a lot of personal information to be read alongside the text which itself almost inevitably contains particular resonances, repetitions or intensities that also mark the place of the personal (*Forum*, 1996: 1150). Norman Holland argues that 'objectivity' in criticism was the result of a nineteenth-century attempt to gain a scientific respectability for literary studies, a claim dispelled by postmodernism, yet oddly still fostered by its attachment to hegemonic theory (*Forum*, 1996: 1147). For many, objectivity in criticism can be seen as masking the partiality of a given critical viewpoint: 'When we invoke objectivity and universality, we appeal to power and mystify our personal investments so as to speak for everyone', Claudia Tate writes (*Forum*, 1996: 1148). The alternative is to write with a modesty which acknowledges the limits of one's knowledge and understanding, and leaves space for interaction with others. For George Wright, the difference may be one of perceiving one's work in a less assuming way as 'a probably flawed contribution to a continually interesting dialogue' rather than as 'another stolid block in the great pyramid of objective scholarship' (*Forum*, 1996: 1160).

For many the argument is a political one: the recognition that objectivity, though deriving its authority from its claim to universality, was the preserve of the privileged and excluded multiple viewpoints, has led to the personal in criticism being used, just as autobiography has, as a place of cultural intervention, empowering otherwise marginalised groups. Most of the contributors to the *Forum* were women but many (also) spoke from minority positions as gay, immigrant, black, Chicano or Asian. For these writers personal criticism seemed to offer a way of inserting their difference into a discourse which was otherwise oblivious to it, 'seizing the initiative of utterance', as Claudia Tate declares. 'If nothing else', she writes, 'the possibility of a multitude of personal expressions enables those who are silenced to speak'(*Forum*, 1996: 1148). For Carole Boyce Davies, putting oneself into one's scholarship, locating oneself in history, is less a choice than a necessity for groups such as 'African Americans, Caribbeans, women, and leftists' who, without the luxury of neutrality, must counter how they are already marked by the dominant culture (*Forum*, 1996: 1154). The hope for all these writers is that the introduction of the personal does not stop there – it is never an end in itself – but precipitates a change in the academy and how our ways of knowing are framed.

Of those respondents who expressed reservations, disappointment or opposition to personal criticism, the most surprising is Mary Ann Caws. Her book, *Women of Bloomsbury* (1990), contained an influential preface entitled 'Personal Criticism: A Matter of Choice' in which she advocated a move away from impersonality in critical writing towards a greater intimacy. Writing about women, she believed at that time, should attempt to get very close, stylistically, to its subject, even 'mingle' with the lives of the women being written about (Caws, 1990: 2). Retrospectively, she is worried about how the pronouns 'I' and 'we' can exclude others and how her tentative style probably emanated from, and served to reinforce, a feminine timidity: ' I wanted to be both passionate and compassionate but I could not express my wanting in a form hard enough ... My personalizing criticism seemed weak to me. It felt like a lesser form that knew it was lesser' (*Forum*, 1996: 1160–1). Caws' change of mind is interesting. For critics whose move into personal criticism arose out of a suspicion of, or a sense of exclusion from, the kinds of authority invested in objectivity, the idea that personal criticism can also silence others, making it hard to offer oppositional arguments, or draw back from the kind of involvement and relatedness which Caws offered in her earlier work, may seem paradoxical. For many respondents to the *Forum*, however, an investment in the personal, even though aimed at demonstrating a connection between 'subjectivity and the subject' in scholarship, sits awkwardly with any theoretical or political interrogation of it. How can people argue with 'lived reality', Richard Flores asks (*Forum*, 1996: 1166), whilst Ruth Perry sees the personal being used more often as a substitute for the political in contemporary criticism than as a way of probing their connection. We need, she contends, 'to engage in a political analysis of private meanings' (*Forum*, 1996: 1166). For its most severe detractors, personal criticism is inevitably embedded in the power structures of the academy and further contributes to the academic star system, the cult of personality in literary studies. Some – those who have 'names' – are asked to 'do' personal criticism at conferences, while others must mutely listen (*Forum*, 1996: 1167). What makes personal criticism more than a rhetorical device, a way of giving criticism, against a postmodern scepticism, the semblance of authenticity? Can writing about oneself ever be, of itself, radical, given that it participates in a genre – autobiography – which, however anxiously it does it, still underwrites the subject?

PERFORMANCES OF THE PERSONAL

In her book *Getting Personal* (1991), in which she took as her context 'the current proliferation in literary studies of autobiographical or personal criticism', Nancy Miller employed the term 'performance' to describe her own move towards 'self-figuration' in criticism (1991: 1). The term performance is a resonant one, suggestive of Miller's 'use' of the personal as a way of marking a specific time and place in the history of feminist criticism, though it is not a term she particularly interrogates. In *Touching Feeling*, however, Eve Kosofsky Sedgwick has provided her own genealogy of this word (2003: 3–8). Citing, first of all, J. L. Austin's influential work on performative utterances, on that particular group of sentences where to utter the sentence is not to *describe* doing a thing, but to do it ('I apologise'; 'I promise'; 'I bequeath'), she then outlines the way its meaning was extended from a closed set of grammatical instances to a more generalised property of language by deconstructionist critics. Famously, Jacques Derrida argued that Austin's examples could not be contained by specific contexts and intentions but were open to interpretation. Whilst Austin tried to differentiate between performative utterances which are pure or serious, and those, including fictional examples, spoken, for instance, by an actor on a stage, which are not, Derrida's point is that such a distinction cannot be maintained. There is no context where language does not share the characteristics of the literary, that is, where meaning can be present to itself, and does not have to be inferred or constructed, drawing on previously repeated instances. In this sense the performative, rather than drawing on a context outside itself which can fix its meaning, instead produces the context which supposedly underlies it. Only convention and shared assumptions make it appear otherwise (Derrida, 1982). For Sedgwick, whose book instigates an important dialogue of her own with deconstruction, the term performativity also has another lineage in contemporary usage, that deriving from the dramatic or theatrical. The connection between the two meanings of performative as non-referential and as dramatic is, Sedgwick avers, by no means assured and founders on the notion of intentionality (2003: 7).[2] Judith Butler's work has been crucial in this respect. In Butler's early book, *Gender Trouble*, the idea that gender depended on repeated performances which take on the illusion of naturalness could be illustrated through the 'drag act' where the self-conscious theatricality of the performer demonstrated something important about the imitative nature of gender itself (Butler, 1990: 137). As such Butler's work seemed for many readers to be advocating performance – in the theatrical sense – as a space of radical, willed resistance or as a deliberate intervention into gender politics. In retrospect Butler has re-stated her position stressing instead the discursivity of the performative and effecting a distinction between theatrical performance as a discrete, embodied event, chosen by the performer (the drag act, for instance), and the performative as a compulsory repetition of norms:

Performance as bounded 'act' is distinguished from performativity insofar as the latter consists in a reiteration of norms which precede, constrain, and exceed the performer and in that sense cannot be taken as the fabrication of the performer's 'will' or 'choice'; further, what is 'performed' works to conceal, if not disavow, what remains opaque, unconscious, unperformable. The reduction of performativity to performance would be a mistake. (Butler, 1993: 234)

For Butler the question of intentionality can only be approached by understanding the ways in which the subject is constituted. The 'I' cannot simply preside over discourse, selecting and discarding different positions, since it has already been constituted by them. To become the subject of feminist theory – to speak in the name of feminism – is also to invoke an institutional history that 'positions' me through both inclusion and exclusion; it is in turn to produce utterances that can never be fully owned by me but which will be made to signify elsewhere and in a way which 'I' may not recognise. However, for Butler, this notion, which seems so detrimental to any idea of the subject as agent, becomes instead enabling and works to release 'me' into another field of possibility. Because she believes the subject is constituted through norms which must be repeated over time, and because it is therefore never fully and finally constituted, it becomes the site of a permanent instability and 'resignifiability', able to be endlessly constituted anew. For Butler all norms are 'haunted by their own inefficacy' and try anxiously to 'install and augment their jurisdiction' (1993: 237); however, it is also this very weakness that opens up the possibility of their re-articulation and transformation, a process with an uncertain outcome, which may or may not be subversive.

In *Getting Personal* Nancy Miller's response to those same anxieties about the subject and its agency is to try to find a different place from which to write, one which uses the wager of 'a limited personalism' to interrogate theory or 'turn it back on itself' (1991: xiv). In an earlier essay, 'Changing the Subject: Authorship, Writing and the Reader', Miller had complained about the 'self-censorship' which seemed to be the outcome of both theories of the subject and gender identity in the 1980s. Her own point of critical intervention was to attempt to claim for women a different historical relation to the 'I':

The postmodernist decision that the Author is Dead and the subject along with him does not, I will argue, necessarily hold for women, and prematurely forecloses the question of agency for them. Because women have not had the same historical relation of identity to origin, institution, production that men have had, they have not, I think (collectively) felt burdened by too much Self, Ego, Cogito, etc. (Miller, 1988: 106)

The problem, however, with any attempt on the part of women – or other disenfranchised groups – to instate themselves in the position of the subject and claim the right to speak for themselves, is that they could do so only by excluding others, by reproducing the same model of subjecthood they were contesting. 'Speaking as' emerged, as Miller acknowledges, as 'an equally problematic form of representativity', even as it, through multiplying differences, challenged the assumption of a universal subject who could speak for all (1991: 20). In a later book, *But Enough about Me*, Miller returns to a moment of crisis within feminism, which she dates to the mid eighties, when 'women of colour refused a definition of feminism that by the whiteness of its universal subject did not include them' (Miller, 2002: 42). Feminism at this time encountered the problem that there was no unified constituency of 'women' and every attempt to clarify one produced disunity, an internal contestation by groups who felt themselves to be marginalised. If personal criticism is Miller's attempt to ground her critical authority in something less contentious, because more personal, than her representative status within feminist theory, she is still haunted by the problem of community, by the question of who she is writing for. 'How can I propose a reflection about an ethics in criticism (an ethics requires a community) from these individualistic grounds?' (Miller, 1991: xiv). Her writing takes the risk that it simply *will* matter to others (1991: 24). In *But Enough about Me* she attempts to relegate feminist theory to a prior moment within her career, looking to 'new generations' to address the problem of the 'new commonalities among women' in a 'postfeminist age'. Through this autobiographical genre she imagines herself addressing a different, less specialised audience (Miller, 2002: 66, 2). However, questions about what those commonalities might be and who her audience is refuse to go away. Indeed they become, as Miller proposes it, the motivating force behind memoir writing: 'Memoir is the record of an experience in search of a community, of a collective framework in which to protect the fragility of singularity in the postmodern world' (2002: 14).

Going back to the earlier *Getting Personal*, we can see that, despite the fact that Miller sets her performance at a critical distance from postmodern theories of the subject, and looks to the personal to provide a different mode of situatedness and embodiment, her writing is profoundly performative in that it replays different discursive and theoretical positions. 'I became a feminist critic along with a certain history' she writes in *But Enough about Me* (2002: 42). The history that she writes is not linear but instead one where different discourses overlap, producing unpredictable conjunctions of meaning. In the 'Preface' to *Getting Personal*, Miller comments on the importance of metaphor in her own work as a figure displaying the movement of meaning round an absent centre, creating new combinations in order 'to imagine in the material of language what has not yet come' (Miller, 1991: xii). Though Miller announces that her book is about 'personal criticism', her critical position is best described as a process of bringing prior critical discourses into new combinations, reading her 'self' within their contours and their omissions.

In the first chapter of *Getting Personal* what this means is putting Jane Tompkins' essay 'Me and My Shadow' alongside Roland Barthes, or rather, inserting into the middle of her essay an 'intermezzo' or interlude about Barthes, which seems, in a formal sense too, to disturb the boundaries between the two critics. Initially, Tompkins' essay is presented as a manifesto for personal criticism, which has, through its risk-taking, 'electrified' Miller (Miller, 1991: 4). Her difference from Tompkins is in their relation to theory, and the excursion into the writing of Roland Barthes is a means of negotiating this difference. The critic who famously wrote that 'the author is dead' is also the writer who initiated feminist critics – Miller cites Jane Gallop here – into a more subjective mode:

Despite his polemic against the 'person' and celebration of the empty 'subject' of language, Barthes modelled the possibility of personal criticism through his own extremely sophisticated manipulation of theoretical discourse, which not only made visible the traces of a writing body, but imposed the manners of a strongly biographized – biographemized – rhetorical *personality*. (Miller, 1991: 9)

If, for Miller, Gallop, through reference to Barthes, provides one turn of the screw towards theory, this is challenged by Barbara Christian who turns the argument back to the 'reality', including race, that Barthes' 'metaphysical' language fails to address. For Miller the question of 'whether theory can be personalized and the personal theorized'

(1991: 21), is not one that can be resolved. Rather it is an 'unfolding phenomenon' (1991: 19), which leads her, as a writer, in different directions. She, as writer, is at the place where these different discourses converge, where their relations to each other can be rehearsed, re-played, to create new possibilities of writing. A conclusion may seem to be emerging, therefore, that personal criticism offers no way out of the problems of critical discourse and the fate of the subject always to be 'defaced' by language, as Paul de Man argued in relation to autobiography (de Man, 1979: 919–30).[3] It may seem from this, too, that every critical performance will always inevitably become yet another form of the performative.

For Miller, though, there is something else, something she experiences in relation to Tompkins' text that will not 'go away' (1991: 7), a residue that she associates with embarrassment. Tompkins famously challenges critical propriety in the essay by referring to her need to go to the bathroom. The problem she introduces is one of the relation between 'myself' as a subject within critical debate and 'just myself as a person sitting here in stockinged feet, a little chilly because the windows are open, and thinking about going to the bathroom. But not going yet' (Tompkins, 1993: 28). Miller finds that for her students the discomfort or embarrassment which the essay produces in them has to do with Tompkins' seeming disparagement of the very critical authority they are working to acquire in their own writing. Tompkins is ceding power by representing herself in this way; she is undermining her own critical credibility (Miller, 1991: 28). Miller herself speculates about Tompkins' anger. Having been made to feel embarrassed for introducing a personal voice into a professional context, and realising that 'the public–private dichotomy' is a 'hierarchy', and 'a founding condition of female oppression', Tompkins' response is to say 'to hell with it' (Tompkins, 1993: 25). In the flagrant exposure of 'wanting to go to the bathroom' Tompkins exposes herself twice over, drawing attention to her physicality – her bodily functions – *and* letting her feelings show. ' "She" is making a spectacle of herself. "She," as has often been said of me, is "being emotional".' This leads Miller to her ongoing anxiety about personal criticism: 'Is the personal critic necessarily alone, immured in isolation?' (Miller, 1991: 23). The connection between these points, however, is not altogether clear. If one part of the anxiety or feelings of discomfort which Miller names 'embarrassment' has to do with being looked at, it seems the other is about not being seen at all.

Eve Kosofsky Sedgwick, drawing on the work of recent psychologists on shame, has suggested that this important affect has much to do with the complexity of the relationship between self and other, identity and sociability. Shame, according to the developmental model she draws on, arises very early in the infant's life when the mother or caregiver refuses to play her part in a mutual, mirroring gaze. Sedgwick quotes the psychologist Michael Franz Basch: 'The shame-humiliation response, when it appears, represents the failure or absence of the smile of contact, a reaction to the loss of feedback from others, indicating social isolation and signalling the need for relief from that condition' (2003: 36). The characteristic expressions of shame, the averted gaze or downwards look are, as the psychologist Silvan Tomkins suggests, ambiguous. The wish to look and be looked at continues even as one looks away; as, for example, when a child 'covers his face in the presence of strangers' only to peek through his fingers 'so that he may look without being seen' (Tomkins, 1995: 134). For Sedgwick, shame is not to do with repression so much as with a desire to communicate: it indicates both a break in the circuit of communication and 'a desire to reconstitute the interpersonal bridge' (2003: 36). Shame could be seen, therefore, as poised at a threshold, looking both ways, towards a painful individualism, and towards the pleasure of connection. Sedgwick sees it as the necessary 'lining' of self-display or exhibitionism; the risk of performance is that the regard that is sought will be refused (2003: 38). Indeed it is possible to see shame itself as a kind of performance – the person experiencing shame displays signs which make them supremely visible. What shame performs is the 'question of identity' and the grounds of connection with others. This performance, which is bound up with 'spectacle', seems difficult to recuperate under performativity and maybe gives us a way to go beyond it. In *But Enough about Me*, Miller writes: 'As always, it's in the private stories behind the public statements, as much as in the collective pronouncements and manifestos, that the history of feminism continues to remain – however embarrassingly – alive' (2002: 67). The embarrassment Miller refers to has to do with youthful sexual incidents which seem incompatible with mature feminist insight, and yet help to summon up the world out of which seventies feminism emerged. However, this embarrassment could also be seen as the very condition of feminism's 'life', of a community posited on the possibility of connection. In *Getting Personal* Miller describes seventies feminism in terms of a *possibility*, a sense that there *might be* in some indeterminate future time 'enough feminist teachers out there to collaborate – as opposed to lonely brave souls in hostile environments' (1991: 16). Just as the individual comes into being tremulously on that threshold of recognition, so too does the community. The move from 'I' to 'we', which Miller argues is at the basis of feminism, ultimately means that neither historically can be fixed in their place, but must be permanently open to the risk of new and different recognitions (1991: 16)

For Miller the 'point' of her encounter with Tompkins' essay is reached in *Getting Personal* when she makes the connection between 'showing and anger', the 'spectacle' of gender and the angry refusal of feminine invisibility on Tompkins' part (1991: 22–3). However, the spectre of a vulnerability which is not fully acknowledged surely inhabits both. In a chapter entitled 'The Marks of Time' in *But Enough about Me* Miller explores the problem of appearance and ageing, of how one goes on recognising oneself over time. The cultural narrative which is offered to women is a process of decline in one's appearance from some 'youthful moment', a high point of sexual attractiveness; the challenge of ageing is to construct a different narrative through which the facial and bodily signs can be read 'otherwise' (Miller, 2002: 88). For Miller the narrative that emerges is one of expanding recognitions. Having reached the age her mother was in a family photograph, she confronts for the first time how she may be like her (2002: 78). Increasingly those who are thought of as old, different, beyond recognition, come to inhabit one. The culminating recognition is of a changing relation with death: 'It's only in one's sixties, I think, that it becomes possible to see the anxiety about appearance that often haunts one's fifties as a way of displacing or postponing – the crisis of mortality. Far easier to obsess about the signs of ageing . . . than reflect upon death' (2002: 108). Death offers the ultimate commonality but also, of course, marks a limit to identification. Miller notes in *Bequest and Betrayal: Memoirs of a Parent's Death*: 'The biography of the dying other is as much about what we can't know as what we do. In its final moments the declining parental body insists on the necessity of separation, on the limits of truth' (Miller, 1996: 53). Autobiography, as Miller points out, has often been seen as the history of a becoming. It has tended to emphasise the 'gain' which lies on the other side of loss, the ability of the child to reclaim their own story, to inscribe themselves into the space of the parental absence (1996: 54). Self-recognition becomes the positive outcome of a painful separation; a newly acquired autonomy propels the child into authorship. But does not this offer too simple an explanation of the role of the 'other' in autobiography? Do we not also learn through what Miller calls an 'ethics of disidentification' (2002: 120), through being able to identify across difference, through challenging the very limits of who we think we are?

HISTORY AND AUTOBIOGRAPHY

Carolyn Steedman's influential memoir *Landscape for a Good Woman*, which was written, like Miller's *Bequest and Betrayal*, in the aftermath of her mother's death, opens with the uncompromising scene of her dying which, though not witnessed by Steedman, is represented with a starkness that is intended to remove the screens and challenge the discourses of death:

> Like this: she flung up her left arm over her head, pulled her knees up, looked out with an extraordinary surprise. She lived alone, she died alone: a working-class life, a working-class death. (Steedman, 1986: 2)

It is important, of course, that this is a 'working-class death'. By inserting class difference into the place where it might seem to have lost its resonance, she insists on its unacknowledged significance everywhere. Taking her own life as material – a working-class childhood in the 1950s – Steedman explores a disjunction between the particularities of class and the dominant narratives that organise our understanding of childhood, gender and social class, the stories that structure both autobiography and history. The 'specificity of place and politics has to be reckoned with', she tells us, 'in making an account of anybody's life, and their use of their own past' (1986: 6). Her memoir therefore addresses an absence and rebuts too easy an assumption of similarity between women's lives.

For Steedman, using her memories means coming upon the resistances produced by experiences which cannot be easily translated into 'neutral' metaphors. Steedman draws attention to the way, for instance, the psychoanalytic case study is supported by images which it does not recognise as deeply embedded in class – a jewel-case, a pair of pearl earrings, a nursemaid – and questions whether this same structure could contain 'the stuff of the world outside the gate in this way: streets, food, work, dirt' (1986: 77). One moment from her own childhood works powerfully to illustrate this, challenging Sigmund Freud's psychoanalytic model of the father's symbolic power. Steedman remembers her father picking bluebells and then being caught and humiliated by the forest keeper. What difference does it make, she asks, when the father's 'position in a household is not supported by recognition of social status and power outside it' (1986: 72). How is it possible to derive an account of human culture, as Freud does, from the position and role of the father, when he can be rendered vulnerable in social terms, shamed in the eyes of a child?

For Steedman, writing autobiographically is not an end in itself. The personal has a 'use' historically. It provides particular material images through which social reality can be interrogated (Probyn, 1993: 105), and it is historical understanding which gives value to the writing. In a later essay about *Landscape for a Good Woman*, Steedman writes: 'I am very eager to tell readers, close to the beginning of the book, that what they are about to read is not history. At the end, I want those readers to say that what I have produced is history; which would please me much more than anything else' (Steedman, 1992: 45). The question of what constitutes history, of course, is not easily answered and it is also one of the functions of Steedman's writing to argue that most historical narratives are maintained by marginalising others and that the truths of history are complex and incomplete, always open to new evidence and interpretations. For Steedman, this marks the major difference between autobiography and history: autobiography ends in the figure of the writer doing the telling; it is a '*confirmation* of that self that stands there telling the story' (1992: 49). History, on the other hand, gives her the chance of finding other narratives, of rescuing herself from the 'bleak knowledge' of what happened to her. It is history, also, which offers the possibility of community, a common mode of cognition, a shared sense of historicity, if not of history (1992: 49–50).

At one point in this essay Steedman asks the question 'what am I hiding through my use of history?' (1992: 44). In Miller's reading of *Landscape for a Good Woman* she finds it hard, despite Steedman's warnings against it, and despite the obvious differences between them, not to find resemblances with her own life and relationship with her mother, not to read, in some sense, 'with her' (Miller, 1996: 62). What does history deny? What does class conceal? The repudiation of likeness, the need for separation fuels Steedman's narrative and explains why she offers an account of autobiography solely in terms of autonomy and individuation, without reference to the role of others in the constitution of the story. Yet, returning to the first memorable scene of the memoir and the description of the mother's dying, it is possible, as Miller argues, to see class itself being used as a screen, depriving Steedman of the ability to see the resemblances between Beauvoir's description of her mother's dying and her own (Beauvoir, 1969: 83). For Miller the body in pain brings exposure to the witness as well. 'In the end, what we retain is less the fact that class markers divide bodies – the screen that blocks the gaze of the dying poor – than the fact that bodies demand our attention' (Miller, 1996: 92). What is also screened or partitioned, Miller suggests, is the daughter's 'rage of longing at work in her own project', her own anger and vulnerability (1996: 92). If history is Steedman's salvation – it gives her another professional identity – it also subsumes personal vulnerability into a form of more abstract knowledge. It is history which can then be allowed to have the characteristics of openness and vulnerability, and within whose terms a sense of community can emerge.

Steedman has offered an important account of how the personal can function as an interpretive device which can provide new understandings of cultural narratives. She has also offered an autobiographical speaking position in her memoir which seems to bypass many of the thorny problems of subjecthood (Anderson, 2001: 110–11). However, by making history as a form of knowledge provide an overarching rationale for her writing, the particular meaning – or ethical weighting – of the personal gets lost. Why does it matter? For Miller personal criticism, partly also a rhetorical style, is a way of participating in an ongoing discussion about what the subject is and how we imagine our relation to others, about writing and the kinds of recognitions it allows. Though it goes well beyond the scope of this chapter, it is interesting to ponder how the recognition of vulnerability in ourselves may be the best way of expanding our recognition of others. Which lives are 'grievable', Judith Butler has asked recently. Which do we refuse to count as worthy of mourning? (Butler, 2004: 32). Her question asks us to acknowledge how important it is to open ourselves up to loss and mourning, to understand our exposure to each other, our interdependence. She suggests in the most serious and disturbing fashion how dangerous it may be for ourselves, but also for our politics, to deny our own vulnerability, our violability to each other.

NOTES

1. See Eve Sedgwick's plea for a wider exploration of critical approaches and for an 'ecology of knowing' (1997).
2. See also Jon McKenzie's illuminating essay (1998: 217–35).
3. De Man believed that autobiography enacted a linguistic dilemma, since writing about the self will also be a form of displacement of the self. An author calls attention to his face, his reflection, but he can do so only through personification, through using figurative language. The autobiographical subject is disfigured or 'defaced' by tropes. See Anderson (2001: 12–13).

BIBLIOGRAPHY

Anderson, Linda (2001), *Autobiography*, London: Routledge.
Ascher, Carol, Louise DeSalvo and Sara Ruddick (eds) (1984), *Between Women*, Boston: Beacon Books.
Austin, J. L. (1976), *How to Do Things with Words*, Oxford: Oxford University Press.

Basch, Michael Franz (1976), 'The Concept of Affect: A Re-Examination', in *Journal of the American Psychoanalytic Association* 24.

Beauvoir, Simone de (1969), *A Very Easy Death*, Harmondsworth: Penguin.

Butler, Judith (1990), *Gender Trouble: Feminism and the Subversion of Identity*, New York and London: Routledge.

(1992), 'Contingent Foundations: Feminism and the Question of "Postmodernism"', in *Feminists Theorize the Political*, ed. Judith Butler and Joan W. Scott, New York: Routledge.

(1993), *Bodies That Matter: On the Discursive Limits of 'Sex'*, New York: Routledge.

(2004), *Precarious Life: The Powers of Mourning and Violence*, London and New York: Verso.

Caws, Mary Ann (1990), *Women of Bloomsbury*, London: Routledge.

Cixous, Hélène and Catherine Clément (1975/1986), *The Newly Born Woman*, trans. Betsy Wing, Minneapolis: University of Minnesota Press.

de Man, Paul (1979), 'Autobiography as De-Facement', in *Modern Language Notes* 94.

Derrida, Jacques (1982), 'Signature Event Context', in *Margins of Philosophy*, trans. Alan Bass, Chicago: Chicago University Press.

Du Plessis, Rachel Blau (1986), 'For the Etruscans', revised version published in *The New Feminist Criticism*, ed. Elaine Showalter, London: Virago.

Forum (1996), in *PMLA* 111.

Freedman, Diane P., Olivia Frey and Frances Murphy Zauhar (eds) (1993), *The Intimate Critique: Autobiographical Literary Criticism*, Durham, NC: Duke University Press.

Gallop, Jane (1988), *Thinking through the Body*, New York: Columbia University Press.

Kristeva, Julia (2002), *Intimate Revolt: The Powers and Limits of Psychoanalysis*, trans. Jeanine Herman, New York: Columbia University Press.

McKenzie, Jon (1998), 'Genre Trouble: (The) Butler Did It', in *The Ends of Performance*, ed. Peggy Phelan and Jill Lane, New York: New York University Press.

Miller, Nancy (1988), *Subject to Change: Reading Feminist Writing*, New York: Columbia University Press.

(1991), *Getting Personal: Feminist Occasions and Other Autobiographical Acts*, London and New York: Routledge.

(1996), *Bequest and Betrayal: Memoirs of a Parent's Death*, Oxford: Oxford University Press.

(2002), *But Enough about Me: Why We Read Other People's Lives*, New York: Columbia University Press.

Moi, Toril (1985), *Sexual/Textual Politics: Feminist Literary Theory*, London: Methuen.

Probyn, Elspeth (1993), *Sexing the Self: Gendered Positions in Cultural Studies*, London and New York: Routledge.

Rich, Adrienne (1980), *On Lies, Secrets and Silence: Selected Prose 1966–1970*, London: Virago.

Sedgwick, Eve Kosofsky (1997), 'Paranoid Reading and Reparative Reading', in *Novel Gazing: Queer Readings in Fiction*, Durham, NC: Duke University Press.

(2003), *Touching Feeling: Affect, Pedagogy, Performativity*, Durham, NC: Duke University Press.

Showalter, Elaine (1977), *A Literature of Their Own: British Women Novelists from Brontë to Lessing*, London: Virago.

Steedman, Carolyn (1986), *Landscape for a Good Woman*, London: Virago.

(1992), *Past Tenses: Essays on Writing, Autobiography and History*, London: Rivers Oram Press.

Tomkins, Silvan (1995), *Shame and Its Sisters: A Silvan Tomkins Reader*, ed. Eve Kosofsky Sedgwick and Adam Frank, Durham, NC: Duke University Press.

Tompkins, Jane (1993), 'Me and My Shadow', in *The Intimate Critique: Autobiographical Literary Criticism*, ed. Diane P. Freedman, Olivia Frey and Frances Murphy Zauhar, Durham, NC: Duke University Press.

CHAPTER 9

Black feminist criticism

Arlene R. Keizer

What is generally understood to be black feminist criticism is a body of critical and creative work written by women of African descent in the United States. While black feminisms have arisen in other sites of the African diaspora, for example, in Europe and Latin America, the United States has been the site of the most sustained black feminist critical discourse. Contemporary black feminist criticism came into being in the late 1960s and early 1970s, fostered by the Civil Rights Movement and developed in conjunction with the Second Wave of American feminism, which was dominated by white women, and the Black Power and Black Arts movements, which were dominated by black men.[1] Late twentieth-century black feminist critics and writers, like their white counterparts, have been invested in the connections between their present-day analyses and those of their foremothers in the eighteenth and nineteenth centuries; in other words, establishing a sense of continuity between black women's struggles and critical approaches to literature and culture in previous eras and in the present has been a foundational concern. Furthermore, a major thematic and structural element of black feminist criticism, from its roots in the era of slavery to the present, has been its simultaneous attention to multiple oppressions and multiple categories of analysis. From Frances Beale's concept of 'double jeopardy' (1970) – the conjoined effects of racial and gender discrimination – to Kimberlé Crenshaw's 'intersectionality' (1989/2000) – a more complex model of the ways in which black women function as a nexus at which several forms of discrimination work together – black feminist critics have articulated the layered effects of racism and sexism.[2]

This chapter traces the history of black feminist literary criticism through the concepts articulated by its most important exponents. African American women fiction writers, dramatists and poets have been essential to the development of the field. These creative writers themselves have written critical essays establishing key concepts, and their fictional work has provided the ground for literary critics' articulation of black feminist theoretical approaches. The year 1970 was a high-water mark in the publication history of African American women's critical and creative work. Toni Morrison's novel *The Bluest Eye*, Alice Walker's novel *The Third Life of Grange Copeland*, Maya Angelou's memoir *I Know Why the Caged Bird Sings* and Toni Cade's anthology *The Black Woman* were all published in this year. Each of these texts highlights the obstacles to freedom for African American women, focusing in many cases on black men's physical and psychological oppression of black women in the context of white-supremacist domination of all black people. Some of the major issues established in this fiction and these collected essays are the need for sexual self-determination and economic empowerment, the struggle against the psychic pain of racism and sexism, the possibility of coalition across the lines of race, gender, sexual orientation and class, and black women's passionate and persistent strategies of self-formation, self-recovery and self-expression.

THEORISING BLACK FEMINIST CRITICISM

As both fiction writer and essayist, Alice Walker has been an extremely important figure in black feminist literary criticism. Her essays 'In Search of Our Mothers' Gardens', originally published in *Ms.* magazine in 1974, and 'Looking for Zora', published in *Ms.* the following year, enjoined women to recognise the everyday creativity of their female ancestors as artistic creation and modelled a method for recovering the work of previous generations of black women writers. In 'Saving the Life That Is Your Own: The Importance of Models in the Artist's Life' (1976), Walker describes her 'desperate need to know and assimilate the experience of earlier black women writers, most of them unheard of by you and me, until quite recently' (Walker, 1983: 9) and demonstrates how finding Zora Neale Hurston's work validated her own choice of a writer's life. In conjunction with her later coinage of the term 'womanism' to distinguish black feminism from white feminism, Walker's critical insights could well be dubbed a 'vernacular theory' of African American women's cultural production.[3]

The Combahee River Collective's 'A Black Feminist Statement' and Barbara Smith's 'Toward a Black Feminist Criticism' both date from 1977 and were the first attempts to theorise systematically the issues delineated above. Though not focused specifically on literary analysis, The Combahee River Collective's 'Statement' functioned as an empowering manifesto for black feminist literary critics. Simultaneously a brief history of black feminism, a collective self-definition and a call for action, the 'Statement' was evidence of the public, political existence of a black feminist standpoint. Smith's 'Toward a Black Feminist Criticism' linked the general concerns of black feminism with the work of literary criticism for the first time. Smith begins with an acknowledgement of the radical, original nature of her enterprise:

> I do not know where to begin. Long before I tried to write this I realized that I was attempting something unprecedented, something dangerous merely by writing about Black women writers from a feminist perspective and about Black lesbian writers from any perspective at all. These things have not been done. (Smith, 1977/1982: 157)

Excoriating racist white male and white feminist critics and sexist black male critics, Smith traces the denigration and exclusion of black women's fiction, poetry and drama in American literary critical discourse. She then proceeds to delineate two principles that might distinguish a black feminist approach to literature: first, the critic's assumption that black women's writing in the US constitutes a literary tradition, 'that thematically, stylistically, aesthetically, and conceptually Black women writers manifest common approaches to the act of creating literature as a direct result of the specific political, social, and economic experience they have been obliged to share' (1977/1982: 164). The second guiding principle for black feminist critics 'would be for the critic to look first for precedents and insights in interpretation within the works of other Black women. In other words she would think and write out of her own identity and not try to graft the ideas or methodology of white/male literary thought upon the precious materials of Black women's art' (1977/1982: 164). Though these principles may seem simple, they have been hotly contested in debates between black feminist critics and within African American literary critical circles more generally; I outline the major strands of this debate below.

Deborah McDowell's 1980 essay, 'New Directions for Black Feminist Criticism', was a direct response to Barbara Smith's article and the conversations that it engendered. While Smith assumes that the black woman critic will choose to write about black women's literary output, McDowell questions this assumption, noting that, while she uses the term 'black feminist criticism' in much the same way that Smith does, she leaves open the possibility that black women critics might choose to analyse a variety of literary works, not only those written by women of African descent. One problem raised by McDowell's formulation in this essay is that she seems to assume that black women's approaches to their chosen subject matter would be inherently progressive, since she argues that 'the term [black feminist criticism] can also apply to any criticism written by a Black woman regardless of her subject or perspective' (McDowell, 1980/ 1994: 433). Nevertheless, McDowell's essay further enriched the development of black feminist criticism by calling for greater definitional and methodological rigor, by emphasising the need for critics to be widely knowledgeable about African American literature, and by questioning the degree to which black feminist criticism could effect political change. On this final point, McDowell clearly wants to retain some sense of hope in the interaction between political activism and feminist literary criticism, but she injects an important cautionary note into a discourse that assumes the mutually beneficial relationship between these two enterprises, asking:

What ideas, specifically, would Black feminist criticism contribute to the [Black feminist] movement? Further, even though the proposition of a fruitful relationship between political activism and the academy is an interesting (and necessary) one, I doubt its feasibility. I am not sure that either in theory or in practice Black feminist [literary] criticism will be able to alter significantly circumstances that have led to the oppression of Black women. (1980/1994: 433)

McDowell's questioning of the automatic link between black feminist theory and political activism undeniably marked a turning point in the history of the field, the point at which many of its major practitioners began to investigate some of the enterprise's most significant founding assumptions, as black feminist criticism became more established as an area of academic enquiry.

Barbara Christian's *Black Women Novelists: The Development of a Tradition* (1980) was another landmark, the first full-length critical work to posit the existence of an African American women's literary tradition. In this book, Christian enacts a black feminist criticism of the kind envisioned by Smith. After a first section in which she traces the early history of American literary and cultural stereotypes of black women and demonstrates the ways in which nineteenth-century African American writers responded to these stereotypes, Christian goes on to explicate the ways in which Paule Marshall, Toni Morrison and Alice Walker have created characters through which to explore imaginatively the challenges faced by African American and Caribbean American women, both historically and in the present. *Black Women Novelists* set a high standard for the critical works to follow, with its simultaneous attention to craft and to socio-economic and political contexts. Like Smith, Christian directly addresses the disturbing precedent in which black women's literary texts are treated sociologically, in other words, as transparent examples of the conditions of black women's lives. Christian's consistent attention to literary technique serves as a corrective to this tendency.

Black Women Novelists and Christian's subsequent collection of essays *Black Feminist Criticism: Perspectives on Black Women Writers* (1985) both inspired and were challenged by later works of black feminist literary analysis. Hazel Carby's *Reconstructing Womanhood: The Emergence of the Afro-American Woman Novelist* (1987) is a case in point. Carby uses her introduction to critique the major existing statements on the nature of black feminist criticism – those of Smith, McDowell and Christian – and to assert her own materialist approach to nineteenth- and early twentieth-century black women's narratives and novels. One of Carby's most useful interventions is her critique of the notion that the body of work by African American women writers necessarily constituted a 'tradition'. *Reconstructing Womanhood* called attention to 'the theoretical and historical questions raised by the construction of a tradition of black women['s] writing' (Carby, 1987: 14).

Hortense Spillers, Claudia Tate, Mae Henderson, Nellie McKay, bell hooks, Audre Lorde, Valerie Smith, Frances Smith Foster, Carole Boyce Davies, Mary Helen Washington and others further expanded the field in several different directions, exploring, amongst other issues, sexuality, intergenerational co-operation and conflict, the continuing influence of African culture upon African American literature and the turn towards African-diaspora studies. These developments are outlined below.

In an extraordinary series of essays published in the 1980s and 90s (and now collected in the volume *Black, White, and in Color: Essays on American Literature and Culture*), Hortense Spillers initiated an enquiry into the relationship between psychoanalysis and African American literature and culture. From a black feminist perspective, in notoriously challenging but always rewarding prose, Spillers has sought to determine whether Freudian and Lacanian theories can legitimately and usefully be applied to African American texts and contexts and to explore the results of juxtaposing psychoanalytic theory with black literature and culture. 'Mama's Baby, Papa's Maybe: An American Grammar Book', ' "The Permanent Obliquity of an In(pha)llibly Straight": In the Time of the Daughters and the Fathers' and ' "All the Things You Could Be by Now, if Sigmund Freud's Wife Was Your Mother": Psychoanalysis and Race' are her best-known and most influential essays. Spillers' conclusions – for example, that psychoanalytic theory may apply only by accident to African American literature and culture, because of the ways in which

American slavery ruptured the African American family, and that the traumatic marks on the body of the slave constitute 'an American grammar' (Spillers, 1987/2003: 209) that is transferred across generations within African American culture – are both generative and contested. More than any other theorist, Spillers has succeeded in bringing the issues central to psychoanalytic thought and critical race studies into productive tension with one another.

A number of other critics have taken up the challenge posed by Spillers' work and produced psychoanalytic readings of African American literary texts (for example, Claudia Tate, *Psychoanalysis and Black Novels: Desire and the Protocols of Race*, and Mae Henderson, 'Toni Morrison's *Beloved*: Re-Membering the Body as Historical Text', the most convincing of the many psychoanalytic readings of *Beloved*). Asian Americanist critics such as Anne Cheng and Sarita See have also clearly drawn upon Spillers' groundbreaking essays in their analyses of psychoanalysis and multi-ethnic literatures.[4]

The remarkably prolific bell hooks (Gloria Watkins) has been one of the great popularisers of black feminist theory and criticism. Reaching out to audiences within and outside the academy, hooks, in her many books, has often been the first black feminist theorist to articulate a problem of significance to black feminists as a group. For example, 'Reconstructing Black Masculinity', which appeared in *Black Looks: Race and Representation* (1992), uses the unconventional black men hooks remembers from her childhood to argue for the alternatives to patriarchal masculinity already embedded within African American culture. While black feminist criticism has always included a critique of patriarchy, few have articulated in theoretical terms the ways in which black men have diverged from the model presented by white patriarchal culture and might do so more deliberately in the future. Though not a literary critic, hooks has written about African American literature in illuminating ways, and her writing on film and popular culture has made a substantial contribution to these fields.

In addition to her poetry and her experimental autobiography (her 'biomythography', as she calls it), Audre Lorde has contributed groundbreaking essays to the enterprise of black feminist criticism. 'The Master's Tools Will Never Dismantle the Master's House', 'Poetry Is Not Luxury' and 'Uses of the Erotic: The Erotic as Power' are three of the most influential of her critical works. Lorde argues powerfully for the critical value of difference in anti-racist, anti-sexist and anti-heterosexist struggles. With Barbara Smith, Lorde was one of the most articulate advocates for solidarity between straight and lesbian feminists. More recently, Evelyn

Hammonds, in 'Black (W)holes and the Geometry of Black Female Sexuality' (1994/2002), has utilised queer theory to approach the issue of black women's sexual identities across the spectrum. Hammonds argues for a 'politics of articulation', a project of identifying 'what makes it possible for Black women to speak and to act' (Hammonds, 1994/2002: 316). By making visible the fact that the silence surrounding black female sexuality within African American culture is not simply a void but an absence that is being actively produced, Hammonds shifts the discourse in a richly suggestive way. These black feminist critics have been central to the project of reclaiming black female sexuality from its distortion either by denigrating stereotypes or by the code of respectability traditionally imposed by African American middle-class culture.

The work of Sylvia Wynter and Carole Boyce Davies has been profoundly important in extending the diasporic reach of black feminist criticism. Their focus on literary representations of women of African descent in the Caribbean and women whose identities are constructed through travel between the US, the Caribbean and the European metropoles has helped to create African-diaspora studies, one of the main strands of black literary and cultural criticism today. While Paul Gilroy's masculinist paradigm of the 'Black Atlantic' is the model often privileged within the field, Wynter, Davies and other black feminist critics have insisted upon the necessity and, indeed, the transformative power of viewing the African diaspora through the lens of gender and the experiences and literary works of women.

An overview of black feminist criticism would not be complete without a mention of our 'fellow travellers' – black feminist critics who are not black women. Some of the most significant figures in this group are Barbara Johnson, Michael Awkward, and more recently Madhu Dubey and Kevin Everod Quashie; over the past twenty-five years, these critics and several others have made major contributions to black feminist theory. One of the debates in this field has been whether or not one needs to inhabit a black female body in order to express a black feminist perspective. On the one hand, the emergence of black feminist critiques from those socially positioned elsewhere is a very positive development, indicating the powerful influence of black feminist literary and cultural criticism on the academy at large. On the other hand, while critical essays on the combined effects of race, gender and class abound, the number of critics articulating black feminist positions remains small.

Black feminist critics' bold articulations of their standpoints have provoked firestorms of criticism at key moments in the development of

African American literary criticism. In the late 1980s and early 90s, for example, a fierce debate ensued over the use of poststructuralist theory in African American literary criticism. Though gender was not the main issue in this debate, the opposing forces broke down along gendered lines. Barbara Christian's 'The Race for Theory' (1987) was the opening salvo in this battle, followed by essays by Joyce A. Joyce, Henry Louis Gates Jr, Houston Baker and Michael Awkward.[5] Christian argued that poststructuralist theory had taken over the world of literary criticism, and that this new definition and elevation of theory within the discipline was having a negative effect on African American literary critics and criticism, displacing methods of reading derived from within black literature and culture. Joyce went further, accusing critics like Gates and Baker of denying 'blackness or race as an important element of literary analysis of Black literature' (Joyce, 1987a/2000: 292) and 'adopt[ing] a linguistic system and an accompanying world view that communicate to a small, isolated audience' (1987a/2000: 294). Gates', Baker's and Awkward's replies were varied, but in essence they asserted the value of applying a range of critical perspectives to African American literary texts and argued that 'Afro-American critical engagement of literary theory . . . has indeed deepened our received knowledge of the textual production of black writers' (Awkward, 1988/2000: 332).

In retrospect, one can read this controversy as a fight to determine how African American literary studies would be institutionalised in historically white colleges and universities. Though established in the late nineteenth century by figures such as W. E. B. Du Bois, Martin Delany, Anna Julia Cooper and Frances E. W. Harper, African American Studies was not recognised as a legitimate field of academic enquiry by white colleges and universities until the student strikes of the late 1960s and early 1970s forced many campuses to acknowledge their problematic exclusion of black intellectual traditions and contributions. The major participants in the debate over 'theory' and African American literature were, for the most part, the first generation of black academicians on their respective campuses. (As late as 1980, Barbara Christian, for example, was the first black woman to achieve tenure at the University of California, Berkeley). The establishment of African American Studies programmes was influenced heavily by the cultural force of the Black Power and the Black Arts movements, but as these movements waned and were critiqued from within, many new questions about the field had to be answered. What critical models would (or should) be used to discuss African American literary texts? How was African American textual production different from the production of texts in other literary traditions? Was there (and should there be) an African American literary canon? If so, what was included? What excluded? Because so much American literary criticism ignored or denigrated African American writers and their works, how would it be possible to draw upon this literary critical tradition while critiquing its entrenched racism? In 1987, when Christian published 'The Race for Theory', none of these questions had been answered definitively, and many are still lively motors of ongoing debate. As Christian notes, the ascendancy of 'theory' in US academic circles was taking place at the moment that literatures by people of colour were finally being recognised in these same institutions of higher education. One major tenet of the Black Arts Movement – the idea that African American literature should be evaluated by methods and standards derived from African American culture – was now being challenged by the rise of largely European literary and critical theory in the new setting in which African American literary criticism found itself. As noted above, critics like Barbara Smith had clearly accepted this tenet and rearticulated it with reference to black feminist criticism. Other black feminist critics – Spillers, Henderson, Carby and Valerie Smith, to name a few – were far less hostile to European/Euro-American literary and critical theory, both utilising and critiquing this body of work in their books and essays. However, Gates and Baker were the two African American literary critics who, above others, came to be identified with the project of linking poststructuralist theory and African American literature and culture.

From the vantage point of the early twenty-first century, revisiting the debate over the theoretical models appropriate to African American literature is a painful process, one that mostly reveals how durable the discourse of black authenticity remained in the late 1980s. Joyce fundamentally questioned whether Gates, Baker and other black male critics embracing structuralism and poststructuralism were 'black enough'. Rather than focusing primarily on the appropriateness of European/Euro-American critical models as tools for analysing black literature, as Christian did, Joyce accused these black male critics of being self- and culture-hating. This history has had significant implications for perceptions of black feminist criticism. Far too often, black feminist criticism has been associated with essentialism and presumed to have an anti-theoretical bias. As this general discussion has shown, black feminist critics are no more likely than their counterparts in other areas of literary study to eschew engagement with contemporary literary and cultural theory. While some black feminist critics have engaged with European/Euro-American literary and critical theory, others, like the sociologist Patricia Hill Collins in her influential *Black Feminist Thought* (1990) have mined the traditions of

African American culture for their theoretical value. Still others have merged these two approaches. What has emerged in contemporary black literary criticism is an expanded array of options for analysing texts, and black feminist approaches have been critical to this development.

THE WORK OF RECOVERY

Thus far, this chapter has traced the theoretical trajectories of black feminist criticism. It is equally important to direct attention to the work of literary recovery and dissemination that has been essential to the development of the field. Like many areas of study that became institutionalised in mainstream colleges and universities in the 1970s (women's studies, cultural studies, ethnic studies), black feminist criticism has been established in large part through the publication of anthologies and book series. Deborah McDowell's series of novels by black women writers, published by Beacon Press, and Henry Louis Gates' Schomburg Library of Nineteenth-Century Black Women Writers were two of the most extensive and effective republication ventures, making available works that had fallen out of print years before. Gates' rediscovery and republication of *Our Nig* by Harriet Wilson and *The Bondwoman's Narrative* by Hannah Crafts were also significant events for black feminist criticism. Mary Helen Washington has been a prolific anthologiser of African American women's fiction. Her *Black-Eyed Susans: Classic Stories by and about Black Women* (1975) and *Midnight Birds: Stories by Contemporary Black Women Writers* (1980) were critical to the development of a wide readership for African American women's writing as black feminist criticism was coming into being. From classics like Gerda Lerner's 1972 volume *Black Women in White America* and Cherríe Moraga and Gloria Anzaldúa's 1981 collection *This Bridge Called My Back: Writings by Radical Women of Color* to *Recovering the Black Female Body: Self-Representations by African American Women*, edited by Michael Bennett and Vanessa Dickerson in 2001, anthologies have highlighted new directions in the field at each stage of its evolution.

The critical and creative work of the formidably successful Toni Morrison reflects the entire trajectory of black feminist theory. In her masterful use of Black English as a vernacular form through which one can see the values of African American culture at work and as a literary language, Morrison has employed the very best of the theory derived from the Black Arts Movement. More recently, Morrison's foray into a full-length literary critical argument – *Playing in the Dark* (1992) – demonstrates her engagement with contemporary theory of many kinds, as does her post-modernist novel *Jazz*. Her writing career, sustained over more than three decades, signals that, however threatened by erasure the work of black women writers remains, conditions now are better than they have ever been for black feminist writers and critics.

Overall, black feminist literary criticism as a field is characterised by the dynamic interplay between the work of literary recovery – work that was absolutely necessary to the establishment of the idea of a black women's literary and critical tradition – and the work of theorising black women's social positioning and literary representations of black female experience. In the aforementioned debates over the use of poststructuralist theory in African American literary criticism, the symbiotic relationship between the work of recovering and analysing lost texts and the work of theorising the tradition as a whole was often lost. Restoring the balance between these two essential aspects of the critical enterprise, as well as continuing to develop in new directions, is the task ahead of the new generation of black feminist critics.

NOTES

1. The Civil Rights Movement in the United States was the post-Second World War drive by African Americans (and supporters across the racial/ethnic spectrum) to end *de facto* and *de jure* segregation in all aspects of American life. One of the major victories in this battle was the landmark legal case *Brown v. Board of Education* (1954), in which an African American family sued the Topeka, Kansas Board of Education over school segregation. In their decision in this case, the US Supreme Court declared 'separate but equal' public facilities to be unconstitutional. The Civil Rights Movement, largely integrationist in its goals, was succeeded by the Black Power Movement, in which black activists argued that African Americans needed to organise amongst themselves in order to become truly liberated. The Black Arts Movement is often described as the cultural arm of the Black Power Movement. Writers and artists turned to black vernacular and popular culture – especially Black English, the blues, jazz and other forms of black music – as the source of a new black aesthetic.
2. See Beale (1970) and Crenshaw (1989/2000).
3. See Baker (1984).
4. See Cheng (2001) and See (2002).
5. See Joyce A. Joyce's 'The Black Canon: Reconstructing Black American Literary Criticism' (1987a) and Henry Louis Gates Jr and Houston A. Baker Jr's replies – ' "What's Love Got to Do With It": Critical Theory, Integrity, and the Black Idiom' (1987) and 'In Dubious Battle' (1987). Joyce responded to their responses in ' "Who the Cap Fit": Unconsciousness and Unconscionableness in the Criticism of Houston A. Baker, Jr. and Henry Louis Gates, Jr' (1987b).

Michael Awkward's 'Appropriative Gestures: Theory and Afro-American Literary Criticism' (1988) is largely a response to Christian's 'The Race for Theory' (1987). Finally, Joyce revisits this debate in 'The Problems with Silence and Exclusiveness in the African American Literary Community', published in 1993–4. The initial exchange between Joyce, Gates and Baker was published in *New Literary History* 18 (Winter 1987). All of these essays are reprinted in Winston Napier's essential collection *African American Literary Theory: A Reader* (2000).

BIBLIOGRAPHY

Abel, Elizabeth, Barbara Christian and Helene Moglen (eds) (1997), *Female Subjects in Black and White: Race, Psychoanalysis, Feminism*, Berkeley: University of California Press.

Awkward, Michael (1988/2000), 'Appropriative Gestures: Theory and Afro-American Literary Criticism,' reprinted in Napier (2000).

(1989), *Inspiriting Influences: Tradition, Revision and Afro-American Women's Novels*, New York: Columbia University Press.

(1995), *Negotiating Difference: Race, Gender, and the Politics of Positionality*, Chicago: University of Chicago Press.

Baker, Houston A., Jr (1984), *Blues, Ideology, and Afro-American Literature: A Vernacular Theory*, Chicago: University of Chicago Press.

(1987/2000), 'In Dubious Battle', reprinted in Napier (2000).

Beale, Frances (1970), 'Double Jeopardy: To Be Black and Female', in Cade (1970).

Bennett, Michael and Vanessa D. Dickerson (eds) (2001), *Recovering the Black Female Body: Self-Representations by African American Women*, New Brunswick, NJ: Rutgers University Press.

Bobo, Jacqueline (ed.) (2001), *Black Feminist Cultural Criticism*, Malden, MA: Blackwell.

Braxton, Joanne M. and Andrée Nicola McLaughlin (eds) (1990), *Wild Women in the Whirlwind: Afra-American Culture and the Contemporary Literary Renaissance*, New Brunswick, NJ: Rutgers University Press.

Cade, Toni (1970), *The Black Woman*, New York: Mentor–New American Library.

Carby, Hazel V. (1987), *Reconstructing Womanhood: The Emergence of the Afro-American Woman Novelist*, New York: Oxford University Press.

Cheng, Anne Anlin (2001), *The Melancholy of Race: Psychoanalysis, Assimilation, and Hidden Grief*, Oxford: Oxford University Press.

Christian, Barbara (1980), *Black Women Novelists: The Development of a Tradition, 1892–1976*, Westport, CT: Greenwood Press.

(1985), *Black Feminist Criticism: Perspectives on Black Women Writers*, New York: Pergamon.

(1987/1990), 'The Race for Theory', in *The Nature and Context of Minority Discourse*, ed. Abdul R. JanMohamed and David Lloyd, New York: Oxford University Press.

(1990), ' "Somebody Forgot to Tell Somebody Something": African-American Women's Historical Novels', in Braxton and McLaughlin (1990).

Collins, Patricia Hill (1990), *Black Feminist Thought: Knowledge, Consciousness, and the Politics of Empowerment*, London: HarperCollins Academic.

Combahee River Collective (1977/1981), 'A Black Feminist Statement', in Moraga and Anzaldúa (1981).

Crenshaw, Kimberlé (1989/2000), 'Demarginalizing the Intersection of Race and Sex: A Black Feminist Critique of Antidiscrimination Doctrine, Feminist Theory and Antiracist Politics', in James and Sharpley-Whiting (2000).

Davies, Carole Boyce (1994), *Black Women, Writing and Identity: Migrations of the Subject*, New York: Routledge.

Davis, Angela Y. (1981), *Women, Race and Class*, New York: Random House.

(1998), *Blues Legacies and Black Feminism: Gertrude 'Ma' Rainey, Bessie Smith, and Billie Holiday*, New York: Pantheon.

Dubey, Madhu (1994), *Black Women Novelists and the Nationalist Aesthetic*, Bloomington: Indiana University Press.

(2003), *Signs and Cities: Black Literary Postmodernism*, Chicago: University of Chicago Press.

duCille, Ann (1993), *The Coupling Convention: Sex, Text, and Tradition in Black Women's Fiction*, New York: Oxford University Press.

Foster, Frances Smith (1993), *Written by Herself: Literary Production by African American Women, 1746–1892*, Bloomington: Indiana University Press.

Gates, Henry Louis, Jr (1987/2000), ' "What's Love Got to Do With It": Critical Theory, Integrity, and the Black Idiom', reprinted in Napier (2000).

(ed.) (1990), *Reading Black, Reading Feminist: A Critical Anthology*, New York: Meridian–New American Library.

Giddings, Paula (1984), *When and Where I Enter: The Impact of Black Women on Race and Sex in America*, New York: William Morrow.

Gilroy, Paul (1993), *The Black Atlantic: Modernity and Double Consciousness*, Cambridge, MA: Harvard University Press.

Hammonds, Evelyn (1994/2002), 'Black (W)holes and the Geometry of Black Female Sexuality', reprinted in Wallace-Sanders (2002).

Henderson, Mae G. (1991), 'Toni Morrison's *Beloved*: Re-Membering the Body as Historical Text', in Spillers (1991).

hooks, bell (1984), *Feminist Theory: From Margin to Center*, Boston: South End Press.

(1989), *Talking Back: Thinking Feminist, Thinking Black*, Boston: South End Press.

(1992), *Black Looks: Race and Representation*, Boston: South End Press.

Hull, Gloria T., Patricia Bell Scott and Barbara Smith (eds) (1982), *All the Women Are White, All the Blacks Are Men, But Some of Us Are Brave*, Old Westbury, NY: The Feminist Press.

James, Joy and T. Denean Sharpley-Whiting (eds) (2000), *The Black Feminist Reader*, Malden, MA: Blackwell.

Johnson, Barbara (1998), *The Feminist Difference: Literature, Psychoanalysis, Race and Gender*, Cambridge, MA: Harvard University Press.

Joyce, Joyce A. (1987a/2000), 'The Black Canon: Reconstructing Black American Literary Criticism', reprinted in Napier (2000).

(1987b/2000), ' "Who the Cap Fit": Unconsciousness and Unconscionableness in the Criticism of Houston A. Baker, Jr. and Henry Louis Gates, Jr.', in Napier (2000).

(1993–4/2000), 'The Problems with Silence and Exclusiveness in the African American Literary Community', reprinted in Napier (2000).

Lerner, Gerda (ed.) (1972), *Black Women in White America: A Documentary History*, New York: Vintage-Random.

Lorde, Audre (1984), *Sister Outsider: Essays and Speeches*, Freedom, CA: The Crossing Press.

McDowell, Deborah (1980/1994), 'New Directions for Black Feminist Criticism', reprinted in *Within the Circle: An Anthology of African American Literary Criticism from the Harlem Renaissance to the Present*, ed. Angelyn Mitchell, Durham, NC: Duke University Press.

Moraga, Cherríe and Gloria Anzaldúa (eds) (1981), *This Bridge Called My Back: Writings by Radical Women of Color*, New York: Kitchen Table/Women of Color Press.

Morrison, Toni (1992), *Playing in the Dark: Whiteness and the Literary Imagination*, New York: Random House.

Napier, Winston (ed.) (2000), *African American Literary Theory: A Reader*, New York: New York University Press.

Peterson, Carla L. (1995), *'Doers of the Word': African American Women Speakers and Writers in the North (1830–1880)*, New York: Oxford University Press.

Quashie, Kevin Everod (2004), *Black Women, Identity, and Cultural Theory: (Un)becoming the Subject*, New Brunswick, NJ: Rutgers University Press.

Rose, Tricia (2003), *Longing to Tell: Black Women Talk about Sexuality and Intimacy*, New York: Picador.

See, Sarita (2002), ' "An Open Wound": Colonial Melancholia and Contemporary Filipino American Texts', in *Vestiges of War 1899–1999: The Philippine–American War and Its Aftermath*, ed. Angel Velasco Shaw and Luis Francia, New York: New York University Press.

Smith, Barbara (1977/1982), 'Toward a Black Feminist Criticism', in Hull, Scott and Smith (1982).

(ed.) (1983), *Home Girls: A Black Feminist Anthology*, New York: Kitchen Table/Women of Color Press.

Smith, Valerie (1998), *Not Just Race, Not Just Gender: Black Feminist Readings*, New York: Routledge.

Spillers, Hortense J. (1987/2003), 'Mama's Baby, Papa's Maybe: An American Grammar Book', in Spillers (2003).

(ed.) (1991), *Comparative American Identities: Race, Sex, and Nationality in the Modern Text*, New York: Routledge.

(2003), *Black, White, and in Color: Essays on American Literature and Culture*, Chicago: University of Chicago Press.

Tate, Claudia (1992), *Domestic Allegories of Political Desire: The Black Heroine's Text at the Turn of the Century*, New York: Oxford University Press.

—— (1998), *Psychoanalysis and Black Novels: Desire and the Protocols of Race*, New York: Oxford University Press.

Walker, Alice (1983), *In Search of Our Mothers' Gardens: Womanist Prose*, San Diego: Harcourt Brace Jovanovich.

Wall, Cheryl A. (ed.) (1989), *Changing Our Own Words: Essays on Criticism, Theory and Writing by Black Women*, New Brunswick, NJ: Rutgers University Press.

Wallace, Michele (1978), *Black Macho and the Myth of the Superwoman*, New York: Dial Press.

Wallace-Sanders, Kimberly (ed.) (2002), *Skin Deep, Spirit Strong: The Black Female Body in American Culture*, Ann Arbor: University of Michigan Press.

Washington, Mary Helen (ed.) (1975), *Black-Eyed Susans: Classic Stories by and about Black Women*, Garden City, NY: Anchor.

—— (ed.) (1980), *Midnight Birds: Stories by Contemporary Black Women Writers*, Garden City, NY: Anchor.

—— (ed.) (1987), *Invented Lives: Narratives of Black Women 1860–1960*, New York: Doubleday.

White, Deborah Gray (1985), *Ar'n't I a Woman: Female Slaves in the Plantation South*, New York: Norton.

Williams, Patricia J. (1991), *The Alchemy of Race and Rights*, Cambridge, MA: Harvard University Press.

Wynter, Sylvia (1990), 'Beyond Miranda's Meanings: Un/silencing the "Demonic Ground" of Caliban's "Woman"', in *Out of the Kumbla: Caribbean Women and Literature*, ed. Carole Boyce Davies and Elaine Savory Fido, Trenton, NJ: Africa World Press.

CHAPTER 10

Lesbian feminist criticism

Caroline Gonda

Any historical account of lesbian feminist criticism must, sooner or later, grapple with a myth of origins. The myth itself is not always the same, but certain features remain constant. I could begin by invoking Laura Doan's keynote address to the international Lesbian Lives conference in Dublin in 2004, a conference marking ten years of lesbian lives, studies and activism since the publication of Doan's critical anthology, *The Lesbian Postmodern*. In her conference speech, Doan emphasised the need to create a new genealogical model of lesbian studies and to dislodge what she called 'this now calcified origin narrative': the narrative of lesbian feminism's collision with, and defeat by, queer theory (Doan, 2004). Other participants at the conference – Linda Garber and Paulina Palmer, for example – likewise voiced their dissent from this dominant narrative, pointing out the unacknowledged connections between lesbian feminist thought and queer theory, and the injustice of the narrative's stereotypes: queer theory as 'sexy, vital, pluralistic and fun', lesbian feminism as the opposite (Palmer, 2004).

Ten years earlier, a different yet strikingly similar myth of origins was dominating lesbian and gay studies, as Kathleen Martindale noted: the story of 'how the American feminist sex wars over sexual representation in the early 1980s created lesbian category trouble, broke up the feminist consensus, realigned lesbians with gay men and then brought forth the newest kid on the block: lesbian postmodernism' (Martindale, 1997: 1). Here, as in the 'calcified origin narrative' attacked by Doan, the point seems to be the overthrow of old-style, monolithic and unsexy lesbian feminism in favour of something new, bright, flashy and male-influenced. The function of lesbian feminism in these narratives is to be what Marilyn Farwell calls 'the monster Error', a powerful but slow-moving beast conquered by theoretical sophistication (Farwell, 1996: 195). The conflict is also presented as an intergenerational one: a story of queer daughters rebelling against maternal sexual repression (Creet, 1991) or, in Lillian Faderman's wry analogy, of lesbian feminism as 'like the mother – who had been "very advanced" in her youth – whose daughter, having just come of age, rudely rejects all mama's ideas as dated and dowdy though she only half understands them . . . running off with strange young men' instead of following in her mother's footsteps (Faderman, 1997: 221).

Whatever these myths of origin see as the conquering hero or rebel, they agree on what has been defeated or displaced: lesbian feminism as mother, monster or monolith. That is to say, they take for granted the origins of lesbian feminist criticism in a particular, late twentieth-century, historical moment and political movement. Lesbian feminist criticism, such as Bonnie Zimmerman's essay 'What Has Never Been: An Overview of Lesbian Feminist Criticism' (1981/1985), emerges from, and defines itself against, the criticism produced by second-wave feminism in the 1970s. Its political contexts are shaped by texts such as Adrienne Rich's 'Compulsory Heterosexuality and Lesbian Existence' (1980/1986), with its notion of the lesbian continuum, and Radicalesbians' 'The Woman Identified Woman' (1970/1988), with its insistence on lesbianism as political choice rather than innate sexuality. Interesting and valuable as these ideas are, however, this is not where lesbian feminist criticism begins.

Criticism shaped by lesbian and feminist concerns pre-dates the rise of second-wave feminism and lesbian feminism's emergence from it. This earlier criticism is sometimes overlooked because of its origins outside the academy, though some recent accounts (for example Barrett and Cramer, 1997; Martindale, 1997; Schuster, 1998; Castle, 2003) have acknowledged the importance of key figures. A classic example of this criticism is Jeannette H. Foster's encyclopaedic work on the representation of lesbians and lesbianism from antiquity to the mid-twentieth century, *Sex Variant Women in Literature* (1956/1985). A work of immense scholarship and erudition, the result of forty years' independent research, with extensive coverage of literature in English, French and German, Foster's book was published at her own expense, after a frightened university press refused to honour its contract, and subsequently reprinted by feminist and lesbian presses (1975, 1985). One of Foster's first and most dedicated readers, Barbara Grier, herself became the author of just such another invaluable but often inadequately acknowledged labour of love, *The Lesbian in Literature* (1967). An annotated and categorised bibliography of around three thousand items, published by the lesbian periodical *The Ladder*, its earlier incarnations had been circulated in laboriously hand-typed, manually duplicated form (Tilchen, 1981: xi). These works of early lesbian feminist criticism were fuelled by the personal passion and engagement of curious, hungry readers and writers, seeking enlightenment about female homosexuality (Foster) or compiling a

'Treasure Map' (Grier, as described by Tilchen, 1981: xi). Such researches were not only institutionally unsupported but also executed at personal risk: Judy Grahn's study *Another Mother Tongue* (Grahn, 1984), begun in 1964, took twenty years to complete, delayed partly by her burning of her notes at a time of raids on private houses by police searching for gay material (Martindale, 1997: 115).

Much early lesbian feminist criticism was concerned to identify literary lesbians and lesbianism: lesbian authors, lesbian texts, lesbian characters or lesbian images (to borrow the title of Jane Rule's 1975 book). Another work too often dismissed or overlooked in academic studies, Rule's *Lesbian Images* gains power over representation by analysing it. As Marilyn Schuster notes, Rule's dual perspective as lesbian novelist and lesbian reader is the book's strength: 'In that book, as in her own fiction, Rule was charting new territory: reading as a writer, but also as a lesbian looking for stories that would help her map what it means for a woman to love women and to articulate that desire in language' (Schuster, 1998: 89).

In lesbian feminist literary criticism as in traditional literary criticism, many of the most significant theorists have been poets or writers of fiction themselves: Adrienne Rich, Audre Lorde, Jane Rule, Judy Grahn, Gloria Anzaldúa, Nicole Brossard, Gillian Hanscombe and Suniti Namjoshi, Judith Barrington and Patricia Duncker, to name but a few. Betsy Warland's collection *InVersions: Writings by Dykes, Queers, and Lesbians* (1991/1992) is a prime example of the interplay between creative and critical in lesbian feminist writing, and also of the importance of the personal and the autobiographical in lesbian feminist criticism.

Personal writing has had a chequered history in lesbian feminist criticism, as elsewhere in feminist criticism. Reclaimed from triviality by that central feminist tenet, 'the personal is political', personal and autobiographical writing could become a powerful moral and political weapon in lesbians' insistence that heterosexual feminism must recognise its own blind spots and attend to the particularities of lesbian experience. In turn, however, lesbian feminism would come under attack, in the 1980s, for its failures to take account of class and racial differences (Moraga and Anzaldúa, 1981/1983; Martin, 1987/1996), as well as for its doctrinaire stance on sexual practices (Vance, 1984; Nestle, 1987; Allison, 1995). Poststructuralist theories of sub-jectivity led to a questioning of the very notions of the self and its personal experience as essentialist (Fuss, 1989; Scott, 1991/1993). Attacked for both political narrowness and essentialism, it might indeed seem, as Sally Munt suggested, that the personal had become 'the one discourse we now love to hate' (Munt, 1992: xv); but this pronouncement appears premature (or rather, the wheel has come full circle). Lesbian feminist criticism still has recourse to the power of experience, even if it has become customary to problematise 'experience' (for example, O'Driscoll, 1996; Emery, 2002).

Reading, both as personal practice and source of theory, has been a frequent concern of such criticism. Some critics write about the change in perspective created by reading as a lesbian, adopting Adrienne Rich's model of 're-vision – the act of looking back, of seeing with fresh eyes, of entering an old text from a new critical direction' (Rich, 1971/1980: 35). For these lesbian feminist critics, the 'mind that has been implanted in us' (Fetterley, 1981: xxii) is not simply a male one, it is what Monique Wittig calls 'The Straight Mind', the way of thinking 'which throughout the centuries built heterosexuality as a given' (Wittig, 1992: xvi). Toni McNaron, for example, recalls how reading Virginia Woolf pushed her to recognise her own 'indoctrination into compulsory heterosexuality as a literary scholar', a training so strong that her personal relationships with women had not initially dislodged it, and wryly notes the need to 'scour off years of heterosexist rust' from her 'reading antenna' (McNaron, 1997: 12). Formulating 'a theory for lesbian readers', Jean Kennard suggests adopting a practice of 'polar reading' which allows for engagement with an alien text while maintaining one's lesbian perspective on it and one's lesbian distance from it (Kennard, 1984/1985).

Other lesbian feminist critics write about the importance of reading in lesbian self-formation (for example, Hennegan, 1988; Lynch, 1990/1992; Hastie, 1993). Alison Hennegan chronicles the unexpected benefits of 'becoming a lesbian reader' in a period before the rise and proliferation of widely available, openly lesbian writing, including the pleasures of learning Greek, reading Enid Blyton and rewriting Jane Austen and Charles Dickens to create same-sex pairings (Hennegan, 1988). Reading between the lines and against the grain becomes, in these accounts, a characteristically lesbian activity (Munt, 1992, argues that lesbians are particularly skilled in deconstruction). It is also one which can lead to unease, however: Luzma Umpierre describes her sense of being placed as a lesbian voyeur in relation to the 'tantalizing' text (Umpierre, 1996). Marilyn Farwell expresses her reservations that making the lesbian reader the location of lesbian meaning in a text 'might lead to a solipsism I am reluctant to endorse' (Farwell, 1996: 198).

Solipsism, as much as essentialism, can be a danger in personal writing, and at times lesbian feminist criticism which puts the critic and her experience centre stage can come perilously close to it. When Elizabeth Meese's *(Sem)Erotics: Theorizing Lesbian: Writing* (Meese, 1992) is punctuated by passionate love letters from 'L' to 'L' ('L' as 'Elle', 'Lesbian', 'Lover', 'Letter-writer'?), or indeed from 'L' to 'V and V' (Virginia and Vita, in the chapter on Woolf and Sackville-West), are we dealing with flamboyant, risk-taking creativity, or with a public display of the private (as opposed to the personal)? As Kevin Kopelson has remarked, those of us fortunate enough to work in lesbian or gay studies have a tendency 'to put ourselves on – or over – the line'; I would add that it's not always easy to tell which is which (Kopelson, 1994: [vii]). The place of the self in lesbian feminist criticism is difficult to define: I think Meese gets away with it, just, but it's a close-run thing. The boundaries between critic and text, or indeed between critic and author, can become blurred, as can the boundaries between different literary genres. Ruth Salvaggio rightly notes that, in Alice Parker's writing on Nicole Brossard, 'as in the writing of other lesbian critics and theorists, theory bends toward poetry' (Salvaggio, 1997: 58); but theory also bends towards autobiography and prose fiction. It can be hard to know what it is that lesbian feminist critics really want to be writing.

The question of lesbian feminist criticism's relationship to other genres and disciplines has been a complex one, made more so by the importance of practitioner critics and by lesbian feminist criticism's ambivalent relation to the academy. Attempts to define the boundaries of lesbian literature and criticism have come from novelists (Harris, 1977) as well as academics (Stimpson, 1981); from poets with academic pasts (Hanscombe and Namjoshi, 1991) or without (Grahn, 1985); from journalists and campaigners in mixed gay political movements (Hennegan, 1980; 1985) and from professors of Women's Studies (Zimmerman, 1981/1985). Lesbian feminist criticism may be something enabled by the academy (Meese, 1992, sees the freedom conferred by tenure as essential to her lesbian feminist critical writing) or carried on necessarily outside it, even in opposition to it (Bennett, 1982; Segrest, 1982). The rise of lesbian and gay studies and queer studies departments and courses has, in the US especially, raised questions of where, academically, lesbian feminist criticism 'belongs' (Zimmerman, 1996).

Even within the academy, lesbian feminist criticism has had to work out its relationship to other disciplines, including history, philosophy and cultural studies, as well as to other forms and schools of criticism and critical theory, including mainstream feminist criticism, gay and lesbian studies, queer theory, poststructuralism, performance theory and postmodernism. The borderline between lesbian feminist criticism and lesbian feminist philosophy has often been difficult to fix, particularly given the strength of lesbian feminist criticism's engagement with ethics. Jeffner

Allen's diverse collection, *Lesbian Philosophies and Cultures* (1990), is a prime example of such work, but one could also point to Judith Roof's *A Lure of Knowledge* (1991) or indeed to the work of Judith Butler (1990, 1991, 1993). Butler's notion of gender performativity has been a powerful shaping force in much recent lesbian feminist criticism and queer theory, as has Eve Kosofsky Sedgwick's work on homosexuality and the closet (1990, 1993). Important though these theories are, Biddy Martin suggests, there is a danger that such work, with its 'focus on a homo/hetero division', results in a disavowal of femininity and indeed feminism, constructing the latter as the 'anti-sexual, identificatory muck out of which any good queer must pull him- or herself' (Martin, 1996: 10).

Lesbian feminist criticism has been profoundly influenced by some essays which do not focus specifically on literary texts, and which are themselves political as much as literary. Adrienne Rich's 'Compulsory Heterosexuality and Lesbian Existence' (1980/1986) is perhaps the most obvious example of this. Rich's idea of a 'lesbian continuum' along which *all* female-female relations could be situated was attacked both for essentialism and for occluding the specificity of lesbians' experience; yet her indictment of heterosexuality as not natural but 'compulsory', ideologically imposed and reinforced as a norm, remains a powerful one. Rich's pamphlet 'Women and Honor: Some Notes on Lying' (1975/1980) is still unmatched in its account of the forces which deform relations between women in a patriarchal society. Audre Lorde's 'Uses of the Erotic: The Erotic as Power' reclaims the erotic for women as 'creative energy empowered', and as a force which informs and connects 'our language, our history, our dancing, our loving, our work, our lives' (Lorde, 1978/1984: 55). Lorde's complex self-identification as 'Sister Outsider' (1984) vitally emphasises the importance of difference, which she defines as 'that raw and powerful connection from which our personal power is forged' (1979/1984: 112).

As Linda Garber has argued, however, the rise of 'high theory' in the late 1980s and the 1990s produced a tendency to classify these works as activism rather than theory. Unlike Salvaggio, who examines how 'theory bends toward poetry', Garber contests the hierarchical placing of theory *above* poetry, and argues for the recognition of poetry *as* theory (Garber, 2001). In the case of Gloria Anzaldúa's *Borderlands/La Frontera: The New Mestiza* (1987), for example, Garber notes how academic criticism focuses on Anzaldúa's theoretical prose writings and ignores the poetry which makes up more than half the book. Garber's *Identity Poetics: Race, Class, and the Lesbian-Feminist Roots of Queer Theory* (2001) takes up Sharon Holland's challenge, in '(White) Lesbian Studies', to the split between activist and academic discourse: 'lesbian feminists in the terrain of lesbian writings have constructed a historical arena filled with the Steins and Woolfs of the world, a world where black lesbians don't produce "literature" and "theory," but they do produce "activism" and, therefore, "politics" ' (Holland, 1996: 252).

What counts as 'literature' or 'theory', and what the focus of criticism should be, are questions which have exercised lesbian feminist criticism from its early days. By the beginning of the 1990s, some critics were already noting the emergence of a 'lesbian canon', with all the narrowing of focus and hardening of orthodoxies which canon-formation entails. Lyndie Brimstone challenges the exclusion of Maureen Duffy's novels from this canon (1990), while Suzanne Raitt's collection, *Volcanoes and Pearl Divers*, emphasises 'neglected lesbian authors and texts' rather than 'the ones that many lesbians have heard of: Audre Lorde, Virginia Woolf, Willa Cather, and so on' (Raitt, 1995: xiii). With the exception of Woolf, Radclyffe Hall and latterly Jeanette Winterson, the lesbian canon has tended not to include many British writers. The balance of Jay and Glasgow's *Lesbian Texts and Contexts* (1990/1992) is not untypical: Woolf, Hall, Winterson and, perhaps more surprisingly, George Eliot appear along with a few French or Francophone writers (Brossard, Wittig, Jovette Marchessault), but the collection focuses mainly on US writers, including Emily Dickinson, Willa Cather, H. D., Gertrude Stein, Djuna Barnes, Patricia Highsmith, Ann Allen Shockley, Paula Gunn Allen, Barbara Deming and Audre Lorde.

Paradoxically, even as a lesbian canon was emerging, lesbian feminist criticism was struggling with questions of definition. As Annamarie Jagose notes, the same questions keep recurring: Terry Castle's question, 'What is a lesbian fiction?' (Castle, 1993: 66), rearticulates 'what almost a decade earlier Zimmerman identified as "a special question" for lesbian critics: "When is a text a 'lesbian text'...?" ' (Jagose, 1994: 13). Dorothy Allison recalls Bertha Harris' declaration that 'there was no such thing as a lesbian novel, because no little female books ever ran off with other little female books'; for Allison in the 1970s, wanting a category of 'lesbian fiction' which would validate her own life and work, Harris' pronouncement was enraging (Abraham, 1996: xxiii). The Dutch author Anja Meulenbelt, like Harris, sees sexuality as not resident in texts: 'Novels are not lesbian ... Novels have no sexual preference' (quoted in Smith, 1997: 15).

Even if critics could agree on what a lesbian text was, however, should lesbian texts be the sole or chief focus of lesbian feminist criticism – and if so, what *kind* of lesbian texts? Paulina Palmer, writing in the early 1990s, notes regretfully lesbian feminist critics' preference for producing readings 'against the grain' of high art and canonical literature, rather than attending to explicitly lesbian writing (Palmer, 1993). Catharine Stimpson (1981) and Elizabeth Meese (1992), however, have bemoaned what they see as lesbian critics' comparative neglect of 'difficult' or 'experimental' literature; Bonnie Zimmerman notes the impact on lesbian fiction of readers' desire for something 'accessible, entertaining, and just "correct" enough to be a bit bland' (Zimmerman, 1990/1992: 19). Political and aesthetic judgements, it seems, are unlikely to tally, and lesbian feminist criticism may vary dramatically in its sense of what makes something worthwhile as an object of study. Two pieces from the same collection (Lilly, 1990) present a striking contrast in this respect: Diane Hamer's essay on the 1950s lesbian 'pulp' novels of Ann Bannon, and Gillian Spraggs' analysis of the love poetry of Sylvia Townsend Warner and Valentine Ackland. Hamer sees Bannon's importance as cultural rather than literary, arguing that Bannon's '*range* of possible trajectories to lesbianism' and her 'emphasis on choice and on diversity' make her 'an important landmark for us, as lesbian feminists embarking on the construction of our history' (Hamer, 1990: 70). Spraggs' essay is uncompromising in its emphasis on the literary merit of Warner's and Ackland's poetry, carefully discriminating in its close readings of individual poems, not all of which Spraggs thinks equally strong; keeping both aesthetics and politics firmly in view, the essay also makes very clear the exceptional nature of this erotic poetry between women, its pioneering achievement, and what is lost by its being out of print (Spraggs, 1990).

These two contrasting essays foreshadow the territorial struggle between the claims of poetry and narrative as proper objects of lesbian feminist critical study. Paula Bennett, whose work on Emily Dickinson as lesbian poet (1990) has completely transformed Dickinson studies, argues that 'Poetry is the literary genre in which lesbian writers have flourished and to which they have contributed the most' (Bennett, 1995: 100). Bennett sees the roll-call of US poetry by lesbian and bisexual women as far more distinguished than that of American women's prose fiction, in which, with few exceptions, 'the major voices ... have historically been straight' (1995: 100). Ambiguity, Bennett argues, may be the key to poetry's success here, since it enables lesbian poets to avoid the institutionalised heterosexuality of the novel, dominated as that form has been by the marriage plot. Unlike Gillian Hanscombe and Suniti Namjoshi, who see the traditions of lyric poetry as fraught with difficulty for lesbians because lyric 'imagery itself [is] gender role stereotyped' (1991: 157), Bennett sees 'the lyric voice of the lesbian poet' as freed by not needing to make either her persona or that of her beloved specifically gendered (Bennett, 1995: 100). In effect, women poets could adopt the traditionally male persona and thus, Bennett argues, 'carv[e] out, as it were, a lesbian space' (1995: 102). For Hanscombe and Namjoshi, the difficulty of articulating specifically lesbian desire nevertheless persists: how to identify *both* speaker *and* beloved as female without rupturing the lyric tradition (1991: 157)? Bennett's valuing of poetry over prose fiction is not altered by lesbian novelists' achievements; instead, she argues that 'where lesbian novelists have been at their strongest (as in Barnes, Virginia Woolf, and Monique Wittig), they have also written something closer to poetry than prose', as have 'a number of recent prose-poet theorists ... [and] those poets who also tried their hands at fiction – Stein, HD, and Lorde, in particular' (1995: 100).

Despite some important work on particular poets and on the lesbian poetic tradition,[1] and despite some collections which include poetry, narrative and, more rarely, drama,[2] lesbian feminist criticism has tended to focus more on narrative than on poetry. In 1996, the year after Bennett's essay on US lesbian poetry, three books devoted to narrative appeared: Julie Abraham's *Are Girls Necessary? Lesbian Writing and Modern Histories*, Marilyn Farwell's *Heterosexual Plots and Lesbian Narratives*, and Judith Roof's *Come As You Are: Sexuality and Narrative*. Abraham and Farwell both engage with the problem already outlined by Bennett: the marriage plot and the difficulty of escaping the institutionalisation of heterosexuality in prose fiction. Following Rachel Blau DuPlessis, who sees the romance plot as suppressing or marginalising the possibility of female-female bonds (1985), Abraham suggests that the novel's inability to escape from the romance plot, whether in reproducing it or in reacting against it, prompted many twentieth-century lesbian writers to turn to history or 'histories' instead. The result, Abraham argues, is that their works have been overlooked by critics who focus on 'the lesbian novel', narrowly defined, rather than looking at 'lesbian writing' (Abraham, 1996). Farwell adopts DuPlessis' notion of 'writing beyond the ending' to explore the ways in which lesbian narratives *can* escape from heterosexual plots. These ways include privileging female bonding and breaking up male bonding; using sexual sameness to disrupt the gendered oppositions between active and passive which often structure narrative; and undermining the authority of traditional narrative, for example by using multiple plots and voices. Noting the tendency of lesbian feminist criticism on narrative to focus either on formally traditional works (Zimmerman, 1990/1992; Palmer, 1993) or on experimental ones (Meese, 1992; Roof, 1991), Farwell argues for a notion of lesbian narrative which would include both. Her project, as she describes it, is an 'attempt to answer two large critical and theoretical questions – what is the lesbian in a lesbian narrative, and what is the narrative structure that accommodates, contains, or repels this lesbian' (Farwell, 1996: 196).

Whereas Abraham and Farwell analyse female-authored lesbian narrative, Roof is concerned to theorise the relationship between narrative and sexuality, and the place of lesbianism in that relationship. Her chosen texts include works by both men and women, and narratives in different media and genres – films as well as novels and short stories, psychoanalytic writings as well as self-declared fictions. A more recent study of lesbianism and narrative, Annamarie Jagose's *Inconsequence: Lesbian Representation and the Logic of Sexual Sequence* (2002), likewise explores not lesbian narratives but the narrativisation of lesbianism, again ranging across works by both sexes and in different media; her final chapter analyses a photographic essay illustrating a lurid sexological treatise on lesbianism.[3]

As my comparison of Abraham and Farwell with Roof and Jagose above might indicate, lesbian feminist criticism of narrative has proceeded in very different ways – and with widely divergent critical allegiances. The stylistic choices which result from those allegiances have themselves become an issue, particularly in relation to poststructuralist influences on lesbian feminist critical writing. Margaret Cruikshank, in her foreword to *The New Lesbian Studies*, voices her dismay at much recent lesbian and gay writing in 'obscure and needlessly difficult language' which, she says, 'reminds me of priestcraft. Some scholars seem to be writing only for each other. Their language may be an emblem of power, a sign of initiation' (Cruikshank, 1996: xi–xii). To those who claim that 'complex ideas require difficult language', Cruikshank writes, 'My retort is brief: read bell hooks, read Gloria Anzaldúa' (1996: xii).

In Kathleen Martindale's provocative formulation, 'feminists and lesbians had to choose: be pure but old-fashioned, or become trendy but difficult. In effect, the sex wars became the text wars. If you didn't keep up with your reading, you couldn't play' (Martindale, 1997: 10). In a world of 'paper lesbians and theory queens' (1997: 30), the choice might seem to be between lesbian theorising as 'smart and sexy' or as 'naive and puritanical' (1997: 54). High-performance rhetorical criticism has sometimes behaved as if being 'smart and sexy' is sufficient as an end in itself, or as if the power of performance is self-justifying. Even a more charitable reading would have to acknowledge that it *is* about power, about the pleasure and admiration one may feel in seeing a lesbian feminist critic successfully take on the great white fathers at their own game. But at my back, I always hear other voices: the voice of Catherine Morland, in *Northanger Abbey*, confessing with unintentional satiric brilliance that 'I cannot speak well enough to be unintelligible' (Austen, 1818/1990: 103); or the voice of Audre Lorde, reminding us that 'the master's tools will never dismantle the master's house' (Lorde, 1979/1984: 112).

As I suggested at the start of this chapter, recent lesbian feminist criticism has sought to move beyond the antagonistic view of lesbian feminism and queer theory, and to acknowledge the connections between the two.[4] The scope of lesbian feminist criticism now includes far more than the lesbian canon: though particular periods ('Sapphic Modernism') and authors (Woolf, Radclyffe Hall, Winterson) may continue to attract the lion's share of critical attention, there is a lively interest in popular culture and genre fiction (for example in works by Griffin, Munt and Palmer) as well as in visual media. Cartoons, including Alison Bechdel's *Dykes to Watch Out For* series, and alternative 'zines', such as *Hothead Paisan: Homicidal Lesbian Terrorist*, have been recent favourites (see Martindale, 1997). The historical and textual focus of lesbian feminist criticism nevertheless remains strong, as it has been from the first.

The relationship between historical and textual considerations has not been an easy one, however; the disciplinary boundary between literature and history has seen numerous border skirmishes over the function of literary texts as historical evidence, material for close reading, or both. The desire to establish an historical as well as literary tradition of lesbianism, a genealogy or record of our existence, has also been problematised by the difficulty of reading and interpreting works from earlier periods. Alison Hennegan, in one of the earliest British attempts to grapple with these difficulties, notes how often critics and social historians have dismissed the lesbian implications of pre-twentieth-century exchanges between women by appealing to changes in linguistic, emotional and physical conventions; whatever we post-Freudians might think, it doesn't mean *that* (Hennegan, 1980). The meanings of romantic friendship, explored so extensively by Lillian Faderman in *Surpassing the Love of Men* (1979/1981/1985), have been especially problematic. Faderman's work asserts a continuous tradition of women-loving women, but – like Rich's notion of the 'lesbian continuum' – it has been criticised both for essentialism and for de-sexing lesbianism. With the discovery and publication of coded but sexually explicit nineteenth-century diaries by the Yorkshire heiress Anne Lister (Whitbread, 1988; 1992), lesbian history took a fresh turn. The link between sexual *practices* and sexual *identity* remains problematic, however. Is lesbian sexual identity a modern invention, socially constructed through the work of sexologists such as Havelock Ellis (1897)? Were there, as Terry Castle mischievously formulates it, 'no lesbians before 1900' (1993: 241 n. 10)? Was there, as Emma Donoghue's *Passions between Women* suggests, something we can recognise as 'British lesbian culture' in the seventeenth and eighteenth centuries (1993)? And what role should or can the evidence of literature play in all this?

Recent historical lesbian feminist criticism has often turned to discourse analysis for a solution of these difficulties. Valerie Traub analyses 'lesbian' and 'lesbianism' as 'rhetorical effects' in early modern England (2002), while Susan Lanser argues for a reading of 'the sapphic body as transgressive text' (2003). Terry Castle, criticised in some quarters as essentialist for her book *The Apparitional Lesbian* (1993), seems to have found a middle path between essentialism and constructionism in her anthology *The Literature of Lesbianism* (2003). Castle still clearly believes in the existence, and indeed the *visibility*, of lesbians and lesbianism before the era of the sexologists, but she focuses on lesbianism as a subject of discourse: what people have said about it, and how it became increasingly 'thinkable' between the Renaissance and the late twentieth century.

Castle's anthology is one of a number of historically wide-ranging works of its kind in recent years. Other notable examples have been Lillian Faderman's *Chloe Plus Olivia: An Anthology of Lesbian Literature from the Seventeenth Century to the Present* (1994/1995), Emma Donoghue's *What Sappho Would Have Said: Four Centuries of Love Poems between Women* (1997) and two anthologies which go all the way back to Sappho: Gillian Spraggs' *Love Shook My Senses: Lesbian Love Poems* (1998) and Alison Hennegan's *The Lesbian Pillow Book* (2000). Anthologies and collections, both of essays and other writings, have had a significant place in lesbian feminist criticism.[5] Their importance reflects the collectivity of lesbian feminist endeavour, but also the need to collect information, types of representation, ways of thinking about lesbianism over a wide historical span. These recent anthologies, especially those by Faderman, Hennegan and Castle, represent a return to some of lesbian feminist criticism's earliest concerns, to the search for lesbians in literature and the literature of lesbianism rather than lesbian literature or literature by lesbians. Like the anthologies by Donoghue and Spraggs, they also represent a return to lesbian feminist criticism's origins in personal quests and treasure maps, and in years of passionate and curious reading. The range of publishers involved, from Columbia University Press (Castle) to Penguin (Faderman), British trade publishers Hamish Hamilton (Donoghue) and

Fourth Estate (Hennegan) to The Women's Press (Spraggs), suggests that in its oldest form lesbian feminist criticism is still alive and well both in and out of the academy. Which is as it should be.

NOTES

1. For example, Bennett (1990), Donoghue (1998), Garber (2001), Grahn (1985), Spraggs (1990 and 1991).
2. For example Griffin (1993b), Raitt (1995), Hobby and White (1991), Jay and Glasgow (1990/1992), Warland (1991/1992).
3. For other works on narrative see Castle (1993), Duncker (2002), Lanser (2001), O'Driscoll (1996), Palmer (1993), Schuster (1998), Smith (1997), Zimmerman (1990/1992).
4. For more on this, see Heather Love's chapter in this volume.
5. See Allen (1990), Barrington (1991), Cruikshank (1982), Doan (1994), Freedman et al. (1985), Griffin (1993b), Heller (1997), Hobby and White (1991), Jay and Glasgow (1990/1992), Moraga and Anzaldúa (1981/1983), Munt (1992), Raitt (1995), Warland (1991/1992), Wolfe and Penelope (1993), Zimmerman and McNaron (1996).

BIBLIOGRAPHY

Aaron, Jane and Sylvia Walby (eds) (1991), *Out of the Margins: Women's Studies in the Nineties*, London: Falmer Press.
Abelove, Henry, Michèle Aina Barale and David Halperin (eds) (1993), *The Lesbian and Gay Studies Reader*, New York and London: Routledge.
Abraham, Julie (1996), *Are Girls Necessary? Lesbian Writing and Modern Histories*, New York and London: Routledge.
Allen, Jeffner (ed.) (1990), *Lesbian Philosophies and Cultures*, Albany: State University of New York Press.
Allison, Dorothy (1995), *Skin: Talking about Sex, Class and Literature*, London: Pandora.
Anzaldúa, Gloria (1987), *Borderlands/La Frontera: The New Mestiza*, San Francisco: Aunt Lute Books.
Austen, Jane (1818/1990), *'Northanger Abbey', 'Lady Susan', 'The Watsons' and 'Sanditon'*, ed. John Davie, with a new introduction by Terry Castle, Oxford: Oxford University Press.
Barrett, Eileen and Patricia Cramer (eds) (1997), *Virginia Woolf: Lesbian Readings*, New York and London: New York University Press.
Barrington, Judith (ed.) (1991), *An Intimate Wilderness: Lesbian Writers on Sexuality*, Portland, OR: Eighth Mountain Press.
Bennett, Paula (1982), 'Dyke in Academe (II)', in Cruikshank (1982).
    (1990), *Emily Dickinson: Woman Poet*, Hemel Hempstead: Harvester Wheatsheaf.

(1995), 'Lesbian Poetry in the United States, 1890–1990: A Brief Overview', in Haggerty and Zimmerman (1995).

Brimstone, Lyndie (1990), ' "Keepers of History": The Novels of Maureen Duffy', in Lilly (1990).

Brossard, Nicole (1985/1988), *The Aerial Letter*, trans. Marlene Wildeman, Toronto: The Women's Press.

Butler, Judith (1990), *Gender Trouble: Feminism and the Subversion of Identity*, London: Routledge.

(1991), 'Imitation and Gender Insubordination', in Fuss (1991).

(1993), *Bodies That Matter: On the Discursive Limits of 'Sex'*, London: Routledge.

Castle, Terry (1993), *The Apparitional Lesbian: Female Homosexuality and Modern Culture*, New York: Columbia University Press.

(ed.) (2003), *The Literature of Lesbianism: A Historical Anthology from Ariosto to Stonewall*, New York: Columbia University Press.

Creet, Julia (1991), 'Daughter of the Movement: The Psychodynamics of Lesbian S/M Fantasy', in *differences* 3.

Cruikshank, Margaret (ed.) (1982), *Lesbian Studies: Present and Future*, Old Westbury, NY: The Feminist Press.

Cruikshank, Margaret (1996), 'Foreword', in Zimmerman and McNaron (1996).

Doan, Laura (ed.) (1994), *The Lesbian Postmodern*, New York: Columbia University Press.

(2004), 'Lesbian Studies after *The Lesbian Postmodern*: Toward a New Genealogy', plenary address at conference 'Lesbian Lives XI: Lesbian Lives, Studies and Activism since *The Lesbian Postmodern*', 13–15 February, University College Dublin, Ireland.

Donoghue, Emma (1993), *Passions between Women: British Lesbian Culture, 1668–1801*, London: Scarlet Press.

(ed.) (1997), *What Sappho Would Have Said: Four Centuries of Love Poems between Women*, London: Hamish Hamilton.

(1998), *We Are Michael Field*, Bath: Absolute Press.

Duncker, Patricia (2002), *Writing on the Wall: Selected Essays*, London: Pandora.

DuPlessis, Rachel Blau (1985), *Writing Beyond the Ending: Narrative Strategies of Twentieth-Century Women Writers*, Bloomington: Indiana University Press.

Ellis, Havelock (1897), *Studies in the Psychology of Sex*, vol. 1: *Sexual Inversion*, London: University Press.

Emery, Kim (2002), *The Lesbian Index: Pragmatism and Subjectivity in the Twentieth-Century United States*, Albany: State University of New York Press.

Faderman, Lillian (1979/1981/1985), *Surpassing the Love of Men: Romantic Friendship and Love between Women from the Renaissance to the Present*, London: The Women's Press.

(ed.) (1994/1995), *Chloe Plus Olivia: An Anthology of Lesbian Literature from the Seventeenth Century to the Present*, Harmondsworth: Penguin.

(1997), 'Afterword', in Heller (1997).

Farwell, Marilyn (1996), *Heterosexual Plots and Lesbian Narratives*, New York and London: New York University Press.

Fetterley, Judith (1981), *The Resisting Reader: A Feminist Approach to American Fiction*, Bloomington: Indiana University Press.

Foster, Jeannette H. (1956/1985), *Sex Variant Women in Literature*, Tallahassee, FL: Naiad.

Freedman, Estelle B., Barbara C. Gelpi, Susan L. Johnson and Kathleen M. Weston (eds) (1985), *The Lesbian Issue: Essays from SIGNS*, Chicago: University of Chicago Press.

Fuss, Diana (1989), *Essentially Speaking: Feminism, Nature and Difference*, New York: Routledge.

(ed.) (1991), *Inside/Out: Lesbian Theories, Gay Theories*, London: Routledge.

Garber, Linda (2001), *Identity Poetics: Race, Class, and the Lesbian-Feminist Roots of Queer Theory*, New York: Columbia University Press.

Gay Left Collective (eds) (1980), *Homosexuality: Power and Politics*, London: Allison and Busby.

Grahn, Judy (1984), *Another Mother Tongue: Gay Words, Gay Worlds*, Boston: Beacon Press.

(1985), *The Highest Apple: Sappho and the Lesbian Poetic Tradition*, San Francisco: Spinsters Ink.

Greene, Gayle and Coppélia Kahn (eds) (1985), *Making a Difference: Feminist Literary Criticism*, London: Methuen.

Grier, Barbara (1967/1981), *The Lesbian in Literature*, 3rd edn, Tallahassee, FL: Naiad.

Griffin, Gabriele (1993a), *Heavenly Love? Lesbian Images in Twentieth-Century Women's Writing*, Manchester: Manchester University Press.

(ed.) (1993b), *Outwrite: Lesbianism and Popular Culture*, London: Pluto.

Haggerty, George E. and Bonnie Zimmerman (eds) (1995), *Professions of Desire: Lesbian and Gay Studies in Literature*, New York: The Modern Language Association of America.

Hamer, Diane (1990), ' "I Am a Woman": Ann Bannon and the Writing of Lesbian Identity in the 1950s', in Lilly (1990).

Hanscombe, Gillian and Suniti Namjoshi (1991), ' "Who Wrongs You, Sappho?": Developing Lesbian Sensibility in the Writing of Lyric Poetry', in Aaron and Walby (1991).

Harris, Bertha (1977), 'What We Mean to Say: Notes toward Defining the Nature of Lesbian Literature', in *Heresies* 3.

Hastie, Nicki (1993), 'Lesbian BiblioMythography', in Griffin (1993b).

Heller, Dana (ed.) (1997), *Cross-Purposes: Lesbians, Feminists, and the Limits of Alliance*, Bloomington and Indianapolis: Indiana University Press.

Hennegan, Alison (1980), 'Here, Who Are You Calling a Lesbian?', in Gay Left Collective (1980).

(1985), 'What Lesbian Novel?', in *Women's Review* 1.

(1988), 'On Becoming a Lesbian Reader', in Radstone (1988).

(ed.) (2000), *The Lesbian Pillow Book*, London: Fourth Estate.

Hoagland, Sarah Lucia and Julia Penelope (eds) (1988), *For Lesbians Only: A Separatist Anthology*, London: Onlywomen Press.

Hobby, Elaine and Chris White (eds) (1991), *What Lesbians Do in Books*, London: The Women's Press.

Holland, Sharon P. (1996), '(White) Lesbian Studies', in Zimmerman and McNaron (1996).

hooks, bell (1991), *Yearning: Race, Gender and Cultural Politics*, London: Turnaround.

Jagose, Annamarie (1994), *Lesbian Utopics*, New York: Routledge.

  (2002), *Inconsequence: Lesbian Representation and the Logic of Sexual Sequence*, Ithaca, NY: Cornell University Press.

Jay, Karla and Joanne Glasgow (eds) (1990/1992), *Lesbian Texts and Contexts: Radical Revisions*, London: Onlywomen Press.

Jones, Sonya L. (ed.) (1998), *Gay and Lesbian Literature since World War II: History and Memory*, Binghamton, NY: Harrington Park Press.

Kennard, Jean E. (1984/1985), 'Ourself behind Ourself: A Theory for Lesbian Readers', in Freedman et al. (1985).

Kittredge, Katharine (ed.) (2003), *Lewd and Notorious: Female Transgression in the Eighteenth Century*, Ann Arbor: University of Michigan Press.

Kopelson, Kevin (1994), *Love's Litany: The Writing of Modern Homoerotics*, Palo Alto, CA: Stanford University Press.

Lanser, Susan (2001), 'Sapphic Picaresque, Sexual Difference, and the Challenge of Homo-Adventuring', in *Textual Practice* 15.

  (2003), 'Queer to Queer: The Sapphic Body as Transgressive Text', in Kittredge (2003).

Lilly, Mark (ed.) (1990), *Lesbian and Gay Writing*, London: Macmillan.

Lorde, Audre (1978/1984), 'Uses of the Erotic: The Erotic as Power', in Lorde (1984).

  (1979/1984), 'The Master's Tools Will Never Dismantle the Master's House', in Lorde (1984).

  (1984), *Sister Outsider: Essays and Speeches*, Freedom, CA: The Crossing Press.

Lynch, Lee (1990/1992), 'Cruising the Libraries', in Jay and Glasgow (1990/1992).

Martin, Biddy (1996), *Femininity Played Straight: The Significance of Being Lesbian*, New York: Routledge.

  (1987/1996), 'Lesbian Identity and Autobiographical Differences', in Martin (1996).

Martindale, Kathleen (1997), *Un/Popular Culture: Lesbian Writing after the Sex Wars*, Albany: State University of New York Press.

McNaron, Toni (1997), 'A Lesbian Reading Virginia Woolf', in Barrett and Cramer (1997).

Meese, Elizabeth A. (1992), *(Sem)Erotics: Theorizing Lesbian: Writing*, New York and London: New York University Press.

Moraga, Cherríe and Gloria Anzaldúa (eds) (1981/1983), *This Bridge Called My Back: Writings by Radical Women of Color*, New York: Kitchen Table/ Women of Color Press.

Munt, Sally (ed.) (1992), *New Lesbian Criticism: Literary and Cultural Readings*, Hemel Hempstead: Harvester Wheatsheaf.

Nestle, Joan (1987), *A Restricted Country*, Ithaca: Firebrand Books.

O'Driscoll, Sally (1996), 'Outlaw Readings: Beyond Queer Theory', in *Signs* 22.

Palmer, Paulina (1993), *Contemporary Lesbian Writing: Dreams, Desire, Difference*, Buckingham and Philadelphia: Open University Press.

(2004), conference presentation on 'Queer Theory and Lesbianism: Debating the Issues', at 'Lesbian Lives XI: Lesbian Lives, Studies and Activism since *The Lesbian Postmodern*', 13–15 February, University College Dublin, Ireland.

Parker, Alice (1993), 'Under the Covers: A Synaesthesia of Desire (Lesbian Translations)', in Wolfe and Penelope (1993).

Radicalesbians (1970/1988), 'The Woman Identified Woman', in Hoagland and Penelope (1988).

Radstone, Susannah (ed.) (1988), *Sweet Dreams: Sexuality, Gender and Popular Fiction*, London: Lawrence and Wishart.

Raitt, Suzanne (ed.) (1995), *Volcanoes and Pearl Divers: Essays in Lesbian Feminist Criticism*, London: Onlywomen Press.

Rich, Adrienne (1971/1980), 'When We Dead Awaken: Writing as Re-Vision', in *On Lies, Secrets and Silence: Selected Prose 1966–1978*, London: Virago (1980).

(1975/1980), 'Women and Honor: Some Notes on Lying', in *On Lies, Secrets and Silence: Selected Prose 1966–1978*, London: Virago (1980).

(1980/1986), 'Compulsory Heterosexuality and Lesbian Existence', in *Blood, Bread and Poetry: Selected Prose 1979–1985*, London: Virago (1986).

Roof, Judith (1991), *A Lure of Knowledge: Lesbian Sexuality and Theory*, New York: Columbia University Press.

(1996), *Come As You Are: Sexuality and Narrative*, New York: Columbia University Press.

Rule, Jane (1975/1989), *Lesbian Images*, London: Pluto.

Salvaggio, Ruth (1997), 'Skin Deep: Lesbian Interventions in Language', in Heller (1997).

Schuster, Marilyn (1998), 'Inscribing a Lesbian Reader, Projecting a Lesbian Subject: A Jane Rule Diptych', in Jones (1998).

Scott, Joan W. (1991/1993), 'The Evidence of Experience', in Abelove et al. (1993).

Sedgwick, Eve Kosofsky (1990), *Epistemology of the Closet*, Berkeley: University of California Press.

(1993), *Tendencies*, Durham, NC: Duke University Press.

Segrest, Mab (1982), 'I Lead Two Lives: Confessions of a Closet Baptist', in Cruikshank (1982).

Smith, Patricia Juliana (1997), *Lesbian Panic: Homoeroticism in Modern British Women's Fiction*, New York: Columbia University Press.

Spraggs, Gillian (1990), 'Exiled to Home: The Poetry of Sylvia Townsend Warner and Valentine Ackland', in Lilly (1990).

(1991), 'Divine Visitations: Sappho's Poetry of Love', in Hobby and White (1991).

(ed.) (1998), *Love Shook My Senses: Lesbian Love Poems*, London: The Women's Press.

Stimpson, Catharine (1981), 'Zero Degree Deviancy: The Lesbian Novel in English', in *Critical Inquiry* 8 (1981–2).

Tilchen, Maida (1981), 'The Legendary Lesbian Treasure Map', in Grier (1967/1981).

Traub, Valerie (2002), *The Renaissance of Lesbianism in Early Modern England*, Cambridge: Cambridge University Press.

Umpierre, Luzma (1996), 'Lesbian Tantalizing in Carmen Lugo Filippi's "Milagros, calle Mercurio" ', in Zimmerman and McNaron (1996).

Vance, Carole S. (ed.) (1984), *Pleasure and Danger: Exploring Female Sexuality*, London: Routledge and Kegan Paul.

Warland, Betsy (ed.) (1991/1992), *InVersions: Writings by Dykes, Queers, and Lesbians*, London: Open Letters.

Whitbread, Helena (ed.) (1988), *I Know My Own Heart: The Diaries of Anne Lister 1791–1840*, London: Virago.

(1992), *No Priest but Love: Excerpts from the Diaries of Anne Lister, 1824–1826*, Otley, West Yorkshire: Smith, Settle.

Wittig, Monique (1992), *The Straight Mind and Other Essays*, Hemel Hempstead: Harvester Wheatsheaf.

Wolfe, Susan J. and Julia Penelope (eds) (1993), *Sexual Practice, Textual Theory: Lesbian Cultural Criticism*, Cambridge, MA and Oxford: Blackwell.

Zimmerman, Bonnie (1981/1985), 'What Has Never Been: An Overview of Lesbian Feminist Criticism', in Greene and Kahn (1985).

(1990/1992), *The Safe Sea of Women: Lesbian Fiction 1969–1989*, London: Onlywomen Press.

(1996), 'Placing Lesbians', in Zimmerman and McNaron (1996).

Zimmerman, Bonnie and Toni A. H. McNaron (eds) (1996), *The New Lesbian Studies: Into the Twenty-First Century*, New York: The Feminist Press at the City University of New York.

CHAPTER 11

Men and feminist criticism

Calvin Thomas

INTRODUCTION: AT THE MERCY OF LANGUAGE

If 'men and feminism' share a complicated history, the complications may be thought to arise from the sheer impossibility of the relationship itself. After all, when Stephen Heath kicks off his contribution to *Men in Feminism* by stating that 'Men's relation to feminism is an impossible one' (1987: 1), the assertion seems transparent. For while feminism must by definition desire the end of systemic male dominance, domination apparently remains the largest part of 'what it means to be a man'. As Heath points out, 'no matter how "sincere," "sympathetic" or whatever, we [men] are always also in a male position which brings with it all the implications of domination and appropriation, everything precisely that is being challenged, that has to be altered' (1987: 1). Or, as John Stoltenberg puts it, 'under patriarchy, the cultural norm of male identity consists in power, prestige, privilege, and prerogative *as over and against* the gender class women. That's what masculinity is. It isn't something else' (1974/2004: 41). Hence the impossibility, the deadlock.

To foreground this deadlock is to begin on an unpromising note, and there's a certain bleak irony in thus commencing my account. For historical narration, at least in its modern sense, usually involves some notion of promise, some modicum of faith in progress, some hope for the ameliorative transformation of a social reality deemed inadequate in relation to some animating ideal of freedom, justice or equality. A progressive historical narrative must dive into the wreckage of the past to account for the grim tensions of the present while casting a bright eye toward the possible reconciliations of the future. It would thus be contrary to the redemptive spirit of history to begin on the sour note of deadlock, as if to suggest that, when it comes to men and feminism, we are only ever on the road to nowhere.

To foreground deadlock even further, I would ask the reader to note that the very phrase 'hence the impossibility, the deadlock' lacks predication, fails to act or complete itself as a sentence. Representing 'deadlock' in a way that deadlocks representation, I have here resorted to 'enactment', a literary device. But if I now call attention to this device (and such 'laying bare' is itself a literary device), I do so to suggest, by means of metonymic juxtaposition (yet another device), the essentially *literary* 'nature' of what is inscribed in the phrases that precede it: 'what masculinity is', 'what it means to be a man'. What I thus mean to suggest is that there is no question of anyone's ever having been 'a man' outside the socially devised meanings – inherently literary, or at least linguistic – of manhood. Systemic male dominance reproduces itself by reproducing dominance as *the meaning* of maleness, the dominant way that men understand, read and write, enact themselves *as men*. Feminism attempts to lay bare this cycle of violence by insisting that the 'reproductive activity' involved in perpetuating male dominance isn't genetic, chromosomal, natural or inevitable, but rather *linguistic, semiotic, textual* and *representational*. For even if 'man' is a biological animal, he is nonetheless 'an animal at the mercy of language' (Lacan, 2002: 253). Even if it is still 'a man's world' – insofar as it is still predominantly men who own and control the global means of production – that 'world' must still be produced, must, in Stuart Hall's words, still 'be made to mean' (Hall, 1998: 1050). And if the world can be 'made to mean' only in language – for where else can meaning reside? – language itself 'is, by nature, fictional' (Barthes, 1981: 87).

The implications of these claims – all the seemingly 'real men' in this 'man's world' are 'made' and 'at the mercy' of a language that isn't natural but fictional, hence not 'real' – are unsettling, if not quite 'castrating'. But how do they *really* pertain to a history of men and feminist *literary* criticism? What does the assertion that language is 'fictional' *really* mean? Fiction, after all, by definition, is not real. But obviously fiction exists, and is of course made of language. Language, though it too obviously exists, also is not real. Words function as words only by virtue of *not* being identical to the phenomena in the world that they designate. To *mean* 'elephant', the word 'elephant' cannot *be* an elephant. Language cannot *be* 'real', or it wouldn't *exist*, wouldn't *mean*. A certain 'no to the real', an inevitable 'not really' – and hence a thoroughgoing fictionality – form the condition of possibility for linguistic meaning.

Obviously, these considerations complicate 'history' as an inscription *in language* of what 'really' happened. That 'the world must be made to mean'; that human social reality operates as a system of meanings; that we as human beings are grammatical subjects who 'move and have our being' only within the 'symbolic order' of language: all of these ideas follow from the so-called 'linguistic turn' in the human sciences that occurred in the West in the latter half of the twentieth century.[1] In terms of the history of men and feminist literary criticism, there are two major consequences that follow this re-interpretation of the world. One is that literary analysis *per se* assumes a broader cultural and political significance: not just poems, novels and plays but 'all the world' becomes figuratively readable (and potentially rewritable) as social text. The other consequence of the linguistic turn is the unsettling idea that not only literary genres but *gendered identities* can be opened up to textual analysis, exposed as 'punitively regulated cultural fictions' (Butler, 1990: 140) rather than natural givens. 'Manhood' and 'masculinity' also become readable and potentially rewritable as social texts. Men – not simply male characters in male-authored dramas but the 'real men' who authored these texts – come to be seen not as *masters* but as *effects* of 'literary devices', no less fictional than their various symbolic or mythological representatives, from Jason the Argonaut and Jesus Christ to James Bond and G. I. Joe.

The 'linguistic turn' is thus a crucial moment in the history of men and feminism because it undermines what Heath calls 'the usual justification for the status quo' – the tautology that 'men are men and that's that' (1987: 1). As we will see, it also compromises 'God and nature' as the two strongest ideological alibis of the reproduction of systemic male dominance. At the very least, the linguistic turn has allowed (some) men to participate, however problematically, in the writing of a feminist political imaginary, to imagine social reality and themselves otherwise by envisioning reinscriptions of masculinity in which 'dominance' need not be the largest part of 'what it means to be a man'. In other words, the confluence of literary theory after the linguistic turn with a feminist vision of overcoming male dominance radically *ungrounds* the deadlock that I began by foregrounding. This confluence doesn't make the history of the relationship between men and feminism any less complicated. It only makes it possible, and perhaps even promising.

FABRICATING MEN

In his introduction to *Feminism and Masculinities*, Peter F. Murphy writes that 'Male authors of pro-woman and pro-feminist works span at least twenty-five hundred years and represent a vitally rich tradition.' He also suggests that 'an intellectual history of male authors who have supported women's rights and causes is long overdue' (2004a: 1). Although his introduction does not 'provide such a wide-ranging history', Murphy does offer 'an abridged overview of this critical tradition' that features an impressive roster of men's names, from Aristophanes to Bertrand Russell. Further noting that his 'initial research has identified a minimum of 250 male advocates of women's rights', Murphy points out that 'since 1960, the field of feminist masculinities' – pro-feminist studies of masculinity by men – 'has burgeoned' (2004a: 18n1). If the 'rich tradition' of pro-feminist male writing actually spans twenty-five hundred years, it might seem rather miserly to focus only on the last forty. But there are compelling reasons for such a limited focus. Prior to the twentieth century, outbursts of male feminist advocacy were sporadic, isolated and relatively unconnected to broader feminist movements. Even in the early twentieth century, male involvement in 'first-wave feminism' – which 'endorsed the franchise for women, equal opportunities in the professions, access to higher education, and the elimination of restrictions in marriage' (Murphy, 2004a: 8) – was limited both in numbers and to and by the liberal, egalitarian goals of the first-wave movement itself.

But a number of factors converge in what Murphy calls the 'crucial change in the relationship between feminism and men in the 1960s and 1970s' (2004a: 9). First, the advances in reproductive technology and legal access to abortion that gave women unprecedented control over their own bodies correspondingly gave Western 'second-wave feminism' more social, political and economic traction than its predecessors were able to gain. Second, the fact that the women's liberation movement developed historically 'in the context of the New Left, the civil rights movement, and opposition to the war in Vietnam' (Murphy, 2004a: 9) meant not only that second-wave feminism's goals were often more radical than those of its predecessors (desiring utter transformation of the entire patriarchal/ racist/ heterosexist/ imperialist/ military-industrial complex rather than merely greater equality within it); this historical context also meant that the women's liberation movement co-emerged with forms of political activism in which many radical men were already involved. Even if the concept of sexual politics turned many male leftists into myrmidons of masculinist privilege, some men responded more productively to the challenges of feminist critique:

When the personal, emotional, sexual experiences of women's lives gained significance as legitimate social concerns with political consequences, men were forced to examine their own socially constructed roles as men ... No longer is masculinity the known, unexamined, natural phenomenon that it had been taken to be. Beginning in the 1960s, men start to apply feminism to an examination of their own lives as men in a patriarchal society. (Murphy, 2004a: 9–10)

Significantly, however, by the late 1970s and early 1980s, the 'real' sites of cultural change were no longer 'the streets' but the academic seminar rooms.

If in the late 1960s university radicalism involved students and professors chucking the Chaucer and heading for 'the streets', a decade later radicalism was being routed back into classrooms through the defiles of sexually politicised textuality. Even as late as the mid 1970s, a straight white male student in a typical graduate programme in literary studies in the US or UK would be trained in only canonical literature and study only traditional literary criticism from metaphysical Platonism to 'apolitical' formalism. He would, in other words, learn little that did not support, reproduce or naturalise his own privileged position in patriarchal society. A decade or so later, however, that student's counterpart would more likely be poring over debates about the exclusions of the canon, reading about the politics of the signifier, looking into the male gaze, boning up on 'the meaning of the phallus' or immersing himself in the fluidities of *écriture féminine*: in other words, he would learn little that did not decentre, desediment or denaturalise his position in (and as an agent of) male domination. If that student did 'turn feminist', he most likely negotiated his turn in the context of the 'linguistic turn'. Even if he didn't enroll in a specific course in feminist theory; even if his theory class didn't include a specific section on gender and sexuality; even if he read only the 'big daddies' of European theory (Hegel, Marx, Nietzsche, Freud, Barthes, Foucault, Lacan, Derrida); even if he read only Terry Eagleton's popular *Literary Theory: An Introduction*: that male student nonetheless exposed himself to a conceptual barrage that foregrounded and ungrounded his privileged position as a *gendered* subject in language.

Thus I consider 'literary theory' to be the third factor in the 'crucial change' in the relationship between men and feminism that has occurred in the last forty years. I do not mean to suggest that all the men who turned to or with feminism during this time were necessarily academic intellectuals. I do however suggest that from the late 1960s on 'theory' had a significant enough impact inside and outside universities to make possible a fundamental (if anti-foundational) rethinking of what 'really happens' in language, in history, in texts, in 'the streets', 'between the sheets' or in any of the other discursive conduits through which systemic male dominance is socially reproduced.

'NO HELP FROM ABOVE, NO FOUNDATION BELOW'

It would require a small library of books to examine the ways the afore-mentioned 'big daddies' of theory have influenced transformative feminist critique.[2] But before considering some of the overtly 'male feminist' statements of the early 1980s, I would like to touch upon two male figures whose work, though not intentionally feminist, nonetheless made such statements possible. Particularly, I will consider Karl Marx and Roland Barthes in relation to my earlier claim that the linguistic turn in theory negated 'God and nature' as the major alibis of male domination.

It does not take a radical feminist genius to recognise that patriarchal rule is all the more easily maintained if grounded in the premise that 'the world' was created by an Almighty Male Deity who still Lords over His creation. Nor should it take much genius – though it may require some existential courage – to arrive at the corresponding conclusion that the 'death' of this AMD might be a promising precondition for ending patriarchy itself. It was of course no feminist but Friedrich Nietzsche who turned the phrase 'God is dead' (1887/1974: 181). But it was Marx who declared that 'the criticism of religion is the premise of all criticism' and that the 'basis of irreligious criticism is this: *man makes religion*; religion does not make man' (1844/1978: 53). I cite Marx here not because I think there were any specifically feminist intentions behind his declarations, but because I feel that under present historical circumstances, which witness the baleful recrudescence of global (and explicitly anti-feminist) religious fundamentalisms, *any* pertinently feminist criticism should subscribe to what Marx called 'the premise of all criticism': man makes religion. A feminist revision of this premise might be: man makes religion for a variety of reasons, not all of them oppressive or contemptible, but *primarily* in ways that serve the interests of patriarchy and *mainly* for the purpose of its maintenance. Correspondingly, I feel that men with feminist aspirations, in interrogating their own relationships to power, would do well to extirpate in themselves any nostalgia for the 'God and nature' that have always been integral to the reproduction of systemic male dominance. The man who would be feminist has got to get over 'God'.

As for 'nature': Marx argues that it is the protracted labour of *working on* (and against) nature that makes history only ever humanly made, and thus makes 'man' himself humanly made. In *The German Ideology*, Marx writes:

Men can be distinguished from animals by consciousness, by religion or anything else you like. They themselves begin to distinguish themselves from animals as soon as they begin to *produce* their means of subsistence ... By producing their means of subsistence men are indirectly producing their actual material life. (1932/1978: 150)

It is from Marx, then, that we get the 'historical materialist' import of the first part of Stuart Hall's sentence: the world must be *made*; the human world is only ever humanly fabricated; only humans are responsible for it.

But we get the semiotic kicker – the world must be made *to mean* – from Roland Barthes. In 'Men, Feminism: The Materiality of Discourse', Cary Nelson points out that:

Men may ... make contributions to feminism without intending to. I don't imagine, for example, that Roland Barthes was thinking of feminism when he began to rethink the semiotics of sexual difference in *S/Z*, but the book has proven nonetheless useful for some feminists. If one wished to map the whole territory of feminism, then some lines of affinity, influence, and rearticulation will have to run to Barthes. (1987: 167)

Here the line of influence I wish to trace runs not to *S/Z* but to Barthes' 1957 *Mythologies*, particularly the concluding essay, 'Myth Today'. There Barthes invaluably argues that 'myth' does not represent a particular narrative *content* but performs a specific ideological *function*: 'it transforms history into nature' (1957/1972: 129). Establishing the real political signifi-cance of 'semiology' as the study of signs and signification, Barthes writes: 'Semiology has taught us that myth has the task of giving an historical intention a natural justification, and making contingency appear eternal' (1957/1972: 142). As he explains:

Myth is constituted by the loss of the historical quality of things: in it, things lose the memory that they once were made ... [Myth] has turned reality inside out, it has emptied it of history and has filled it with nature, it has removed from things their human meaning so as to make them signify a human insignificance ... *Myth is depoliticized speech*. One must naturally understand *political* in its deeper mean-ing, as describing the whole of human relations in their real, social structure, in their power of making the world. (1957/1972: 142–3)

Returning to a particular instance of 'mythological signification' he has examined – a *Paris Match* cover depicting a black soldier saluting the French flag – Barthes then writes: 'In the case of the soldier-Negro ... what is got rid of is certainly not French imperiality (on the contrary, since what must be actualized is its presence); it is the contingent, historical, in one word: *fabricated*, quality of colonialism' (1957/1972: 143).

I rehearse Marx and Barthes at such length to stress the need to under-stand labour and language as the *actually* fabricative, the really fictional bases not only of the assertion that 'the world must be made to mean' but of the actualised world itself. I also want to underscore the 'global' importance of that assertion to any productive or *working* understanding of the history of men and feminism. If we (men) can grasp what Marx posited as the real material basis of history as humans 'making the world', if we can grasp what Barthes posited as the contingent and *fabricated* quality of a force as *real* as colonialism, then we should more easily be able to understand and work with what feminist theorists have more recently posited as the contingent and fabricated realities of our bodies, our selves, our texts and their mutual co-implication in the fabricated realities of male domination. We could better understand Judith Butler when she writes: 'It is not clear to me that reality is something settled once and for all, and we might do well to urge speculation on the dynamic relation between fantasy and the realization of new social realities' (1987/2004: 36).

MEN IN/AND/ON/FOR/AGAINST/WITH/WITHOUT/DOING (AND BECOMING UNDONE BY) FEMINISM

I have argued for Marx and Barthes as intellectual preconditions not simply for understanding Judith Butler but for men's actively participating in the historical realisation/fabrication of new feminist social realities. Of course, it does not hurt my argument that one of the more active participants in this project – Stephen Heath – is both a committed cultural materialist and an English translator of major work by Roland Barthes.

Heath's 1982 book *The Sexual Fix* critiques 'sexological' discourses from nineteenth-century medical treatises and Freudian psychoanalysis, to sex researchers Alfred Kinsey and Masters and Johnson, to the plethora of 1970s pop psychology/sexual self-help books that, in Heath's opinion, did not 'liberate' but rather coerced readers into believing they *had* to be 'erotically fulfilled' and 'fully orgasmic'. The fact that *The Sexual Fix* is also a work of literary criticism, treating canonical authors such as Thomas Hardy, Henry James and D. H. Lawrence as well as contemporary popular novelists like Erica Jong and Lisa Alther, underscores Heath's basic argument that 'sexology' is not the objective observation of immutable natural fact that it pretends to be but is, in fact, an ideological fiction. And for Heath 'sexology' can only be an ideological fiction because the 'object' it purports to observe – sexuality – is itself only such a fiction. Heath writes:

[T]here is no such thing as sexuality; what we have experienced and are experiencing is the fabrication of a 'sexuality', the construction of something called 'sexuality' through a set of representations – images, discourses, ways of picturing and describing – that propose and confirm, that make up this sexuality to which we are then referred and held in our lives, a whole *sexual fix* precisely; the much-vaunted 'liberation' of sexuality ... is thus not a liberation but a myth, an ideology, the definition of a new mode of conformity (that can be understood, moreover, in relation to the capitalist system, the production of a commodity 'sexuality'). (1982: 3)

For Heath, then, 'sex' too must be made to mean; it is only ever 'a matter of meaning and meanings' (1982: 153). But, Heath adds, 'to say that sexuality does not exist as such is not at all to deny the reality of the sexual in human life . . .; on the contrary, it is the beginning of an attempt to displace the particular and limiting representation of it that we know today as "sexuality"' (1982: 3).

To unfix the sexual fix, then, one must demythologize, denaturalise, attempt to turn 'nature' back into 'history'. But one makes this attempt while understanding that 'history' can never be anything other than a 'set of representations – images, discourses, ways of picturing and describing', that one can displace a particular and limiting representation only with another (hopefully less limiting) representation: *real* political struggles can never cease to be struggles in and over meaning. Heath makes these points, laying out the basic tenets of anti-essentialist, semiotic political analysis, when he takes up the question of whether there can be an 'essential male or female language, immediate and inevitable, determined by the sex' (1982: 120). For Heath there can be no such language because:

in any given instance, men do not *necessarily* speak or write male positioning discourse nor women *necessarily* female positioning discourse; the link between sex (in the sense of gender) and the sexual is not direct – there is no natural expression of one's sex – but is always mediated, realized in language in use in society, in discourses, is always a matter of representations . . . If the sexual were not this cultural fact, there would be no hope of any transformation. (1982: 120)

Clearly, Heath wants to displace 'natural fact' with 'cultural fact' because without the possibility of such displacement *there would be no hope of any transformation.* Just as clearly, Heath does hope to transform, wants to participate in the transformative feminist critique of the essentialist sexual fix. But nowhere in *The Sexual Fix* does Heath call himself a 'male feminist'. In a sense, he does not need to affix himself with such a designation: the book itself suggests that it is unnecessary for a male writer to declare or even think of himself as 'a feminist' to produce usefully feminist work.

And yet questions of whether or not and if so exactly how a man can be useful to feminism were actively debated in academic circles in the 1980s. In 1984, the Society for Critical Exchange sponsored two sessions on the question of 'Men in Feminism' at the annual Modern Language Association Convention in Washington, DC. Participants included Heath, Paul Smith, Andrew Ross, Judith Mayne, Elizabeth Weed, Alice

Jardine and Peggy Kamuf. In 1987, the papers presented at these sessions were published, along with work by other prominent scholars and theorists (Jane Gallop, Jacques Derrida), in Jardine and Smith's *Men in Feminism*.

Since nearly all of the contributors to this collection are literary critics, most of the essays feature an acute self-consciousness about the way relations of power are inscribed in language. Indeed, one of the key problems to emerge in the 1980s was the question of how to designate men's potentially productive relations to feminism without unconsciously reproducing men's historically abusive relationships with women. Whether by intentional design or not, the conjunctions, prepositions and linking verbs that have appeared in various book and essay titles – and, with, on, in, doing – all tend to conjure objectionable images of matrimony ('and'), false symmetry ('with'), mounting ('on') or even rape, the penetrative violence of phallic breaking and entering ('in', 'doing'). The conjunction in the title of this chapter would be an example; the linking preposition in *Men in Feminism* would be another; while the linking verb in Tom Digby's collection *Men Doing Feminism* (1998) would be conspicuously still another. With acute self-consciousness, Paul Smith, in his contribution to *Men in Feminism*, takes 'some large part of responsibility' for its 'at least provocative, perhaps offensive' title, and then announces that:

> The provocation, the offence, the trouble that men now are for feminism is no longer . . . simply a matter of men's being the object or *cause* of feminism . . . Men, some men, now . . . are entering feminism, actively penetrating it . . . for a variety of motives and in a variety of modes, fashions. That penetration is often looked upon with suspicion; it can be understood as yet another interruption, a more or less illegal act of breaking and entering, for which these men must finally be held to account. Perhaps the question that needs to be asked, then, by these men, with them, for them, is to what extent their irruption (penetration and interruption) is justified? is it of any political use to feminism? to what extent is it wanted? (1987: 34)

All of the essays in *Men in Feminism*, and most of the writings concerning male feminism that come after it, attempt to answer these questions of justice, use and desire. In my estimation, some of the more significant answers in *Men in Feminism* come from Smith's co-editor, Alice Jardine, and I will consider her recommendations and their consequences shortly. First, however, I would like to examine a particular moment in *Men in Feminism*, a critical exchange that reveals the way masculinist resistance to feminist insights and traditionalist reaction against theory's linguistic turn are both indentured to a sort of crypto-theological nostalgia for a sense of the divine legitimation of masculinist tradition.

PREHISTORICAL MAN (1986)

Nancy K. Miller's 'Man on Feminism: A Criticism of His Own' responds to Denis Donoghue's 'A Criticism of Her Own', an antagonistic review of feminist literary scholarship, as well as a set of gripes about deconstruction, that appeared in *The New Republic* in 1986 and is reprinted in its entirety in *Men in Feminism*. Donoghue registers many complaints here but is particularly dismayed that feminist critics attempt to bring the question of literary merit down into the realm of the merely social. Employing a well-worn 'New Critical' tactic of dismissing any but a formalist approach to literature, Donoghue opines that 'The question of literary merit, as distinct from sociological interest, is rarely raised by feminist critics. When it is, the argument is desperate. We are to believe that literary criteria are incorrigibly man-made values, and are compromised by the power they enforce' (Donoghue, 1987: 149). In her rejoinder, Miller responds not desperately but perfectly: 'Why, yes, Denis, we really believe that literary criteria are man-made. What else might they be? Divine?' (Miller, 1987: 143).

Though a man like Donoghue may not explicitly believe that literary criteria are literally handed down like stony commandments from a Heavenly Father, only an unconscious assumption of the immaculate conception of literary values could account for his incredulity towards the feminist argument that such values do not spring from any deity's mighty loins but are all-too-humanly produced. In other words (Miller's own), Donoghue, caught with his pants down, 'displays his unexamined relation to *ideology*' (Miller, 1987: 142), to what Louis Althusser would call the '*Amen – So be it*' (1971: 181) of ideological interpellation.

Pointing out that 'the term [man-made] seems to be a kind of negative buzzword in his lexicon of conservative doxa', Miller reveals Donoghue objecting to that term in another piece of journalism, this one castigating postmodernism in the *New York Times Book Review*. She writes: 'Donoghue opposes "man-made" to an "artist's desire for spontaneity or an original relation to the world"; "man-made" images are "quotations from quotations"' (1987: 276n4). One might compare, however, Donoghue's 'artist's desire' to these quotations from Barthes' 'The Death of the Author':

A text is not a line of words releasing a single 'theological' meaning ... but a multi-dimensional space in which a variety of writings, none of them original, blend and clash. The text is a tissue of quotations drawn from the innumerable centres of culture ... [T]he writer can only imitate a gesture that is always anterior, never original. His only power is to mix writings ... Did he wish to express himself, he ought at least to know that the inner 'thing' he thinks to 'translate' is itself only a ready-formed dictionary, its words only explainable through other words, and so on indefinitely . . . In precisely this way literature . . . by refusing to assign a 'secret', an ultimate meaning, to the text (and to the world as text), liberates what may be called an anti-theological activity, an activity that is truly revolutionary since to refuse to fix meaning is, in the end, to refuse God and his hypostases – reason, science, law. (1977: 146–7)

Just as Nietzsche saw the 'death of God' as the birth of exhilarating possibility (1887/1974: 280), so feminism welcomes 'the death of the author' as one condition of possibility for refusing the sexual fix, refusing to be fixed *in or by* the monolithically authorised 'meaning' or regulatory fiction of gender. While Donoghue's 'artist' yearns for an 'original relation to the world' that presumably not only mirrors but holds communion with God's Fathering of the wor(l)d, Barthes' scriptor affirms that the inner 'thing' or essence he wants to express in writing is itself an always already fabricated dictionary, an ensemble of 'quotations of quotations' drawn neither from God nor nature but 'from innumerable centres of culture' and from the 'world as text'. But while such citational refraction causes Donoghue's artist to despair, the recognition of the 'historically produced nature' of nature gives Barthes' decidedly deicidal scriptor cause for radical optimism. For in the secular faith of social constructionism, there is no cultural centre that cannot be decentred, no dictionary that cannot be rewritten. As Mark Seltzer puts it, 'if persons and things are constructed, they could, at least in principle, be constructed differently' (1990: 144). Or as Michel Foucault writes, speaking specifically (but perhaps not exclusively) for and of male homosexuals, 'Maybe the target nowadays is not to discover what we are but to refuse what we are . . . We have to promote new forms of subjectivity through the refusal of this kind of subjectivity that has been imposed on us for several centuries' (1983/2000: 336).

THE LIVING END(S) OF MAN

Since the 1980s, some of us men have responded to the feminist critique, the linguistic turn and the so-called 'crisis of masculinity' by attempting to historicise, denaturalise or otherwise refabricate our gendered identities, to 'refuse what we are' so as to 'promote new forms of subjectivity' and realise new social realities. Others, however, have attempted to ignore, refute or rage against all these 'castrating' feminist and social constructionist arguments, to remythologise the Male Self and revive a resolutely singular form of masculine subjectivity that is imputed to be as old as the hills. Outside the strictly academic context, while the late 1980s saw the publication of works like John Stoltenberg's *Refusing to Be a Man* (1989), the decade's end also witnessed the rise of the 'mythopoetic men's movement' and the publication of Robert Bly's bestseller *Iron John* (1990). Relatively few were the men who took courage from Stoltenberg's refusal compared to the legions comforted by Bly's hard-assed assertion that 'the structure at the bottom of the male psyche is still as firm as it was twenty thousand years ago' (1990: 230). According to the mythopoeticists, these legions of contemporary men, softened and wounded by feminist attacks, had lost touch with that timelessly firm bottom and thus needed – not only for their own good but for the greater benefit of society itself – to reconnect with so-called 'Zeus energy', which Bly blithely defines as 'male authority accepted for the good of the community' (1990: 22).[3]

Returning, however, to the 1980s academic context: if the first Modern Language Association sessions on 'Men in Feminism' took place in 1984, that year also saw the publication of K. K. Ruthven's anti-feminist *Feminist Literary Criticism: An Introduction*. I have nothing to say about this volume – *except* that I would have hoped such phrases as 'feminist ideologies' (1984: vii), 'feminist terrorism' (1984: 10) and 'the more ridiculous manifestations of feminist criticism' (1984: 14), would have safely consigned it to the historical dustbin (particularly, after 11 September, 2001, the phrase 'feminist terrorism'). So I was unpleasantly surprised to open a *2002* book on masculinity that trundled out the following Ruthvenism as an epigraph: 'I object to a strategy which situates men in such a way that the only speaking positions available to them are those of tame feminist or wild antifeminist' (DiPiero, 2002: 1; Ruthven, 1984: 9). I too would object to that 'strategy' if it were all that transformative feminist critique had ever made available. But feminism has actually been more generous – both in the strategies and speaking positions it has offered to men and in its observations concerning men and their desires – than these two particular men would allow. As a conceptual field, feminism is considerably more generous and varied than, say, mythopoeticism. For all their ritualised treks to the 'wilderness' to reconnect with 'Zeus energy' as the timeless truth of male desire, the leaders and followers of the mythopoetic men's movement were only wildly conventional, and hence quite tamely anti-feminist, in their thinking.

Stephen Heath, on the other hand, is neither tame nor anti-feminist in *The Sexual Fix* or in his contribution to *Men in Feminism*. And yet I do think that several of Heath's positions in *Men in Feminism* were superannuated by Alice Jardine later in that very volume. These would include his already cited opening salvo – 'Men's relation to feminism is an impossible one' (Heath, 1987: 1) – and his observation that while 'female sexuality is a bad question from a rotten history ... "male sexuality" is a good question from a rotten history that could not pose it' (1987: 14). Heath implies that history is still too rotten for the good question of male sexuality to be posed by men. Jardine, however, suggests that the time is overripe for men to inquire into male bodies and sexualities and that such inquiry could be the very condition of possibility for a productive male relation to feminism. Taking her cue from Hélène Cixous' statement that 'men still have everything to say about their sexuality, and everything to write' (1981: 247), and from Luce Irigaray's observation that 'The bodily in man is what metaphysics has never touched' (cited in Jardine, 1987: 61), Jardine touches on a number of matters other than female sexuality that men who want to be useful to feminism could start taking up, including 'the penis and balls, erection, ejaculation (not to mention the phallus) ... homosexuality, blood, tactile pleasure, pleasure in general, *desire* ... Now this *would* be talking your body, not talking *about* it' (1987: 61). Ending her essay 'on a more literary note', Jardine raises questions about 'narrative structure' and 'problems of enunciation, voice, and silence' (1987: 61). Then, addressing her male reader in the second person, she asks:

> Can you think through the heterogeneity of the subject without putting the burden of the demised universal subject onto the female? And most important, when you're reading men's books, whether new or old, are you up to taking Nietzsche seriously?:
> What has *the Man* not been able to talk about?
> What is *the Man* hiding?
> In what respect is *the Man* mistaken?
> You see, you have all your work before you, not behind you. We, as feminists, need your work. We don't need your Odor di Uomo. We need you as traveling *compagnons* into the twenty-first century. (1987: 61)

Still in the twentieth century, in 1988, at yet another MLA session on 'Men in Feminism', Jonathan Culler presented 'Five Propositions on the Future of Men in Feminism', the fourth of which was that 'if men want to do feminist work their most productive strategy might be, as Alice Jardine has suggested, to investigate not feminine sexuality but masculine sexuality ... and the construction of the male subject' (1994: 188). And in fact the 'future' did play out along more or less Jardinean lines, for the following years saw a great blossoming of studies on male sexualities, male bodies and male subjectivities.[4] The ethical impulse animating many of these studies involved the idea that since idealist metaphysics has always repressed male embodiment and denied male vulnerability (to, say, death) by displacing the 'matters' of 'the body' onto 'the feminine' (an analytical point first made by Simone de Beauvoir in *The Second Sex*), a discursive embrace of repressed male embodiment by men might help dissolve that thanatical displacement.[5]

But the conclusion that some men reached in attempting this embrace was that even if, as Jardine put it, our work was before us and not behind us, our writing should begin to address not only the physically 'before' but the corporeal 'behind': that is, not only the 'fronts' we put up – 'penis and balls, erection, ejaculation' – but the behinds we generally put down or shut tight, which not even Jardine had seen fit to mention. Despite her omission, however, what *the Man* has in fact not been able to talk about is not only the phallus, which Jacques Lacan says 'can play its role only when veiled' (2002: 277), but the rectum, which Leo Bersani calls 'the grave in which the masculine ideal . . . of proud subjectivity is buried' (1987: 222). There was, in other words, a decidedly 'rectal turn' in critical discourse on 'embodied masculinity' in the 1990s, a new *feminist* focus on the male anus as a site of penetration, liminality and significant leakage. This turn followed variously from Jardine's recommendations, from Bersani's AIDS-related essay 'Is the Rectum a Grave?', from renewed critical interest in the excessive visions of 'excremental philosopher' Georges Bataille, from political reworkings of Julia Kristeva's treatment of abjection by Iris Marion Young and Judith Butler and from the general emergence and spread of 'queer theory' in the early part of the decade. The turn provoked assorted critical efforts, on the part of male and female, straight and queer feminist theorists to demean proudly phallic subjectivity, to queer straight masculinity and to reconfigure or otherwise open up the heterosexual male body to and through the radical avenue of analism.[6]

I will return to the 'rectal turn' and its possible ethical/political significance for male feminism in a moment. First I want to consider the way the 1980s 'question of male feminist criticism' got folded, as it were, into the provocative origamis of queer theory in the 1990s. Donald E. Hall points out that 'the first high-profile use of the term "queer theory" was in a special issue of the feminist journal *differences* from the summer of 1991' (2003: 55). So the term as such was not exactly in play in 1990 when Joseph A. Boone and Michael Cadden published *Engendering Men: The Question of Male Feminist Criticism*. This collection, however, not only featured essays by men who would soon become leading voices in queer theory (Michael Warner, Ed Cohen and Lee Edelman, for examples) but it performed one of queer theory's most valuable services – exposing the presumption of heteronormative privilege at work in other putatively progressive discourses. In particular, Boone critiques Jardine and Smith's *Men in Feminism* for its heterosexism and its general neglect of gay men's support of academic feminist interventions:

At this historical juncture, many of the men in the academy who are feminism's most supportive 'allies' *are* gay. Somehow this fact and its implications have often been forgotten in many of the discussions surrounding the 'male feminist' controversy, especially those represented in the *Men in Feminism* volume. From Heath's to [Rosi] Bradotti's essay, too many of the generalizations made about men's desire to become a part of feminism *take for granted* the 'heterosexual' basis of that desire – the predominant imagery of penetration is but one clue to the preponderance of these assumptions. In contrast, a recognition of the influence of gay men working in and around feminism has the potential of rewriting feminist fears about 'men *in* feminism' as a strictly heterosexual gesture of appropriation. (Boone, 1990: 23)

If, however, *Engendering Men* assuaged any feminist anxieties about penetrative prepositional appropriation (relax, girls – gay men want only to work *around* you, not thrust into you), the text may not have eased concerns about what Luce Irigaray called 'hom(m)osexuality', which she considered merely another 'alibi for the smooth workings of man's relations with himself' (1974/1985: 172). After all, 'to work around' can also mean 'to avoid'. The issues thus raised are a complicated part of a complicated history that was anything but simplified by the rise of queer theory: recognising the continuing structural solidarity of misogyny and homophobia within systemic male dominance, we must also acknowledge the heterosexism that still circulates among some straight feminist women, the misogyny that still obtains among some gay men and the potential for avoiding feminism, or ignoring women altogether, opened up by straight male feminism's embrace of the queer.[7] *Engendering Men* in no way avoided feminism, but it did in a sense cut *women* out of the picture. While *Men in Feminism* may have largely excluded gay men (excepting Craig Owens), the volume at least featured a salutary gender parity in terms of the authorship of its essays, and its cover illustration depicts two androgynous figures facing each other and engaged in conversation; *Engendering Men*'s essays are all male-authored, and its cover illustration shows only nude male figures, foregrounding in fact a young man's slightly upturned behind.

I mention this detail less to criticise *Engendering Men* – a strong and valuable collection – than to return to the 'rectal turn' and the decidedly abject body-talk that saturated feminist and queer masculinity studies in the 1990s. Obviously, feminist suspicions about men who 'broke and entered' into feminism only to keep 'feminine sexuality' as the object of their controlling gaze may be further exacerbated when a male theorist peers up his own ass and insists on calling *that* dark speculation 'feminist'. But what in my view makes the rectal turn more than male mooning, but instead a potentially 'productive strategy' for those men who 'want to do feminist work', is that the rectal turn can also represent a re-enfleshed effort to think through the heterogeneity of the subject without putting the onerous burden of abjection – 'the mode by which Others become shit' (Butler, 1990: 134) – onto the feminine. In other words, if 'the construction of the male subject' has always depended upon the punitive abjection of a 'feminized' other, then to dismantle this projective mode from within would seem an urgent male feminist task of resignification. To try to become not a 'universal' but an ethically non-abjecting subject 'is not to cease to be male but to try to make that role into less of an agent of oppression and disregard' (Culler, 1994: 188). Such making, even if it means men's seemingly self-indulgent (if possibly self-shattering) narcissistic masochism, even if it seems to mean men's merely messing (with) themselves, may also mean men's trying to make less of a misogynist mess in and of a world that must be made to mean.

   In the end, then, we return to the question of making, of word-making and world-making, and of the possible corrigibility of 'man-made values' from the perspective of feminism 'both as a methodology for interpreting literary texts and as a socio-political ground for acting in the world' (Morgan and Davis, 1994: 189). The 'rich tradition' and complicated history of male feminist writing has indeed travelled into the twenty-first century, if mainly in the forms of masculinity studies and queer theory. The question of whether or not such theoretical studies qualify as feminism or do anything at all to assist transformative feminist critique remains quite open – and is not, in any case, to be declared closed by the likes of me. Although I'm not sure that in 2007 it would still be as 'tendentious and appropriative for a man to call what he is doing feminism' (Culler, 1994: 187) as it seemed to Jonathan Culler and others in 1988, I agree with him that it is probably still 'preferable' for a man 'not to claim to be doing feminist readings, leaving it to others to describe his criticism as they think fit' (1994: 187). Such a man, ever at the mercy of a language that is by nature fictional, can only hope that his fabrications will have somehow made a real difference. In the meantime, in all truth, he can only promise that he will continue to lie – with and for feminism.

NOTES

1. In the essay 'Structure, Sign, and Play in the Discourse of the Human Sciences', Jacques Derrida describes the 'event' of the linguistic turn as the moment when 'language invaded the universal problematic' and 'everything became discourse' (1966/1978: 280). For Derrida, the main lesson of the linguistic turn is that 'there is nothing outside the text' (1997: 258). Psychoanalyst Jacques Lacan 'universalizes' the linguistic turn by conflating the 'no to the real' that makes language possible with the paternal prohibition against incest that founds the human social order. For Lacan the human subject is at the same time a linguistic subject and an oedipal subject: just as the word cannot *be* the real thing it *means*, the subject cannot *be* ('at one' with the mother) and *mean* (in language). The human subject is subjected to the 'symbolic order' – an order of symbols and the order to symbolise. 'Man speaks', says Lacan, but only 'because the symbol has made him man' (2002: 65).

2. On Hegel, see Butler (1987) and Ferguson (1993); on Marx, see Barrett (1988); on Nietzsche, see Oliver (1995); on Freudian and Lacanian psychoanalysis, see Grosz (1990), Shepherdson (2000) and Moi (2004); on Barthes and Foucault, see Schor (1987) and McNay (1992); on Derrida and deconstruction, see Elam (1994).

3. For feminist responses, see Ferber (2000/2004) and Kimmel (1995). For a more sympathetic reading, see Gardiner (2002b).

4. See Silverman (1992), Lehman (1992), Goldstein (1994), Thomas (1996), Schoene-Harwood (2000), Robinson (2000), Gardiner (2002a), Tuana (2002), Still (2003) and Murphy (2004a). The interdisciplinary journal *Men and Masculinities*, edited by Michael S. Kimmel, began publication in 1998 and features the best pro-feminist male writing on masculinity.

5. Judith Butler writes: 'Women are "Other" according to Beauvoir in so far as they are defined by a masculine perspective that seeks to safeguard its own disembodied status through identifying women generally with the bodily sphere... By defining women as "Other," men are able ... to dispose of their [own] bodies, to make themselves other than their bodies – a symbol potentially of human decay and transience, of limitation generally – and to make their bodies other than themselves. From this belief that the body is Other, it is not a far leap to the conclusion that others *are* their bodies, while the masculine "I" is a noncorporeal soul' (1987/2004: 28). In using the adjective 'thanatical', I merge 'Thanatos', the name that Freud gives to the death-drive, with 'fanatical'.

6. See Bersani (1987), Bataille (1985), Kristeva (1982), Young (1990), Butler (1990, 1993), Hall (2003), Miller (1991), Edelman (1999), Pronger (1998), Waldby (1995), Gardiner (2000) and Thomas (1996, 2002a, 2002b).

7. In regard to the potential for male feminism and queer theory to ignore women, see Modleski (1991) and Walters (1996). On the pros and cons of 'straight queer theory' see Thomas (2000) – ambivalently pro – and Schlichter (2004) – unambivalently con.

BIBLIOGRAPHY

Althusser, Louis (1971), *'Lenin and Philosophy' and Other Essays*, trans. Ben Brewster, New York: Monthly Review Press.

Barrett, Michèle (1988), *Women's Oppression Today: The Marxist/Feminist Encounter*, London and New York: Verso.

Barthes, Roland (1957/1972), *Mythologies*, trans. Annette Levers, New York: Hill and Wang.

(1977), *Image-Music-Text*, trans. Stephen Heath, New York: Noonday.

(1981), *Camera Lucida: Reflections on Photography*, trans. Richard Howard, New York: Noonday.

Bataille, Georges (1985), *Visions of Excess: Selected Writings 1927–1939*, ed. Allan Stoekl, Minneapolis: University of Minnesota Press.

Bersani, Leo (1987), 'Is the Rectum a Grave?', in *October* 43 (Winter).

Boone, Joseph A. (1990), 'Of Me(n) and Feminism: Who(se) Is the Sex That Writes?', in *Engendering Men: The Question of Male Feminist Criticism*, ed. Joseph A. Boone and Michael Cadden, New York and London: Routledge.

Bristow, Joseph (1992), 'Men in Feminism: Sexual Politics Twenty Years On', in *Between Men and Feminism*, ed. David Porter, London and New York: Routledge.

Butler, Judith (1987), *Subjects of Desire: Hegelian Reflections in Twentieth-Century France*, New York: Columbia University Press.

(1987/2004), 'Variations on Sex and Gender: Beauvoir, Wittig, Foucault', in *The Judith Butler Reader*, ed. Sarah Salih, Malden, MA: Blackwell.

(1990), *Gender Trouble: Feminism and the Subversion of Identity*, London and New York: Routledge.

(1993), *Bodies That Matter: On the Discursive Limits of 'Sex'*, London and New York: Routledge.

Bly, Robert (1990), *Iron John: A Book about Men*, Reading, MA: Addison-Wesley.

Cixous, Hélène (1981), 'The Laugh of the Medusa', in *New French Feminisms*, ed. Elaine Marks and Isabelle de Courtivron, New York: Schocken.

Culler, Jonathan (1994), 'Five Propositions on the Future of Men in Feminism', in *Men Writing the Feminine: Literature, Theory, and the Question of Genders*, ed. Thaïs E. Morgan, Albany: State University of New York Press.

Derrida, Jacques (1966/1978), *Writing and Difference*, trans. Alan Bass, Chicago: University of Chicago Press.

(1997), *Of Grammatology*, corrected edition, trans. Gayatri Chakravorty Spivak, Baltimore: Johns Hopkins University Press.

Digby, Tom (ed.) (1998), *Men Doing Feminism*, New York and London: Routledge.

DiPiero, Thomas (2002), *White Men Aren't*, Durham, NC: Duke University Press.

Donoghue, Denis (1987), 'A Criticism of Her Own', in Jardine and Smith (1987).

Edelman, Lee (1999), '*Rear Window*'s Glasshole', in *Outtakes: Essays in Queer Theory and Film*, ed. Ellis Hanson, Durham, NC: Duke University Press.

Elam, Diane (1994), *Feminism and Deconstruction: Ms. en Abyme*, New York and London: Routledge.

Ferber, Abby L. (2000/2004), 'Racial Warriors and Weekend Warriors: The Construction of Masculinity in Mythopoetic and White Supremacist Discourse', in *Feminism and Masculinities*, ed. Peter F. Murphy, Oxford: Oxford University Press.

Ferguson, Kathy E. (1993), *The Man Question: Visions of Subjectivity in Feminist Theory*, Berkeley: University of California Press.

Foucault, Michel (1983/2000), 'The Subject and Power', in *The Essential Works of Foucault, 1954–1984*, vol. III: *Power*, ed. James D. Faubion, trans. Robert Hurley, New York: The New Press.

Gardiner, Judith K. (2000), '"South Park," Blue Men, Anality, and Market Masculinity', in *Men and Masculinities* 2:3 (January).

(ed.) (2002a), *Masculinity Studies and Feminist Theory*, New York: Columbia University Press.

(2002b), 'Theorizing Age and Gender: Bly's Boys, Feminism, and Maturity Masculinity', in Gardiner (2002a).

Goldstein, Laurence (ed.) (1994), *The Male Body: Features, Destinies, Exposures*, Ann Arbor: Michigan University Press.

Grosz, Elizabeth (1990), *Jacques Lacan: A Feminist Introduction*, London and New York: Routledge.

Hall, Donald E. (2003), *Queer Theories*, New York: Palgrave.

Hall, Stuart (1998), 'The Rediscovery of "Ideology"', in *Literary Theory: An Anthology*, ed. Julie Rivkin and Michael Ryan, New York: Blackwell.

Heath, Stephen (1982), *The Sexual Fix*, London: Macmillan.

(1987), 'Male Feminism', in Jardine and Smith (1987).

Irigaray, Luce (1974/1985), *Speculum of the Other Woman*, trans. Gillian G. Gill, Ithaca: Cornell University Press.

Jardine, Alice and Paul Smith (eds) (1987), *Men in Feminism*, New York: Methuen.

Jardine, Alice (1987), 'Men in Feminism: Odor di Uomo or Compagnons de Route?,' in Jardine and Smith (1987).

Kimmel, Michael (ed.) (1995), *The Politics of Manhood: Profeminist Men Respond to the Mythopoetic Men's Movement (and the Mythopoetic Leaders Answer)*, Philadelphia: Temple University Press.

Kristeva, Julia (1982), *Powers of Horror: An Essay on Abjection*, trans. Leon S. Roudiez, New York: Columbia University Press.

Lacan, Jacques (2002), *Ecrits: A Selection*, trans. Bruce Fink, New York: Norton.

Lehman, Peter (1992), *Running Scared: Masculinity and the Representation of the Male Body*, Philadelphia: Temple University Press.

Marx, Karl (1844/1978), 'Contribution to the Critique of Hegel's Philosophy of Right: Introduction', in *The Marx-Engels Reader*, 2nd edn, ed. Robert C. Tucker, New York: Norton.

(1932/1978), *The German Ideology*, in *The Marx-Engels Reader*, 2nd edn, ed. Robert C. Tucker, New York: Norton.

McNay, Lois (1992), *Foucault and Feminism*, Boston: Northeastern University Press.

Miller, D. A. (1991), 'Anal *Rope*', in *Inside/Out: Lesbian and Gay Theory*, ed. Diana Fuss, New York: Routledge.

Miller, Nancy K. (1987), 'Man on Feminism: A Criticism of His Own', in Jardine and Smith (1987).

Modleski, Tania (1991), *Feminism without Women: Culture and Criticism in a 'Postfeminist' Age*, New York: Routledge.

Moi, Toril (2004), 'From Femininity to Finitude: Freud, Lacan, and Feminism, Again', in *Signs: Journal of Women in Culture and Society* 29:3.

Morgan, Thaïs E. and Robert Con Davis (1994), 'Two Conversations on Literature, Theory, and the Question of Gender', in *Men Writing the Feminine: Literature, Theory, and the Question of Genders*, ed. Thaïs E. Morgan, Albany: State University of New York Press.

Murphy, Peter F., (ed.) (2004a), *Feminism and Masculinities*, Oxford: Oxford University Press.

(2004b), 'Introduction', in Murphy (2004a).

Nelson, Cary (1987), 'Men, Feminism: The Materiality of Discourse', in Jardine and Smith (1987).

Nietzsche, Friedrich (1887/1974), *The Gay Science*, trans. Walter Kaufmann, New York: Vintage.

(1887/2000), *On the Genealogy of Morals*, in *Basic Writings of Nietzsche*, ed. Walter Kaufmann, New York: Modern Library.

(1889/1990), *The Twilight of the Idols*, trans. R. J. Hollingdale, New York: Penguin.

Oliver, Kelly (1995), *Womanizing Nietzsche: Philosophy's Relation to the 'Feminine'*, New York and London: Routledge.

Pronger, Brian (1998), 'On Your Knees: Carnal Knowledge, Masculine Dissolution, Doing Feminism', in Digby (1998).

Robinson, Sally (2000), *Marked Men: White Masculinity in Crisis*, New York: Columbia University Press.

Rubin, Gayle (1975), 'The Traffic in Women: Notes on the "Political Economy" of Sex', in *Toward an Anthropology of Women*, ed. Rayna R. Reiter, New York: Monthly Review Press.

Ruthven, K. K. (1984), *Feminist Literary Criticism: An Introduction*, Cambridge: Cambridge University Press.

Schlichter, Annette (2004), 'Queer at Last? – Straight Intellectuals and the Desire for Transgression', in *GLQ: A Journal of Lesbian and Gay Studies* 10:4 (September).

Schoene-Harwood, Berthold (2000), *Writing Men: Literary Masculinities from Frankenstein to the New Man*, Edinburgh: Edinburgh University Press.

Schor, Naomi (1987), 'Dreaming Dissymmetry: Barthes, Foucault, and Sexual Difference', in Jardine and Smith (1987).

Sedgwick, Eve Kosofsky (1993), *Epistemology of the Closet*, Berkeley: University of California Press.

Seltzer, Mark (1990), 'The Love Master', in *Engendering Men: The Question of Male Feminist Criticism*, ed. Joseph A. Boone and Michael Cadden, New York and London: Routledge.

Shepherdson, Charles (2000), *Vital Signs: Nature, Culture, Psychoanalysis*, New York and London: Routledge.

Silverman, Kaja (1992), *Male Subjectivity at the Margins*, London: Routledge.

Smith, Paul (1987), 'Men in Feminism: Men and Feminist Theory', in Jardine and Smith (1987).

Still, Judith (ed.) (2003), *Men's Bodies*, Edinburgh: Edinburgh University Press.

Stoltenberg, John (1974/2004), 'Toward Gender Justice', in Murphy (2004a).

— (1989), *Refusing to Be a Man: Essays on Sex and Justice*, Portland, OR: Breitenbush Books.

Thomas, Calvin (1996), *Male Matters: Masculinity, Anxiety, and the Male Body on the Line*, Urbana: University of Illinois Press.

— (ed.) (2000), *Straight with a Twist: Queer Theory and the Subject of Heterosexuality*, Urbana: University of Illinois Press.

— (2002a), 'Must Desire Be Taken Literally?', in *Parallax* 8:4.

— (2002b), 'Re-enfleshing the Bright Boys: Or, How Male Bodies Matter to Feminist Theory', in Gardiner (2002a).

Tuana, Nancy, et al. (eds) (2002), *Revealing Male Bodies*, Bloomington: Indiana University Press.

Waldby, Catherine (1995), 'Destruction: Boundary Erotics and the Refigurations of the Heterosexual Male Body', in *Sexy Bodies: The Strange Carnalities of Feminism*, ed. Elizabeth Grosz and Elspeth Probyn, New York and London: Routledge.

Walters, Suzanna Danuta (1996), 'From Here to Queer: Radical Feminism, Postmodernism, and the Lesbian Menace (Or, Why Can't a Woman Be More Like a Fag?)', in *Signs: Journal of Women in Culture and Society* 21:4.

Young, Iris Marion (1990), 'Abjection and Oppression: Dynamics of Unconscious Racism, Sexism, and Homophobia', in *Crises in Continental Philosophy*, ed. Arleen B. Dallery and Charles E. Scott, with Holley Roberts, Albany: State University of New York Press.

Poststructuralism and beyond

Introduction to Part III

Gill Plain and Susan Sellers

The chapters in this section introduce what might be termed a 'paradigm shift' in feminist literary criticism. This is a period in which the meaning of 'woman' as a signifying term is subject to its most radical destabilisations – and hence what it means to be a feminist or to practice feminist literary criticism undergoes significant change. In Part II of the book, 'woman' as a situated, socio-cultural entity was problematised. As the essays demonstrated, there was a movement outwards from white, middle-class feminism to an acknowledgement of the diversity of women's lives, experiences and creativity. To think about women was also to think about gender: masculinity as much as femininity became available for interrogation and reinscription. Feminism began to ask fundamental questions regarding language and human subjectivity, and these questions were, simultaneously, the subject of intense debate in a range of complementary theoretical discourses, from linguistics to psychoanalysis. While poststructuralism was examining the role played by language in individual and social formation, psychoanalysis was analysing the construction of gendered identity in the embryonic adult, and postcolonialism was focusing attention on the socio-economic reality of the subaltern 'other'. From diverse directions new hybrid forms of feminist literary criticism emerged that, while continuing to examine the complexity of gendered identities in contemporary society, also brought renewed energy to ongoing debates questioning the status of the term 'woman' as a coherent theoretical point of origin.

The increased hybridity of feminist literary criticism and its intersection with complementary discourses gives a somewhat different shape to the chapters of Part III. The writers in this section spend more time explaining theoretical concepts and movements and less time on the tangible literary critical products of these debates. Given the diversity of discourses that feminism now brings together, it has become harder to define the key texts of feminist literary criticism, and indeed it is questionable whether there would be anything to gain from establishing a canon of poststructuralist feminist thought. Nonetheless, the bibliographies for the individual chapters will direct readers to examples of criticism in practice, and this further reading will provide material evidence of the literary value of these multi-vocal encounters. It should also be noted that the projects of 'literary' criticism have themselves expanded to embrace developments in media, film and technology. The text itself has become a hybrid and interdisciplinary concept, and the contributors to Part III draw on sources as diverse as autobiography, film and hypertext to illustrate their discussions.

Inevitably, then, Part III is characterised by an extensive cross-fertilisation of ideas, as aspects of the work of key theorists and practitioners will appear in different contexts in different chapters. These connections are evident from the outset as Claire Colebrook's chapter on feminist criticism and poststructuralism examines the enormously influential and provocative work of some of Calvin Thomas' 'big daddies' of literary theory. Colebrook traces the tradition of Western metaphysics that recognises only 'man' and offers succinct accounts of the philosophical, psychoanalytical and material challenges to such foundational thought. Through an examination of the philosophical problems that have necessitated feminism and feminist enquiry, this chapter prepares the ground for the more detailed examinations of key 'feminist' thinkers such as Kristeva, Irigaray, Cixous, Spivak, Anzaldúa, Butler, Sedgwick and Haraway that can be found in the subsequent chapters. The work undertaken by Colebrook is paralleled by Madelon Sprengnether's survey of feminist criticism and psychoanalysis. Sprengnether goes back to Freud, the 'father' of analysis and the progenitor of the unconscious, in order to map the problems and the promise that psychoanalysis has held for female subjectivity and feminist critical practice.

As was the case in the earlier sections of the book, all the chapters aim to provide a lucid introduction to complex material, but there is also a crucial element of reappraisal as the contributors aim to dissipate some of the myths that have come to surround such problematically monolithic concepts as 'French' feminist criticism. The totalising impulses of critical practice have resulted in the construction of categories that do not adequately represent the territory they are meant to cover, and 'French' feminist theory is a case in point. This complex corpus of European writing about the body and textuality has, as Judith Still explains, been reduced to the discussion of a handful of feminist writers in French. The desire to reduce difference to a critically manageable homogeneity is equally the subject of Chris Weedon's account of postcolonial feminist criticism. The Eurocentric gaze, argues Weedon, subjects Third World women to inappropriate Western ideological pressures, silencing them and depicting them as ignorant victims. The attempt to bring feminisms from disparate contexts into line with Western praxis is futile and destructive, as the meanings of 'Third World' feminisms can only be understood and evaluated in their own contexts. Postcolonial feminist writing and criticism emerges from socially specific struggles, and until Western feminism learns to listen to these voices it is unlikely to move beyond an appropriative position. But while writing might indeed be a way to achieve new modes of understanding difference, this potential is limited by the familiar problem of finding a position from which to speak. As Weedon observes, access to the institutions of publishing and distribution – and, indeed, the dominance of the English language – are material factors which have the potential to silence the 'other', leaving postcolonial criticism with limited and distorted 'canons' of women's writing. Recuperating texts and voices is as important to the contemporary practice of feminist literary criticism as it was forty years ago when women academics first started looking for a 'literature of their own'.

Equally important to the ongoing practice of feminist literary criticism is the relationship between activism and the academy. If it might have seemed from the development of poststructuralism that feminist literary criticism had left its activist origins behind then, as Heather Love observes, the advent of queer acted as a timely reminder that the personal is still political. The textual practice of queer theory is defiantly political, and in the era of AIDS and right-wing retrenchment in both Britain and the USA, queer theory restated the fundamental feminist point that the construction of bodies is a matter of the utmost concern. The work of Weedon and Love reminds us that within feminist literary criticism there is a complex and ongoing negotiation between the deconstruction and the reconstruction of the subject. Woman is both textual and embodied, a historically contingent sign that bears many radically different meanings. But, as Stacy Gillis demonstrates, woman is also a technologically mediated concept – the impact of which will have inevitable implications for both feminist criticism and women's lives. In the penultimate chapter we encounter the idea that woman might now be no more than a cypher in a disembodied universe. Can feminism, or literature, continue to have meaning in a hypertextual, virtual environment? This question is central to Gillis, whose chapter weighs the problematic technological exploitation of women, and their frequent exclusion from the online community, against the liberatory possibilities of hybrid cyborgic embodiment. It is also implicit in the conclusions of Susan Gubar, whose Postscript argues for the continuing relevance of feminist literary criticism in a world where not all bodies are virtual and society still limits the possibilities of gendered subjectivity.

Part III of this volume has seen the figure of woman dismantled, fragmented, displaced and queered. She has equally been silenced, outside and beyond. Throughout these theoretical and political transformations, though, the text has remained a space within which actual women have constructed and reconstructed the narrative possibilities of their lives, where the unthinkable is imagined and the impossible is achieved. For women as writers and as readers, textuality enables, facilitating new critical and creative encounters. Beyond this, for the feminist critic, all texts and all bodies have come to matter, and feminism has transgressed its own boundaries in a series of productive encounters with its others. Our contemporary understanding of gender is a product of the encounter between feminism, poststructuralism and psychoanalysis, but the linguistic body has not obliterated the tangible body – even if it has demanded a recognition of the ultimate unknowability of its form. The delight and the value of feminist literary criticism is its multiplicity. Each of the many feminisms described in this book continues to exist and to produce constructive new readings of the world, its texts and its bodies. Above all, these multiple feminisms continue to demand an attention to the problems of representation and subjectivity. Whether the woman's body is virtual, textual, queer or situated in a Third World context, it remains a female embodiment and subject to the prescriptive power of gender. Feminist literary criticism offers us a set of fluid and incisive tools for writing and reading this body, and the history of feminist literary criticism explains why it is essential that we continue to use them.

CHAPTER 12

Feminist criticism and poststructuralism

Claire Colebrook

POSTMODERNISM AND POSTSTRUCTURALISM

In contrast with the term 'postmodernism', it is possible to give a quite strict sense to 'poststructuralism'. Whereas postmodernism encompasses movements in the arts, theory and popular culture, and is dated variously depending upon just which modernism the 'post' is seen to qualify, poststructuralism refers to a quite specific consequence of accepting the premises of structuralism. Structuralism insists that no term has meaning in itself but can only be identified in relation to other terms; poststructuralism investigates the emergence of systems of relations. Poststructuralism is often identified as a general movement including the works of Jacques Derrida, Michel Foucault, Luce Irigaray, Julia Kristeva, Jean-François Lyotard, Jacques Lacan and Gilles Deleuze, all of whom both accepted and criticised aspects of the structuralist movement. Poststructuralism might also be marked by the threshold date of May 1968 (the Paris student uprising that challenged the authority of party-political action), when French thinkers turned away from directly Marxist forms of politics. Far from thinking that ideology might be unmasked by a proletariat who had a direct experience of labour and capital, post-68 thinkers paid more attention to ideology as a positive, constructive and semi-autonomous force (Althusser, 1972). Literature would therefore be neither a reflection nor a distortion of reality but a crucial component in the recreation of conditions of consciousness. The 'unhappy marriage' that had existed between Marxism and feminism, which had tried to explain women's condition on the basis of the division of labour, could now give way to forms of feminism attentive to the images, figures, metaphors and myths through which both men and women live their reality. If structuralism had insisted on the ways in which thought and subjectivity were already determined by systems not decided by, or present to, consciousness, *post*structuralism demonstrated that such systems were intrinsically unstable. Literature would play a crucial role in iterating the binaries through which gender had been constituted *and* would allow for a critical reflection on those very binaries. The text was neither an historical document that might disclose women's real social conditions nor a simple representation of false conscious-ness or stereotypes; literature could be read as creative of differences, as productive of systems. While ordinary language was oriented towards judge-ment, literature played with the sounds, marks, rhythms and syntax that are 'normally' repressed. Literature could therefore be considered as directly revolutionary (Kristeva, 1974/1984) or even incestuous – destroying the boundary between the judging subject and the chaos or excess of the real.

While Derrida, Deleuze, Kristeva, Irigaray, Foucault and Lyotard offer different philosophies and responses to the problem of sexual difference, they all share some common features which have quite direct consequences for problems of feminist thought. Indeed, while it is neither possible nor desirable to define a single model for poststructuralist theory, there is nevertheless a shared ground of debate and different ways of approaching the same *post*structuralist condition. It is therefore necessary to begin with the seemingly revolutionary moves of structuralism in order to see the ways in which poststructuralism both radicalised structuralist claims and accused structuralism of being complicit with Western metaphysics.

FROM STRUCTURALISM TO POSTSTRUCTURALISM

Structuralism is the theory that no term or identity has any being in itself; terms can only be produced through relations. In linguistic terms this means that no word can have sense unless it is part of a language that comprises relations among words and concepts (Saussure, 1983); while in terms of social phenomena, no event can have meaning in isolation (Barthes, 1957/1972). We only know that the whiteness of a wedding dress signifies purity because of a system of fashion and religious conven-tions, and we only associate red traffic lights with the command to stop because of the three-colour system that organises possible responses at road intersections. Nothing is meaningful in isolation, and so we might say that nothing has any identity in isolation. The moment we want to say that something *is* something we have marked it out, differentiated it and therefore understood its relation to what it is not. One might conclude, then, that terms like male and female (and certainly what counts as conventionally masculine or feminine) can only be understood or exist in a system of relations; it would not be possible to identify a self-sufficient, pre-linguistic and intrinsic femininity (Culler, 1976).[1]

However, the relation between structuralist theory and sexual difference goes well beyond the claim that gender is conventional or socially constructed. One of the problems raised by the structuralist project is the *genesis* of structure. It is this problem that structuralism 'solved' by turning to sexual difference and it is also this problem that *post*structuralism has repeatedly revisited and problematised (Irigaray, 1974/1985). If no being or entity has an intrinsic meaning, and if we have to impose some system or set of relations onto the world to give it meaning, how do we explain the emergence of structure and how do we think about *what is structured?* The answer, for structuralists and those who followed the structuralist theory of kinship, lay in the image of woman (Rubin, 1975). We become cultural by abandoning our biological immediacy; culture is therefore the other of nature and immediacy and, for humans at least, our image or figure of the natural and immediate is 'Woman'. According to Claude Lévi-Strauss, culture takes the form of a system of relations: we do not just live the world in immediate animal desire, but defer our desires in accord with the demands of culture.[2] The entry into this system takes the form of a prohibition of incest: we abandon the first object of desire – the mother who meets all our bodily needs – and establish relations of alliance with other families, whose women we exchange for those of our own (Lévi-Strauss, 1969). Culture begins, then, with the exchange of women. Woman becomes that first desired and denied object that is renounced in order that we might recognise each other as cultural subjects. It is possible to read poststructuralism as a problematisation of this structuralist logic.

DERRIDA AND STRUCTURE

Jacques Derrida began his philosophical career exploring the question of genesis. How do systems of meaning or difference emerge, and how do we think their emergence? How is it possible to give an account of the origin of meaning without already drawing on the structure we are setting out to explain? In one of his most important essays Derrida offers a critique of the structuralist answer to this problem, by exposing the apparently neutral viewpoint adopted by Claude Lévi-Strauss and showing how any attempt to explain the emergence of structure must already rely on a set of differences (Derrida, 1978).

This has immediate relevance for feminist criticism, as it both precludes the possibility of a pure, neutral and universal viewpoint, and at the same time demonstrates that any simple abandonment of universality merely becomes another universalism. By claiming to do no more than observe particulars – to be a mere empiricist or 'bricoleur' – Lévi-Strauss represses the ways in which his observations are nevertheless located, determined and (for Derrida) metaphysical. Derrida argues that any attempt to explain relative systems has to adopt some point of view outside those systems, some point of truth: there is always *one* term that opens a structure and that cannot be accounted for within the structure.[3] For poststructuralism, then, any posited structure has to be delimited by at least one term that cannot be reduced to the structure, and which therefore precludes closure. In Lévi-Strauss' anthropology this inaugurating term is 'incest' or the prohibition of the original union with the mother. On the one hand, incest is outside culture; the desire for the mother is the natural and pre-cultural given that must be renounced in order for the world to be mediated by cultural relations. On the other hand, we know incest prohibition as a feature of all cultures, as a cultural universal. It appears as 'naturally' cultural, or as the 'cultural' phenomenon required by nature.

The fact that Lévi-Strauss sees *woman* as the original prohibited object does not concern Derrida directly, although it was this aspect of structuralism that became pertinent for the theories of sexuality in poststructuralist psychoanalysis. For whatever the empirical truth of Lévi-Strauss' theory, the Western literary tradition does evidence an intense investment in the notion of an original maternal plenitude. This runs from the *Timeaus*, where Plato argues that the original creation of the world occurs with a father figure giving form to a chaotic unbounded and formless motherly body of matter, to Romantic images of Mother Nature and modernist fantasies of an original fluid feminine principle that might revivify a rigid and systematised civilisation. Derrida is less interested in the *specific* images that have been used to figure the 'outside' of the system of differences than he is in the necessity that *no* structure can remain closed. His key point is that *any* text that seeks to account for the origin of meaning, system and difference has to assume a point from which that difference might be viewed, mastered and defined. This, according to Derrida, is the necessary impossibility that governs our thinking. What cannot be thought is a system of differences, or play, that has no centre, ground or origin.

The problem of *post*structuralism is, then, whether we can think difference *positively*: not as a difference *from* some neuter term, such as the differentiation of nature by culture, or the difference of woman from the generic 'man', but difference that has no identity, origin or privileged figure. Such a concept of difference would be directly revolutionary for sexual politics precisely because 'man' has always been thought of in terms of what Derrida refers to as an 'onto-theological humanism'. 'Man' is the being who recognises what is other than, or different from, himself in order that he may be the point from which difference is represented, mastered and contained. Positive difference, by contrast, would be decentred and multiple, neither the difference between two terms nor the differentiation of some grounding substance. Derrida refers to the notion of 'invagination' to challenge 'phallogocentrism', or the idea of a single originating logic. Whereas Western thought has been dominated by the idea of a seminal reason that can always give birth to itself and be unified, self-present and dominant, the figures of 'hymen' and 'invagination' are used by Derrida to depict the active creation of borders between inside and outside. There is no origin that is *then* doubled or copied; rather, in the beginning is the 'fold' that produces the first term – man – only by marking woman as a lesser or derived complement (Derrida, 1981).

SEXUAL DIFFERENCE AND THE CRITIQUE OF HUMANISM

In an essay on Martin Heidegger (1983), Derrida explores the difficulty of liberating philosophy from specified images of humanity or 'man'. Observing that the human has always been defined through tropes of self-fathering – man defines himself and gives himself his own essence – Derrida argues that the concept of 'man' is not some sexist term *within* philosophy that might be erased or modified. Rather, for Derrida, our experience of the world as *present*, as the same through time and subsisting in its being despite experiences of difference, requires an implicit concept of 'man' – some persisting human tradition that can always recognise itself and assume a common world that can be rendered meaningful and objective. The very notion of universal truth or transcendental truth requires some presupposed 'we', some common space of 'man' (Derrida, 1989).

The implications of these arguments for literary criticism are manifold. We cannot just dismiss the figure of 'man' as one ideological image among others, for the very idea of truth, objectivity and even meaning – an ongoing tradition that can be recalled, reinvigorated and re-lived – presupposes a common underlying subject, a 'we'. The figure of 'man' as self-determining, devoid of any determined essence and without foundation – a figure that might seem so radical in twentieth-century thought – is really one more form of 'onto-theology' where one being provides the ground and source for all being. What has to be repressed, both in traditional humanism and in more recent notions of the self as socially constructed is that which lies outside self-determination. This is why *literature* is so important for deconstruction, but also why deconstruction is so important for feminist approaches to literature. If it is the case that any attempt to think of truth, subjectivity or consciousness *in general* must always be articulated in some specific way, then the philosophical ideal of pure truth or presence is not possible. Ideas of truth, universality and meaning will always draw on normative and singular figures. However, one cannot simply dismiss this project of presence. To admit that we are all socially, discursively or culturally constructed presents 'culture', 'discourse' or 'society' as a new transcendental foundation, or one more 'we'. Derrida's own project is therefore twofold: on the one hand, he uses figures of the hymen, invagination, the fold and choreographies to imagine non-hierarchical concepts of difference; on the other hand, he demonstrates the figures or tropes through which the project of pure truth has been articulated. Such tropes have often been explicitly sexual, having to do with images of self-fathering, insemination, mastery and auto-affection. Certain figures create a hierarchy between the pure and productive origin on the one hand and the derivative, fictive simulation on the other. The figure of the voice as that which, unlike dispersed writing, feels itself speak; the image of self-fathering or insemination as that which creates and springs forth from itself; the image of the sun, as the source of all illumination and form; and the image of the phallus as the giver of life and spirit to matter and chaos: all these figures are not *simply* metaphors, for they inaugurate a difference between literal and figural, active and passive – a difference without which the tradition of meaning and sense would not have been possible.

At a more complex level, philosophy's contamination by writing is not simply an identification of metaphors in the text of philosophy, it is also a sophisticated argument about time and space. It is not the case, Derrida argues, that we have space or time as simple givens; on the contrary, both space and time have to be synthesised. The continuity of time is given through a connectedness of appearances, as causal sequence; while the distribution of space is given as a relation among points. Whereas Immanuel Kant had argued that there must have been a subject who synthesises time and space, Derrida argues that no such synthesising subject can be assumed or intuited. Instead, he argues that *writing* or *écriture* is one way of thinking a linkage or synthesis in which not all elements can be brought together, commanded and held present. Writing names a relation to that which resists and remains; a text is never in command of itself, and no point in the text can be taken as the centre or point of origin. Both the figure of woman and the literary text are significant here. First, man is the figure of onto-theological humanism: a being who has experiences of an outside – matter, difference, time, space – only so that he can recognise and return to himself as the subject who gives birth to and maintains experience. Woman, then, would be one way of thinking that which metaphysics has always repressed or left unthought. In opposition to the voice of man which gives birth to itself and is in command of itself, woman has always represented a passive, sensible and unthinking materiality. Ultimately, though, Derrida has a utopian thought where we move beyond such oppositional figures to 'choreographies' of difference. Here, the literary text, particularly the modernist literary text, is capable of 'saying anything' and moving beyond the propositional structure of the philosophical statement, which necessarily posits some truth or present.

In Derrida's reading of Mallarmé's *Un Coup de Des*, for example, Mallarmé describes a complex mime in which a character already 'quotes' from previous mimes and texts. The character *in* the mime pretends or mimes a character from another mime. Whereas philosophy creates a clear distinction between a truth and a double or copy of that truth produced by mimesis, Mallarmé's writing refuses all borders between original and copy. It thereby presents the opening or production of a temporal and spatial multiplicity. In mime there is neither an original event that is then represented, nor a real world that is then doubled by fiction. Mallarmé's mime quotes from previous mimes and stories, himself miming or copying what is already a copy. Mallarmé's text *folds* before and after, inside and outside through a play of reflections, imitations and quotations. Indeed, in both Derrida and other thinkers of his time (such as Deleuze and Foucault) the 'fold' becomes a central term for the undoing of the notion of an origin or subject that precedes play and simulation. There is no privileged or hierarchically elevated term; the distinction between inside and outside, self and other, before and after, are 'unfolded' from one multiplying and decentred text. A literary text often folds its inside into its outside – referring to itself as a text or fiction. A literary text can therefore 'say' anything, for even a *factual* literary statement, such as 'This is a novel', has a curious status in a literary text. The very frame that would mark off a text as fiction is itself, when placed in fiction, neither inside nor outside. If, then, philosophy is a phallogocentrism – the positing of one presence that expresses itself in a truth to be read, repeated, mastered and maintained – literature is an *invagination*: a creation of differences, or folds, where no term is primary, originating, self-sufficient or in control.

On the one hand, then, Derrida's deconstruction does suggest that philosophy has a sex. The figures of the phallus, insemination and self-fathering have enabled the production of an ultimate and originating presence that can recognise and return to itself. On the other hand, while Derrida acknowledges a certain necessity to the concept of truth – for insofar as we speak and *mean* we intend some presence beyond the mere figure of the literary text – he does not regard sexual difference as a privileged figure, and does imagine an overcoming of the binary nature of this difference.

PSYCHOANALYTIC POSTSTRUCTURALISM

A stronger argument for the relation between what Derrida referred to as the 'metaphysics of presence' and sexual difference was put forward by a number of feminist poststructuralists who accepted crucial premises from psychoanalysis. Sexual difference, here, would not be the socially coded, represented and conventional opposition between male and female, but a recognition of the difference that renders such binaries complex. One way of understanding the terrain of poststructuralist feminism is to see it as a debate between the critical aspects of deconstruction and the positive claims for a specifically sexual difference of Lacanian psychoanalysis. Psychoanalytically inspired feminists, such as Luce Irigaray, rejected the idea that 'phallogocentrism' was a necessary system. Woman had, Irigaray conceded, been defined as the figure through which man comes to know, master and differentiate himself, but one could also imagine another mode of subjectivity. Such a mode would be sexually different and autonomous. Woman would not be man's other. Irigaray therefore read the texts of Western philosophy to show the ways in which theories of the 'subject' were always figures of a self who distances himself from matter, the sensible and the dispersed and finds himself as the centre of reason and representation. If woman had been depicted as this opaque and unthinking passive materiality then she would be the place to begin a thought of genuine sexual difference. Here, the self would not be *self-inaugurating* but would become a self only by relating to what is not oneself. Feminists who took up the poststructuralist challenge were therefore poised between two possibilities. One response, following Derrida, might be critical: the sexual binary is part of a logic that needs to be deconstructed (Cornell, 1992). Another approach might ask just *whose* logic this was, and *whose* subjectivity was being dispersed (Braidotti, 1991). This would also yield two responses to literature: feminists could look at the ways in which 'woman' was figured in the text as that which needs to be mastered, differentiated, rendered intelligible and represented. Alternatively, feminists could take up

Irigaray's challenge of reading as a woman: one would not read the text as an object to be mastered, but relate to the text *ethically* as another subject with its own relations, desires and intentionality (Felman, 1993). An ethical reading would not relate to the text as bearing some sense to be fully comprehended, but would recognise that the text – like the other person in a relation of love – must always present itself as enigmatic; there is always an excess or lacuna that cannot be recuperated or mastered. Contemporary feminism has maintained this ambivalent relationship to sexual difference: if sexual difference is one figured binary among others then literary interpretation remains critical, but if sexual difference is positive then one might imagine other modes of reading, other relations towards the text.

One recent answer to this deconstructive insistence that we are always within relations, and that the sexual scene is one set of relations among others, comes from the Lacanian Slavoj Žižek. According to Žižek sexual difference is *the* fantasy frame through which all scenes are read. The very phenomenon of sense or having a world *to be read or understood* requires that we have some fantasy of an ultimate master who knows that truth. We make sense of our world and relations to others, then, through the fantasy of paternal law – a master presumed to know – and a maternal 'beyond' or that which is limited by law and prohibition. So, Lacan is not arguing for the literal truth of Oedipus – that the child desires his mother, is threatened by castration and then identifies with his father – but only for the ways in which we use the oedipal frame to make sense of our textual condition. It is because we exist in a cultural world of relations, systems, structures and signifiers – never being at one or fully present to ourselves – that we imagine that *there must have been* some ultimate *jouissance* that has been prohibited. It is not, then, that *there is* woman, which is then renounced. Rather, from our position of mediation we posit that which is beyond mediation. Derrida's position that we can never know the truth or the universal in its pure form, but only in its specified figures is, Žižek argues, really just a form of common sense (Žižek, 1994). For Žižek, Lacan more rigorously offers the formulae for sexual difference that analyse the ways in which we live this impossible relation to the truth. To occupy the masculine position is to be submitted to an order of prohibition, where we all acknowledge that our desires must be articulated through the discourse of the other, but also to the fantasy that there is a place 'beyond' the order of prohibition. To occupy the feminine position is, by contrast, to be liberated from this fantasy of a 'beyond' the law, an ultimate *jouissance* or plenitude.

This yields a number of possibilities for feminist literary criticism. Critically, one might read the ways in which the text produces woman as object. Lacan's own seminars referred to the woman of courtly love who, through the practices, poetry and rituals of unattainability, *produced* the feminine as that which would – if attained – yield enjoyment (Lacan, 1992). This generates what Lacan refers to as an ethics of dependence that can only be overcome if we confront the possibility that 'Woman does not exist'. In the courtly love tradition, and in a modernity dominated by the oedipal fantasy, it is imagined that *jouissance* might be achieved if only one could attain the prohibited object. In fact, it is the *delay* in attaining the longed-for object that instates woman as the place of 'truth'. Woman is therefore a symptom; the subject's fascination with *this* unattainable woman merely covers over the truth that there is *no* Woman, that 'Woman does not exist'. Each subject, and each text, is therefore structured around the particular fragment or symptom that seems to stand in the way of full enjoyment. 'I' am a subject only insofar as there is always a desire for what goes beyond the symbolised world of attainable objects; and there is always one object that stands in the way of this fantasised beyond, an object around which my desire circles.

In his debates with Judith Butler, it is this formula for sexual difference that Žižek defends against what he takes to be Butler's 'postmodernism'. Butler, Žižek argues, is too simply historicist, wanting signifying systems to be malleable and arbitrary (Žižek, 2001). They therefore disagree with regard to the relations between the Imaginary, the Symbolic and the Real – ways in which the Symbolic (our submission to a system of relations) is lived through fantasy (the Imaginary, where we posit some original oedipal scene) and the real (that which we posit as resisting all symbolisation). Butler argues both that kinship systems need not be heterosexual *and*, like other feminists such as Drucilla Cornell, that we can refigure the sexual fantasy (or Imaginary) through which we relate to our condition of being (Butler, 1993). Cornell argues for the necessary difference between the imaginary ideal of Woman and specific and particular women; Butler argues for other forms of the Imaginary, beyond the heterosexual matrix where it is *man's* supposedly normal and normative desire that structures the symbolic. For Žižek, however, there is one formal feature that cannot be included within history or symbolic systems and that is the split of sexual difference: the opposition between an ultimate Real and the symbolic figuring of that real. Sexual difference is the way we imagine the split, gap or non-relation that constitutes us as subjects. Without some prohibited or unattainable real we would have no desire, and we would therefore not be marked as singular subjects. By privileging performativity, or the capacity of signifying systems to become undone through their own necessary operations of repetition, Butler misses – Žižek argues – that necessary and transcendental dialectic. We only know or live the real through some determined system, but we also necessarily imagine a 'real' beyond that system and it is the sexual other – woman – who is the figure of the beyond, or what Lacan refers to as the *Ding an Sich* (thing in itself). For Žižek, then, sexual difference is *the* problem or way in which we live this gap between what we can say or know and what *is*.

A more liberating Lacanian response to the formulae of sexual difference has come from Joan Copjec, who presents one of the most rigorous critiques of structuralist or constructivist notions of gender. According to Copjec, the idea that each historical period or culture is relative, each representing gender in its own way, remains blind to the transcendental problem of sexual difference (Copjec, 1994). The problem is transcendental precisely because it is a necessary condition of our being that we take up some relation to our bodily, biological or sexual emergence. We cannot know or grasp the nondiscursive, but we cannot simply reduce all that *is* to its mode of being known or lived:

Desire is produced not as a striving for something but only as a striving for something else or something more. It stems from the feeling of our having been duped by language, cheated of something, not from our having been presented with a determinate object or goal for which we can aim. Desire has no content – it is for nothing – because language can deliver to us no incontrovertible truth, no positive goal. (Copjec, 1994: 55)

This has two crucial consequences. Like many earlier Lacanian feminists (Mitchell, 1974; Gallop, 1982), Copjec insists that Lacan is not offering sexual difference as a norm so much as diagnosing the fantasy frame through which we live norms and, indeed, reality as such. Second, Copjec reads a radical possibility in this fantasy of sexual difference. Unlike Žižek who enjoins us to 'enjoy your symptom', Copjec quotes another Lacanian imperative: 'Imagine there's no Woman'. If there were no ultimate *jouissance* beyond the realm of prohibition, and if there were no plenitude whose loss might explain the subject's lack, then we would no longer see woman as a redemptive promise, but would live without dependence on some ultimate truth or foundation (Copjec, 2002).

If we accept Copjec's argument, then the act of literary criticism and reading becomes directly political. Feminist criticism would not be ideo-logical – in the sense of exposing distorted or stereotypical representations of women – but would work with the hypothesis that the very idea of representation is itself already gendered. For it is the fantasy of some true being beyond the order of signification that is given in the figure of woman. If it is the *fantasy* of woman that creates a certain structure of sexual difference whereby we live our mediated desire as directed to some prohibited 'beyond', then only a critical reading of those fantasmatic structures would allow for an ethical act. It is this more promising and active relation to the imaginary that has led many feminists, Copjec included, to look towards the work of Gilles Deleuze. Deleuze can still be considered a poststructuralist, for he is highly critical of the idea that the world is simply mediated through some system of signs. Instead, he is concerned with the historical emergence of sign systems. More importantly, his work with Félix Guattari was directly concerned with the history of 'oedipal man': how is it that we came to think of ourselves as subjected to language (Deleuze and Guattari, 1983), and why did woman appear as the prohibited object *par excellence*? For Deleuze 'becoming-woman' marked the opening of true thinking: we would no longer accept a difference between signs on the one hand and signifying man on the other, for we would be able to imagine multiple points of view, each opening out onto their own world. If Irigaray had argued that there needed to be at least two sexes in order to relate to the world and others ethically, Deleuze raised the possibility of 'a thousand tiny sexes' – desires not reducible to the image of signifying, representing and oedipal man (Deleuze and Guattari, 1988). Alongside the critical poststructuralist feminisms that used the figure of woman to undermine the system of metaphysics, there were also feminists oriented towards more positive, often utopian, programmes of thinking. The two figures who were most important for thinking beyond the idea of 'a' system to which 'we' are subjected were Deleuze and Irigaray (Lorraine, 1999; Olkowski, 1999).

POSITIVE DIFFERENCE

From its first readings Irigaray's work was charged with the problem of 'essentialism', even though it was the very logic of essence that her work set out to dismantle (Moi, 1985). Without some concept of essence – as that which remains the same through time and allows for identity and truth to become known – Western metaphysics would not have had a world for the subject *to represent*. Irigaray's *Speculum of the Other Woman* (1974/1985) examined the ways in which this relation between a world to be represented and the subject who faithfully repeats and mirrors that world had been articulated. At its simplest level Irigaray uncovered a persistent sexual metaphorics at the heart of Western metaphysics: the truth that is to be known is passive, unchanging, determined, in-itself and objective, while the knower is active, determining, self-governing and present to himself. Knowledge is presented through figures of light, penetration, unity, form-giving, mastery and activity: figures through which masculinity has also been defined. That which is to be known or mastered is formless, chaotic, awaiting illumination and there to be taken up and re-presented: figures through which the female body has been given as the complement of male knowledge. But there is a far more complex argument at work in *Speculum* than the isolation of metaphors. First, the very logic of metaphor that would distinguish between a literal ground and a figural overlay is already part of the sexual logic of Western metaphysics that has presented being as something present, and the subject as a knower who gives form to the presence. Second, it is not just that man has been associated with the reasoning and mastering subject and woman with the passively viewed object; Irigaray looks at the very structure of knowing and isolates a sexual morphology. In her famous reading of Plato's cave allegory, for example, the men who stare at the shadows on the wall of the cave are captured by merely secondary appearances until they can turn around and look at the source of light, the one true rational ground of knowing. Thus, knowledge is presented as a turn away from appearance towards an orienting logic: the light of reason is the subject's proper way of knowing. This turn towards logic and reason becomes, with Descartes' theory of the subject as one who perceives the world, and with Kant whose subject gives form to the world, a logic of the same. The subject only encounters what is other than himself in order that he might turn back and see himself seeing, recognise himself as the origin of all being.

Knowledge has always used images of ground, foundation, substance, matter or being that will enable the subject to exercise his forming, knowing, exercising and determining power. If there were another mode of knowing – not a subject creating himself through a passive medium but a subject who related to another body *as other* – then autonomy would not take the form of giving a law to oneself but of recognising the difference of oneself. Irigaray's ethics of sexual difference (Irigaray, 1984/1993) therefore goes beyond critique to morphology: to *another* mode of relation that might draw on the figure of woman. Perhaps the most fruitful assessment of the literary implications of this manoeuvre was that of Shoshana Felman. Lacan's psychoanalysis was already, according to Felman, a rec-ognition that our condition in this world is not one of knowledge but of *reading*, where the enigma of the speaking other will always create spectral effects. The ethics of reading lies, then, not in grasping and repeating what the text or other *means* but in paying attention to the ways in which the other eludes a full comprehension, the ways in which it creates the promise but not fulfilment of sense. This is given a feminist rendering in Felman's work on *Don Juan*, where she argues that all language is sexual – for language places us in a desiring relation to an other – while all sexuality is linguistic, as the other is given only to be read, interpreted and desired (Felman, 2003). In her essay 'Women and Madness: The Critical Phallacy' (1991), Felman argues that the tradition of grasping the text's sense suffers from the logic whereby the reader only finds himself and his own desires; a feminist reading would attend to what the text does not present but only veils. Felman argues that her own project is an extension of Irigaray's critique of Western metaphysics' sexual binarism, where woman is there to be discovered and brought to light. But how, Felman asks, can we talk about woman if 'woman' is precisely that which cannot speak in Western metaphysics? How could this otherness be given voice? Rather than claiming to speak *as* a woman, for such a speaking position would take its place within the norms of criticism, Felman looks at how texts produce these loci of unreadability. Every text has a silence, enigma or madness which criticism has traditionally explained or interpreted. We need a literary practice, Felman argues, that will demonstrate the ways in which 'woman' has been created in the text as that which requires interpretation.

In some ways, then, Irigaray's project for sexual difference or thinking a relation of the self that would not be dominated by mastery, cognition or judgement could be compared to the work of Julia Kristeva. Kristeva's significant contribution to poststructuralism lay in her challenge to the linguistic paradigm. Language is not, she insisted, a system of differences beyond which lies the undifferentiated and unthinkable. On the contrary, her early work argued that the first traces through which we live and think are embodied, marked out in the first touches, caresses and sounds of infancy (Kristeva, 1977/1980). Her later work paid attention to cultural experiences of otherness that would undermine the subject who is set against a world to be known (Kristeva, 1988/1991). Kristeva's emphasis was on the *genesis* of the subject. Before there is a subject of judgement who represents and masters the world through a system of signs (or what she refers to as the 'thetic' subject), there is a body that relates to otherness through touch, sound and rhythm, and does not have a clear distinction between self and mother. We become subjects only through distancing ourselves from that original maternal *jouissance*. For this reason, Kristeva argued that gender was 'metaphysical' – neither arbitrary nor essential but the structure through which we have come to think what is essential and which can, therefore, be transformed. For this reason her work was often preferred to

Irigaray's putative essentialism (Moi, 1985), particularly throughout the
1980s when many feminists expressed anxieties about the body as a deter-
minant of sexual identity.

However, the anti-linguisticism implicit in Kristeva's work came to the
fore in the 1990s and allowed for a far more fruitful relation between
feminism and poststructuralism. Rosi Braidotti in *Patterns of Dissonance*
(1990) had astutely pointed out that just as women were beginning to create
some form of identity, certain forms of poststructuralism dismissed *any*
form of embodiment or sexual difference as constructed, relative or arbitrary. Braidotti argued that the seemingly liberating arguments regarding
the end of humanism were ways of neutralising sexual difference. Neither
an essential sexual identity nor a mere play of neutral difference would
provide the way forward; instead criticism needs to look at the specific ways
in which subjects are sexed, the specific patterns of desire or dissonance
through which bodies speak, desire and move. Elizabeth Grosz was also
offering a far less linguistic approach to embodiment and, like Braidotti,
turning to Deleuze's work on the positivity of desire to overcome the
notion that 'we' are constructed through language. By 1994 Grosz had
made the body a central concern for poststructuralist feminism: there is not
a subject who constructs their reality, nor a subject constructed by language
(Grosz, 1994). Instead, there are bodies whose desire, movements and
relations create *through time* a border between self and other, inside and
outside, bodily surface and world. In 1993 Judith Butler wrote *Bodies That
Matter* to correct the impression of her work as being dominated by the
linguistic paradigm, but the very publication of this book signalled a
radical shift in feminist thinking. Whereas talk of the body had once
appeared to be a naïve essentialism or biologism, by the 1990s feminists
were arguing that the idea of the subject as *not* affected by the body merely
repeated the centuries-old concept of 'man' as the negation of the body,
materiality, sensibility and the feminine.

To see the force of this problem we need only look at Judith Butler's
Gender Trouble (1990). Butler's ostensible argument was a critique of the
sex/gender distinction, or the idea that our biological sex is given meaning
and gendered identity through culture. The idea of a pre-linguistic sex,
though, is itself produced through language. Reality is not some pure
biological matter that is then experienced and articulated. Rather, Butler
takes up Derrida's notion of iteration and performativity. Something can
have identity or be said to be only if it remains the same through time or
is repeated. For something to be capable of repetition, then, it must
already have marked out *within itself* that which might be iterated. That

is, a sign – such as the phoneme of a language – can only be repeated if something in the singular instance is marked as repeatable: we all have different ways of pronouncing the 'a' in 'dance', but a speaker recognises what is the same through all the repeated differences, and so we have found what is repeatable or iterable in any one case. So there is no presence in itself that is then repeated, something *is* only in its repeatability. There can only be a sexual identity or essence – who I really am – if there is that which would remain the same through time. But if something requires repetition in order to be and has no identity in itself then the very repetition that makes it possible may also be destabilising. I am feminine because I walk, act, touch, dress, speak and relate to others in an identifiable way; and it is this *performance* that produces the sense that there must have been some 'I' who preceded and performed these acts.

Performativity creates its own ground. And it can also, because it is repeatable, undo itself. Cases of drag, camp, mime, trans-gendering, and literary character in general, display gender as a constitutive performance and not the overlay of some preceding essence. It is not that there are women and *then* a practice of romantic novel writing that 'stereotypes' femininity. Rather, it is the novelistic practice that creates a certain style of femininity that *then* allows for the illusion of the *real* sex beneath the stereotype. Butler's work has always been a complex negotiation of post-structuralist thinking. She draws upon Foucault's notion of the body as given identity through its relations (Foucault, 1979), at the same time as she criticises Foucault for failing to consider subjection. Only if we consider the ways in which selves are *at odds* with the relations that grant them an ongoing identity will we be able to make sense of the politics of gender. Butler therefore argues that gender is a necessary condition of being a subject, for one must speak *as* someone, but that there are always those who are at odds with this condition. For this reason she has challenged the binary of sexual difference, arguing that as long as we understand selves to be either male or female there will be those who are incapable of perform-ing in ways that are recognised. This can have radical implications when one considers practices such as drag that combine incommensurable norms of selfhood and tragic consequences when one considers trans-gendered individuals whose bodies have been forced to occupy one of two genders.

Far from denying the body by seeing it as produced through language, Butler argues that both language and bodies share the same structure of performativity. 'Woman' can only be a concept if it covers more than one case, but this means it can also be quoted, parodied, satirised or simply questioned. Women exist as a group only because of social norms that survive through repetition, so the repetition of those norms in disjunctive circumstances – say, when I claim both to be a woman *and* desire a woman – will alter that norm's stability.

Butler's work, then, emerges from one of two poststructuralist strategies for reading Irigaray. The first of these sees Irigaray as critical, arguing that the West had produced woman as language's embodied other. One would therefore need to adopt the voice of woman strategically (Spivak, 1990), ironically (Cornell, 1991) or with a sense of drag and parody (Butler, 1990). The second emphasis on Irigaray's work came from feminists who were less perturbed by essentialism. Elizabeth Grosz argued that Irigaray had a commitment to morphology, or the ways in which thought is imbricated with the relations we have to our bodies; bodies were not simply *constructed* as gendered (Grosz, 1994). One way to consider the body positively was to see mind as an idea of the body (Gatens, 1996); in order to think of a self we require some image or figure, and it has been the male body that has been imagined as the 'human' body. What imaginaries might be produced if we considered the female body? Irigaray, then, was also arguing that there had always been some figure of the female body at work in the metaphysical tradition, and that if such a tradition could be articulated positively it might open new ethical relations.

It is this emphasis on the positivity of the body, and the refusal of the idea that we are *subjected* to language, that explains the recent turn in feminism to the work of Gilles Deleuze. Whereas Irigaray had argued for a 'sensible transcendental' – that is, that one's very relation to being is given through bodily relations – Deleuze argued for a transcendental empiricism (Deleuze, 1994). Deleuze's approach was one of immanence: no being can set itself outside life and explain life. Language, bodies, culture, structures, signs and the virtual planes of memory, potential and affects are all real and all within life. This has crucial consequences for feminism. Ridding the world of *a* being that explains all other beings entails destroying the illusion of a subject who constructs, knows, represents or gives forms to reality. Instead of the 'man' of reason who perceives his world, Deleuze and Guattari write of a 'plane of immanence', a 'chaosmos' or a life that expresses itself in infinite durations, including the concepts of philosophy, the affects of art and the functions of science (Deleuze and Guattari, 1994). Their notorious concept of 'becoming-woman' was an attempt to think of the world not from the stable point of view of a 'man' who watches time go by and eventually arrives at some point of mastery. Instead of replacing 'man' with some arbitrary and undifferentiated chaos, they argued that life *is* its changes, and that a becoming is what it is only in its encounters. Life might produce thought, but such a potential remains virtual unless certain encounters occur. The mouth must become capable of language, the hand capable of using tools, bodies capable of social groupings, social groupings capable of producing the conditions for relaxed contemplation: only then will something like philosophy emerge. Philosophy, in turn, will change with subsequent contingent encounters; we think differently today because of visual technologies, and we may make even more difference if we consider inhuman durations (for example, the time of machines, of animals, of environments and bodies).

Deleuze and Guattari's affirmation of becoming-woman has been criticised for producing 'woman' once again as the metaphor or figure for the progress of subjectivity in general. Yet only if we overcome what Deleuze refers to as the 'image of thought', or the idea we have of good sense, of man as a being who speaks, masters, acts and interprets his world, can we arrive at a life that is composed of multiple observers, durations and potentialities. In terms of literary criticism this means that woman will no longer be the figure for the text's concealed or hidden depths, and there will no longer be an oedipal frame of reading whereby we are necessarily submitted to a system we cannot master. Rather, to read would be to look at texts as styles of thought that 'counter-effectuate' the image of man that has always stopped us from thinking. If 'man' has been produced as the subject of common sense and good sense, then literary texts show us that image in production. This means that literary criticism is not so much interpretation – what the text conceals – as production: the text is a composite or actualisation of virtual potentials. In this regard all reading is a form of becoming-woman.

NOTES

1. The debate about the relationship between feminism and postmodernism has been intense and complex but has tended to focus around the issue of identity: on the one hand, postmodernism and its challenge to essentialism and grand narratives threatens any notion of a coherent women's movement grounded in an appeal to essence; on the other hand, this very anti-foundationalism places women (and men) in a position of ongoing critical and open-ended debate (Elam, 1994).
2. This emphasis on submission and subjection is maintained by Judith Butler (1997), who insists that the condition for autonomy or speaking *as* a subject necessarily requires not being fully in command or possession of either one's self or one's self as gendered.
3. We might compare this to feminist attempts at 'situated knowledges' or 'standpoint theory' (Weeks, 1998).

BIBLIOGRAPHY

Althusser, Louis (1972), *'Lenin and Philosophy' and Other Essays*, trans. Ben Brewster, London: Verso.

Barthes, Roland (1957/1972), *Mythologies*, trans. Annette Lavers, London: Cape.

Braidotti, Rosi (1990), *Patterns of Dissonance: A Study of Women in Contemporary Philosophy*, Cambridge: Polity Press.

Butler, Judith (1990), *Gender Trouble*, New York: Routledge.

(1993), *Bodies That Matter: On the Discursive Limits of 'Sex'*, New York: Routledge.

(1997), *The Psychic Life of Power*, Stanford: Stanford University Press.

Copjec, Joan (1994), *Read My Desire: Lacan against the Historicists*, Cambridge, MA: MIT Press.

(2002), *Imagine There's No Woman: Ethics and Sublimation*, Cambridge, MA: MIT Press.

Cornell, Drucilla (1991), *Beyond Accommodation: Ethical Feminism, Deconstruction, and the Law*, New York: Routledge.

(1992), *The Philosophy of the Limit*, New York: Routledge.

Culler, Jonathan (1976), *Saussure*, London: Fontana.

Deleuze, Gilles (1994), *Difference and Repetition*, trans. Paul Patton, New York: Columbia University Press.

Deleuze, Gilles and Félix Guattari (1983), *Anti-Oedipus: Capitalism and Schizophrenia*, trans. Robert Hurley, Mark Seem and Helen R. Lane, London: Athlone.

(1988), *A Thousand Plateaus: Capitalism and Schizophrenia*, trans. Brian Massumi, London: Athlone.

(1994), *What Is Philosophy?*, trans. Hugh Tomlinson and Graham Burchell, New York: Columbia University Press.

Derrida, Jacques (1969), 'The Ends of Man', in *Philosophy and Phenomenological Research* 30.

(1978), *Writing and Difference*, trans. Alan Bass, London: Routledge and Kegan Paul.

(1981), *Dissémination*, trans. Barbara Johnson, London: Athlone.

(1983), 'Geschlecht: Sexual Difference, Ontological Difference', in *Research into Phenomenology* 13.

(1989), *Edmund Husserl's 'Origin of Geometry': An Introduction*, trans. John P. Leavey, Lincoln: University of Nebraska Press.

Elam, Diane (1994), *Feminism and Deconstruction: Ms. en abyme*, London: Routledge.

Felman, Shoshana (1991), 'Women and Madness: The Critical Phallacy', in *Feminisms: An Anthology of Literary Theory and Criticism*, ed. Robyn R. Warhol and Diane Price Herndl, New Brunswick, NJ: Rutgers University Press.

(1993), *What Does a Woman Want?: Reading and Sexual Difference*, Baltimore: Johns Hopkins University Press.

(2003), *The Scandal of the Speaking Body: Don Juan with J. L. Austin, or Seduction in Two Languages*, trans. Catherine Porter, Stanford: Stanford University Press.

Foucault, Michel (1979), *The History of Sexuality*, vol. I, trans. Robert Hurley, London: Allen Lane.

Gallop, Jane (1982), *Feminism and Psychoanalysis: The Daughter's Seduction*, London: Macmillan.

Gatens, Moira (1996), *Imaginary Bodies: Ethics, Power and Corporeality*, London: Routledge.

Grosz, Elizabeth (1994), *Volatile Bodies*, Sydney: Allen and Unwin.

Irigaray, Luce (1974/1985), *Speculum of the Other Woman*, trans. Gillian C. Gill, Ithaca, NY: Cornell University Press.

(1984/1993), *An Ethics of Sexual Difference*, trans. Carolyn Burke and Gillian C. Gill, London: Athlone.

Kristeva, Julia (1974/1984), *Revolution in Poetic Language*, trans. Margaret Waller, New York: Columbia University Press.

(1977/1980), *Desire in Language: A Semiotic Approach to Literature and Art*, ed. Leon S. Roudiez, trans. Thomas Gora, Alice Jardine and Leon S. Roudiez, Oxford: Blackwell.

(1988/1991), *Strangers to Ourselves*, trans. Leon S. Roudiez, London: Harvester Wheatsheaf.

Lacan, Jacques (1992), *The Ethics of Psychoanalysis, 1959–1960: The Seminar of Jacques Lacan*, ed. Jacques-Alain Miller, trans. Dennis Porter, London: Tavistock/Routledge.

Lévi-Strauss, Claude (1969), *The Elementary Structures of Kinship*, trans. James Harle Bell, John Richard von Sturmer and Rodney Needham, Boston and London: Beacon Press.

Lorraine, Tamsin (1999), *Irigaray & Deleuze: Experiments in Visceral Philosophy*, Ithaca, NY: Cornell University Press.

Mitchell, Juliet (1974), *Psychoanalysis and Feminism*, New York: Pantheon Books.

Moi, Toril (1985), *Sexual/Textual Politics: Feminist Literary Theory*, London: Methuen.

Olkowski, Dorothea (1999), *Gilles Deleuze and the Ruin of Representation*, Berkeley: University of California Press.

Rubin, Gayle (1975), 'The Traffic of Women: Notes on the Political Economy of Sex', in *Toward an Anthropology of Women*, ed. Rayna R. Reiter, New York: Monthly Review Press.

Saussure, Ferdinand de (1983), *Course in General Linguistics*, ed. Charles Bally and Albert Sechehaye with Albert Riedlinger, trans. Roy Harris, London: Duckworth.

Spivak, Gayatri Chakravorty (1990), *The Post-Colonial Critic: Interviews, Strategies, Dialogues*, ed. Sarah Harasym, New York: Routledge.

Weeks, Kathi (1998), *Constituting Feminist Subjects*, Ithaca, NY: Cornell University Press.

Žižek, Slavoj (1994), *The Metastases of Enjoyment: Six Essays on Woman and Causality*, London: Verso.

(2001), *Did Somebody Say Totalitarianism?: Five Interventions in the (Mis)use of a Notion*, London: Verso.

CHAPTER 13

Feminist criticism and psychoanalysis

Madelon Sprengnether

Feminism, psychoanalysis and literary interpretation have more in common than their early histories might seem to suggest – or promise. Each of these intellectual and socially engaged activities is based on premises (about text, psyche and culture) that undermine familiar or received wisdom. At times, they seem to ignore one another, but often they have coincided – and collided – in startling and productive ways. What follows is an overview of a challenging set of engagements – beginning with Freud's analyses of female hysterics in the 1890s, continuing into the 1920s with the first wave of feminist encounter with Freud, jumping to the early second-wave critique of Freud's oedipal phallocentrism, then moving to an interrogation of the possibilities of pre-oedipal subversion into something that we might describe as our current decentred, post-Freudian, post-postmodernist era.

STORIES OF ORIGIN

The story of psychoanalysis, insofar as it may be said to begin with Freud's co-authored *Studies on Hysteria* (1895/1986), may also be said to begin with a woman – referred to as Anna O. in the case history reported by Freud and his mentor Josef Breuer. Anna O., who suffered from partial paralysis and aphasia (an inability to speak in her native German, though she was capable of speaking English, French and Italian), is described by Freud and Breuer as effecting her own cure by freely associating each of her symptoms to their point of origin in her conflicted feelings about nursing her father in his last illness. It was Breuer who stumbled on this method – which Anna termed 'chimney sweeping' – by visiting her on a daily basis and allowing her to talk in an uninhibited way.[1] But if a woman's speech provided Freud with his model of the 'talking cure', it also helped to set the boundaries of his thinking about women and gender. There is a clear hierarchy in this story. The woman babbles; her physician interprets. He may learn from her, but the implication is clear. He knows her better than she knows herself.[2]

The story of (Euro-American) feminism has a different point of origin. This is a story in which women argue for their own rights. Consider the following figures on both sides of the Atlantic: Harriet Taylor, Mary Wollstonecraft, Harriet Tubman, Angelina Grimke, Susan B. Anthony, Fanny Wright. In this narrative, even Anna O. appears – under her true name Bertha Pappenheim – as a woman who spent the majority of her life (after her encounter with Breuer) opposing white slavery and advocating for abused women and neglected children.[3] In this story, women speak for themselves and are clear about what they need and want.

There is no question that the gains of feminism in the socio-political realm could not have been (and cannot be) achieved without a strong political organisation and a cogently argued agenda. Yet it is intriguing to speculate that Anna O.'s experience with Breuer did actually relieve her internal conflicts, freeing her to live a richly self-determined life in the world. Such a story might suggest possibilities for alliance between feminism and psychoanalysis, although a story of this kind would not become available (in theoretical terms at least) until something close to our own era.

FREUDIAN AMBIVALENCE(S)

Although Freud's early studies in hysteria and his monumental work *The Interpretation of Dreams* (1900/1986) do not depend on a gender-marked narrative, his later drive theory does. As he elaborated his concept of an oedipal stage of development, his thinking tilted in the direction of a necessary correlation between the achievement of masculine identity (in men) and the patriarchal organisation of culture and civilisation. Less varied and flexible than his inquiry into the mind's capacity to deceive itself in dreams or symptomatic behaviour, this aspect of Freud's thought created a 'problem' for many of his early women followers, while constituting a direct challenge to second-wave feminists seeking to deconstruct the post-Second World War ideology of woman as wife, mother and homemaker. Taken together, Freud's oedipal paradigm of civilisation and corresponding theories of feminine development, emphasising women's condition of lack, or 'castration', seemed to authorise the conservatism of the 1950s regarding women's roles and capabilities.[4]

Ironically, Freud's own writings give evidence of his ambivalence about what it means to be a woman, but the signs of this ambivalence would not become fully 'readable' until new strategies of feminist literary interpretation became available. A brief review of Freud's 'Ur' dream in *The*

Interpretation of Dreams, the work that he expected to launch his career in the field of psychoanalysis, demonstrates the degree to which Freud's own texts offer themselves to feminist deconstruction.

In this dream, Freud inspects the mouth of a woman he calls Irma and finds curly structures therein.[5] He also palpates her chest through her clothes and concludes that her symptoms are physiological (rather than neurotic or psychological), caused by a contaminated injection adminis- tered by a colleague. Freud explains in detail how the dream is meant to deliver the following message: I am not responsible for Irma's pains; rather, someone else is. Freud uses this dream to illustrate his thesis: that dreams give expression to a secret or repressed wish. Once Freud has elucidated this wish – to exonerate himself from responsibility for Irma's symptoms – he feels satisfied that he has plumbed the dream.

In the story of Irma, we may discern the real-life ordeal of Emma Eckstein, a young patient of Freud's, whom he referred to his friend Wilhelm Fliess for nasal surgery to cure her sexual neurosis. The surgery was bungled by Fliess, who left gauze packing in Emma's nose, causing infection. When the gauze was removed, Emma haemorrhaged so severely that she nearly died. Freud, who could not stand the sight of blood, fainted during this scene, perhaps also regretting his own nasal surgery at the hands of Fliess. Initially horrified by the outcome of Emma's surgery, Freud wrote anxious reports to Fliess on her slow progress toward recovery, which included several more bleeding episodes. Gradually, however, Freud began to convince himself that Emma's bleeding was hysterically motivated, hence exonerating Fliess from charges of wrongdoing. In the end, Freud managed not only to dissociate himself from Emma and her vulnerabilities, but also to persuade himself that her sufferings were neurotic in origin.[6]

While many have commented on the elements of Emma's story that are encoded in Freud's Irma dream, and some have perceived a homoerotic subtext in the relationship between Freud and Fliess, no one has fully appreciated the implications of Freud's unconscious identification with Emma/Irma in the light of his later construction of femininity as a con- dition of violation.[7] Freud's interpretation of the Irma dream, which locates him firmly in the role of physician, effectively conceals the degree to which he also sees himself as a victim, thus paving the way for his hierarchical construction of the relationship between masculinity and femininity. Ironically, the instability of Freud's dream interpretation opens the possibility of deconstructing this relationship. If, in the short run, Freud's oedipal paradigm achieved supremacy, over time, it has worn thin, if not actually dissolved.

Interestingly, many of Freud's women patients – including the indomitable Emma Eckstein – later became psychoanalysts. Many of them made theoretical contributions of their own, participating in scientific meetings and publishing psychoanalytic papers. Evidently, they saw no contradiction between Freud's conservative pronouncements on woman's role in society (including the second-class nature of femininity) and the professional lives they led in the world. However, while women such as Loe Kann, Sabina Spielrein, Marie Bonaparte and Lou-Andreas Salomé remained loyal to Freud and his theories of femininity, others began to chafe. These women, who did not necessarily break with Freud, offered modifications of his theories of feminine development, which contained subversive possibilities.[8]

Helene Deutsch, for instance, who published a seemingly conservative study of female masochism, also wrote about the significance of the mother-infant relationship, a topic that Freud failed to explore. Melanie Klein, who considered herself Freud's true heir, undermined his emphasis on the primacy of the phallus through her theorisation of the child's relationship to the breast. Anna Freud, the youngest of Freud's six children and self-appointed keeper of the flame, not only pioneered the field of child analysis, but also introduced empirical study as an important component of its development.[9] Such women, though clearly deferential to Freud, also had minds of their own. One early woman follower, Karen Horney, even had the temerity to break with him and found her own school.[10] The post-First World War 'new woman' not only embraced Freud's implicit message of liberation from Victorian models of repression, but she took them one step further – into an implicit critique of the patriarchal order that upheld the normative construction of the relationship between the sexes.

FAST FORWARD

Fast forward to 1950s America, where Freud's ideas flourished in an atmosphere far removed from their origin. Freud's understanding of the relationship between the sexes, as based in his concepts of female castration, penis envy and the Oedipus complex, offered a means of rationalising a desire to re-establish order and stability in a society whose internal workings had been profoundly disrupted.

In the aftermath of the Second World War, women left their wartime jobs, compelled to return to husbands and children to cultivate the 'feminine' arts of housekeeping and child-rearing. The ideal of the nuclear family – father, mother and one or two children raised in a single-family home, apart from grandparents, aunts, uncles, cousins – prevailed, finding representation in visions of suburban tract housing, commercial advertising and television. In this new kind of 'bunker' mentality, Freud's theorisation of women as fundamentally lacking and hence vulnerable to 'envy' of male physical endowment and achievement seemed plausible. Women, in this view, should learn to accept their inferior physical status and fate. In these years, the history of Freud's early women followers – including their unconventional ideas and life choices – went missing, and it was not until the early 1960s, with a new generation of activist women, that another level of questioning began to arise. Two benchmark books, Simone de Beauvoir's *The Second Sex* (1953) and Betty Friedan's *The Feminine Mystique* (1963), presented cogent arguments against the philosophical and cultural ideologies that relegated women to inferior status in society and in the home. Suddenly there was an outpouring of books interrogating received wisdom about women, and the (retrospectively named) second wave of feminism was born.

In this heady moment, two more influential books appeared, each of which helped to jump-start feminist literary criticism through a targeted critique of Freud: Kate Millett's *Sexual Politics* (1971) and Germaine Greer's *The Female Eunuch* (1971). While Millett offered an analysis of phallocentrism as represented in the works of male authors such as D. H. Lawrence and Norman Mailer, Greer went for the jugular of Freud's failure to imagine an independent and robust form of female sexuality. Both books authorised new forms of interpretation, using psychoanalysis (with its subtextual method of interrogation) to undermine assumptions about women's inferiority.

In the wake of de Beauvoir, Friedan, Millett and Greer, critiques of male-authored literature in terms of its gender biases and sexist portrayals of women abounded.[11] Suddenly, the characterisation of women as virgins, mothers or whores became visible and subject to analysis, as women gleefully attacked the bases of Freud's assumptions about women. Once again, Freud himself provided fuel for the fire, as feminists scrutinised his texts for evidence of gender bias, making use of his own hermeneutic assumptions. A celebrated case in point is Freud's first extended narrative of analysis, that of a young woman (referred to him by her father) whom he named Dora. Published in 1905, 'Fragment of an Analysis of a Case of Hysteria' was designed to demonstrate Freud's theory of the sexual origins of female hysteria, although it is also widely regarded among psychoanalysts as the moment when he began to formulate his idea of transference.

The richly polysemic nature of Freud's writing, however, lends itself to multiple levels of interpretation.

Steven Marcus was among the first to remark on the similarity between Freud's manner of case history writing and that of the novelists and short story writers of his time. Freud himself commented on the degree to which his case histories resemble the form of the short story (without seeming to comprehend the implications of his admission). For Marcus, Freud is an 'unreliable narrator' (1976: 70) familiar to critics like himself as a manifestation of literary modernism. Feminists have adopted Marcus' insight and extended it. The Dora case history may be the most closely read text by feminists seeking to deconstruct and transform Freud's assumptions about women.[12]

In Freud's narrative, a young woman undergoes a brief treatment by him for a number of troubling symptoms, including nervous cough, catarrh and vaginal discharge of unknown origin. As her tale unfolds, many storylines begin to develop and proliferate. Her father, who has suffered from syphilis, is impotent (Freud claims), yet is having an affair with the wife of a friend. The friend, known as Herr K., focuses his erotic attentions on the adolescent Dora, who rebuffs him. Dora's mother, who may or may not be aware of what is happening, occupies herself with obsessive housekeeping. In this hot-house atmosphere, Dora is also called upon to nurse her father in his many episodes of illness. Freud concludes: that Dora fantasises fellatio with her impotent father (because he is incapable of intercourse); that she resents his relationship with Frau K. (towards whom she also feels erotically inclined); that she feels aroused by the attentions of Herr K. (a supposedly virile male); but also repudiates her arousal, hence succumbing to hysteria. Dora's problem, according to Freud, derives from her unwillingness to admit her sexual fantasies regarding her father and her desire to have intercourse with his friend, Herr K.

The upshot of this story is that Dora, a reluctant subject from the beginning, not only did not accept Freud's interpretation, but also took matters into her own hands, leaving treatment. Freud's reconstruction of their interaction occurred in the charged atmosphere of her rejection. We do not know what Anna O. thought about her involvement with Breuer, nor do we have any record of Emma Eckstein's response to the mishandling of her nasal surgery. Freud's Dora (subsequently identified as Ida Bauer) also remains something of a mystery.[13] Yet we do have Freud's extended interpretation of what happened between them. In this light, it seems apparent that he imposed his views of normative femininity and heterosexuality on a young woman who had good reason to resist his interpretation of her desire(s).

Feminist readers of this case history easily find fault with Freud's inappropriate treatment of Dora, who appears as something of a heroine – not unlike Ibsen's Nora – for walking out on him. In Dora's silent resistance, they find authorisation for their own vocal scepticism. Why should a fourteen-year-old girl respond with enthusiasm to the sexual advances of an older man? Even granting that Dora actively fantasises her father's sex life with Frau K., why should she assume that they practise fellatio? How might we construe the following: the position of Dora's mother, the role of the governess seduced and dismissed by Herr K., Dora's relationship with Frau K., and her attraction to the painting of the Madonna in the Dresden museum? Like the Dream of Irma's injection, the Dora case history yields a number of intriguing narrative subtexts, in the light of which Freud's oedipal construction of Dora's desire (for her father and for Herr K.) appears highly questionable.

Freud focuses on Herr K.'s natural attractiveness as a man, rather than the sordid situation in which he presses his courtship, thus deflecting our attention from Dora's father, a decidedly unvirile male. By insisting on Dora's desire for Herr K., Freud produces a normative heterosexual scenario that acts as a screen for the impotence of her father. Here, as elsewhere in Freud's body of work, the emphasis on masculine aggression barely conceals another layer of anxiety about helplessness and passivity. Beginning with Irma/Emma, Freud both exhibits and denies this anxiety, which he associates with the damaged condition he regards as 'feminine'. As Freud demonstrates in his dream analyses, however, his own texts may be read for what they displace and repress as much as for what they explicitly reveal. There are multiple 'Freuds' who inhabit the works we assign to him as author. At least one of these is a man who regards himself as wounded or lacking.[14]

THE SPHINX CONFRONTS OEDIPUS

Although Freud himself was unable to theorise the period of the child's earliest phase of development, including its relationship to the shadowy figure of the mother, his followers were less hesitant. Otto Rank (1952), who posited the idea of birth as trauma, was among the first to begin to explore what happens prior to the child's awareness of the father's authority and threat of castration. The infant's involuntary expulsion from the body of its mother, Rank suggested, may provide its first experience of separation, or 'castration', hence obliterating Freud's crucial distinction between the sexes. To his credit, Freud briefly entertained this notion, but did not,

finally, endorse it. Instead, he reaffirmed the centrality of the father's
prohibition on incest as the defining factor in the (male) child's abandonment of his tie to his mother and subsequent submission – and final
accession – to patriarchal authority.

Yet the (necessary, compelling and insufficiently theorised) figure of the
mother continued to beckon. Two converging, but also philosophically
opposed, understandings of the pre-oedipal period emerged in Freud's
wake. One owes its origin to a body of writings evolved over time, now
commonly referred to as 'Object Relations' theory. The other derives from
the work of a single figure, Jacques Lacan. What these two traditions share
is a fascination with the pre-oedipal period and its potential for the
reformulation – and subversion – of oedipal norms.

Object Relations theory evolved from the writings of a cluster of British
and American analysts, who took issue with Freud's assumption that the
child's ego is self-contained, or narcissistic.[15] Instead, they maintained, a
baby develops selfhood in the context of its relationship with its earliest
caregiver(s), typically the mother. This fundamental shift introduced a new
phase of psychoanalytic inquiry, redirecting attention from the father's
oedipal authority to the pre-oedipal period and the figure of the mother.
These thinkers, following the lead of Anna Freud and Melanie Klein in
pioneering the field of child analysis, also observed actual mother-child
interactions, hence underscoring the importance of empirical study in the
evolution of theory.

Just as feminist literary critics made use of psychoanalytic methods to
interrogate sexist assumptions in male-authored texts, they later employed
Object Relations theory to scrutinise the subject of mothering.[16] This
activity complemented their ongoing efforts to recover 'lost' women writers and re-evaluate texts by women relegated to the margins of the literary
canon.[17] The nearly universal practice of women's care of children (hitherto considered natural and hence unworthy of study) constituted a new
field of inquiry. Given the diversion of female energy into this activity and
its consequences for women's creative production – as analysed by Tillie
Olsen's *Silences* (1978) and Adrienne Rich's *Of Woman Born* (1976) – the
need for understanding the sources of women's investment in mothering
now seemed urgent.

Incorporating Object Relations theory into her analysis, Nancy
Chodorow, in her groundbreaking book *The Reproduction of Mothering*
(1978), offered an elegant, psycho-social explanation for why mothers raise
daughters who mother. Our current social arrangements, she argued,
support the way in which daughters identify with their mothers (including

their gender roles), whereas sons are encouraged to separate and distinguish themselves from their maternal origins. These primary dispositions have life-long consequences in the ways that women are inclined to foster and value close affiliative ties, while men seek competition and the rewards of individual achievement. To alter this set of psychological conditions, Chodorow maintained, would also require altering the conditions of childrearing that induce them.

For Chodorow, psychology is rooted in mutable cultural practices, yet the immediate impact of her argument was to open a space for a revaluation of women's relationships with one another – as mothers, daughters, sisters, friends, lovers. Object Relations theory, viewed through Chodorow's powerful lens, offered a means of exploring the intensity of female bonds, a genuinely new subject in the field of literary interpretation. Classic women authors, such as Jane Austen, the Brontë sisters and George Eliot received new scrutiny – not for their conventional romantic plots, but for the ways they shrewdly assessed their heroines' economic conditions, range of social choices and relationships with other women. Modernist writers, including H. D., Djuna Barnes, Gertrude Stein and Virginia Woolf, commanded new interest and respect – not only for their literary innovations, but also for their lesbian life styles and the traces of these affiliations in their writing.

Whereas Freud posited a mother whose lack led to the daughter's bitter disappointment in her, recognition of her own castration, development of penis envy and final wish for a baby, Object Relations theory offered a more positive scenario, emphasising the daughter's attachment to her mother as her first love. In both accounts, the achievement of a heterosexual orientation in girls required explanation, but Object Relations theory presented a softer view of this process and had the advantage of offering feminists a way to 'normalise' female homosexuality. In her influential essay 'Compulsory Heterosexuality and Lesbian Existence' (1980), Adrienne Rich coined the phrase 'lesbian continuum' to highlight the significance of intimate relations among women (whether as sisters, friends or lovers) over the course of women's lives. If a daughter's passionate first love is directed towards a woman, Rich argued, it makes sense for this current of feeling to persist over time, seeking and finding other female objects. Heterosexual attachments, in this view, develop as an overlay on a matrix of woman-to-woman connection. Blending theory with practice, feminist literary critics made use of these insights to interpret neglected aspects of women's writing, such as the lesbian subtext(s) in Emily Dickinson's poetry or Willa Cather's prose, as well as to encourage reception of the work of younger, openly lesbian writers.[18]

Daughters, it seemed, were finally having their day. But what about mothers? Who could adequately theorise their subjectivity – or imagine their liberation? While Olsen and Rich articulated the cost of women's exclusive childrearing, Chodorow bravely proposed a more practical solution – shared parenting. In the meantime, an alternate approach to this set of issues emerged in France – as an outgrowth of feminist responses to Jacques Lacan's re-interpretation of Freud.

Juliet Mitchell's *Psychoanalysis and Feminism* (1974) introduced Anglo-American feminists to the complex French thinker Jacques Lacan. Psychoanalysis, she argued, describes (rather than prescribes) gender arrangements under patriarchy. As such, it illuminates the unconscious structure of this particular social organisation, rather than confirming its universality. In essence, Mitchell pointed to the arbitrary nature of collectively held and unconsciously inscribed belief-systems regarding women. Like Chodorow, she emphasised the material and social organisation of the unconscious. Yet her reliance on Lacan led to different subjects and emphases in feminist literary criticism.

Jacques Lacan, who was profoundly influenced by the surrealist and Dada movements of his generation, attacked the emerging phenomenon of ego psychology, which he deemed a betrayal of Freud's insights into the revolutionary workings of the unconscious. He offered a re-reading of Freud's texts – mediated by contemporary developments in linguistics and structuralism – as a means of restoring a proper emphasis on the radical instability of conscious mental life.[19] Lifting Freud's theory of castration out of the realm of physical threat ('if you violate the incest taboo and try to have sex with your mother, your father will cut off your penis') into that of language, Lacan posited the notion of the phallus as signifier – a (more or less) arbitrary marker of the child's entry into the Symbolic Order of language and culture. Although patriarchal social organisation requires such a move, it is not authorised by anatomy. In this view, patriarchy is something of a sham – so why not have some fun with it? One senses Lacan's wry critique of phallocentrism and implicit alliance with the party of the devil, but also his unwillingness finally to overturn Freud's oedipal paradigm. With hindsight, one can detect Lacan's ambivalence. On the one hand, he seemed to side with those who would valorise the pre-oedipal phase of fluid psychic organisation. On the other, he seemed to endorse the necessity of the child's entry into the order of language and culture, represented by the name ('nom') and threat of castration ('non') of the father. Lacan played one side against the other, nimbly moving back and forth across this boundary, simultaneously subverting and affirming the structure of patriarchy.

A group of 'French' feminists (most prominently Hélène Cixous, Luce Irigaray and Julia Kristeva) exploited the weakness in Lacan's position, by focusing on the potential of his formulation of the pre-oedipal period to disrupt the order of language, hence patriarchy. Valorising the fragmented and disorganised rhythmic pulsions and babblings of the child as an aspect of its fluid boundary state in relation to its mother, these women imagined new forms of writing. Such writing, they maintained, would imitate or recreate the preverbal condition of the child (male or female), prior to the imposition of the father's name and law. This form of writing could be practiced by men as well as women, and many male precursors were invoked (for example, Nietzsche, Joyce, Genet). In effect, certain forms of *avant-garde* writing received new consideration through this philosophic/psychoanalytic lens. It also authorised, and helped to inaugurate, innovative forms of women's writing. Cixous, Irigaray and Kristeva – all intimately acquainted with the philosophical traditions Lacan inherited and invoked – played with the formal structures of language in order to interrogate these traditions. The difference between these women and Lacan was that they imagined the possibility of transforming the existing social order.

Cixous, Irigaray and Kristeva took Lacan's formulation of the pre-oedipal period (termed the Imaginary) seriously. While paying lip service to his account of the movement from the Imaginary to the Symbolic (hence the intervention of the phallus), they also violated the prescriptiveness of this narrative by giving imaginative 'voice' to the Imaginary. Whereas Lacan seemed to advocate a delicate balancing act, in which he could simultaneously celebrate the condition of *'jouissance'* (where all boundary conditions were suspended) and also maintain the necessity of accepting the conventional sexual positions defined by patriarchy, these women were less ambivalent about embracing the joyous indeterminacy of the Imaginary.

Hélène Cixous, who celebrated the eruption of unconscious energies in men's writing, also found special authorisation for this capacity in women's experience of maternity. 'How could the woman', she asked, 'who has experienced the not-me within me, not have a particular relationship to the written?' (Cixous and Clément, 1986: 90). For Cixous, the body of the mother, which must make a space for the inclusion of an absolute 'Other', becomes a model for the kind of discourse that allows itself to be traversed by the voice of the ultimate other, the unconscious. She draws an analogy between the process of parturition, and that of ecstatic speech. 'Voice! ... That, too, is launching forth and effusion without return. Exclamation, cry, breathlessness, yell, cough, vomit, music. Voice loses. She leaves. She loses. And that is how she writes, as one throws a voice – forward, into the void'. Famously, Cixous concluded, 'woman must write her body' (1986: 94–5).

Luce Irigaray, in *Speculum of the Other Woman* (1985a), indicted the tradition of Western philosophy for its exclusion of women's sexual difference. Freud's construction of femininity, she argued, is a special instance of this phenomenon. In Freud's account, she maintained, there is only one sexual organ – the penis. Measured against this norm, women can only be found wanting. There is no room in such a view for the plurality of women's sexual organs (clitoris, vulva, vagina) or desires. In *This Sex Which Is Not One* (1985b), she elaborated on this conviction, suggesting that women's sexuality is multiple and diffuse, thus undermining the singular status (and authority) of the phallus. Women's two- (or perhaps four-) lipped vulva is never completely open, nor closed, thus provoking analogies with the process of speech itself. Finally, she extends this analogy into the realm of the mother-child relationship, which begins in a condition of radical two-ness, hence violating the (phallic) fiction of self-contained individuality and consciousness. In 'And the One Doesn't Stir Without the Other', Irigaray lyrically evokes the condition of pregnancy, through the voice of a young woman addressing her mother: 'Of the two of us, who was the one, who the other? What shadow or what light grew inside you while you carried me? And did you not grow radiant with light while I lived, a thing held in the horizon of your body?' Later, she extends this meditation into a reverie about the mutual openness and connection of women's bodies: 'From your/my mouth, an unending horizon. In you/me and out of you/me ... Neither wide open nor sutured. Not rent, but slightly parted' (Irigaray, 1981: 65–7).

Even Julia Kristeva, who essentially agreed with Lacan's account of the child's necessary movement from the Imaginary to the Symbolic, was impelled to theorise a pre-Symbolic form of communication, rooted in the reproductive function and the child's pre-oedipal bond to its mother. She conceived of a prelinguistic, 'semiotic' phase, marked by fluid drives, pulsions and energies that later find expression through disruptions of Symbolic discourse. At the same time, she suggested that a woman's experience of pregnancy, in its condition of doubled selfhood, might afford special access to semiotic expression. 'A mother', she states in 'Stabat Mater', where she imagines the Virgin's maternal discourse, 'is a continuous separation, a division of the very flesh. And consequently a division in language' (Kristeva, 1986: 178).

But is there such a thing as a writing specific to women? Does not such a notion reinscribe the categories of sexual difference that French feminists (and others) have sought to undermine? While critical debates raged around this issue, the net effect was increasing attention to the writing practices of actual women: a win/win situation.

DECONSTRUCTION AND AFTER

Though proceeding from different philosophical assumptions, Object Relations theory and Lacanian theory both directed attention to the pre-oedipal period and the mother-infant relationship. Each modified and challenged Freud's oedipal construct, but neither displaced or overturned it, the Oedipus complex and the Symbolic Order remaining key to entry into language and culture. Feminists were bound to become dissatisfied with this impasse.

Help came from different quarters. While Michel Foucault cogently argued the case that sexual identities are constructed in social and material ways and hence historically contingent, Jacques Derrida pulled the rug out from under the assumption that separation from a state of plenitude (maternal or otherwise) occurs as a result of paternal intervention (physical or otherwise).[20] Rather, Derrida maintained, we experience lack (or castration) as a condition of being, or origin (Derrida, 1976, 1975). Together, Foucault and Derrida challenged the foundations of the oedipal, and heterosexually normative, narrative of cultural acquisition.

For Derrida, who attacked Lacan's structuralist model of linguistics, the phallus is not a privileged signifier. Instead, he argued, there never existed a condition of fusion between words and meanings, between signifier and signified. As a result, everyone (no matter how young) is cast into the condition of seeking a 'supplement' for something that is felt as missing or lacking. We do not arrive into a condition of lack (or castration) through the acquisition of language. Rather, we are born into it. For Foucault, who questioned normative constructions of gender and sexuality (including psychoanalytic categories of so-called 'perversion'), there never was a state in which gender identity or roles were self-evident or biologically prescribed. Rather, historically specific relationships of power that circulate through and define culture impose (and shape) them. Both of these thinkers were well acquainted with Freud, and both challenged him at the core of his assumptions about how individual subjects come into being and assume sex/gendered positions in society. Together, they mounted a formidable challenge to the psychoanalytic establishment, fuelling the work of feminists seeking to integrate a variety of disciplinary approaches – philosophy, history, political science, sociology and

anthropology – into literary studies. The synthesis that has emerged from
this volatile set of confrontations has helped to define current trends in
psychoanalytic theory as well as feminist literary criticism.

The writing of Judith Butler crosses many of these disciplinary boundaries. Versed in Freud, as well as Lacan, Derrida, Foucault and the post-
Marxist tradition of Theodor Adorno, Louis Althusser, Walter Benjamin,
Antonio Gramsci and others, Butler confronts the question of 'femininity'
and painstakingly deconstructs it (as these male thinkers did not in terms
of the reality of women's lives) in order to construe a more flexible and
open-ended construction of women's gender identities, sexual choices and
life destinies. So-called 'femininity', as she maintains, reflects the
culture's needs, power relations and ideologies, rather than a psychoanalytically ordained condition. In this view, women *perform* femininity,
rather than submitting to or deviating from an anatomically or biologically
prescribed script.[21] Psychoanalysis, in turn, has responded to such challenges by revising its previous convictions regarding sex/gender
practices and identities. Women are no longer regarded as anatomically
deficient, hence relegated to positions of service to men and children.
Nor is homosexuality considered a 'perversion', much less a category of
mental illness. Contemporary psychoanalytic theories recognise the diversity that characterises gender roles and sexual practices in most human
societies.

All of these are favourable (and long overdue) developments. But what
does psychoanalysis have to offer feminism (or literary studies) in our
current multiracial, multiethnic, multicultural global context? Some recent
movements, I believe, have merit – not only in terms of how we view
women's place(s) in society, but also in terms of how we understand
historical memory. Intersubjective theory and trauma theory, both of
which arose towards the end of the twentieth century, have each contributed to the ways that contemporary psychoanalysts (in theory as well as
clinical practice) approach the complexities of gender and culture.

INTERSUBJECTIVE THEORY

At the heart of intersubjective theory is an understanding of the necessary
implication of transference (the patient's projection onto his/her analyst of
the structure of prior painful and unresolved relationships) with countertransference (the analyst's response to his/her patient on the basis of his/her
own painful and unresolved experiences). In this model, the analyst is no
longer in the position of the 'one who is supposed to know', a position that

Lacan also laboured to deconstruct, but rather in that of the one who reflects – on both his/her patient's conflicts, and his/her own. In order to make sense of the patient's history of prior relationships, the analyst must also take into account and make productive use of his or her own history of neurotic engagement.

What Freud theorised – but most likely did not practice – was a model of neutrality, in which the analyst did not respond out of his/her own history of conflict(s), but rather 'heard' and interpreted the patient's (hitherto) incoherent narrative. This assumption, in turn, established a structure of mastery and submission, Freud's treatment of Dora being a case in point. It was not only Dora who projected her conflicted desires onto Freud, in her narrative of painful sexual ambivalence, but also Freud who projected his need for a normative heterosexual resolution into his interpretation of Dora's wishes and fantasies. While Freud came to understand the crucial role of transference, he did not articulate a concept of countertransference, much less speculate how the countertransference (properly utilised) might become an analytic tool.

Recognition of the analyst's subjective investment in the analytic process, although adumbrated in the work of Sandor Ferenczi, one of Freud's early followers, did not achieve full consideration and respectability until Stephen A. Mitchell, and others, brought it to light.[22] In this view, the so-called mastery of the analyst does not derive from an unalterable set of theoretical principles, but rather from his or her historical moment, cultural position, depth of interior questioning and degree of self-understanding. In correspondence with trends in other disciplines, which highlight the role of the observer in the theorisation of the observed, psychoanalysis began (at last) to acknowledge its implication in history and individual subjectivity. Contemporary psychoanalytic feminism – as exemplified by the work of Jessica Benjamin, Muriel Dimen, Adrienne Harris, Bonnie Litowitz and others – is grounded in this set of assumptions. Intersubjective theory (a refinement of Object Relations theory) has thus succeeded in redefining the position of the analyst in psycho-social-cultural terms. Trauma theory meanwhile has re-introduced psychoanalysis to the realm of (so-called) material reality.

TRAUMA THEORY

Although Freud himself inaugurated this field of study, he subsequently abandoned it. Early in his career, he assumed that a history of sexual seduction in childhood was responsible for the neurotic symptoms he observed in his patients. Gradually, however, he moved away from a one-to-one formulation of the relationship of the external to the internal world, to embrace a more nuanced paradigm of conscious/unconscious functioning. As a result, he focused on the role of unconscious fantasies in neurotic conflicts and inhibitions. This shift from the inter-psychic (in today's terms intersubjective) to the intra-psychic realm had powerful implications for the future of psychoanalysis as a discipline.

Trauma theory emerged in the 1960s from several areas of social concern: recognition of the prevalence of violence against women and children (rape, battering, incest); identification of the phenomenon of post-traumatic stress disorder in (Vietnam) war veterans; and awareness of the psychic scars inflicted by torture and genocide, especially in regard to the Holocaust.[23] Although Freud never denied the reality of incest in the stories he heard from his early women patients, he chose to direct his attention to the drama of internal conflict instead. Similarly, the psychic shocks and disillusionments incurred by the Great War caused Freud to speculate about the kinds of pathology (flashbacks, recurring nightmares and compulsive repetitive behaviour) inflicted by war experience.[24] Yet his inclination towards grand narrative led him away from an investigation of how traumatic experience affects individuals towards the realm of universal theory, culminating in his formulation of the 'death instinct'.

In the field of trauma studies, feminists have played (and continue to play) a major role, by calling attention to issues that specifically affect women and children, for example, physical and/or sexual abuse, female sexual slavery, genital mutilation, the practices of suttee, bride burning and 'honour' killing, not to mention rape as a routine weapon of terrorism. Studies in cognitive neuroscience, moreover, support the assumptions embedded in trauma theory – that the mind confronted with an overwhelming experience tends to isolate the memories associated with this experience in specific areas of the brain that are inaccessible to conscious recall and (hence) integration into the subject's ongoing narrative of his or her life history (Kolk, 1985). So-called talk therapy (of the sort that Freud advocated in his psychoanalytic methodology) does not fully access these split-off (often dissociated) areas of neuro-subjective awareness.

The point here is not so much that Freud was wrong as that he failed to comprehend the myriad ways in which individual subjects are shaped by their experience of being born to and raised by specific parents or care-givers, subject to unique conditions of class, racial, national and cultural influences at a particular historical moment. Together, intersubjective theory and trauma theory have begun to address these imbalances.

MOURNING FREUD

Freud is central to an understanding of the meanings and trajectories of the twentieth century. Yet, as I suggested earlier, there is no single Freud, whose work can be understood in monolithic terms. If the intellectual history of the second half of the twentieth century has taught us anything, it is that the value of Freud's texts lies precisely in their polyvalence and polysemy, exemplifying the very aspects of conscious/unconscious interplay that first engaged him. Reading Freud along a certain axis it is possible to authorise a number of psychoanalytic lines of thinking that he would not have consciously agreed to, much less anticipated. Many, if not most, of Freud's followers (including women) have done just that. Earlier I suggested that a reading of Freud's texts that traces his concern with the condition and gender position he associated with a primary wound (castration) might offer feminists a way not only to deconstruct his thinking about femininity, but also to dissolve the link between oedipal theory and patriarchy. In closing, I would like to sketch the outlines of such a reading – not to debunk Freud, but rather to make use of his work to open new possibilities for psychoanalytic feminism.

The pre-oedipal emphasis of much post-Freudian thinking paved the way for a reconfiguration of Freud's oedipal theory without challenging it at the core. Yet, if one takes the assumptions of these lines of thinking seriously, they lead to an account of origins that displaces the concept of a threatened loss (castration) with one that has always already occurred. In this sense, there is no distinction between the sexes – at least in regard to having or not having the actual (penis) or fantasmatic (phallus) symbol of power. Both Lacan and Derrida were right. Patriarchy (according to Lacan) is an arbitrary social construct – albeit one that persists in representing itself as necessary. Even more radically, Derrida proposed that insofar as patriarchy depends on the phallus as signifier, it founds itself on quicksand. Lacan, in addition, imagined the primitive ego as undefined, if not splintered or dissolved into random energies. In order for the ego to pull itself together, he argued for the necessity of a 'mirror stage', a moment in which the child conceives itself as a (falsely) coherent entity, either through the reflection of its mother's gaze, or through the perception of itself as an imagistic whole in an actual mirror. Derrida was invested in what happens if the ego refuses, evades, or simply acknowledges, its state of incoherence. In this respect his style(s) of writing also resemble the innovative writing practices of French feminists. Judging from his, and their, examples, it is possible to write (that is to say engage with the order of language and culture) in ways that suggest the multiple possibilities of consciousness that coexist at any given moment of time within a single 'person'. In each of these accounts, the ego is a fragile, amost illusory, construct. What I want to propose is that this particularly useful way of thinking for our time also has its roots in a submerged or subtextual Freud.

The Freud of popular imagination (based in part on his unsmiling, cigar-wielding photographic representation) is a rather forbidding figure, a father to be reckoned with. Read from this angle, his texts affirm Oedipus as the guarantor of patriarchal culture and authority. From another angle, a more vulnerable, even tentative Freud emerges – a boy, let's say, who looks to his mother rather than his father for love, comfort and confirmation of his burgeoning selfhood.[25] Increasingly in biographies and reminiscences of Freud and his followers, this particular child may be glimpsed. But he also appears (symptomatically perhaps?) in the interstices of Freud's own writings.

In *The Ego and the Id* (1923/1986: 29), a relatively late work, Freud speculates about the primitive formation of the ego as 'a precipitate of abandoned object-cathexes', hence an outgrowth of a process of painful separation. In this view, the ego is a product of childhood mourning – of the mother, her breast(s) or the fantasy of originary symbiosis or plenitude – so archaic as to elude memory and, to some degree, theoretical formulation. There is no evocation of the father, his penis/phallus or threat of castration here. Rather, the infant's loss of its mother's body, coveted gaze or exclusive attention signals a fall from grace into individual subjecthood, along with the necessity of finding alternate (symbolic) means of connection and communication. It hardly matters how or when this loss occurs – whether in the mother's womb (certainly a possibility given what we know about this complex two-in-one condition), during the process of parturition (as Otto Rank speculated) or after. The point is that Freud imagined such a primary loss in imagery that he later attributed to the oedipal drama of castration.

As early as 1917, in 'Mourning and Melancholia' (1917/1986: 253), Freud was thinking about loss (in metaphoric terms) as a wound. In this essay, he states that 'the complex of melancholia behaves like an open wound, drawing to itself cathectic energies ... and emptying the ego until it is totally impoverished'. But the analogy goes back even further, being first introduced in 1895 when he described melancholia to his friend Wilhelm Fliess as analogous to 'an internal haemorrhage ... which operates like a wound' (Masson, 1985: 103–4). Such a wound, he concludes, constitutes a 'hole ... in the psychic sphere'. The ego, for Freud, is an elegiac, or memorial construct – not so much a thing in itself as a tribute to absence.[26] Both sexes are subject to this melancholy condition, hence equally vulnerable or wounded. Freud's elaboration of the Oedipus complex, with its emphasis on the father's physical and social authority, masked this painful reality – as if (paradoxically) to shore up the façade of the Victorian culture he was born into, whose false pieties about sex and family life he actively strove to dismantle. The twentieth century's history of two world wars, genocidal conflict, cultural modernity and postmodernity, combined with new global configurations of wealth and power, have succeeded in redefining the nature of patriarchal authority. No longer the romanticised psychic structure that Freud conceived – based on the visible, genital emblem of male superiority – patriarchy reveals itself for what it is: an arbitrary assumption of power, founded in a set of widely shared belief systems, historical conditions and material, social practices, which combine to instil and compel individual (and sometimes mass) assent.

Oedipus with a small 'o', if you wish.

It may seem ungenerous to fault Freud for not having imagined the world we inhabit today. I hope I have not left that impression. Rather, I have tried to indicate how time-bound, yet also useful, his texts have proved for feminists who have laboured to detect the loopholes in his arguments regarding sexual difference(s) and practices, and the construction of social authority, while also proposing flexible, productive and challenging alternatives.

NOTES

1. Anna O.'s affliction, which involved a variety of physical symptoms, was understood by Freud and Breuer as a form of hysteria, an illness most often diagnosed in female patients. The Greek origin of the word hysteria – from *hysteros*, meaning 'womb' – predisposed physicians to consider hysteria (once thought to derive from the literal displacement of the womb) as a disease of women. As a part of his medical training in neurology, Freud studied in Paris with the celebrated Jean Martin Charcot, who regularly staged public demonstrations of his women patients acting out various symptoms under hypnosis. Josef Breuer's treatment of Anna O. was more individual, intimate and ultimately therapeutic. Under light hypnosis, Anna recalled feelings and incidents relating to her father's recent illness and death, which corresponded (in symbolic ways) to her physical symptoms. With Breuer as facilitator and sympathetic listener, Anna performed her own cure by following her seemingly unconnected thoughts, fantasies and reminiscences to their source in the painful circumstances surrounding her father's death. Although Breuer did not choose to pursue the implications of this unusual case, Freud grasped its

potential for revolutionising the understanding of hysteria as an illness based in psychology, rather than neurology. For an account of the meanings of hysteria in literary, historical and socio-cultural terms see Showalter (1985a).

2. Dianne Hunter (1985) analyses Anna O.'s 'hysterical' speech – ungrammatical, disjointed, polylingual – as a protofeminist revolt against her strict, puritanical upbringing.

3. Ernest Jones revealed Anna O.'s identity (1953: 223–6). For other accounts of her life see Edinger (1968), Ellenberger (1970), Freeman (1972) and Rosenbaum (1984).

4. Freud composed three essays specifically addressing the question of femininity: 'Some Psychical Consequences of the Anatomical Distinction between the Sexes' (1925), 'Female Sexuality' (1931) and 'Femininity' (1933). In them, he makes clear that he regards the girl child as 'castrated' owing to her lack of a penis and hence subject to 'penis envy', a condition she must overcome if she is to follow the normative path to femininity, which includes a shift of focus from the clitoris to the vagina in adult sexual relations and a passive orientation towards men. Although Freud affirms a basic bisexual disposition in boys and girls, leading the small girl to act as aggressively as a boy and to behave in other respects like a 'little man' (1933: 118), she relinquishes this character in the face of her recognition of 'castration'. Lacking the penis, the organ that symbolises activity and social power, she must accept her condition of physical deprivation and subordinate social position – or suffer the consequences of neurosis. In *Totem and Taboo* (1913), Freud developed an argument that equates the achievement of human civilisation with recognition of the incest taboo, which prohibits the boy from acting on his sexual desire for his mother. Because the father enacts this prohibition through his threat of castration, the foundations of civilisation are inherently phallic and patriarchal. Freud's theories of femininity both derive from and support these hypotheses.

5. Freud's Irma dream has drawn voluminous commentary (Sprengnether, 2003). I am indebted to Max Schur (1966), Erik Erikson (1954) and Jim Swan (1974), all of whom emphasise Freud's unconscious identification with his patient.

6. Jeffrey Masson, who edited the full correspondence between Freud and Fliess (1985), also published a scathing account of Freud's detachment from Emma's suffering as he convinced himself of its origin in hysteria – as opposed to medical malpractice (1984).

7. Max Schur (1966) was the first to make a connection between Freud's Irma and Emma Eckstein. Garner (1989) and Koestenbaum (1988) make cogent arguments for the homoerotic aspect of Freud's relationship with Fliess.

8. Lisa Appignanesi and John Forrester (1992) discuss Freud's relationships with these early women followers. For more information regarding Freud's relationship to Lou-Andreas Salomé see Roazen (1969/1986) and Pfeiffer (1966/1985). Aldo Carotenuto (1982) describes the romantic entanglement of Sabina Spielrein with Carl Jung, her disenchantment and subsequent flight to Vienna, where she aligned herself with Freud. Vincent Brome (1983), the biographer of Ernest Jones (who lived with Loe Kann for many years), offers

a vivid portrait of her, as does Jones himself in his autobiography, *Free Associations* (1959). For Marie Bonaparte's role in the Freud family's emigration from Vienna, see Peter Gay (1988). For her views on femininity and female sexuality, see *Female Sexuality* (1953).

9. Helene Deutsch wrote about female masochism in 'The Psychology of Women in Relation to the Function of Reproduction' (1925), 'The Significance of Masochism in the Mental Life of Women' (1930) and *The Psychology of Women* (1946). Yet she also stressed the significance of women's reproductive function and the importance of the mother-child relationship. Like many contemporary women, she experienced conflict between the demands of motherhood and a career, which she describes in her autobiography, *Confrontations with Myself* (1973). Melanie Klein, while professing absolute allegiance to Freud, introduced significant modifications into his theory of childhood sexuality by assuming that infants fantasise about the mother's breast – as gratifying or potentially devouring. From this point of departure, she elaborated her theory of infant development as beginning with a 'paranoid-schizoid position', in which affective objects (such as the breast) are conceived as alien to the self, followed by the 'depressive position', in which the infant internalises its hitherto split-off desire and aggression toward the mother's breast, hence enabling some form of integrated selfhood. Klein's major theoretical contributions are contained in *Love, Guilt and Reparation* (1975b) and *Envy and Gratitude* (1975a). See also Juliet Mitchell's sensitive introduction to her work in *The Selected Melanie Klein* (Mitchell, 1986) and Phyllis Grosskurth's accessible biography (Grosskurth, 1986). The significance of Anna Freud's contribution to the field of child analysis (and hence to theorisation of the pre-oedipal period) has remained somewhat unexplored, although her independence from her famous father has been thoroughly documented by her biographer, Elisabeth Young-Bruehl (1988).

10. Horney challenged Freud's conception of female sexuality as based in castration and penis envy, suggesting that cultural forces also play a role in the formation of feminine identity. Like Freud's male followers Alfred Adler, Wilhelm Stekel and Carl Jung, she defected from his group to develop her own distinctive body of theory and clinical methodology. See *The Neurotic Personality of Our Time* (1937), *New Ways in Psychoanalysis* (1939) and Susan Quinn's biography (1987).

11. This field is too vast to cover, but one representative area is feminist criticism of Shakespeare, which flourished in the 1980s and 1990s, owing in part to the landmark publication of *The Woman's Part: Feminist Criticism of Shakespeare* (Greene et al., 1980). See also the integration of feminism and psychoanalysis in Garner et al.,(1985).

12. Commentary on the Dora case history is quite extensive. See Bernheimer and Kahane (1985).

13. Many have written on aspects of the Bauer family history. See Deutsch (1957), Rogow (1978), Ramas (1980) and Decker (1991).

14. See Sprengnether (1990, 1995a, 1995b and 2003).

15. Central figures in the early development of this continuously evolving body of theory are: John Bowlby (1969), W. R. D. Fairbairn (1952), Harry Guntrip (1968), Melanie Klein (1975a and 1975b), Marion Milner (1969) and D. W. Winnicott (1971) in the UK and Frieda Fromm-Reichmann (1959/1974), Margaret Mahler (1968) and Harry Stack Sullivan (1953) in the US. Psychoanalytic feminists who have been influenced by this approach include: Jessica Benjamin (1988), Nancy Chodorow (1978), Muriel Dimen (2003), Dorothy Dinnerstein (1976), Jane Flax (1990), Carol Gilligan (1982) and Adrienne Harris (2005).

16. See Abel (1989), Hirsch (1989), Gardiner (1985), Lilienfeld (1980) and Suleiman (1985).

17. Gilbert and Gubar (1979) and Showalter (1977) are particularly influential in this regard.

18. See Bennett (1990) and Lindemann (1999).

19. A core grouping of Lacan's texts is gathered in *Ecrits* (1977). For a lucid exposition of his body of work, see Ellie Ragland-Sullivan (1986). David Macey (1988) places his work in relation to his cultural milieu.

20. See, in particular, Foucault's *The History of Sexuality* (1978).

21. This is an oversimplification of Butler's argument in *Gender Trouble* (1990). She amplifies the psychoanalytic dimensions of her position on the relationships between body, sex, discourse and power in *Bodies That Matter* (1993).

22. See, in particular, *The Clinical Diary of Sandor Ferenczi* (1988).

23. Bessel van der Kolk (1966) provides a useful summary of this body of theory in 'History of Trauma in Psychiatry'. See also Herman (1992), Terr (1990) and, for the literary uses of trauma theory, Caruth (1996).

24. In *Beyond the Pleasure Principle* (1920), Freud returned to the question of how external events may impact on the mind in devastating ways. Here he speculates on the phenomenon of 'repetition compulsion', using as an example the repeated nightmares suffered by soldiers returning from the front.

25. The official biography of Freud, as promulgated by Ernest Jones (1953) and Peter Gay (1988), emphasises his oedipal strivings and self-conceived heroic identity. Reading his life and work along a pre-oedipal axis, however, leads to a different conception of both the man and his writing. See Sprengnether (1990, 1995a and 1995b).

26. I first suggested this way of understanding the ego in *The Spectral Mother* (1990). I have since discovered that Hans Loewald preceded me in viewing the ego as a memorial structure that arises out of mourning (1976/1980). Others who have made use of this concept from a feminist perspective include Krier (2001) and Jonte-Pace (2001).

BIBLIOGRAPHY

Abel, Elizabeth (1989), *Virginia Woolf and the Fictions of Psychoanalysis*, Chicago: Chicago University Press.

Appignanesi, Lisa and John Forrester (1992), *Freud's Women*, New York: Basic Books.

Beauvoir, Simone de (1953), *The Second Sex*, trans. H. M. Parshley, New York: Knopf.

Benjamin, Jessica (1988), *The Bonds of Love: Psychoanalysis, Feminism and the Problem of Domination*, New York: Pantheon.

Bennett, Paula (1990), *Emily Dickinson: Woman Poet*, New York: Harvester Wheatsheaf.

Bernheimer, Charles and Claire Kahane (eds) (1985), *In Dora's Case: Freud–Hysteria–Feminism*, New York: Columbia University Press.

Bonaparte, Marie (1953), *Female Sexuality*, New York: International Universities Press.

Bowlby, John (1969), *Attachment and Loss*, vol. 1, London: Hogarth Press.

Brome, Vincent (1983), *Ernest Jones: A Biography*, New York: Norton.

Broner, E. M. and Cathy Davidson (eds) (1980), *The Lost Tradition: Mothers and Daughters in Literature*, New York: Frederick Ungar.

Butler, Judith (1990), *Gender Trouble: Feminism and the Subversion of Identity*, London: Routledge.

(1993), *Bodies That Matter*, New York: Routledge.

Carotenuto, Aldo (1982), *A Secret Symmetry: Sabina Spielrein between Freud and Jung*, trans. Arno Pomerans, John Shepley and Krishna Winston, New York: Pantheon.

Caruth, Cathy (1996), *Unclaimed Experience: Trauma, Narrative, History*, Baltimore: Johns Hopkins University Press.

Chodorow, Nancy (1978), *The Reproduction of Mothering: Psychoanalysis and the Sociology of Gender*, Berkeley: University of California Press.

Cixous, Hélène and Catherine Clément (1986), *The Newly Born Woman*, trans. Betsy Wing, Minneapolis: University of Minnesota Press.

Decker, Hannah S. (1991), *Freud, Dora, and Vienna 1900*, New York: Free Press.

Derrida, Jacques (1975), 'The Purveyor of Truth', in *Yale French Studies* 52.

(1976), *Of Grammatology*, trans. Gayatri Chakravorty Spivak, Baltimore: Johns Hopkins University Press.

Deutsch, Felix (1957), 'A Footnote to Freud's "Fragment of an Analysis of a Case of Hysteria"', in *Psychoanalytic Quarterly* 26.

Deutsch, Helene (1925), 'The Psychology of Women in Relation to the Function of Reproduction', in *International Journal of Psychoanalysis* 6.

(1930), 'The Significance of Masochism in the Mental Life of Women', in *International Journal of Psychoanalysis* 11.

(1946), *The Psychology of Women*, 2 vols, London: Research Press.

(1973), *Confrontations with Myself*, New York: Norton.

Dimen, Muriel (2003), *Sexuality, Intimacy, Power*, Hillsdale, NJ: Analytic Press.

Dinnerstein, Dorothy (1976), *The Mermaid and the Minotaur: Sexual Arrangements and Human Malaise*, New York: Harper and Row.

Eagleton, Terry (1983), *Literary Theory: An Introduction*, Minneapolis: University of Minnesota Press.

Edinger, Dora (1968), *Bertha Pappenheim – Freud's Anna O*, Highland Park, IL: Congregation Solel.

Ellenberger, Henri (1970), *The Discovery of the Unconscious*, New York: Basic Books.

Erikson, Erik (1954), 'The Dream Specimen of Psychoanalysis', in *Psychoanalytic Psychiatry and Psychology: Clinical and Theoretical Papers*, ed. Robert P. Knight and Cyrus R. Friedman, New York: Hallmark-Hubner.

Fairbairn, W. R. D. (1952), *An Object Relations Theory of the Personality*, New York: Basic Books.

Felman, Shoshana (1987), *Jacques Lacan and the Adventure of Insight: Psychoanalysis in Contemporary Culture*, Cambridge, MA: Harvard University Press.

Ferenczi, Sandor (1988), *The Clinical Diary of Sandor Ferenczi*, ed. Judith Dupont, trans. Michael Balint and Nicola Jackson, Cambridge, MA: Harvard University Press.

Flax, Jane (1990), *Thinking Fragments: Psychoanalysis, Feminism and Post-modernism in the Contemporary West*, Berkeley: University of California Press.

Foucault, Michel (1978), *The History of Sexuality*, vol. I, trans. Robert Hurley, New York: Pantheon.

Freeman, Lucy (1972), *The Story of Anna O.*, New York: Walker.

Freud, Sigmund (1900/1986), *The Interpretation of Dreams*, in *Standard Edition*, vol. IV, Freud (1986).

(1905/1986), 'Fragment of an Analysis of a Case of Hysteria', in *Standard Edition*, vol. VII, Freud (1986).

(1908/1986), 'Creative Writers and Day-Dreaming', in *Standard Edition*, vol. IX, Freud (1986).

(1913/1986), *Totem and Taboo*, in *Standard Edition*, vol. XIII, Freud (1986).

(1917/1986), 'Mourning and Melancholia', in *Standard Edition*, vol. XIV, Freud (1986).

(1920/1986), *Beyond the Pleasure Principle*, in *Standard Edition*, vol. XVIII, Freud (1986).

(1923/1986), *The Ego and the Id*, in *Standard Edition*, vol. XIX, Freud (1986).

(1925/1986), 'Some Psychical Consequences of the Anatomical Distinction between the Sexes', in *Standard Edition*, vol. XIX, Freud (1986).

(1931/1986), 'Female Sexuality', in *Standard Edition*, vol. XXI, Freud (1986).

(1933/1986), 'Femininity', in *Standard Edition*, vol. XXII, Freud (1986).

(1986), *The Standard Edition of the Complete Psychological Works of Sigmund Freud*, ed. James Strachey, London: Hogarth.

Freud, Sigmund and Josef Breuer (1893–5/1986), *Studies on Hysteria*, in *Standard Edition*, vol. II, Freud (1986).

Friedan, Betty (1963), *The Feminine Mystique*, New York: Norton.

Fromm-Reichmann, Frieda (1959/1974), *Psychoanalysis and Psychotherapy: Selected Papers*, Chicago: University of Chicago Press.

Gallop, Jane (1982), *The Daughter's Seduction: Feminism and Psychoanalysis*, Ithaca, NY: Cornell University Press.

Gardiner, Judith (1985), 'Mind Mother: Psychoanalysis and Feminism', in *Making a Difference: Feminist Literary Criticism*, ed. Gayle Greene and Coppelia Kahn, London: Methuen.

Garner, Shirley Nelson (1989), 'Feminism, Psychoanalysis, and the Heterosexual Imperative', in *Psychoanalysis and Feminism*, ed. Richard Feldstein and Judith Roof, Ithaca, NY: Cornell University Press.

Garner, Shirley Nelson, Claire Kahane and Madelon Sprengnether (eds) (1985), *The (M)other Tongue: Essays in Feminist Psychoanalytic Interpretation*, Ithaca, NY: Cornell University Press.

Gay, Peter (1988), *Freud: A Life for Our Time*, New York: Norton.

Gilbert, Sandra and Susan Gubar (1979), *The Madwoman in the Attic: The Woman Writer and the Nineteenth-Century Literary Imagination*, New Haven: Yale University Press.

Gilligan, Carol (1982), *In a Different Voice: Psychological Theory and Women's Development*, Cambridge, MA: Harvard University Press.

Greene, Gayle, Carol Thomas Neely and Carolyn Ruth Swift Lenz (eds) (1980), *The Woman's Part: Feminist Criticism of Shakespeare*, Urbana-Champaign: University of Illinois Press.

Greer, Germaine (1971), *The Female Eunuch*, New York: McGraw Hill.

Grosskurth, Phyllis (1986), *Melanie Klein: Her World and Her Work*, New York: Knopf.

Guntrip, Harry (1968), *Schizoid Phenomena, Object Relations and the Self*, London: Hogarth Press and Institute of Psychoanalysis.

Harris, Adrienne (2005), *Gender as Soft Assembly*, Hillsdale, NJ: Analytic Press.

Herman, Judith (1992), *Trauma and Recovery*, New York: Basic Books.

Hirsch, Marianne (1989), *The Mother/Daughter Plot: Narrative, Psychoanalysis, Feminism*, Bloomington: Indiana University Press.

Horney, Karen (1937), *The Neurotic Personality of Our Time*, New York: Norton.
(1939), *New Ways in Psychoanalysis*, New York: Norton.

Hunter, Dianne (1985), 'Hysteria, Psychoanalysis, and Feminism: The Case of Anna O', in Garner, Kahane and Sprengnether (1985).

Irigaray, Luce (1981), 'And the One Doesn't Stir Without the Other', trans. Helene Vivienne Wenzel, in *Signs* 7.
(1985a), *Speculum of the Other Woman*, trans. Gillian C. Gill, Ithaca, NY: Cornell University Press.
(1985b), 'When Our Lips Speak Together', in *This Sex Which Is Not One*, trans. Catherine Porter with Caroline Burke, Ithaca, NY: Cornell University Press.

Jacobus, Mary (1986), *Reading Woman: Essays in Feminist Criticism*, New York: Columbia University Press.

Janet, Pierre (1901), *The Mental State of Hystericals*, trans. Caroline Rollin Corson, New York: Putnam.

Jardine, Alice (1985), *Gynesis: Configurations of Woman and Modernity*, Ithaca, NY: Cornell University Press.

Jones, Ann Rosalind (1985), 'Writing the Body: Toward an Understanding of L'Ecriture Féminine', in *The New Feminist Criticism: Essays on Women, Literature, Theory*, ed. Elaine Showalter, New York: Pantheon.

Jones, Ernest (1953), *The Life and Work of Sigmund Freud*, vol. 1, New York: Basic Books.

(1959), *Free Associations*, New York: Basic Books.

Jonte-Pace, Diane (2001), *Speaking the Unspeakable: Religion, Misogyny and the Uncanny Mother in Freud's Cultural Texts*, Berkeley: University of California Press.

Klein, Melanie (1975a), *Envy and Gratitude & Other Works 1946–1963*, New York: Delacorte.

(1975b), *Love, Guilt and Reparation & Other Works 1921–1945*, New York: Delacorte.

Koestenbaum, Wayne (1988), 'Privileging the Anus: Anna O. and the Collaborative Origin of Psychoanalysis', in *Genders* 3.

Kolk, Bessel van der (1966), 'History of Trauma in Psychiatry', in *Traumatic Stress: The Effects of Overwhelming Experience on Mind, Body, and Society*, New York: Guilford Press.

(1985), 'Inescapable Shock, Neurotransmitters, and Addiction to Trauma: Toward a Psychology of Post Traumatic Stress', in *Biological Psychiatry* 20.

Krier, Theresa (2001), *Birth Passages: Maternity & Nostalgia, Antiquity to Shakespeare*, Ithaca, NY: Cornell University Press.

Kristeva, Julia (1986), 'Stabat Mater', in *The Kristeva Reader*, ed. Toril Moi, New York: Columbia University Press.

Lacan, Jacques (1977), *Ecrits: A Selection*, trans. Alan Sheridan, London: Tavistock.

Lilienfeld, Jane (1980), 'Reentering Paradise: Cather, Colette, Woolf and Their Mothers', in Broner and Davidson (1980).

Lindemann, Marilee (1999), *Willa Cather: Queering America*, New York: Columbia University Press.

Loewald, Hans (1976/1980), 'Perspectives on Memory', in *Papers on Psychoanalysis*, New Haven: Yale University Press.

Macey, David (1988), *Lacan in Contexts*, London: Verso.

Mahler, Margaret (1968), *On Human Symbiosis and the Vicissitude of Individuation*, New York: International Universities Press.

Marcus, Steven (1976), 'Freud and Dora: Story, History, Case History', in *Representations: Essays on Literature and Society*, New York: Random House.

Marks, Elaine and Isabelle de Courtivron (eds) (1981), *New French Feminisms*, New York: Schocken Books.

Masson, Jeffrey (1984), *The Assault on Truth: Freud's Suppression of the Seduction Theory*, New York: Farrar Straus Giroux.

(ed. and trans.) (1985), *The Complete Letters of Sigmund Freud to Wilhelm Fliess, 1887–1904*, Cambridge, MA: Harvard University Press.

Millett, Kate (1971), *Sexual Politics*, New York: Doubleday.

Milner, Marion (1969), *The Hands of the Living God: An Account of a Psycho-Analytical Treatment*, London: Hogarth.

Mitchell, Juliet (1974), *Psychoanalysis and Feminism*, New York: Pantheon.

(ed.) (1986), *The Selected Melanie Klein*, London: Hogarth.

Mitchell, Stephen A. (1993), *Hope and Dread in Psychoanalysis*, New York: Basic Books.

Moi, Toril (1985), *Sexual/Textual Politics: Feminist Literary Theory*, London: Methuen.

(1986), *The Kristeva Reader*, New York: Columbia University Press.

Ogden, Thomas (1997), *Reverie and Interpretation: Sensing Something Human*, Northvale, NY: Jason Aronson.

Olsen, Tillie (1978), *Silences*, New York: Delacorte.

Paris, Bernard J. (1994), *Karen Horney: A Psychoanalyst's Search for Self-Understanding*, New Haven: Yale University Press.

Pfeiffer, Ernst (ed.) (1966/1985), *Sigmund Freud and Lou Andreas-Salomé Letters*, trans. William and Elaine Robson-Scott, New York: Norton.

Quinn, Susan (1987), *A Mind of Her Own: The Life of Karen Horney*, New York: Simon and Schuster.

Ragland-Sullivan, Ellie (1986), *Jacques Lacan and the Philosophy of Psychoanalysis*, Urbana: University of Illinois Press.

Ramas, Maria (1980), 'Freud's Dora, Dora's Hysteria: The Negation of a Woman's Rebellion', in *Feminist Studies 6*.

Rank, Otto (1952), *The Trauma of Birth*, New York: Robert Brunner.

Roazen, Paul (1969/1986), *Brother Animal: The Story of Freud and Tausk*, New York: New York University Press.

Rich, Adrienne (1976), *Of Woman Born: Motherhood as Experience and Institution*, New York: Norton.

(1980), 'Compulsory Heterosexuality and Lesbian Existence', in *Signs* 5.

Rogow, Arnold (1978), 'A Further Footnote to Freud's "Fragment of an Analysis of a Case of Hysteria"', in *Journal of the American Psychoanalytic Association* 26.

Rose, Jacqueline (1986), *Sexuality in the Field of Vision*, London: Verso.

Rosenbaum, Max (1984), 'Anna O. (Bertha Pappenheim): Her History', in *Anna O.: Fourteen Contemporary Reinterpretations*, ed. Max Rosenbaum and Melvin Muroff, New York: The Free Press.

Schur, Max (1966), 'Some Additional "Day Residues" of the "Specimen Dream of Psychoanalysis"', in *Psychoanalysis – A General Psychology: Essays in Honor of Heinz Hartman*, ed. Rudolph M. Lowenstein, Lottie M. Newman, Max Schur and Albert J. Solnit, New York: International Universities Press.

Showalter, Elaine (1977), *A Literature of Their Own: British Women Novelists from Brontë to Lessing*, Princeton: Princeton University Press.

(1985a), *The Female Malady: Women, Madness, and English Culture, 1830–1980*, New York: Pantheon.

(ed.) (1985b), *The New Feminist Criticism: Essays on Women, Literature, Theory*, New York: Pantheon.

Sprengnether, Madelon (1990), *The Spectral Mother: Freud, Feminism and Psychoanalysis*, Ithaca, NY: Cornell University Press.

(1995a), 'Mourning Freud', in *Psychoanalysis in Contexts*, ed. Anthony Elliott and Stephen Frosh, London: Routledge.

(1995b), 'Reading Freud's Life', in *American Imago* 52.

(2003), 'Mouth to Mouth: Freud, Irma, and the Dream of Psychoanalysis', in *American Imago* 60.

Suleiman, Susan (1990), *Subversive Intent: Gender, Politics and the Avant-Garde*, Cambridge, MA: Harvard University Press.

Sullivan, Harry Stack (1953), *The Interpersonal Theory of Psychiatry*, ed. Helen Swick Perry and Mary Ladd Gawel, New York: Norton.

Swan, Jim (1974), 'Mater and Nannie: Freud's Two Mothers and the Discovery of the Oedipus Complex', in *American Imago* 31.

Terr, Lenore (1990), *Too Scared to Cry: Psychic Trauma in Childhood*, New York: Harper and Row.

Winnicott, D. W. (1971), *Playing and Reality*, London: Tavistock.

Young-Bruehl, Elisabeth (1988), *Anna Freud: A Biography*, New York: Simon and Schuster.

CHAPTER 14

French feminist criticism and writing the body

Judith Still

This chapter will first take an historical perspective on writing the body in the context of 'French feminism', considering what was at stake in writing the body in the 1970s and 1980s. The very expressions 'writing the body' and 'French feminism' pull us in the direction of the Anglophone reception of the work of Hélène Cixous, Luce Irigaray and Julia Kristeva. I shall analyse the main charges made against this work, and conclude by asking what positive and productive readings of this work are now possible. This will incorporate a brief consideration of some more recent work by these three women writers.

TERMINOLOGY

Both 'writing the body' and 'French feminism' are expressions used, at least in the Anglophone critical community, as shorthand to refer almost exclusively to writings by Cixous, Irigaray and Kristeva. These three authors are brought together for the convenience of our scholarly drive to categorise,[1] and yet they do not present themselves as having anything in common with each other. This article will be no exception since it is engaging with reception as much as with the texts themselves – in such ways are traditions sustained. At the same time commentators on these writers rarely consider them in fruitful dialogue with other women contemporaries. Occasionally other women such as Annie Leclerc or the Canadian Madeleine Gagnon are included, but the 'Holy Trinity' (Moi, 1985) is most commonly considered as if unique albeit representative. Ann Rosalind Jones writes: 'French feminists in general believe . . .' (1986: 361) even though, in the rest of her article, she does indicate a few points of dissent between these 'French feminists' as to the strategies to adopt in attacking phallogocentrism. More recently a volume entitled *French Feminists on Religion* (Joy et al., 2002) includes one extract from Monique Wittig and, unusually, four from Catherine Clément, but of course the other nineteen extracts divide almost equally between the holy trinity. Notoriously, Cixous, Irigaray and Kristeva have been marketed in English as representative of a feminism distinctly French, although many publications over the last twenty years (including the current volume) show how many other kinds of feminism exist in France[2] and indeed how the work of these three writers has had a much more powerful impact outside the French-speaking world. Here I am not only referring to the USA, but could include, for example, Brazil (Oliveira and Still, 1999). In addition, all three are in some ways adopted daughters of France, born respectively in Algeria, Belgium and Bulgaria – and it is important to raise the questions of national identity and race if we are to get a more accurate purchase on their work. The question of Frenchness apart, there is the issue of the appellation 'feminist', a term that has been variously used, questioned and disregarded by all three writers.

Traditional mind-body dualism has been both a contributing cause and an effect of women's historical subordination; feminists have spilled much ink to show women's association with the bodily, and how this has been presented in a negative light. It is played out in literature not only within texts (on the level of representation and form) produced by men and women, but also in the constraints at work on both the production and consumption of women's writing. Hence the assertion of the body in the writings of Cixous, Irigaray and Kristeva, in their different ways, had a startling effect and met with a mixed reception from feminists and non-feminists alike. Two things should be remembered in a discussion of the subordination of the bodily today: the first is the relation of our theories and representations of the body to our changing understanding of animality; the second is the fact that any subordinated term in an opposition will be available for representations of a range of subaltern subjects. Thus the historical downgrading of the material, relative to the spiritual or intellectual, feeds in not only to the traditional understandings of femaleness but also to representations of the working class or of oppressed races and ethnicities. The body gendered female in particular, however, is suffused with the maternal and the range of psychic and economic issues that relate to motherhood and to reproduction. The maternal body is important in evocations of writing the body – but it is simultaneously a material biological reference point, *and* a structure that allows a daughter to suckle her mother, or her lover (male or female), or to give birth to their beloved. If we attempt to dematerialise this writing and let it all drift off into metaphor, then it becomes little more than a poetic, and indeed patriarchal, commonplace: male geniuses have seen themselves as 'giving birth' to their masterpieces, and this spiritual or intellectual birth is, as they see it, of far greater value (and harder work) than common childbirth. If we readers simply attack this writing as 'biological essentialism', then we ignore a vital complexity in order to launch our attack.

WHY SHOULD CIXOUS, IRIGARAY AND KRISTEVA BE ASSOCIATED WITH WRITING THE BODY?

Critiques often begin with an Aunt Sally – Aunt Sally traditionally being a model head of an old African American woman with a clay pipe in her mouth used in a game. The players throw sticks from a distance in order to try to knock the pipe out. It needs no comment. I shall attempt therefore to sketch in some details about the three writers most closely associated with writing the body which, I hope, will not caricature them in order to pull them down. I should prefer to treat them as aunts in the second *OED* sense (the first sense being a biological or marital relation): 'Any benevolent and generally helpful woman'.

Cixous

Cixous first came to the attention of an Anglophone public with 'The Laugh of the Medusa', published in English relatively early (1976), and then *The Newly Born Woman*, not translated until the mid eighties.[3] These texts gained her the reputation of a proponent of *écriture féminine*, a term sometimes mistranslated either literally or conceptually as women's writing. Feminists in university departments of literature in the United States and the United Kingdom had made it one of their priorities, at least from the 1970s onwards, to retrieve from obscurity a number of women writers who had been consigned by a masculine critical orthodoxy to the dustbin of history. Feminist academics sought both to reappraise and republish women writers from earlier periods and also to make sure that contemporary women writers were treated with the seriousness they deserved. This important and difficult project, swiftly tagged 'political correctness' the better to belittle it, contributed to a certain confusion with regard to Cixous' rather different questioning of established orthodoxies. 'Writing the body' is less of a mistranslation although it immediately begs the question 'whose body?'. I consider that the question is posed not only to the opposition between the masculine economy, with its limited supply, and feminine economies of abundance, but also to the boundary between animal and human. But even the sexed opposition (which Cixous' critics seem so sure about) might need to be questioned: a writing economy could be across male and female. Peggy Kamuf carefully analyses some famous 'vertiginous' passages in Cixous, showing how her phrase 'writing is woman's' (Cixous, 1986: 85) assigns each term's meaning to the other, but then 'advances through *contradiction*' (Kamuf, 1995: 77). Later in the passage, Cixous writes: 'Femininity and bisexuality go together ... It is much harder for the man to let himself be traversed by some other'; Kamuf's analysis shows how this claim in fact unsettles any identity, or even non-identity, of both the term *femininity* and the term *man*.

The body described in 'Coming to Writing' with its breath and blood (Cixous, 1991: 10) is a hospitable body, characterised by 'A having without limits, without restrictions, but without any "deposit," a having that doesn't withhold or possess, a having-love that sustains itself with loving, in the blood-rapport' (1991: 4). While it is named *feminine* with all the contradictions that supposes, it also has qualities related to ethnicity or to the lack of a national identity. Cixous, Irigaray and Kristeva all experience exile and (in)hospitality in different ways. Cixous names herself Jewoman; she is 'not at home' (writing) in French (13). She needed to knock before entering. She is in some respects a guest and in others a usurper, and yet there is also love – if only for/in language. Her love for the hospitable French language is complicated: some critics would see her writing style as an assault on the spirit and form of this (neither quite maternal nor paternal) tongue. Others would see her (and vision is important here) as replenishing the language, and even, ironically, as defending it against the most invasive cultural threat: 'An infectious homonymy would be the guardian ... of a French language whose idiom could not be better protected against translation's blood-transfusion than by untranslatable homonymy' (Derrida, 2003: 39, my translation).

Writing the body could be set against two traditional kinds of writing: writing the mind which might involve the transmission (as clearly and transparently as possible) of ideas; and writing the world which might involve the recording or analysis of facts. Realist fiction would then be an imitation of scientific writing of the world, where verisimilitude would take the place of falsifiability as a criterion of judgement. Writing the body, on the other hand, would operate at a different level – closer to the body of the unconscious where the principle of non-contradiction does not apply. This possibility of the coexistence of what might seem to a more 'flat-footed' reader to be mutually exclusive meanings is crucial in Cixous' writing. And the French language, with its allocation of masculine or feminine gender to all nouns, lends itself to a generic gender play: for example, the *elle*, which we learn to translate as *she/her*, can refer to *he/him* (say, referring back to *la personne*, the feminine noun that can refer to a person of either sex) or *it* (say, referring back to *la mer*, the feminine noun for *the sea*).[4]

Irigaray

Irigaray's work covers a wide range of disciplines (most notably philosophy, psychoanalysis, linguistics and theology), but has had little to say directly about literature or literary works as such.[5] Attempts to align her with discussions of 'women's writing' or with Cixous' *écriture féminine* are quite misguided. With regard to women's productions, Irigaray has been far more concerned with the spoken word and with questions of education and pedagogical practice, for instance her work on children's speaking, writing and drawing (1999). However, Irigaray could be associated with the term 'writing the body' insofar as her texts dealing with (male) philosophers and scientists regularly demand that they should write, and acknowledge that they write, as embodied subjects (Irigaray, 2002). At the same time, she has had a very significant impact on literary studies and on the humanities in general – in particular outside France (for example, Stockton, 1994).

Of the various 'French feminists' invoked in this chapter, it is Luce Irigaray who is the most insistent on sexuate difference, sexuate (her preferred translation of *sexué*) understood as covering both biological and social sex and gender. For Irigaray, sexuate difference both exists and is not allowed to exist. Our patriarchal Western society is dominated by sexual (and consequently other kinds of) sameness. This sameness does not only take the form of supposing women to be like men; it is the ideology of French Republicanism and of much apparently egalitarian thinking which by *positing* equality in theory permits real material inequality to flourish in practice, for example in the workplace. Sexual sameness also persistently takes two other forms in Irigaray's analysis: complementarity and opposition (Grosz, 1989: 105–10). Women may be presented as complementary to men or as opposite, but this is still thinking within the straitjacket of the same and women are being measured against that universal phallic yardstick. It is crucial to be clear about what Irigaray understands by a culture of the same, since many of her critics accuse her precisely of attempting to imprison women within a traditional feminine stereotype, for instance peace-loving as opposed to masculine violence. The first translations of her work, *Speculum* and, even more strikingly, *This Sex*

Which Is Not One, met with a strongly bipolar reception that can be summed up by the biological essentialism debate over, in particular, the two lips essay in *This Sex* (1977/1985: 23–33).[6] Most feminists could agree with Irigaray's claim that 'female sexuality has always been conceptualised on the basis of masculine parameters' (23), and with her critique of the degraded representations of women's sexual organs in patriarchal culture (although some readers take issue with what they see as an excessively negative account of heterosexual intercourse). However, she also gives us a lyrical account of the multiple possibilities of women's pleasure, for instance:

She touches herself in and of herself without any need for mediation, and before there is any way to distinguish activity from passivity. Woman 'touches herself' all the time, and moreover no one can forbid her to do so, for her genitals are formed of two lips in continuous contact. Thus within herself, she is already two – but not divisible into one(s) – that caress each other. (1977/1985: 24)

Even more controversially for some of her readers, Irigaray suggests a continuity between the multiplicity of female desire and the possibilities of women's language – 'in what she says, too, at least when she dares, woman is constantly touching herself' (29) – and of a different kind of economy (31). For some readers this is tantamount to the heresy of defining women by their biology, as patriarchy so often has, albeit with a newly positive slant. A quarter of a century later, Irigaray remains unrepentant, and refuses to confess that she was only writing in metaphor all along: 'alluding to the "two lips", I try to give back to the woman that which only she herself can feel of this part of her own body' (2002: 19).

Irigaray is also clear about the urgent need to address the devaluing of the maternal; she shifts the focus from Sigmund Freud's originary patricide, described in his *Totem and Taboo* as the sons banding together to kill their father and chief. For Irigaray, the crime that founds our civilisation is rather an originary matricide which she analyses in 'The Bodily Encounter with the Mother' (1991) via the various maternal deaths in Greek myth, notably the killing of Clytemnestra as represented in the *Oresteia*. Originary is understood here not only in any sense of 'original', but also as 'repeated' (Hodge, 1994: 192). The matricide is another way of approaching her thesis that we live in a monosexual (masculine) economy in which the relationship between subject and object takes precedence over the relationship between two subjects. She is concerned with the exploitation and cultural repression not only of women but also of the natural world.[7]

Kristeva

Kristeva, like Cixous and unlike Irigaray, is a literary critic by training, and, indeed, a novelist. She is also a trained and practising psychoanalyst, and this informs all her work. She was first associated with the term 'writing the body' through her theory of the semiotic, deriving from the pre-oedipal phase, and the symbolic, deriving from the oedipal phase (see *Polylogue* (1977) or *Semiotike* (1979); extracts of both of these are translated in *Desire in Language* (1980)).[8] In an interview from 1977, Kristeva lays out quite clearly her views on women's writing at that time. She distinguishes between three elements: the *radical* nature of writing which cannot be contained in a sexual identity and indeed displaces sexual difference, and the *stylistic* and *thematic* elements which can be discerned in women's writing. She is cautious, however, at the outset even about these stylistic and thematic elements, unsure whether they are specific to women, or to the larger category of 'socio-cultural marginality', or to one particular structure (such as hysteria) amongst the many potential female qualities (Moi, 1987).

Most of Kristeva's earlier work focused on the male *avant-garde* canon, but over the years she has worked on Marguerite Duras (1987/1989) and more recently has devoted books to Hannah Arendt, Colette and Melanie Klein in a deliberate attempt to consider the 'forgotten' feminine genius (2001a, 2001b, 2004). In spite of her words of praise for the Virgin Mary and for motherhood, Kristeva of all French feminists has proved most palatable to Anglophone feminist audiences (Moi, Oliver and Jones for example) – although she still attracts her share of criticism.[9] Kristeva, like Cixous but in a very different style, moves between reference to a biological sexed body, and to the social gender usually attached to that biological sex, and evocation of a psychic sex and sexuality that can prove a great deal more fluid. Thus her writing in praise of maternity does not exclude male mothering even while she gives full weight to the role that women have historically played – and to the pleasure, pain and often material disadvantage that has entailed. In 'Stabat Mater' (1977; in Kristeva, 1983/1987), a lyrical verbalisation of her own pregnancy and the birth of her son is set alongside a theoretical text on motherhood. In her work on male (as well as female) authors she often indicates the power of the maternal. She writes in *Powers of Horror*:

The fact that 'something of the maternal' turns out to motivate that uncertainty I call abjection, makes it clear that literary writing involves the essential struggle which any writer (male or female) engages in with what he names his demon, only in order to signal that it is the reverse or lining of his very being, that it is the other (sex) which works on and possesses him. (1980/1982: 208)[10]

CRITIQUES

The work of these three thinkers (especially Cixous and Irigaray) met with a highly polarised response: on the one hand an enthusiasm that sometimes translated into mimicry, on the other hand an almost vituperative hostility. In the seventies and eighties the critics, such as Morag Shiach or Margaret Whitford, who were able combine an open mind with a degree of critical distance were in the minority.

Ann Rosalind Jones (1986), for example, assumes that Cixous represents all women as equally in touch with their bodies and thus able to produce liberatory writing. While it is possible to snip out quotations from Cixous' work to support such an assertion, it is equally possible to point to her acute awareness of the economic, political, social and other barriers that prevent women from achieving their potential as writers (or as anything else). It is one of the reasons why much of her literary analysis has focused on *male avant-garde* writers. Jones acknowledges Cixous' work on these figures but claims that she is too naïvely optimistic in stressing the 'primacy of multiple, specifically female libidinal impulses in women's unconscious and in the writing of the liberatory female discourses of the future' (1986: 366). However, 'optimistic' assertions (which may function within the textual context poetically as exaltation, or performatively in an exhortation which establishes a horizon of possibility) are (un)balanced with 'realistic' descriptions we can recognise. When writing a 'history' of the UK 'Women in French' group, which included the tale of how difficult we all found it to intervene in discussion after a casually exclusive paper by a distinguished French academic, Diana Knight and myself found the best account of our public paralysis in Cixous:

What Woman in French, whatever her relative and carefully acquired aura of self-confidence, has not recognised herself in Cixous's graphic account of the bodily distress that marks women's attempts to speak in public arenas: 'her heart racing, at times entirely lost for words, ground and language slipping away – that's how daring a feat, how great a transgression it is for a woman to speak – even just open her mouth – in public ... Listen to a woman speak at a public gathering ... She doesn't "speak", she throws her trembling body forwards'. (Knight and Still, 1995: 6)

For Cixous there is positive and creative potential in this feminine proximity to the drives. However, she does not underestimate the negative consequences for women in contemporary patriarchal society.

Jones writes of French feminists' 'assertion of a bedrock female nature' to challenge the systematic repression of 'women's experience'

(1986: 361) – although she then excludes Kristeva from the charge, saying that for Kristeva woman is less of a sex than an attitude (363). This is no more true of Kristeva than it is of Cixous. Jones claims that Irigaray wants women to assert their *jouissance* (364–5). This implies that for Cixous and Irigaray women would *be* a, b, c . . .; would *experience* x, y, z . . .; but that patriarchy buries, veils and undervalues what women are, feel and do. This position is actually much closer to the Anglo-American stance analysed by Toril Moi in the first part of *Sexual/Textual Politics*. The task of feminists would then simply be to reveal and valorise women's nature and experience. It is not so simple for Cixous, Irigaray or Kristeva.

Domna C. Stanton, by contrast, critiques Cixous, Irigaray and Kristeva for their use of the maternal metaphor (1986). In fact the reference to metaphor is quite different in each writer – quotations from Cixous on metaphor cannot be used in application to Irigaray. Cixous' writing has a complex relationship to the figural. We might note occasions when she warns readers against rushing to understand things metaphorically (a reaction that can be more comfortable for us): 'this face is not a metaphor' (1991: 2) or 'I read to live . . . Without metaphor . . . I was raised on the milk of words . . . The language that women speak when no one is there to correct them' (20–1).

Irigaray has written precisely on metaphor as a tool for patriarchal disembodiment in 'Plato's Hystera' in *Speculum*. If we look to her most poetic writing, where we readers might find it easiest to understand what she says as metaphor, we should in fact proceed with caution. In the Preface to *Everyday Prayers*, her collection of poems, she writes: 'there are no metaphors, in the strict sense, in the feminine poems presented in this book' (2004b: 48). She goes on to try to exemplify this point:

So between a beloved lover and a bird, passages are made on behalf of the kinship between them. No creation of images then, but a memory of continuity between human and bird. A bird is the lover who is able to conserve breath in him and use it to love: through flight, through song and through arms. Arms which do not take or detain the other but which shelter in an aerial and light way, like the wings of a bird, or an angel. A bird and an angel – the two being here also related – is the lover who unites body and soul by a transmutation of breaths: a celestial messenger who weathers heaviness and whose flesh speaks in a manner more divine than words themselves.

I have quoted this passage not only because of its rejection of metaphor as a substitution of one thing for another, which privileges the masculine spiritual over the feminine bodily. It is also interesting because in these 'feminine poems' it seems as if the male lover too can cultivate breath in a sensible transcendental – not, we may assume, in the *same* way as the female lover but in communion with her.

H. C. and calling by name

While Cixous continues work as a literary critic (and a teacher), her most significant body of work over the last thirty years lies in her 'fiction' and her writing for the theatre. Although at first she was criticised by some Anglophone critics for what they diagnosed as an essentialism that precluded consideration of racial or class differences (Jones, 1986: 369, 371), her theatre makes clear what was already the case – that cultural and class differences are crucial to her work.[11] Critics may not like her treatment of colonial and postcolonial issues but there is no longer any denying their centrality if we consider her entire oeuvre. I referred above to 'fiction' but such a term could be misleading – and even prose writing is only true in a strict sense since her prose is highly poetic.[12] Important recent publications include a number of hybrid forms that cross generic boundaries and, in particular, the boundary between referential truth and products of the imagination: autofiction or altofiction; texts 'about' close family, friends or animals; the transcription of dreams (2003); notebooks (2004). Derrida comments: 'in her general poetics, each genre remains itself, at home, while offering hospitality generously to the other genre, to the other in any genre that arrives as a parasite, as a ghost or to take its host hostage, always following the same topodynamics of the smaller bigger than the bigger' (2003: 28, my translation). This formulation hints that genre could be understood in more than one sense – and this is quickly made explicit: 'Grafting, hybridisation, migration, genetic mutation multiplies and cancels at once genre and gender differences, literary differences and sexual differences' (28–9, my translation).

Cixous' writing of the body is not only her own or the feminine body, narrowly understood – she expands the parameters of the personal and of sex by affirming, by opening to the other – even as she shows how in practical terms, including political terms, the other may say no. One of the 'light' ways of affirming and opening to the other is calling (by name). We learn the importance of this both from her own words and from Derrida (2002). This calling by name is not quite the same as naming. Cixous is noted for the absence of names in her fictively autobiographical writing – a *pudeur* (or discretion) that conserves secrets and opens up the text to manifold interpretations – as much as for her play on certain key names and the letters and syllables therein (Eve, Georges, Hélène, Jacques to name but four).

In her fiction *Or*, Cixous tells her reader that using someone's name keeps them out of the abyss of nothingness:

But everything begins with proper names. I desire you and keep you and hold you firmly above the void by your name, I pull you from the pit by the braid of a name. There is no minor crime more wounding for me than for me to forget the name of someone who greets me. And the worst thing is that, if I ask that person, whom I've forgotten, what they're called – then I am executing them before their very eyes. But I didn't want to kill the apparition of that person! . . .

Between my cat and myself the pact is in the pronunciation. It is not only that I call her with intensity, but also that between us each time it is a nuptial engagement . . . She hears 'Will you?' and her body racing means yes I do yes, and each time it's for life. I am well aware of this, I never throw out her name like a piece of fish. (1997: 21–2, my translation)

To summarise: the name is like a woven or plaited thread; Cixous cannot bear to forget someone's name – it is like killing them. When she calls her cat's name and the cat comes running it is like a life-time nuptial bond – expressed in the *timbre* (or tone) of her voice as she pronounces the name and the passionate *movement* of the cat's body as she responds.[13] It is important not to throw a gift, such as a loving summons, like a morsel of fish. The manner of giving is as important as the manner of receiving.[14]

Cixous analyses a rather different kind of naming in her writing on her childhood in colonial Algeria. She tells of the haphazard re-naming of streets, districts and towns with French names, including the names of military heroes. She tells of the maids named Fatma, and how even her own beloved maid Aïcha turned out to be called Messaouda. Identities were simple, pre-given and (thus) false:

We always lived in the episodes of a brutal Algeriad, thrown from birth into one of the camps crudely fashioned by the demon of Coloniality. One said: 'the Arabs'; 'the French.' And one was forcibly played in the play, with a false identity. Caricature-camps . . .

The Chorus of the French hurled out with a single voice that the Arabs were: dirty-lazy-incapable-thieves.

It was the reign of the insult and the *apostrophe*. (1998: 156)

One of the impossible identities at the time was 'Berber'. It thus seems all the more appropriate that the very name of Cixous, 'My wild bristling sexual name unclean improper cutting like a Barbary fig, vulnerable, attacked, barbarian' (157), which she thinks of dropping in favour of something less bizarre, turns out, it is suggested, to derive from the name of a Berber tribe (158). That suggestion comes almost like a reward for resisting the temptation of disavowal, for staying faithful to difficulty.

Irigaray and 'I love to you'

Luce Irigaray's recent writing is far less ambiguous with respect to the question 'whose body?' than that of Cixous, Derrida or Kristeva. A culture of sexual difference, a culture of *two* subjects, is, for Irigaray, something that we should be working towards (2001). Of course there is a tension here between different temporalities and modes of experience. We turn back to the past (for instance in search of matriarchal traces) and risk inventing nostalgic utopias; we experience the present time (listening to children's speech for example) and risk the influence of the monoculture that predominates; we imagine future negotiations of sexuate difference – but how can we imagine something truly different, what we do not know at all? Women need to become their own independent ('virgin') subjects before they can enter into the desirable nuptial relationship with another independent and distinct subject. Crucially, that other should be separated from them by a threshold; the culture of two subjects requires a third (space): 'The transcendence between us, this one which is fecund in graces and words, requires an interval, it engenders it also ... it is important that an irreducible distance will remain where silence takes place' (2002: 66).

Envisaging that horizon of the two, feeling that amorous possibility, by practising (yoga) breathing, for example, may begin that *becoming*. Irigaray's work also encourages us to be attentive to (our) language and to work on inventing a different way of speaking (and listening) *with* the other. She suggests, for instance, that verbs, with their different tenses and moods (active, passive, middle passive) will perhaps be more effective than substantives (2002: 59), and that we should privilege verbs which take an indirect rather than a direct object. She tells her readers, for example, that 'I love to you' (the title of one of her books, in French 'j'aime à toi') is more respectful of the two than the more usual formulation ('I love you', 'je t'aime') which risks reducing 'you' to an object of my love. In *The Way of Love* (2002), Irigaray begins with the argument that 'philosophy' means 'the wisdom of love' as much as, or more than, 'the love of wisdom', which is the only meaning that we have chosen to retain from the etymological possibilities. An other kind of speaking relates to an other way of knowing, a way of love, excluded by the dominant scientific (in the broadest sense) community of our day which is wilfully blind to its own bids for power (2002: 104).

Kristeva and maternal experience

It is important to note that all three of these writers have produced important *collaborative* publications. Kristeva's recent collaborative work with Catherine Clément, *The Feminine and the Sacred*, could in many ways be seen as a return to the privileging of motherhood characteristic of *Tales of Love*, written at the time of her son's birth. Motherhood, in the literal sense, is presented as one of the things linking Kristeva and Clément. Quotations from the book can sound naïve: for example, early on Kristeva in New York praises the calm professionalism of African American women in shops and offices:

That has nothing to do with the feverish agitation of emancipated women who, even a few years ago, believed they were liberating themselves by becoming more like men. The ones I saw this time behave like ordinary mothers, and proud to be so, women who quite simply speak up, and, just as simply, conduct the affairs of the city. (Clément and Kristeva, 1998/2001: 11)

She links this to the sacred: 'There is life and women can give it: *we* can give it. Hence time is transformed into an eternity of miraculous instants' (12). However, she does not present motherhood as uniquely serene: 'the mother is never short on the tendency to annex the cherished other, to project herself onto it, to monopolize it, to dominate it, to suffocate it' (57). Nor is the maternal tied solely to the biologically female body:

Outside motherhood, no situations exist in human experience that so radically and so simply bring us face to face with that emergence of the other. The father, in his own, less immediate way, is led to the same alchemy; but to get there, he must identify with the process of delivery and birth, hence with the maternal experience, must himself become maternal and feminine; before adding his own role as indispensable and radical distance. I like to think that, in our human adventure, we can encounter 'the other' – sometimes, rarely – if, and only if, we, men and women, are capable of that maternal experience, which defers eroticism into tenderness and makes an 'object' an 'other me'. (1998/2001: 57).

Clément adds: 'the feminine must be something shared between man and woman' (109). One of the main points of divergence between the two women is what some might term Kristeva's Eurocentrism, and her privileging of Western monotheism against Islam, and others might term Clément's reverse ethnocentrism; it is an important feature of the book's format that the exchange of letters permits each point of view to be challenged by the other.

CONCLUSION

The term 'writing the body' is most strongly associated with the 1980s Anglophone reception of Cixous, Irigaray and Kristeva. The controversies that blazed at that time are somewhat muted now when some would say that we have moved into post-feminism, or that queer theory and post-colonialism are much further up the agenda than feminism *tout court*. However, all three writers continue to publish important material, ena-bling a re-interpretation of their earlier work. Cixous most notably is publishing writing on Algeria that reveals how she has been misread as resolutely Eurocentric and ignorant of the postcolonial dimension. Irigaray emphasises what we can learn from yoga and from Buddhism. Kristeva has addressed issues around immigration, for instance in *Strangers to Ourselves*, and continues to make reference to China and what we can learn from the relationship between yin and yang (Clément and Kristeva, 1998/2001: 169).[15] All three continue to interrogate sexual difference and the sexed body in ways that readers sometimes find uncomfortable. This includes Kristeva and Irigaray's continuing writing on motherhood, and Irigaray's insistence on a culture of two subjects. Motherhood is always a vexed area for feminists; perhaps *because* reproduction is materially and ideologically *essential* for the continued functioning of capitalism and patriarchy it is economically and culturally *devalued*. Yet one of the tricks of real devalua-tion can be an apparent hyperbolic valuation, and this makes the task of revaluation all the harder. I would argue that the most productive way of reading is to interrogate our own discomfort, not to move swiftly to condemn nor to swallow undigested, but to attempt, in good faith, a dialogue between ourselves in our specificity as reading subjects and these various 'other' texts.

NOTES

This chapter was written while on a Major Research Fellowship funded by the Leverhulme Trust to work on hospitality; I should like to express my gratitude to the Trust.

1. For example, Domna C. Stanton (1986) brings the three together to put them on trial for their use of metaphor. There are of course exceptions to the rule. A recent publication edited by Kelly Oliver and Lisa Walsh (2004) rather surprisingly includes only Kristeva of the trinity, preferring instead some

relatively new writers such as Claire Nahon alongside figures such as Gisèle Halimi or Sylviane Agacinski and at least one surprise: Alain Badiou.

2. See the work of Claire Duchen for example. Readers such as *New French Feminisms* (Marks and Courtivron, 1981) and Moi's *French Feminist Thought: A Reader* (1987) also presented a broader picture, but, of the various other French feminists they sought to introduce to an English-speaking public, only Michèle Le Doeuff has received significant attention – and she has not received as much as she deserves.

3. In collaboration with Catherine Clément. First published in France in 1975.

4. In *Messie* (as in many of Cixous' writings) the personal pronouns I, you, he, she (*je, tu, il, elle*) are often ambiguous. The narrator is 'I' but also 'she'. 'She' is also the cat, when it is *la chatte* (a feminine noun to designate specifically a female cat). 'You' is both the lover and the cat; 'he' is also both the lover and the cat when it is *le chat* (a masculine noun to designate a cat of either sex). For example, see 1996: 72–3. My thanks to Gill Rye for directing me to Cixous' writing about her cat(s).

5. It should be noted, however, that Irigaray's first doctorate was on Paul Valéry and that she herself is a prolific writer of poetry. See *Everyday Prayers* (2004b).

6. First published in England in 1981 (America in 1980) in the influential collection *New French Feminisms* (Marks and de Courtivron). See Whitford (1991: 170ff) for an interesting reading of Irigaray's controversial corporeal/sexual vocabulary.

7. See 'How Can We Speak to Each Other with Socialism as Our Horizon?' for her combining of environmental and political issues (2004a: 214–23).

8. For excellent glosses on these terms see Grosz (1989) or Smith (1998).

9. See Anne-Marie Smith for analysis of critiques of Kristeva's work (1998: 35–8), and Still (1991) for some problems of 'translation'.

10. Kristeva's difficult concept-word *abject* from *Powers of Horror* has been much used and abused by a significant audience within and beyond feminism (Still, in Smith, 1997: 221–39).

11. In 'Coming to Writing' there are a number of important references to colonial Algeria for example, 'They teach me … In whose name would I write', 'Nationality? "French." Not my fault! *They* put me in the position of imposture' (1991: 15–16, 19). The same is true of *The Newly Born Woman*.

12. Derrida gives us a felicitous formula for dealing with the question of genre when he refers to Cixous' 'fictions fictively said to be autobiographical' (2003: 18, my translation).

13. For Cixous' relation to the beloved cat that arrived like a miracle, see 'Writing Blind: Conversation with the Donkey', in *Stigmata: Escaping Texts* (1998).

14. Compare the scene in *Osnabrück* (1999: 89), analysed by Hanrahan (2004). The prize morsel of fish must be given up by the mother for the daughter – Cixous gives and betrays as she slips the piece of fish that her mother has given her on to her daughter's plate. The gift has been a key motif in Cixous' (and in Irigaray's) work since the beginning.

15. Kristeva had already published a book about Chinese women (1974/1986), which attracted some hostility from a postcolonial standpoint – notably from Gayatri Spivak. See Whatling in Cady (1991: 39–57).

BIBLIOGRAPHY

Attridge, Derek (ed.) (1992), *Acts of Literature/Jacques Derrida*, London and New York: Routledge.
Bowlby, Rachel (1988), 'Flight Reservations', in *The Oxford Literary Review* 10.
Burke, Carolyn et al. (eds) (1994), *Engaging with Irigaray*, New York: Columbia University Press.
Cady, Andrea (ed.) (1991), *Women Teaching French: Five Papers on Language and Theory*, Loughborough: Studies in European Culture and Society.
Cixous, Hélène (1975), 'Le Rire de la Méduse', in *L'Arc* 61, translated as 'The Laugh of the Medusa', trans. Keith Cohen and Paula Cohen, in *Signs* (Summer 1976).
 (1986), *Entre l'écriture*, Paris: Des femmes.
 (1991), *'Coming to Writing' and Other Essays*, trans. Sarah Cornell, Deborah Jenson, Ann Liddle and Susan Sellers, Cambridge, MA: Harvard University Press.
 (1996), *Messie*, Paris: Des femmes.
 (1997), *Or: les lettres de mon père*, Paris: Des femmes.
 (1998), 'My Algeriance, in Other Words: To Depart Not to Arrive from Algeria', in *Stigmata: Escaping Texts*, trans. Eric Prenowitz, New York and London: Routledge.
 (1999), *Osnabrück*, Paris: Des femmes.
 (2003), *Rêve je te dis*, Paris: Galilée.
 (2004), *The Writing Notebooks*, ed. and trans. Susan Sellers, New York and London: Continuum.
Cixous, Hélène and Catherine Clément (1975/1986), *The Newly Born Woman*, trans. Betsy Wing, Minneapolis: University of Minnesota Press.
Cixous, Hélène and Jacques Derrida (2001), *Veils*, trans. Geoffrey Bennington, Stanford: Stanford University Press.
Cixous, Hélène, Madeleine Gagnon and Annie Leclerc (1977), *La Venue à l'écriture*, Paris: Union Générale d'Editions.
Clément, Catherine and Julia Kristeva (1998/2001), *The Feminine and the Sacred*, trans. Jane Marie Todd, New York: Columbia University Press.
Derrida, Jacques (1992), 'Ulysses Gramophone: Hear Say Yes in Joyce', trans. Tina Kendall with Shari Benstock, in Attridge (1992).
 (2002), *H. C. pour la vie, c'est à dire*, Paris: Galilée.
 (2003), *Genèses, genealogies, genres et le genie: Les secrets de l'archive*, Paris: Galilée.
Duchen, Claire (1986), *Feminism in France: from May '68 to Mitterrand*, London: Routledge.
 (ed.) (1987), *French Connections: Voices from the Women's Movement in France*, Amherst: University of Massachusetts Press.

Fallaize, Elizabeth (1993), *French Women's Writing: Recent Fiction*, Basingstoke: Macmillan.

Gallop, Jane (1986), 'Annie Leclerc Writing a Letter, With Vermeer', in Miller (1986).

Grosz, Elizabeth (1989), *Sexual Subversions: Three French Feminists*, Sydney: Allen and Unwin.

Hanrahan, Mairéad (2004), 'The Place of the Mother: Hélène Cixous' *Osnabrück*', in *Paragraph* 27:1.

Harrison, Nicholas (2004), 'Learning from Experience: Hélène Cixous' "Pieds nus"', in *Paragraph* 27:1.

Hodge, Joanna (1994), 'Irigaray Reading Heidegger', in Burke et al. (1994).

Huffer, Lynne (ed.) (1995), *Another Look, Another Woman: Retranslations of French Feminism*, special issue of *Yale French Studies* 87.

Irigaray, Luce (1974/1985), *Speculum of the Other Woman*, trans. Gillian C. Gill, Ithaca, NY: Cornell University Press.

   (1977/1985), *This Sex Which Is Not One*, trans. Catherine Porter and Carolyn Burke, Ithaca, NY: Cornell University Press.

   (1985/2002), *To Speak Is Never Neutral*, trans. Gail Schwab, London and New York: Continuum.

   (1991), 'The Bodily Encounter with the Mother', in *The Irigaray Reader*, ed. Margaret Whitford, Oxford: Blackwell.

   (1999), *Chi sono io? Chi sei tu? La chiave per una convivenza universale*, Casalmaggiore: Biblioteca di Casalmaggiore.

   (2001), *To Be Two*, trans. Monique M. Rhodes and Marco F. Cocito-Monoc, New York: Routledge.

   (2002), *The Way of Love*, trans. Heidi Bostic and Stephen Pluhacek, London and New York: Continuum.

   (ed.) (2002), *Luce Irigaray: Dialogues around Her Work*, special issue of *Paragraph* 25:3.

   (2004a), *Key Writings*, London and New York: Continuum.

   (2004b), *Prières quotidiennes/ Everyday Prayers*, trans. Luce Irigaray with Timothy Mathews, Paris: Maisonneuve et Larose, and Nottingham: University of Nottingham.

Jacobus, Lee A. and Regina Barreca (eds) (1990), *Hélène Cixous: Critical Impressions*, Amsterdam: Gordon and Breach.

Jones, Ann Rosalind (1986), 'Writing the Body: Towards an Understanding of *l'écriture féminine*', in Showalter (1986).

Joy, Morny, Kathleen O'Grady and Judith L. Poxon (eds) (2002), *French Feminists on Religion*, London and New York: Routledge.

Kamuf, Peggy (1995), 'To Give Place: Semi-Approaches to Hélène Cixous', in Huffer (1995).

Knight, Diana and Judith Still (eds) (1995), *Women and Representation*, Nottingham: WIF Publications.

Kristeva, Julia (1974/1984), *Revolution in Poetic Language*, trans. Margaret Waller, New York: Columbia University Press.

(1974/1986), *About Chinese Women*, trans. Anita Barrows, London: Marion Boyars.

(1977), *Polylogue*, Paris: Seuil.

(1977/1980), *Desire in Language: A Semiotic Approach to Literature and Art*, ed. Léon S. Roudiez, trans. Thomas Gora, Alice Jardine and Léon Roudiez, Oxford: Blackwell.

(1979), *Semiotike: Recherches pour une sémanalyse*, Paris: Seuil.

(1980/1982), *Powers of Horror: An Essay on Abjection*, trans. Léon S. Roudiez, New York: Columbia University Press.

(1981), 'Women's Time', trans. Alice Jardine and Harry Blake, in *Signs* 7:11 (Autumn).

(1983/1987), *Tales of Love*, trans. Léon S. Roudiez, New York: Columbia University Press.

(1987/1989), *Black Sun: Depression and Melancholia*, trans. Léon S. Roudiez, London: Harvester Wheatsheaf.

(2001a, 2001b, 2004), *Female Genius: Life, Madness, Words – Hannah Arendt, Melanie Klein, Colette*, 3 vols, the first two trans. Ross Guberman, third trans. Jane Marie Todd, New York: Columbia University Press (1999–2004).

Lechte, John and Mary Zournazi (eds) (2003), *The Kristeva Critical Reader*, Edinburgh: Edinburgh University Press.

Marks, Elaine and Isabelle de Courtivron (eds) (1981), *New French Feminisms: An Anthology*, Brighton: Harvester.

Miller, Nancy K. (ed.) (1986), *The Poetics of Gender*, New York: Columbia University Press.

Moi, Toril (1985), *Sexual/Textual Politics: Feminist Literary Theory*, London: Methuen.

(ed.) (1987), *French Feminist Thought: A Reader*, Oxford: Blackwell.

Oliveira, Solange Ribeiro de and Judith Still (eds) (1999), *Brazilian Feminisms*, Nottingham: University of Nottingham Monographs in the Humanities.

Oliver, Kelly and Lisa Walsh (eds) (2004), *Contemporary French Feminism*, Oxford: Oxford University Press.

Sellers, Susan (1988), *Writing Differences: Readings from the Seminar of Hélène Cixous*, Milton Keynes: Open University Press.

Shiach, Morag (1991), *Hélène Cixous: A Politics of Writing*, London: Routledge.

Showalter, Elaine (ed.) (1986), *The New Feminist Criticism*, London: Virago.

Smith, Anne-Marie (1997), 'Powers of Transgression/Julia Kristeva', in *Paragraph* 20:3.

(1998), *Julia Kristeva: Speaking the Unspeakable*, London: Pluto Press.

Stanton, Domna C. (1986), 'Difference on Trial: A Critique of the Maternal Metaphor in Cixous, Irigaray, and Kristeva', in Miller (1986).

Still, Judith (1991), 'Can Woman Ever Be Defined? A Question from French Feminism', in Cady (1991).

(1997), *Feminine Economies: Thinking against the Market in the Enlightenment and the Late Twentieth Century*, Manchester: Manchester University Press.

(2007), 'Continuing Debates about "French" Feminist Theory', forthcoming in *French Studies*.

Stockton, Kathryn Bond (1994), *God between Their Lips: Desire between Women in Irigaray, Brontë, and Eliot*, Stanford: Stanford University Press.

Whitford, Margaret (1991), *Luce Irigaray: Philosophy in the Feminine*, London: Routledge.

CHAPTER 15

Postcolonial feminist criticism

Chris Weedon

In its formative years – the late 1960s and 1970s – second-wave feminist criticism in the West had two main aims. The first was to analyse literature as vehicle for reproducing and contesting patriarchal images of women in fictional texts. The second was to identify and analyse the specificity of women's writing. It set out to recover the lost history of women's writing and to identify both a difference of view in women's writing and a feminine aesthetic. By the 1980s, this process was increasingly being questioned by women critics who found both its underlying assumptions and the range of texts and traditions that it privileged narrow and exclusionary. The tendency to focus on the work of white, middle-class, Western, heterosexual women, often under a general heading of 'women's writing', had led to the silencing or marginalisation of issues of class, heterosexism, racism and the colonial legacy as they affected women's cultural production. Moreover, these absences in the important work of recovery that was being undertaken by feminist scholars and publishing houses were beginning to produce new, yet exclusionary, canons.

Even as these debates were being conducted within feminist literary and cultural studies, the increasing influence of poststructuralist, psychoanalytic and postcolonial theories was also making its mark. Such theories questioned the transparency of language, the fixity of meaning, claims to universalism and singular truth. They further problematised the Eurocentric gaze, the sovereignty of intentional subjectivity, authorship and untheorised appeals to global sisterhood and to women's experience. This chapter focuses on how black and 'Third World' feminist critiques both challenged and helped transform early feminist criticism, developing distinctly postcolonial perspectives. Some of the issues raised by black and Third World critics found important echoes in feminist appropriations and developments of poststructuralist theories of subjectivity, language and meaning which were taken up and made to work in the context of postcolonial feminism. The chapter offers an introduction to important issues in postcolonial feminist theory and criticism, including questions of Eurocentrism, voice, colonial modes of representation, racialised difference and the need to make whiteness visible.

THE 'THIRD WORLD' CHALLENGE

Early second-wave Western feminist criticism had a tendency, most clearly articulated in woman-centred work, to downplay differences of class, race, sexuality and location between women. This strategy was aimed at promoting political and personal solidarity and at identifying the specificity of women's writing and a female aesthetic. It could be found to different degrees in liberal, Marxist and radical forms of feminism. Much of the advance in the position of women in the West had rested on liberal humanist discourses of sameness and human rights. Marxist feminists privileged the importance of the analysis of the capitalist mode of production and particularly social class, while radical feminists tended to interpret historically and socially specific practices as effects of global structures of patriarchy. Women as a group were seen to share fundamental oppressions on which feminists everywhere might ground ideas of universal sisterhood and feminist political action. While early radical feminism paid scant attention to forms of power other than patriarchy, since the 1980s radical feminists have paid increasing attention to socially induced differences between women while continuing to stress global structures of patriarchy and sisterhood as a basis for resistance (see Bell and Klein, 1996). Although the emphasising of shared oppression remains an important political strategy within feminism, the history of contemporary feminism has made clear how crucial it is to pay attention to difference and location in understanding and contesting patriarchy. This is a key theme in postcolonial feminist writings that both challenge the Eurocentric gaze and urge the value of Third World feminist perspectives to a global feminism.

In 1984 black American feminist Barbara Smith spoke warmly of being part of a 'Third World' feminist movement: 'And not only am I talking about my sisters here in the United States – American Indian, Latina, Asian American, Arab American – I am also talking about women all over the globe . . . Third World feminism has enriched not just the women it applies to, but also political practice in general' (Smith, 1984/1995: 27). Writing in the United States, Smith used the term 'Third World' in this essay to signify both women in developing countries and minority women in the West. This strategy, often found in feminist writing from the United States, suggests important and empowering possibilities of alliance. Yet, like much Western feminist writing that seeks to embrace the Third World, it also runs the risk of masking the very real differences between First and Third World geographical locations. Like the different structural locations of white and minority ethnic women in Western countries, these geographical differences also have pronounced material effects on whose voices are heard in the international arena. The struggle of Third World women – both in the West and in the developing world – to gain access to the institutions of publishing and peer review to which white Western women have privileged access has been hard fought, as have their attempts to be taken seriously in mainstream Western feminist arenas.[1]

Over the last few decades, postcolonial feminism has become an increasingly important dimension of a wide range of disciplines, such as literary studies, cultural studies, history, development studies, anthropology and social science disciplines concerned with questions of globalisation. In the new millennium most Western feminists now accept a principle that has long been self-evident to Third World women, namely that racism and colonialism cannot merely be seen as the province and concern of non-white or non-Western women. Whiteness itself requires critical attention, and work in feminist history and criticism must of necessity address colonial legacies.

POSTCOLONIAL LITERARY STUDIES AND THE NEED FOR A GENDERED PERSPECTIVE

Fundamental to all forms of postcolonial studies is the view that the history of the West since the early modern period has in large part been a history of the exploitation by European powers of their non-white, non-Western others. Feminist postcolonial critics insist on the gendered nature of this history and look in particular at the relationship between colonialism and patriarchy. The economic and political legacies of colonialism have radically shaped the makeup of societies in both former colonised and colonising nations. Colonialism has not only affected wealth, levels of development and the composition of former colonies and Western societies, but also national cultures, including both literary traditions and popular culture, together with the taken-for-granted meanings of racialised otherness and ethnic difference. Postcolonial studies is a diverse and contested field, covering a range of disciplines and interdisciplinary work. In Anglophone literary studies, postcolonial work developed out of the long established field of Commonwealth Literature, widening its perspectives and bringing in a range of new theoretical perspectives. Much of this work has been done in Commonwealth countries that were former colonies or settler colonies. It has involved both identifying the specificity of the colonial experience, and analysing the relation of former colony to former colonial power (see Ashcroft et al., 1989).

The term 'postcolonial', both in feminist and non-feminist usage, signifies differently according to the context in which it is used. Sometimes it is understood in temporal terms as that which comes after the historically located phenomenon of colonialism. Often it is used as a mode of critique that insists upon questioning both the mechanisms of colonial domination and their ongoing effects in the present. Certain classic texts have come to be seen as foundational for postcolonial studies, for example, the work of Franz Fanon, in particular *The Wretched of the Earth* (1967, original French text 1961), Aimé Césaire's *Discourse on Colonialism* (1972, original French text 1955) and Albert Memmi's *The Coloniser and the Colonised* (1965, original French text 1957). Beyond these key texts, the widespread influence of poststructuralist theory, often linked to feminist postcolonial critics in the field such as Gayatri Spivak (1988, 1990 and 1999) and Chandra Mohanty (1991 and 2003), has led to a focus on the insight that literature can provide into multiple gendered histories, colonial subjectivities and modes of accommodation and resistance. Critics influenced more by Marxism tend to emphasise what they see as larger questions, such as the structures of global capitalism. Ideally, critics argue, postcolonial approaches should facilitate work at both levels. As Henry Schwarz and Sangeeta Ray argue in the *Companion to Postcolonial Studies*, we need to recognise 'that the world is an integrated ensemble of historical and regional processes, and that particular times and places can rarely be separated out from larger patterns if we are to make interpretations capable of producing change' (Schwarz and Ray, 2000: 5).

Equally important in the development of postcolonial literary studies is the foundational work of Edward Said. His seminal text *Orientalism* (1978) drew on the Foucauldian proposition that discourses are relations of knowledge and power.[2] In the case of *Orientalism*, the knowledge of the East produced by the discursive field was, Said argues, imbued with colonial power relations and played an important part in the colonial project. Moreover as knowledge, Said argues, Orientalist writing tells us more about Western constructions of Eastern 'Otherness' than about the societies and cultures that are the objects of study. Some of the themes prominent in *Orientalism* have been taken up and developed from a gendered perspective; for example, Rana Kabani in *Europe's Myths of Orient* analyses the eroticisation of the East (1986: 6). Foucault has been an important influence on the development of feminist postcolonial literary studies precisely because of his stress on relations of power, knowledge and subjectivity, on the material and embodied nature of discourses and on the diffuse and multi-centred workings of power (see Mohanty, 1991 and 2003; Narayan, 1997).

The other major poststructuralist influences in postcolonial studies have been the deconstructive theory of Jacques Derrida and aspects of Lacanian psychoanalysis. Derrida's critiques of the structuring power of binary oppositions in Western culture, of intentional self-present subjectivity and the implication of the self-same in the construction of the other have been of central importance.[3] They have influenced feminist postcolonial critiques of Eurocentrism, of untheorised appeals to global sisterhood and of unproblematised constructions of subaltern women. Derridean deconstruction, as a mode of reading, has also been widely adopted, following the groundbreaking work of critics such as Gayatri Spivak (1987, 1993 and 1999), Homi Bhabha (1990, 1994) and Robert Young (1990 and 1995). Psychoanalytic perspectives have become influential via the work of Franz Fanon and its appropriation by Homi Bhabha and other critics, including feminist critics such as Anne McClintock (1995) and Kalpana Seshadri-Crooks (1994).

Feminist literary studies have played a central role in the development of postcolonial studies. Literary criticism has served as a site for analysing images of colonial societies, for understanding the discursive production of colonial forms of subjectivity and for challenging these. It is also a site for analysing the ways in which colonialism changed both colonisers and colonised. As Ania Loomba (1998) has argued, 'Literature written on both sides of the colonial divide often absorbs, appropriates and inscribes aspects of the "other" culture, creating new genres, ideas and identities in the process. Finally literature is also an important means of appropriating, inverting or challenging dominant means of representation and colonial ideologies' (Loomba, 1998: 70–1).

A defining characteristic of feminist postcolonial literary studies is its commitment to the analysis of history and social specificity and the goal of linking analyses of literary texts to broader social relations. Key areas of work in postcolonial literary studies have included the ways in which power works through language and literary culture to shape meanings, values, subjectivities and identities. The best of this work has attempted to keep power relations of gender, class and race in the frame, seeing them as always integrally related. Some of the most innovative feminist postcolonial literary and cultural criticism has moved in the direction of what might be termed cultural history. This involves reading fictional texts alongside other cultural texts, forms and practices in relation to wider socio-economic developments. A good example of this is Anne McClintock's *Imperial Leather* (1995), which looks at the gendering of imperialism and the role of the feminine in nineteenth-century colonial discourses. McClintock convincingly argues that gender, race and class do not exist in isolation from one another and seeks to analyse the interrelations between Western colonial projects, racist discourse, the cult of domesticity, the reproduction of class- and gender-specific forms of patriarchy and the capitalist market. McClintock draws on feminist, psychoanalytic and social theories to read a rich variety of cultural forms, including novels, advertising, diaries, poetry and oral history.

An important site for developments in feminist postcolonial textual analysis has been travel writing. Sara Mills (1991) focused specifically on gender and the exclusion of women's travel writing from much work on colonialism, while Mary Louise Pratt (1992) examined travel writing as a site for the construction of the domestic subjects of European imperialism. Pratt looks at travel writing as a significant 'contact zone' between coloniser, colonised and domestic readerships in the colonial power, who have little or no direct relationship to colonised others. There is now an extensive literature on travel writing supported by many collections of primary texts.[4]

The relationship between coloniser and colonised is a focal point of both feminist and non-feminist postcolonial studies. It is here that elements of psychoanalytic theory have been particularly important, drawing on the foundational work of Fanon, who theorised the ways in which the binaries underpinning racism and colonialism – understood as relationships – affect subjectivities. More recently Homi Bhabha's work (1984, 1985, 1990) has reinvigorated this area. Drawing on a specific reading of Fanon, and written in part to counteract what he sees as the overly functionalist implications of Said's *Orientalism*, Bhabha's work has privileged the gaps and contradictions produced by the colonial project. Bhabha suggests that Said's use of Foucauldian discourse theory tends to produce an understanding of colonialism as a set of institutions in which Orientalist scholarship and other forms of Orientalist representation serve the reproduction of colonial power relations. Tensions and contradictions become subsumed within a unidirectional will to power. This leads to an overly pessimistic view of the possibilities for negotiation and resistance within colonial contexts. Bhabha brings both psychoanalytic and poststructuralist theories into play, for example, using the concept of mimicry as a way of analysing how in the production of colonised subjects, full control is eluded and communication never fully achieved. In colonial contexts there is always slippage between what is said and what is heard. Bhabha argues that colonial practices produce moments of ambivalence, which open up spaces for the colonised to subvert the master discourse. These ideas have been influential in feminist work, where they complement ideas of gender as masquerade that draw on the important psychoanalytic essay by Joan Riviere (1986, original 1929) and more recent work by Judith Butler (1990 and 1993). Here as in other areas of postcolonial feminism, gender complicates the analysis. Bhabha, for example, uses the concept of 'hybridity' to signify the new forms of subjectivity and culture that are produced by the mixing of colonisers with colonised. From a feminist perspective, what is particularly interesting, however, is the degree to which patriarchal power structures cut across the coloniser/colonised divide and do not allow women the potentially subversive positions and modes of operation open to men.

The position of women in colonial and postcolonial locations is an important focus of feminist postcolonial writing. In their edited collection of essays on Indian colonial history, *Recasting Women* (1990), Kumkum Sangari and Sudesh Vaid argue for the need to understand the 'historical processes which reconstitute patriarchy in colonial India'. In their view, while 'overarching theoretical formulations are helpful and necessary to undertake any work, they need constant testing and overhauling by historically and materially specific studies of patriarchal practice, social regulation and cultural production' (Sangari and Vaid, 1989: 1). The turn to cultural history has been an important influence on feminist postcolonial literary studies and the points that Sangari and Vaid make about history apply equally to feminist scholarship that takes a more narrowly literary focus. Susi Tharu and K. Lalita, for example, argue in their introduction to *Women Writing in India* that 'women's texts from the nineteenth and early twentieth centuries . . . are best read as documents of the writers' engagements with the reworking of their worlds that accompanied British rule in India' (Tharu and Lalita, 1993: 1. 43). In this approach, literary texts cannot be read independently of their contexts and Tharu and Lalita argue that, by the mid-twentieth century, women's writing was participating in the 'profound re-articulation of the political world and of imaginative life that took place in the forties and fifties with the birth of the Indian nation and continues in many ways to underwrite culture and politics into the nineties' (1993: 1. 43). They point out how feminist criticism in India has been concerned with the contexts in which women wrote and read, and the ways in which these contexts have been 'structured and restructured by changing ideologies of class, gender, empire' (1993: 1. 15).

The question of whether dominant cultural forms and practices – be they language, literature, other forms of culture or theory – can be used to challenge hegemony is posed by most feminists. Critics are cautious of trying to use what African American lesbian feminist writer and critic Audre Lorde has termed the 'master's tools' to 'dismantle the master's house' (Lorde, 1984). There is also a widespread problematising of some of the ways in which general theoretical concepts – such as hybridity, *the* postcolonial condition, *the* postcolonial subject or woman – have been employed within postcolonial studies (see Loomba, 1998; Alexander and Mohanty, 1997; Tharu and Lalita, 1993). In particular, some feminist literary critics have questioned the lack of historical specificity residing in these general terms. The message here is one shared by feminist criticism more widely, that is, the need to consider both extra-textual relations and the actual material structure of literary institutions. Colonial relations cannot be interpreted via literary works alone, and the specificity of the text needs both theorising and locating.

FEMINIST PERSPECTIVES ON POSTCOLONIAL CRITICISM

Despite the iconic status of a few key essays that have been repeatedly republished in postcolonial anthologies, most postcolonial feminist critics are still necessarily engaged in the ongoing process of contesting a Eurocentric gaze that privileges Western notions of liberation and progress and portrays Third World women primarily as victims of ignorance and restrictive cultures and religions. This was a central focus of Chandra Mohanty's influential essay 'Under Western Eyes' (1991, revised edition 2001), which argues that much Western feminist writing about Third World women 'discursively colonize[s] the material and historical heterogeneities of the lives of women in the Third World, thereby producing/re-presenting a composite, singular "third world woman" – an image which appears arbitrarily constructed, but nevertheless carries with it the authorizing signature of Western humanist discourse' (Mohanty, 1991: 53). Mohanty points out how Third World women tend to be depicted as victims of male control and traditional cultural practices. In these characterisations little attention is paid to history and difference. Rather Western feminism comes to function as the norm against which the Third World is judged. When, in contrast, Third World women's issues are analysed in detail within the precise social relations in which they occur, then more complex pictures emerge. Mohanty argues that Third World women, like Western women, are produced as subjects in historically and culturally specific ways by the societies in which they live and where they have both voice and agency. Writing in the introduction to the edited volume *Feminist Genealogies, Colonial Legacies, Democratic Futures*, M. Jacqui Alexander and Chandra Mohanty stress the importance of a sense of agency to political struggle for change:

Women do not imagine themselves as *victims* or *dependents* of governing structures but as agents of their own lives. Agency is understood here as the conscious and on-going reproduction of the terms of one's existence while taking responsibility for this process. And agency is anchored in the practice of thinking of oneself as part of feminist collectivities and organizations. This is not the liberal, pluralist individualist self under capitalism. For precisely this reason, decolonization is central to the definition and vision of feminist democracy. (Alexander and Mohanty, 1997: xxviii)

Third World feminists have responded to this call by contesting Western feminist interpretations of patriarchal practices and women's role in relation to them. In Uma Narayan's detailed critique of Mary Daly's classic radical feminist text *Gyn/Ecology* (1979), for example, Narayan challenges what she sees as colonial modes of representation in Daly's treatment of *sati* (the practice of a widow being burnt alive on her deceased husband's funeral pyre). Daly depicts women as the victims of global patriarchy and Narayan argues that while Daly's work addresses Third World women's issues, 'it does so in a manner that misrepresents what is at stake', reproducing 'some common and problematic Western understandings of Third-World contexts and communities' (Narayan, 1997: 45). Comparing Daly's accounts of *sati* and her account of European witch burning in the same book, Narayan points to the absence of historical information provided on *sati*. Daly, Narayan argues, pays no attention to questions of class, caste, religion or geographical location, producing a picture that is too simple and monolithic.

Another key question in postcolonial feminist criticism is who speaks for whom and whose voices are heard in discussions of Third World texts and women's issues. The question of voice was raised by Gayatri Spivak in her influential essay 'Can the Subaltern Speak?' (1988), in which she analyses 'the relations between the discourses of the West and the possibility of speaking of (or for) the subaltern woman' (Spivak, 1988: 271):

Reporting on, or better still, participating in, antisexist work among women of color or women in class oppression in the First World or the Third World is undeniably on the agenda. We should also welcome all the information retrieval in these silenced areas that is taking place in anthropology, political science, history and sociology. Yet the assumption and construction of a consciousness or subject sustains such work and will, in the long run, cohere with the work of imperialist-subject constitution, mingling epistemic violence with the advancement of learning and civilization. And the subaltern woman will be as mute as ever. (Spivak, 1988: 295)

Spivak is sceptical about attempts to construct resistant Third World subjects in scholarly texts. Drawing on Derrida's critique of the knowing subject, she analyses the issues in question in her discussions of the work of Mahasweta Devi (1988), and in her essays on the Rani of Sirmur (1985 and 1999).[5] Here she is profoundly pessimistic about the possibility of giving voice to the subaltern woman, yet she argues that Western women can do better than they have done to date. It is crucial, she suggests, not to make the commonplace mistake of assuming transparent objectivity on the part of the researcher. Feminists need to engage with their subjects: 'In learning to speak to (rather than listen to or speak for) the historically muted subject of the subaltern woman, the postcolonial intellectual systematically unlearns female privilege. This systematic unlearning involves learning to critique postcolonial discourse with the best tools it can provide and not simply substituting the lost figure of the colonized' (Spivak, 1988: 295).

Spivak's work has played a significant role both in defining the field of postcolonial studies and in shaping debates in postcolonial feminism. Her essay 'Three Women's Texts and a Critique of Imperialism' (1985) was an early argument for the importance of historical specificity in the reading of literary texts. Here Spivak argues that there are dangers in reading nineteenth-century texts from a twentieth-century feminist perspective without due attention to the imperialist meanings and values in circulation at the time of the text's production. An understanding of these meanings and the discursive power relation within which they are located points to the implication of women writers and literary texts in the colonial project. The Anglo-American feminist tendency to celebrate texts such as *Jane Eyre* as protofeminist masks the effacement of the colonised woman, in this case Bertha Mason, and the related impossibility of representing the complex subjectivities of colonial subjects. Another influential essay, 'French Feminism in an International Frame' (original 1981, reprinted 1987), analyses the limitations of 'French' feminism, with its disregard of class and race, as an example of Western feminism's objectification of and 'colonial benevolence' towards the Third World woman (Spivak, 1987: 138). Nonetheless, she argues that French feminism's privileging of feminine sexual pleasure, while problematic, can in a deconstructive reading take feminist critics beyond identity and the 'oppressive power of humanism' (1987: 148).

The themes of Spivak's early essays, which include the limitations of Western feminisms, the subaltern woman, agency and colonial discourse are developed in her later works including her broad-ranging text, *A Critique of Postcolonial Reason: Toward a History of the Vanishing Present* (1999). Spivak's work brings into productive dialogue colonial and postcolonial issues and a range of Western theories, principally Marxism, deconstruction, feminism and, via Said, Foucauldian discourse analysis. Her work resists all attempts at establishing totalising theory and, although rooted in literary and textual analysis, is consistently interdisciplinary in scope.

The analysis of difference as inequality is central to postcolonial feminist criticism. In the global context, economic, political, social and cultural factors divide the world into radically different economic zones characterised by extremes of wealth and poverty. Yet these relations of inequality are often also reproduced within developed societies where non-white women most often find themselves in the worst socio-economic positions. Factors that produce difference as oppression include class, ethnocentric and racist practices, and heterosexism. For example the current climate of Islamophobia in the West necessarily has implications for how feminists write about Islam, including literary texts by and about women. Moreover, the position in which women are located within any society often determines what they see as political problems. A key question for postcolonial feminist criticism is how to go beyond the limitations that come from one's location in a particular place at a particular historical moment. If Western feminist criticism is to go beyond the Eurocentric appropriation of the texts of other women, it will have to learn to listen and understand their histories and the social and cultural conditions within which they are placed. Postcolonial feminist criticism requires what African American feminist bell hooks calls 'strategies of communication and inclusion that allow for the successful enactment of this feminist vision', that is a vision that takes diversity seriously (hooks, 1989: 24). For Western feminists it requires, above all, reading non-Western texts, learning contexts and listening to what Third World women themselves have to say.

In both First and Third World contexts, indigenous feminist movements face their own political problems. Trinh T. Minh-Ha, feminist critic and filmmaker, for example, has written of the tendency of Western feminism to disregard differences within indigenous cultures, as well as their differences from the dominant cultures within which they are located

(1989 and 1991). The way in which Western feminism tends to see itself as feminism *per se*, and not to give due regard to indigenous movements and their different forms of feminist intervention, has helped create discursive spaces in which those hostile to feminist movements in Third World contexts have characterised all feminism as by definition Western and therefore as, for example, unpatriotic, un-Islamic, un-Indian and so on. Writing of Indian feminism, Uma Narayan shows how antifeminist forces in India have used the notion of Westernisation selectively to attack those aspects of modern Indian life and politics with which they disagree. Far from being an imitation of Western feminism, Narayan argues, Third World feminism is very much a response to local issues in Third World countries. She describes how feminist groups in India have taken up a wide range of issues including 'dowry-murder and dowry-related harassment of women; police rape of women in custody; issues relating to women's poverty, health and reproduction; and issues of ecology and communalism that affect women's lives'. As elsewhere in the Third World, Indian feminist criticism and activism are 'part of the national political land-scape' and do not merely mimic Western agendas (Narayan, 1997: 13). In Narayan's view, Third World feminists need to challenge 'the larger pictures of Nation, National History, and Cultural Traditions ... that *conceal their own historicity and their own status as representations* – suggest-ing that the nation and its culture are "natural givens" rather than the *historical inventions and constructions* that they are' (20–1). The gender-aware study of national literatures is crucial in this context. This important point is equally applicable to Western nations and, if taken seriously, might make a real contribution to understanding and contesting Western racism and ethnocentrism.

LOOKING FORWARD

All forms of feminist criticism are by definition political, since they are predicated on the recognition of inequalities and the need to transform the structures that produce them. The agenda that has emerged for a non-Eurocentric postcolonial feminist literary and cultural criticism can be said to privilege certain key assumptions. These include a constant recognition of the material relations of inequality that have resulted from colonialism in all its patriarchal, racist and class-specific practices. They include a continuous process of making visible and contesting the racist and ethno-centric meanings that have often become part of the commonsense knowl-edge of Western societies. They involve a commitment to location and historical, social and cultural specificity. They require the bringing together of gender, race and class.

Yet even while recognising the materiality of inequalities, a non-Eurocentric or non-Western feminist criticism needs to learn to think difference in new, non-oppressive ways. Some recent writing by black and Third World women in the West has argued that the diasporic experience of women of colour can create the conditions for breaking down oppressive hierarchical binary categories and liberating difference. This deconstruction of traditional binary oppositions is a move that also informs much postmodern culture. If respect for difference is one of the more positive aspirations of postmodernity, the challenging of boundaries is integral to this project. This is a perspective developed by lesbian Chicana writer and theorist Gloria Anzaldúa in her work and it has profound implications for feminist literary criticism. In her bi-lingual text *Borderlands/La Frontera: The New Mestiza*, Anzaldúa argues that theorists of colour draw on their experience of the margins to develop theories that are both partially outside and inside the Western frame of reference: 'We are articulating new positions in these "in-between," Borderland worlds of ethnic communities and academies, feminist and job worlds' (Anzaldúa, 1987: xxvi). This involves bringing issues of race, class and sexual difference to bear on 'the narrative and poetic elements of a text, elements in which theory is embedded' (1987: xxvi). This work draws on marginal and excluded discourses such as non-Western aesthetics and non-rational modes of interpretation. It involves critiquing the language, framing and assumptions of what counts in hegemonic narratives and recovering indigenous languages, enabling the development of newly inclusive categories (1987: xxvi).

The idea of a cultural hybridity that can challenge existing binary oppositions and hierarchies has also been taken up by black British feminist Heidi Safia Mirza who writes that 'Cultural hybridity, the fusion of cultures and coming together of difference, the "border crossing" that marks diasporic survival, signifies change, hope of newness, and space for creativity' (Mirza, 1997: 16). The social position and lived experience of black and minority ethnic women in predominantly white, exclusive societies like Britain causes a process of disidentification with 'racist British colonizing culture', facilitating instead 'a multi-faceted discontinuous black identity that marks their difference' (1997: 16). These ideas of borderlands, liminal third spaces and hybridity have become important themes in both recent women's writing and feminist criticism.

FEMINISM, EUROCENTRISM AND THE QUESTION OF RACE

For a long time mainstream white Western feminism paid scant attention to the question of race. Racism was seen as secondary to patriarchy and as the problem of non-white women. Many white women took a liberal, colour-blind position, which claimed not to see difference or act upon it. It took a long, hard struggle by black and Third World women to have racism included on the feminist critical agenda. One of the most poignant and powerful critiques of white complacency came from Audre Lorde who wrote that: 'By and large within the women's movement today, white women focus upon their oppression as women and ignore differences of race, sexual preference, class and age. There is a pretence to a homogeneity of experience covered by the word *sisterhood* that does not in fact exist' (Lorde, 1984: 116). Black and Third World critics have argued powerfully that the strong tendency of white women to disregard racism is an effect of white privilege. As Moraga and Anzaldúa put it, 'Racism affects all of our lives, but it is only white women who can "afford" to remain oblivious to these effects. The rest of us have had it breathing or bleeding down our necks' (Moraga and Anzaldúa, 1981: 62).

In recent years the question of whiteness has come to the fore in feminist debates on race and remains a key issue in postcolonial feminist criticism (see Mohanram, 1999). This is largely owing to the impact of black and Third World feminist writing, which argues that the positive recognition of difference and diversity, so necessary to political advance, requires the acknowledgement of privileges. Gloria Anzaldúa explains the dangers of failing to acknowledge this:

Often white-feminists want to minimize racial difference by taking comfort in the fact that we are all women and/or lesbians and suffer similar sexual–gender oppressions. They are usually annoyed with the actuality (though not the concept) of 'differences', want to blur racial difference, want to smooth things out – they seem to want a complete, totalizing identity. Yet in their eager attempt to highlight similarities, they create or accentuate 'other' differences such as class. These unacknowledged or unarticulated differences further widen the gap between white and colored. (Anzaldúa, 1990a: xxi)

QUESTIONS OF INCLUSION AND VOICE

Black and Third World feminist critiques of Western feminism have begun to suggest new ways forward that involve dialogue, respect, located studies and the recognition that binaries are precisely relationships involving both terms. Aboriginal feminist activist and historian Jackie Huggins, for example, argues that: 'Australian historiography has been notably silent about relationships between white women and Black women and, in particular, female employers and their Aboriginal servants' (Huggins, 1998: 28). She describes this as a wall of silence that masks white women's role as oppressors and leads to a 'tendency to equate the situation of white women with that of all women'. She points out that 'when the complex factors of race and gender are considered . . . white women's activities have to be seen as part of the colonisation and oppression of Black women' (28). White Australian women's history of complicity in the oppression of black women has resulted in the alienation of Aboriginal women from the feminist movement. Huggins suggests that this is owing among other things to the failure of the women's movement to address the needs of Aboriginal women, to racism within feminist circles, and feminists' lack of awareness of the structural power relations between black and white women and lack of knowledge of the process of colonisation and its effects on all Aboriginal people (Huggins, 1998: 118).

The reasons that Huggins gives for Aboriginal women's indifference to feminism are symptomatic of problems that beset feminist criticism, not only in Australia, but throughout the Western world. At issue is the failure of white Western women to acknowledge their own privilege and to tackle their implication in and indifference to questions of racism and the legacies of colonialism. This includes a widespread failure to interrogate whiteness, both past and present, and to acknowledge both its structural and everyday effects on non-white women. Failure to address racialised structural privilege leaves black women's position in relation to white women untransformed.

While a starting point for change is for white women to seek out the voices of non-white women – experiential, literary, cultural and theoretical – white women need to be wary of the tendency to appropriate black, Third World and indigenous voices in ways that maintain white power. As Jackie Huggins points out: 'There are also lines of accountability and responsibility to uphold . . . Who has responsibility for what and whom? Who does what? Who takes responsibility for saying things for whom? Who does the saying and the writing? Who gets the feedback and benefit?' (Huggins, 1998: 116). In a similar vein Cherríe Moraga argues that:

Some white people who take up multicultural and cultural plurality issues mean well but often they push to the fringes once more the very cultures and ethnic groups about whom they want to disseminate knowledge. For example, the white writing about Native peoples or cultures displaces the Native writer and often appropriates the culture instead of proliferating information about it. The difference between appropriation and proliferation is that the first steals and harms; the second helps heal breaches of knowledge. (Moraga, 1981: xxi)

Feminist Aboriginal theorist and activist Aileen Moreton-Robinson identifies a further problem in white women's relation to indigenous women – a problem that also transcends the boundaries of the Australian situation. It is the white tendency not to engage with women of colour directly, but through texts and in contexts where women of colour are rarely in a position to contest the ways in which they have been read and appropriated. She argues that 'White feminist academics engage with women who are "Other" predominantly through representations in texts and imaginings. This "Other" offers no resistance and can be made to disappear at will' (Moreton-Robinson, 2000: 183). This form of engagement allows for both the perpetuation of colonial modes of representation and the unquestioned normative status of whiteness. Moreton-Robinson suggests that the failure to interrogate whiteness results in partial readings of indigenous women's writing that omit their challenge to white subjectivity. Thus it is not just a politics of inclusion that is called for, but a thorough questioning of the terms of that inclusion. Moreover, changing the terms of inclusion will require the relinquishing of power by white women. As in any relationships shaped by the legacies of colonialism, white women need to acknowledge the past and take responsibility for the present. This present – itself a product of history – must include their own privileged positions within society and the structural power of whiteness to marginalise and oppress. As Alexander and Mohanty point out, this argument also applies to how white women use the writings of other women: 'Token inclusion of our texts without reconceptualising the white, middle-class knowledge base effectively absorbs and silences us. This says, in effect, that our theories are plausible and carry explanatory weight only in relation to our specific experiences, but that they have no use value in relation to the rest of the world' (Alexander and Mohanty, 1997: xvii).

A knowledge of history is centrally important to acknowledging and confronting Eurocentric or Western perspectives. To be without this knowledge is to be without the tools with which to understand how the present has been formed by the past and how in Uma Narayan's words, 'the project of "Western" culture's self-definition became a project heavily dependent upon its "difference" from its "Others" both internal and external' (Narayan, 1997: 80). The development of a feminist criticism that can take due account of the structural relations that constitute difference must necessarily recognise the often brutal history of colonialism and its role in shaping the modern world. As Narayan argues, 'The contemporary self-definition of many Third-World cultures and communities are also in profound ways political responses to this history' (Narayan, 1997: 80). For this reason understanding this history is necessarily a shared project in which feminists can co-operate: 'Working together to develop a rich feminist account of this history that divides and connects us might well provide Western and Third-World feminists [with] some difficult but interesting common ground, and be a project that is crucial and central to any truly "international" feminist politics' (1997: 80). All postcolonial feminist critics, wherever they are located, can contribute to making the existing social relations that produce hierarchical difference visible. This work is a fundamental prerequisite for social change and requires the positive recognition of difference in the struggle to redefine its meaning and reshape its material effects. In the words of Audre Lorde:

The future of our earth may depend on the ability of all women to identify and develop new definitions of power and new patterns of relating across difference. The old definitions have not served us, nor the earth that supports us. The old patterns, no matter how cleverly rearranged to imitate progress, still condemn us to cosmetically altered repetitions of the same old exchanges, the same old guilt, hatred, recrimination, lamentation and suspicion. (Lorde, 1984: 123)

This is both a challenging and an exciting agenda.

NOTES

1. Much located scholarship that takes account of class, gender, caste and other determinants, produced in former colonised countries, has not gained access to the main publishing outlets in the West and therefore remains relatively unknown outside its immediate context.
2. See Michel Foucault, *The History of Sexuality*, vol. 1 (1981).
3. Deconstruction proposes that we cannot access radical otherness outside language and that our constructions of the other are informed by the traces of our own language and culture.
4. For a bibliography of texts on and about women's travel writing see *Colonial Discourses, Series One, Women, Travel and Empire 1660–1914*, Microfilm, Adam Matthew Publications (1998/9).
5. Mahasweta Devi is one of India's leading writers. Gayatri Spivak has translated two collections of her stories into English, among them the story of the Rani of Sirmur.

BIBLIOGRAPHY

Accad, Evelyne (1996), 'Truth versus Loyalty', in Bell and Klein (1996).

Adam Matthew Publications (1998/9), *Colonial Discourses, Series One, Women, Travel and Empire 1660–1914*, Microfilm, Marlborough.

Alexander, M. Jacqui and Chandra Talpade Mohanty (eds) (1997), *Feminist Genealogies, Colonial Legacies, Democratic Futures*, London: Routledge.

Anzaldúa, Gloria (1987), *Borderlands/La Frontera: The New Mestiza*, San Francisco: Aunt Lute Books.

(ed.) (1990a), 'Haciendo caras, una entrada. An Introduction by Gloria Anzaldúa', in Anzaldúa (1990b).

(ed.) (1990b), *Making Face, Making Soul. Haciendo Caras. Creative and Critical Perspectives by Feminists of Color*, San Francisco: Aunt Lute Books.

Ashcroft Bill, Gareth Griffiths and Helen Tiffin (1989), *The Empire Writes Back: Theory and Practice in Post-Colonial Literatures*, London: Methuen.

Bell, Diane and Renate Klein (eds) (1996), *Radically Speaking: Feminism Reclaimed*, London: Zed Books.

Bhabha, Homi (1984), 'Of Mimicry and Man: The Ambivalence of Colonial Discourse', in *October* 28.

(1985), 'Signs Taken for Wonders: Questions of Ambivalence and Authority under a Tree outside Delhi, May 1817', in *Critical Inquiry* 12.

(1990), *Nation and Narration*, London: Routledge.

(1994), *The Location of Culture*, London: Routledge.

Butler, Judith (1990), *Gender Trouble: Feminism and the Subversion of Identity*, London and New York: Routledge.

(1993), *Bodies That Matter: On the Discursive Limits of 'Sex'*, London and New York: Routledge.

Césaire, Aimé (1972), *Discourse on Colonialism*, New York: Monthly Review Press.

Daly, Mary (1979), *Gyn/Ecology*, London: The Women's Press.

Fanon, Franz (1967), *The Wretched of the Earth*, Harmondsworth: Penguin.

hooks, bell (1989), *Talking Back: Thinking Feminist Thinking Black*, Boston, MA: South End Press.

Huggins, Jackie (1998), *Sister Girl*, Brisbane: University of Queensland Press.

Kabani, Rana (1986), *Europe's Myths of Orient*, London: Pandora Press.

Loomba, Ania (1998), *Colonialism/Postcolonialism*, London: Routledge.

Lorde, Audre (1984), *Sister Outsider*, Freedom, CA: The Crossing Press.

McClintock, Anne (1995), *Imperial Leather: Race, Gender and Sexuality in the Colonial Context*, London: Routledge.

Memmi, Albert (1965), *The Coloniser and the Colonised*, New York: Orion.

Mills, Sara (1991), *Discourses of Difference: An Analysis of Women's Travel Writing and Colonialism*, London: Routledge.

Minh-Ha, Trinh T. (1989), *Woman, Native, Other: Writing Postcoloniality and Feminism*, Bloomington: Indiana University Press.

Minh-Ha, Trinh T. (1991), *When the Moon Waxes Red: Representation, Gender and Cultural Politics*, New York: Routledge.

Mirza, Heidi Safia (1997), *Black British Feminism: A Reader*, London: Routledge.

Mohanram, Radhika (1999), *Black Body: Women, Colonialism and Space*, St Leonards, NSW: Allen and Unwin.

Mohanty, Chandra Talpade (1991), 'Under Western Eyes: Feminist Scholarship and Colonial Discourse', in *Third World Women and the Politics of Feminism*, ed. Chandra Talpade Mohanty, Ann Russo and Lourdes Torres, Bloomington and Indianapolis: Indiana University Press.

(2003), *Feminism without Borders: Decolonizing Theory, Practicing Solidarity*, Durham, NC: Duke University Press.

Moraga, Cherríe (1981), 'Refugees of a World on Fire. Foreword to the Second Edition', in Moraga and Anzaldúa (1981).

Moraga, Cherríe and Gloria Anzaldúa (eds) (1981), *This Bridge Called My Back: Writings by Radical Women of Color*, New York: Kitchen Table/Women of Color Press.

Moreton-Robinson, Aileen (2000), *Talkin' Up to the White Woman*, Brisbane: University of Queensland Press.

Narayan, Uma (1997), *Dislocating Cultures: Identities, Traditions and Third World Feminism*, London: Routledge.

Pratt, Mary Louise (1992), *Imperial Eyes*, London and New York: Routledge.

Riviere, Joan (1986), 'Womanliness as Masquerade', in *Formations of Fantasy*, ed. Victor Burgin, James Donald and Cora Kaplan, London: Methuen.

Said, Edward (1978), *Orientalism*, Harmondsworth: Penguin Books.

(1993), *Culture and Imperialism*, London: Chatto and Windus.

Sangari, Kumkum and Sudesh Vaid (eds) (1990), *Recasting Women: Essays in Indian Colonial History*, New Brunswick: Rutgers University Press.

Schwarz, Henry and Sangeeta Ray (eds) (2000), *Companion to Postcolonial Studies*, Oxford: Blackwell.

Seshadri-Crooks, Kalpana (1994), 'The Primitive as Analyst: Postcolonial Feminism's Access to Psychoanalysis', in *Cultural Critique* 28 (Fall).

Smith, Barbara (1984/1995), 'Black Feminism: A Movement of Our Own', in *Front Line Feminism, 1975–1995: Essays from Sojourner's First 20 Years*, ed. Karen Kahn, San Francisco: Aunt Lute Books.

Spivak, Gayatri Chakravorty (1985), 'Three Women's Texts and a Critique of Imperialism', in *Critical Inquiry* 12.

(1987), 'French Feminism in an International Frame', in *In Other Worlds: Essays in Cultural Politics*, New York: Methuen.

(1988), 'Can the Subaltern Speak?', in *Marxism and the Interpretation of Culture*, ed. Cary Nelson and Lawrence Grossberg, London: Macmillan.

(1990), *The Post-Colonial Critic: Interviews, Strategies, Dialogues*, London: Routledge.

(1999), *A Critique of Postcolonial Reason: Toward a History of the Vanishing Present*, Cambridge, MA: Harvard University Press.

Tharu, Susi and K. Lalita (1993), *Women Writing in India*, 2 vols, London: Pandora Press.

Young, Robert (1990), *White Mythologies: Writing History and the West*, London: Routledge.

(1995), *Colonial Desire: Hybridity in Theory, Culture and Race*, London: Routledge.

CHAPTER 16

Feminist criticism and queer theory

Heather Love

In the late 1990s, several critics took the opportunity to reflect on the relations between feminism, lesbian studies and queer theory. A spate of articles and edited volumes discussed the conflicts and tensions between these fields: some, like the special issue of the feminist journal *differences* (1994) entitled 'Feminism Meets Queer Theory', were sanguine about the possibilities of rapprochement; others such as *Cross-Purposes: Lesbians, Feminists, and the Limits of Alliance* (Heller, 1997) emphasised conflict. It had been a strange couple of decades, marked by the unimaginable gains and tremendous losses of revolution. Stonewall, Women's Liberation, lesbian separatism, the porn wars, HIV/AIDS, the 'invention' of queer theory, lesbian chic, the emergence of transgender politics – all these events had radically transformed the texture of daily life, creating some unlikely coalitions and forever destroying others. While the pace of change had not slowed much, the scene had shifted significantly. Now, the conflicts that had ripped through these communities were being played out largely in academic venues. The fields of women's studies, gay and lesbian studies and queer studies had established themselves in academic departments to a degree that few had dreamed possible during the grittier and more explosive early years of second-wave feminism and Gay Liberation.[1] Although critics were as divided as ever over longstanding questions about the politics of identity, the uses of theory and the relationship between gender and sexuality, one question cut across these differences: 'What happened?'

Many traced the increasing prestige of the study of gender and sexuality to the emergence of queer theory in the late 1980s and early 1990s. While work in lesbian studies had never gained much of a foothold in the academy, increasing attention to Michel Foucault's work on the history of sexuality as well as publications by high-profile critics such as Judith Butler, Eve Kosofsky Sedgwick, Leo Bersani, David Halperin, Michael Warner and D. A. Miller gave the field unprecedented legitimacy. Those who had struggled for the recognition of sexuality as a matter of intellectual and historical significance were pleased by the 'cross-over' success of queer studies; at the same time, many wondered whether such legitimacy could be achieved only at the cost of significant exclusions. Though queer studies emerged out of a range of academic and activist contexts, the theoretical sophistication of early works in the field raised questions of accessibility and access. Could those without training in Continental philosophy make sense of Judith Butler's work on gender performativity? How would David Halperin's radical constructionist history of homosexuality be deployed in the struggle for gay rights? How might one translate Sedgwick's reading of shame in Henry James' *New York Prefaces* into the language of 'real-world' politics?

In addition to struggles over the elite texts and vocabulary that were central to the 'birth of the queer', many people worried over queer's uncompromising stance against the concept of identity. While the value of 'identity politics' and 'strategic essentialism' had been debated during the 1980s, queer emerged at the end of the decade as a movement that understood itself as 'post-identity'. Whereas 'gay' and 'lesbian' might refer to specific and recognisable sexual identities, *queer* evinced a thoroughgoing scepticism about the stability and usefulness of such categories. Queer theorists understood the category of homosexuality as socially constructed and therefore contingent. Rather than affirming gay and lesbian identity, queers focused instead on countering homophobia and at the same time undermining the distinction between homosexual and heterosexual. This approach was not aimed at promoting the assimilation and acceptance of sexual minorities, but rather at examining the process by which the norm and the margin were created. While this brand of anti-identity politics had been tested out in queer activism of the period, many felt that it was out of touch with the real experience and needs of the community. Many people also worried that the blurring of identities advocated by queer activists and scholars made possible the reassertion of age-old hierarchies. Was the newfound prestige of queer theory an effect of academic elitism and male privilege?

While debates about the relationship between queer theory and rights-based gay and lesbian projects were contentious, they did not match the bitter conflicts surrounding the relationship between feminist 'mothers' and queer 'daughters'. The 1998 collection *Coming Out of Feminism?*, edited by Mandy Merck, Naomi Segal and Elizabeth Wright, took this conflict on directly, posing in its title a question on many people's minds: did queer studies 'come out' of feminism in the sense of being indebted to it, or rather in the sense of leaving it behind? Queer theory did depart from feminism, particularly in its focus on sexuality as distinct from gender, but it also borrowed heavily from the methodology of feminist studies. The provocative title implied a series of other questions that would be even more difficult to answer. How else might we understand queer theory as 'coming out' of feminism? Was queer theory 'of woman born'? Did it come out of feminism *that way*? Or did queer theory 'out' the sexuality that was closeted in feminism? And could that sexuality be identified as lesbian? What was the place of sexual pleasure (or 'coming') in the long history of feminism?

Although it is possible to trace a genealogy of queer studies back through gay male activist and intellectual traditions, feminism has also deeply influenced queer scholarship. Lisa Duggan makes this point in the Introduction to the 1996 volume *Sex Wars*:

Some feminist critics of 'queer' theory and politics argue that this term erases gender in the same way that 'gay' without 'lesbian' has done; they invoke a history of 'queer' that aligns it with boy-contexts and boy-meanings. But 'queer' has a girl-history too. During the porn wars, many lesbians who were alienated by lesbian-feminists' homogenizing, white, middle-class, anti-gay-male, antisex discourses, refused the category 'lesbian,' and adopted 'queer' as a mark of separation from such politics, a badge of principled dissidence. Such uses of 'queer' constructed alliances with gay men, and sometimes privileged them over a feminist 'sister-hood.' These alliances have not been constructed on men's terms alone, however. Many women adopt 'queer' as a mark of a particular historical relation to, not a repudiation of, feminism. (Duggan, 1996: 14)

Challenging the idea of a male lineage for queer studies, Duggan draws attention to the importance of conflicts over sexuality in the women's movement in the 1980s. In the 1970s and 1980s, debates over the place of lesbians in feminism and over the politics of pornography, sadomasochism (s/m) and butch/femme made the problem of desire central to the movement.

The emergence of desire as a problem without a solution sparked many of the central methodological insights in queer studies: the separating of sexuality from gender as an analytic category; the radical questioning of the category 'woman'; a critique of the division between public politics and private feelings; a focus on 'sex panics'; the regulation of bodies and practices; and the history of sexually stigmatised communities. Queer theory cannot be understood apart from 'girl-history' and 'girl-meanings', nor can it be separated, finally, from the challenge that desire poses to stable categories of gender, sexual 'orientation' and individual identity.

GENDER PLUS SEX

Before there was such a thing as 'sexuality studies', second-wave feminism made sexuality central. In considering women's experience and its links to more general structural inequalities, feminists addressed topics including family, marriage and childrearing, birth control and abortion, women's health, pornography and other sexualised representations of women, prostitution, domestic and sexual violence, marriage resistance and female friendship and lesbianism. At this point, critics and historians did not make a hard-and-fast distinction between gender and sexuality. Rather, feminist analysis addressed what Gayle Rubin defined as the 'sex-gender system' (1975): the process by which 'raw biological sex' is transformed into a system of inequality. According to such a view it was impossible to separate out biological sex, gendered inequality and sexual behaviour; rather, it was important to see them all as implicated in a larger political economy.

While contemporary feminism continues to treat gender and sexuality as deeply connected, the integrated system that Rubin analysed under the name of the 'sex-gender system' has been challenged over the past couple of decades. The splitting apart of the category woman was largely owing to the efforts of women of colour and working-class women who argued that 'woman' was not a category capacious enough to account for the significant differences between women. In crucial documents such as 'The Combahee River Collective Statement' (1978/1983) and the collections *But Some of Us Are Brave* (Hull et al., 1982), *This Bridge Called My Back* (Moraga and Anzaldúa, 1981) and *Borderlands/La Frontera* (Anzaldúa, 1987), women of colour critiqued the whiteness of second-wave feminism and called for an expanded analysis that would articulate gender with other categories of identity and structures of inequality. In the more general process of the splitting up of the unitary focus on gender, sexuality gradually emerged as a separate analytic category, and, in the late 1980s, as the focus of a separate field.[2]

Lesbianism and desire between women more generally posed both practical and conceptual challenges to the early women's movement. Second-wave feminists could not avoid the question of lesbianism, simply because lesbians made up a big part of the women's community. However, apart from the involvement of actual lesbians, lesbianism as a concept bore a great deal of symbolic weight. A lot of this attention to lesbianism was negative, as women in the mainstream of feminism worried about the image of feminist activism as dominated by 'man-haters'. This tension came to the surface in 1970, when Betty Friedan opposed a NOW (National Organization for Women) initiative for lesbian rights and referred to the 'lavender menace' in the women's movement: as a response, lesbians in 'Lavender Menace' T-shirts protested at the Second Congress to Unite Women in 1970.

The perceived 'threat' of lesbianism to second-wave feminism is not wholly explained either by simple homophobia or by strategic worries about mainstream acceptance. Instead, Friedan's comment indicates an unwanted intimacy: not only were there many lesbians in NOW, but 'love between women' was bound up with the idea of feminist resistance to patriarchy. The same women who staged the 'Lavender Menace' action at the NOW conference formed the group Radicalesbians and published their manifesto 'The Woman-Identified Woman' later that year. The explosive and unpredictable energy of the early movement – sometimes undersold by retrospective accounts – is fully manifest in this early document.[3] They wrote: 'What is a lesbian? A lesbian is the rage of all women condensed to the point of explosion.' This rage is conjured on behalf of women, but it is also directed against those women who would deny others a place in the movement. Although mainstream and straight feminists continued to reject lesbianism, the Radicalesbians defined lesbians as a kind of *avant-garde* for feminism, as a 'fundamental challenge to the basis of the female role' (Radicalesbians, 1970). Women loving women is figured in the manifesto as a way to redefine what it means to be a woman, to throw off men's control and to redirect energy back into the movement. However, while the radical and affirmative vision of 'The Woman-Identified Woman' originally served as a powerful challenge to the category of 'woman', over the course of the decade this understanding of lesbianism ironically served as a way of consolidating and policing the boundaries of this category. Particularly memorable were campaigns to bring lesbian practice into line with feminist theory – not always an easy task for the butches and femmes who had frequented the bars in the years before Women's Liberation and Gay Liberation. This community was made up of working-class women and women of colour who deeply resented the new ideals of gendered behaviour being advocated – and sometimes enforced – by feminist and lesbian-feminist organisations.

Debates over 'role-playing' in lesbian relationships continued throughout the decade, as women struggled with the gap between feminist ideals and the reality of desires and practices. One of the most important articulations of the lesbian-feminist vision was Adrienne Rich's article 'Compulsory Heterosexuality and Lesbian Existence' (1980/2003). Keeping her distance from both pornographic and medical approaches to lesbianism, Rich de-emphasises sexual desire and practice, defining lesbianism instead as a form of female bonding based on a wider spectrum of female experience. She writes, 'I mean the term lesbian continuum to include a range – through each woman's life and throughout history – of woman-identified experience, not simply the fact that a woman has had or consciously desired genital sexual experience with another woman' (Rich, 1980/2003: 27–8). Rich describes lesbianism as an experience defined primarily in relation to gender, not sexuality. Sex itself is less important than relations between women, broadly conceived. In widening the definition of the erotic, Rich turns her attention away from the history of sexually stigmatised populations and the place of lesbianism in such a history.

Rich's essay polarised the lesbian community. For many women, it offered a vision of the possibilities of lesbian existence as life choice that was enriching both politically and personally. Others found Rich's statement profoundly alienating. It seemed far from the experience of actual lesbians, and, as a 2003 retrospective piece by the femme activist and writer Joan Nestle makes clear, was understood as an intervention on behalf of lesbian feminism but against butches and femmes, sex workers and lesbians who practiced s/m (Nestle, 2003: 52). For women like Nestle who had forged their sexual identities in the bars and on the streets in the years before Women's Liberation, Rich's account of lesbianism sounded not only out of touch but condemnatory.

Rich's article sparked responses by women who felt that this feminist vision of lesbianism neglected both the specificity of lesbian experience and the complex realities of sexual practice and desire. Gayle Rubin responded to Rich's piece by articulating the connection between lesbians and other sexual minorities. In her article 'Thinking Sex', she critiqued her own concept of the 'sex-gender system' and argued for the importance of seeing sexuality as distinct from gender:

In contrast to my perspective in 'The Traffic in Women,' I am now arguing that it is essential to separate gender and sexuality analytically to reflect more accurately their separate social existence. This goes against the grain of much contemporary feminist thought, which treats sexuality as a derivation of gender. For instance, lesbian feminist ideology has mostly analyzed the oppression of lesbians in terms of the oppression of women. However, lesbians are also oppressed as queers and perverts, by the operation of sexual, not gender, stratification. Although it pains many lesbians to think about it, the fact is that lesbians have shared many of the sociological features and suffered from many of the same social penalties as have gay men, sadomasochists, transvestites, and prostitutes. (Rubin, 1984/1993: 33)

For Rubin, sex is 'a vector of oppression', one which 'cuts across other modes of social inequality, sorting out individuals and groups according to its own intrinsic dynamics' (22). Rubin's strategic separation of gender and sexuality challenged the lesbian feminist understanding of sexual relations between women as a practice of gender solidarity, and her work offered a way of making sense of the conflict between ideals of sexual desire and practice that had been playing out for years in CR (consciousness-raising) groups, at conferences and in protests. At the same time, Rubin's essay pointed towards a broad coalition of sexual minorities (not the close solidarity of women or gays and lesbians) that would underwrite the emergence of queer politics in the late 1980s.

AM I A WOMAN?

Judith Butler's 1990 book *Gender Trouble: Feminism and the Subversion of Identity* is one of the inaugural texts of queer theory. Combining philosophy, cultural criticism and feminist critique, *Gender Trouble* draws on a long line of feminist challenges to the category of woman. Butler was deeply influenced by Simone de Beauvoir's assertion of the cultural construction of femininity ('One is not born, but rather becomes, a woman' (1949/1989: 267)). Butler also drew on the materialist feminism of the philosopher Monique Wittig, who famously asserted that, because women were defined by their position in the heterosexual matrix, lesbians were not women (1992: 32).

Gender Trouble begins with a direct challenge to the category of woman as the grounding term for feminist criticism and politics. Butler writes:

Recently, [the] prevailing conception of the relation between feminist theory and politics has come under challenge from within feminist discourse. The very subject of woman is no longer understood in stable or abiding terms. There is a great deal of material that not only questions the viability of 'the subject' as the ultimate candidate for representation or, indeed, liberation, but there is very little agreement after all on what it is that constitutes, or ought to constitute, the category of women. (Butler, 1990/1999: 4)

In formulating this challenge, Butler draws on philosophical and psychoanalytic interrogations of the idea of the stable subject as well as specific feminist challenges to the concept of what a woman is or should be. She also draws on Michel Foucault's idea that power operates not only through limiting what subjects can and cannot do, but also by producing particular kinds of subject. Because of power's defining and normalising force, Butler writes that it 'is not enough to inquire how women might become more fully represented in language and politics'. Rather, she argues, '[f]eminist critique ought also to understand how the category of "women", the subject of feminism, is produced and restrained by the very structures of power through which emancipation is sought' (5).

Butler transforms our understanding of the category of woman through her theory of gender performativity. Challenging the idea that gender behaviour follows naturally and inevitably from sexual essence, Butler suggests that gender is a series of repeated and stylised acts that create the illusion of a bodily ground. Her critical attention to gender was sparked by an apparent paradox: that gender is 'so taken for granted at the same time that it [is] violently policed' (xix). According to Butler, subjects are called on to perform strict gender roles and punished when they step out of them; in a strange trick of logic, those same 'command performances' are then taken as evidence that 'normal' gender is natural, biologically determined and inevitable.

Butler's rethinking of the category of woman was not only influenced by the history of feminist criticism and by Foucault's rethinking of subjectivity: it also emerged out of contentious debates within feminist and queer communities. Butler's argument about the performativity of gender depended on examples of butch/femme and drag, practices that had been stigmatised by many lesbian feminists. In the preface to the 1999 edition of *Gender Trouble*, Butler situates this foundational text in queer theory both as an intervention into debates about the relations between lesbianism and feminism and as an attempt to take seriously the practices of sexual and gender subcultures. She writes:

Whereas many feminists in the 1980s assumed that lesbianism meets feminism in lesbian-feminism, *Gender Trouble* sought to refuse the notion that lesbian practice instantiates feminist theory, and set up a more troubled relation between the two terms ... Lesbianism is not the erotic consummation of a set of political beliefs (sexuality and belief are related in a much more complex fashion, and very often at odds with one another). Instead, the text asks, how do non-normative sexual practices call into question the stability of gender as a category of analysis? How do certain sexual practices compel the question: what is a woman, what is a man? If gender is no longer to be understood as consolidated through normative sexuality, then is there a crisis of gender that is specific to queer contexts? (Butler, 1990/1999: xi)

Taking these practices and forms of embodiment and desire seriously, Butler helped to pry open fixed categories and to question the naturalness of gender as well as the presumptive universality of the heterosexual order. In looking at moments of 'gender trouble' as in drag and butch/femme, Butler hoped to show that all gender – even the most 'normal' – was a form of drag. In relation to butch/femme practices, Butler writes, 'The replication of hetero-sexual constructs in non-heterosexual frames brings into relief the utterly constructed status of the so-called heterosexual original. Thus, gay is to straight *not* as copy is to original, but, rather, as copy is to copy' (41).

It would be difficult to overstate the impact of *Gender Trouble* in feminism, literary criticism and queer theory. Still, the book had its critics, many of whom argued that Butler's account of gender performativity was voluntarist and that it did not account for the stubborn material realities of the body. Butler addressed many of these concerns in later writings, but especially in *Bodies That Matter: On the Discursive Limits of 'Sex'* (1993). In this book, Butler reiterated that gender performativity did not imply voluntarism – that just because gender was cultural did not mean that it was utterly flexible or a matter of choice – and she tried to address bodily representations and realities more directly. But still, Butler's writing on drag remained contentious, particularly for a new generation of trans-gender and transsexual critics who took issue with her elevation of drag as an exemplary practice of gender transgression; they argued that the intellectual glamour of queer theory depended on the spectacle of trans-gender marginality. Transgender activists and critics had complained about the positioning of transsexuals, the intersexed and drag queens as exemplary figures in arguments about the flexibility of gender in feminist and lesbian and gay work (for instance, in Marjorie Garber's *Vested Interests*). While Butler was more interested than earlier authors in the lived experience of gender and sexual outlaws, many still had concerns about her attention to transgender embodiment.

Butler's work cleared space for many subsequent accounts of dissident gender, including Kate Bornstein's *Gender Outlaw*, Judith Halberstam's *Female Masculinity* and Anne Fausto-Sterling's *Sexing the Body*. For some transsexual and transgender critics, Butler's revisions of gender perform-ativity still valorised subversion and the 'remaking' of categories usu-ally understood in terms of constraint. Jay Prosser and C. Jacob Hale have criticised the queer ideal of gender flexibility as out of touch with the struggles of many trans people to arrive at stable and habitable positions in the gender system. Resisting the emphasis on drag as an allegory for the unstable production of gender, these critics emphasised the profound challenges facing trans people – citing the murder, for instance, of Venus Xtravaganza, a transwoman featured in Jennie Livingston's documentary *Paris is Burning* (1990) – as well as the inade-quacy of a queer perspective which valorises gender subversion over survival and belonging.[4]

MAKING SEXUALITY CENTRAL

Butler's work on gender drew on Foucault's account of modern disciplinary power and its production of 'normal' subjects. Another important strain of queer theory drew on his account of the imbrication of power and knowledge in modernity. Eve Kosofsky Sedgwick's *Epistemology of the Closet* (1990) began with a discussion of Foucault's account of the 'invention of homosexuality' at the end of the nineteenth century. In *The History of Sexuality* Foucault argued that it was only in the modern period that sexuality became integral to the definition of the person, a development that coincided with the specification of a number of social types defined by their deviant gender and sexual status. Surveying the writings of the sexologists from the end of the nineteenth century, Foucault describes the process by which the homosexual, who had been a 'temporary aberration', became 'a species'. Following Foucault, Sedgwick writes that, 'because modern Western culture has placed what it calls sexuality in a more and more distinctly privileged relation to our most prized constructs of individual identity, truth, and knowledge, it becomes truer and truer that the language of sexuality not only intersects with but transforms the other languages and relations by which we know' (Sedgwick, 1990: 3).

In *Epistemology*, Sedgwick draws a crucial link between knowledge and sexual knowledge, which allows her to make a bold rhetorical claim for the centrality of sexuality in the analysis of culture. She writes that 'an understanding of virtually any aspect of modern Western culture must be, not merely incomplete, but damaged to the degree that it does not incorporate a critical analysis of modern homo/heterosexual definition' (1990: 1). This radical and universalising claim for the importance of sexuality was instrumental in founding the field of queer studies and in finding it a place in the academy (particularly in English Literature departments). While many of the claims in *Epistemology* were new, it also drew on key aspects of feminist methodology. In particular, Sedgwick built on the work of feminists who had made links between gender and apparently unrelated aspects of culture (such as the distinction between the public and the private, or between nature and culture). By seeing the homo-heterosexual divide as central to questions of representation, Sedgwick was able to make a similar claim, arguing that general cultural oppositions like health/illness, innocence/initiation and natural/artificial were deeply bound up with questions of sexual definition. Working through the modernist Anglo-American canon and paying special attention to figures such as Marcel Proust, Herman Melville, Oscar Wilde, Friedrich Nietzsche and Henry James, Sedgwick argued that what D. A. Miller had called the 'open secret' of male same-sex desire was central to the constitution of knowledge in the modern period (Miller, 1989).

Before *Epistemology*, Sedgwick had written *Between Men* (1985), an account of the disavowal of desire in the maintenance of male homosocial relations. The book offered a feminist and anti-homophobic perspective on erotic triangles and male rivalry in literature from the Renaissance onwards. In focusing on the way that both women and gay men suffer as a result of straight male bonding, *Between Men* was less directly concerned with the specificities of gay representation. Yet already after the publication of this book, and especially after *Epistemology of the Closet*, lesbian critics questioned the absence of an extended treatment of female same-sex relations or desire in Sedgwick's work. This concern was summed up in the memorable title of a 1991 article by Blakey Vermeule, 'Is There a Sedgwick School for Girls?'. Critics noted not only the paucity of references to lesbian texts or contexts, but also the fact that the image of female same-sex desire that emerged in Sedgwick's writing seemed to be drawn from a lesbian feminist repertoire that emphasised feminist bonding over down-and-dirty lesbian sex. While Sedgwick made clear that her own investment was in male same-sex relations, readers remained disappointed about a perceived flattening of relations between women in a body of work that offered such a rich and complex account of relations between men.[5]

Despite doubts about the male focus of these founding texts in queer theory, Sedgwick's sustained reflection on her own interest in and attachment to representations of male-male desire has produced some of the most compelling writing to date in queer studies. Sedgwick has not only described the volatility of identity; her writing, with its movements across different forms of desire and identification, has also exemplified that unpredictability. Her often risky accounts of her own shifting identifications have opened the possibility of queer work that operates 'across genders and across sexualities'; at the same time, it has made her image available for identifications by critics working in a range of fields and disciplines.[6] The universalising force of Sedgwick's work as well as her emphasis on cross-identification helped to make *queer* attractive for a host of critics who pushed beyond its original sense of sexual or gender deviance to signify 'the fractal intricacies of language, skin, migration, state'.[7]

The reach and ambition of Sedgwick's arguments in *Between Men* and *Epistemology of the Closet* – her powerful claim that sexuality mattered in the history of Western representation – have proved enabling to queer literary critics. Of course, the fact that sexuality was central to the history of representation, and to literature, was news to no one. Desire – especially queer, perverse or excessive desire – was at the heart of the canon, from Sappho's lyrics to the late novels of Henry James. Roland Barthes had explored the relationship between desire, subjectivity, and textual representation in books like *The Pleasure of the Text*, *S/Z* and *A Lover's Discourse*, while feminist literary critic Barbara Johnson asserted the inextricability of literature and sexuality in *The Critical Difference* (1980: 13). Queer literary critics such as Sedgwick, Leo Bersani, Lee Edelman and D. A. Miller combined such insights about the complex relationship between literature and desire with a new awareness of the structuring effect of the history of sexuality on the history of representation and knowledge.[8]

QUEER DAMAGE

In their 1981 dialogue 'What We're Rollin Around in Bed With', Cherríe Moraga and Amber Hollibaugh discuss the complexities of lesbian sexual experience. They critique the feminist vision of lesbianism as a '"perfect" vision of egalitarian sexuality', one in which women 'could magically leap over our heterosexist conditioning into mutually orgasmic, struggle-free, trouble-free sex' (Moraga and Hollibaugh, 1981/1983: 395). Moraga and Hollibaugh address the distance between their experiences as women of colour from working-class backgrounds who identify (respectively) as butch and femme and the feminist ideal of sex between women. They focus on the significance of pain, trauma and struggles for power in their sexual lives, arguing that sex is not a space separate from larger social difficulties but is infused with them at the deepest level.

At one moment in the essay, Moraga uses the term 'queer' to distinguish her experience from a feminist vision of lesbianism as 'struggle-free' and 'trouble-free':

Most women are not immune from experiencing pain in relation to their sexuality, but certainly lesbians experience a particular pain and oppression. Let us not forget, although feminism would sometimes like us to, that lesbians are oppressed in this world. Possibly, there are some of us who came out through the movement who feel immune to 'queer attack,' but not the majority of us . . . If you have enough money and privilege, you can separate yourself from heterosexist oppression. You can be *sapphic* or something, but you don't have to be queer. (Moraga and Hollibaugh, 1981/1983: 402–3, emphasis in original)

Like Rubin, Moraga sees sexuality as a 'vector of oppression'; she draws a link between lesbians and other sexual minorities vulnerable to 'queer attack'. Queer defines a particular form of homophobic attack; it also names the identity that is formed in relation to such damage. As Moraga uses it, queer means troubled – being queer means acknowledging the problem of desire and the dependence of identity on social injury.

Both the content and the form of 'What We're Rollin Around in Bed With' were crucial to the birth of queer studies. Moraga and Hollibaugh self-consciously take up the feminist tool of consciousness-raising in this piece in order to discuss complex links between their experience and larger structural inequalities. Eschewing both an understanding of lesbianism as pure and the condemnation of particular sexual desires and practices as forms of 'false consciousness', they attempt to talk realistically about their mixed desires. In one example, Hollibaugh discusses her desire for a butch woman, concluding that 'the area you express as *butch* . . . is where in the other world you have suffered the most damage. Part of the reason I love to be with butches is because I feel I repair that damage' (401). For Hollibaugh, butch/femme practice serves as a form of mediation between an intimate sphere and that 'other world' – the larger sphere of social inequality, stigma and violence. In its attempt to move between sex and the social, this dialogue serves as an important bridge between feminist under-standings of the 'personal as political' and queer attention to the damage caused by homophobia.

Acknowledging damage – and incorporating it – was crucial to the turn to queer politics and queer studies in the late 1980s. With the AIDS crisis raging, Reagan in office, and living with the repercussions of the *Bowers* v. *Hardwick* decision supporting the criminalisation of homosexuality, dam-age was all around.[9] Queer Nation was formed in response to this atmos-phere of crisis, as a more radical offshoot of the group ACT UP. In one of their pamphlets from 1990, they discuss their choice of the word queer, emphasising the importance of 'trouble' to the concept:

Queer!
Ah, do we really have to use that word? It's trouble . . . It's forcibly bittersweet and quaint at best – weakening and painful at worst. Couldn't we just use 'gay' instead? It's a much brighter word. And isn't it synonymous with 'happy'? When will you militants grow up and get over the novelty of being different?
Why Queer . . .
Well, yes, 'gay' is great. It has its place. But when a lot of lesbians and gay men wake up in the morning we feel angry and disgusted, not gay. So we've chosen to call ourselves queer. (Anonymous Queers, 1990)

The idea that queer could be reclaimed from its homophobic uses and turned to good use – while still maintaining its link to a history of damage – was crucial to the development of a queer method in the late 1980s and early 1990s. The embrace and 'turning' of queer was based on Foucault's concept of '"reverse" discourse'. Foucault described the way that early homophile movements had taken a 'disqualified' term from a medical lexicon and claimed it as the basis for a new movement for rights.[10] Queer politics, deeply informed by Foucault's critical history of identity, emphasised the importance of stigma in the making of identity and advocated strategic acts of reclamation or resignification.

Butler addressed the importance of damage in the conception of queer identity in her foundational article 'Critically Queer', published in the first issue of the key journal of queer studies, *GLQ: Gay and Lesbian Quarterly* (1993). At the beginning of the article (which was later reproduced in *Bodies That Matter*), Butler asks a series of questions about the dangers and possibilities of taking up a slur as the name for this new movement:

How is it that a term that signaled degradation has been turned – 'refunctioned' in the Brechtian sense – to signify a new and affirmative set of meanings? Is this a simple reversal of valuations such that 'queer' means either a past degradation or a present or future affirmation? Is this a reversal that retains and reiterates the abjected history of the term? . . . Can the term overcome its constitutive history of injury? (Butler, 1993: 223)

Butler describes a transition from degradation to affirmation, and wonders whether queer can mine this history without simply repeating it. There was great excitement about the new forms of political thought and activity emerging from the embrace of this 'forcibly bittersweet' term, but also anxiety about its engagement with past and present forms of hatred.

As well as being concerned with the question of identity and the meaning of slurs, the queer movement was also about feeling bad – the problem of 'waking up in the morning feeling angry and disgusted'. Queer politics broke with the progressive utopian historical vision of some versions of gay liberation and second-wave feminism. At the same time that conditions for the most privileged gays and lesbians were improving, it was hard to hold on to optimistic historical narratives during the darkest days of the AIDS crisis. Queers focused instead on the ongoing problem of homophobia and its material and subjective effects.

The centrality of such perspectives to queer studies is evident in the kinds of subjects its critics take up: gay shame, disidentification, the closet, homosexual panic, masochism, gender dysphoria and so on. An excellent recent example of a book that combines a queer perspective with attention to the specificities of lesbian culture is Ann Cvetkovich's *An Archive of*

Feelings: Trauma, Sexuality, and Lesbian Public Cultures (2003). In this book, Cvetkovich considers the relation between lesbian public cultures and trauma, particularly the trauma of childhood sexual abuse. Looking at a range of materials both popular and elite, she explores the way that queercore bands, lesbian artists and zinesters have negotiated the intimate damage of misogyny and homophobia, arguing that 'Trauma discourse has allowed me to ask about the connection between girls like me feeling bad and world historical events' (Cvetkovich, 2003: 3). Cvetkovich's effort to draw a connection between the everyday and the world historical, between the intimate and the public, recalls early feminist attempts to make the personal political. It also recalls the self-conscious exploration of 'girls feeling bad' that defined some of the best writing of the pro-sex movement – for instance, 'What We're Rollin Around in Bed With'. In such moments, one sees the possibilities for *queer lesbian studies*: tied to the histories of feminism, of lesbian feminism and queer organising; open to a wide range of new materials, both elite and popular; and attentive to the complex experience of women and their bodies marked by both fantastic desires and the real violence of social inequality.

THE PROBLEM OF DESIRE

Desire has been at the heart of many of the conflicts between feminists, lesbians and queers over the past several decades: in anxieties about lesbians being 'too close for comfort' in the early women's movement, in struggles over appropriate gendered behaviour with butches and femmes in lesbian feminist circles, in debates about power and sex in the 1980s and in the emergence of queer studies at the beginning of the 1990s. In these difficult moments, critics and activists divided by powerful differences took on *as a collectivity* a set of impossible questions. Does who you are determine what you want to do? Does what you do make you who you are? Is difference the key to desire? Can you tell the difference between the desire to have and the desire to be? Is a woman who wants another woman still a woman? Is desire possible outside existing structures of power?

In trying to address such questions, many critics have turned to the psychoanalytic theories of Sigmund Freud, Jacques Lacan and their followers, a body of writing still widely recognised as the most rigorous framework for talking about desire.[11] Yet despite its emphasis on desire, gender difference and sexuality, psychoanalysis has had a vexed history within queer studies, for some of the same reasons it has inspired ambivalence in feminist circles. While some queer critics embrace psychoanalysis, for many it is associated with a general politics of normalisation and with the specific pathologisation of homosexuality. In *Saint Foucault*, David Halperin discusses the political consequences of Foucault's critique of psychoanalysis: 'By conceptualizing sexuality as a device whose operation can be analyzed rather than as a thing whose nature can be known, by treating sexuality as the instrument and effect of a series of discursive and political strategies, Foucault translates sex from the realm of individual fantasy to the domain of social power and knowledge' (Halperin, 1995: 121). By taking sexuality out of the realm of the 'merely personal', Foucault makes it political, and so becomes, in Halperin's words, 'the patron saint of queer activism' (121).

That sex is not merely a private matter but is rather central to the transformation of the social world has been a crucial organising idea in second-wave feminism, gay liberation, lesbian feminism, pro-sex feminism and queer politics. The powerful utopianism of these movements is legible in their faith not only that the personal is an aspect of the political but also that it can be a matter for collective discussion. In her book *My Dangerous Desires*, Amber Hollibaugh discusses the link between sexual desires and the desire for social change:

for many of us, [liberation] ... does revolve around the ways we organize our erotic choices. And erotic identities are not just behaviors or individual sexual actions: they represent a much broader fabric that is the weave and crux of our very personhood, a way of mediating and measuring all that we experience, all that we can interpret through the language of our bodies, our histories, our eyes, our hips, our intelligence, our willful, desiring selves. However we've gotten there, erotic identity is not simply a specific activity or 'lifestyle,' a set of heels or ties that dress up the quirk. It is as deep and rich, as dangerous, explosive, and unique as each of us dares to be or become. (Hollibaugh, 2000: 258)

Hollibaugh speaks for a movement that takes sex seriously, that sees it not as a private indulgence but rather as connected to a larger public world. In addition, she emphasises the danger of desire, figuring it as a crisis, an opportunity and a problem. Sexuality as she describes it – as a force at odds with stable identity and with larger social norms – was crucial to the formation of the queer movement. In the twenty-first century, with gay normalisation on the rise, it can be hard to remember that the word queer – now most closely associated with product placement – once seemed to promise revolution. Of course, membership can have its benefits, but it was not what they had in mind, those bad girls who made a point of talking about how bad they felt, and so changed the way we think about women and sex for ever.

NOTES

1. For a sense of the changed material circumstances of queers, feminists, and lesbians, see Moraga and Anzaldúa (1981), *This Bridge Called My Back: Writings by Radical Women of Color* and the later revisiting of the volume, Anzaldúa and Keating (2002), *this bridge we call home: radical visions for transformation*.
2. There are many names for this field of study: sexuality studies, queer studies, LGBTQ (Lesbian Gay Bisexual Transgender Queer) studies, gender studies. As this list demonstrates, the question of the relation between gender and sexuality remains an unsettled issue.
3. In the archives of 1970s feminism one regularly encounters documents whose revolutionary fervour and sheer daring are unparalleled. For example, the *Village Voice* journalism of Jill Johnston, or Valerie Solanas' (1968) S.C.U.M. (Society for Cutting Up Men) Manifesto.
4. See Hale (1998), Prosser (1998) and Stryker and Whittle (2006). Butler has addressed explicitly the importance of what she calls the 'new gender politics' in the introduction to *Undoing Gender* (Butler, 2004).
5. In some later work, Sedgwick has brought her prodigious critical intelligence to bear on representations of lesbian existence. See her essay on Willa Cather in *Tendencies* (1993) and an essay on the Showtime television series 'The L Word' for *The Chronicle of Higher Education* (2004).
6. For the strength and variety of these identifications, see Barber and Clark (2002).
7. In 'Queer and Now' Sedgwick writes, 'a lot of the most exciting recent work around "queer" spins the term outward along dimensions that can't be subsumed under gender and sexuality at all: the ways that race, ethnicity, post-colonial nationality criss-cross with these and other identity-constituting, identity-fracturing discourses, for example. Intellectuals and artists of color whose sexual self-definition includes "queer" – I think of an Isaac Julien, a Gloria Anzaldúa, a Richard Fung – are using the leverage of "queer" to do a new kind of justice to the fractal intricacies of language, skin, migration, state' (Sedgwick, 1993: 8–9). See also Warner (1993) and the 1997 special issue of *Social Text*, 'Queer Transexions of Race, Nation, and Gender'. For queer work that makes such 'fractal intricacies' central, see the 2005 *Social Text* issue 'What's Queer about Queer Studies Now', Anzaldúa (1987), Moraga (1983/ 2000), Ferguson (2003), Quiroga (2001), Gopinath (2005), Rodriguez (2002), Reid-Pharr (2001), Mercer (1994), Somerville (2000), Delany (2001) and Johnson and Henderson (2005).
8. For examples of queer work that makes literature and representation central, see Miller (1989, 2005), Halperin (1990), Dollimore (1991), Sinfield (1994), Traub (2002), Goldberg (1992), Roof (1993), Bartlett (1988), Bray (1995), Koestenbaum (1993/2001), Moon (1991), Dellamora (1994) and Yingling (1990).
9. The *Bowers* v. *Hardwick* decision by the US Supreme Court (1986) ruled that the constitution did not protect the right of individuals to engage in acts of homosexual sodomy. The decision was reversed in 2003 in *Lawrence* v. *Texas*, which extended the right of privacy to all citizens.

10. Michel Foucault describes '"reverse" discourse' in the first volume of *The History of Sexuality*: 'There is no question that the appearance in nineteenth-century psychiatry, jurisprudence, and literature of a whole series of discourses on the species and subspecies of homosexuality, inversion, pederasty, and "psychic hermaphroditism" made possible a strong advance of social controls into this area of "perversity"; but it also made possible the formation of a "reverse" discourse: homosexuality began to speak in its own behalf, to demand that its legitimacy or "naturality" be acknowledged, often in the same vocabulary, using the same categories by which it was medically disqualified' (Foucault, 1977: 101).

11. A brief survey of work in queer psychoanalytic literary criticism might include Bersani (1996), Dean (2000), De Lauretis (1988, 1994), Edelman (1994, 2004), Fuss (1995), Hart (1994, 1998) and Dean and Lane (2001).

BIBLIOGRAPHY

Anon. (1990), *Queers Read This!/I Hate Straights!*, New York: n.p.

Anzaldúa, Gloria (1987), *Borderlands/La Frontera: The New Mestiza*, San Francisco: Aunt Lute Books.

Anzaldúa, Gloria and Analouise Keating (eds) (2002), *this bridge we call home: radical visions for transformation*, New York: Routledge.

Barber, Stephen M. and David L. Clark (eds) (2002), *Regarding Sedgwick: Essays on Queer Culture and Critical Theory*, New York: Routledge.

Barthes, Roland (1970/1974), *S/Z: An Essay*, trans. Richard, Miller, New York: Farrar Straus Giroux.

　(1973/1975), *The Pleasure of the Text*, trans. Richard, Miller, New York: Farrar Straus Giroux.

　(1977/1978), *A Lover's Discourse: Fragments*, New York: Farrar Straus Giroux.

Bartlett, Neil (1988), *Who Was That Man? A Present for Mr. Oscar Wilde*, London: Serpent's Tail.

Beauvoir, Simone de (1949/1989), *The Second Sex*, trans. Howard, Parshley, New York: Vintage (1989).

Bersani, Leo (1996), *Homos*, Cambridge, MA: Harvard University Press.

Bornstein, Kate (1995), *Gender Outlaw: On Men, Women, and the Rest of Us*, New York: Vintage.

Bray, Alan (1995), *Homosexuality in Renaissance England*, New York: Columbia University Press.

Butler, Judith (1990/1999), *Gender Trouble: Feminism and the Subversion of Identity*, New York: Routledge.

　(1993), *Bodies That Matter: On the Discursive Limits of 'Sex'*, New York: Routledge.

　(2004), *Undoing Gender*, New York: Taylor and Francis.

Combahee River Collective (1978/1983), 'The Combahee River Collective Statement', reprinted in *Home Girls: A Black Feminist Anthology*, ed. Barbara Smith, New York: Kitchen Table/Women of Color Press (1983).

Cvetkovich, Ann (2003), *An Archive of Feelings: Trauma, Sexuality, and Lesbian Public Cultures*, Durham, NC: Duke University Press.

Dean, Tim (2000), *Beyond Sexuality*, Chicago: University of Chicago Press.

Dean, Tim and Christopher, Lane (eds) (2001), *Homosexuality and Psychoanalysis*, Chicago: University of Chicago Press.

Delany, Samuel R. (2001), *Times Square Red, Times Square Blue*, New York: New York University Press.

De Lauretis, Teresa (1988), 'Sexual Indifference and Lesbian Representation', in *Theatre Journal* 40 (May).

(1994), *The Practice of Love: Lesbian Sexuality and Perverse Desire*, Bloomington: Indiana University Press.

Dellamora, Richard (1994), *Apocalyptic Overtures: Sexual Politics and the Sense of an Ending*, New Brunswick, NJ: Rutgers University Press.

Dollimore, Jonathan (1991), *Sexual Dissidence: Augustine to Wilde, Freud to Foucault*, New York: Oxford University Press.

Duggan, Lisa (1996), 'Introduction', in *Sex Wars: Sexual Dissent and Political Culture*, ed. Lisa Duggan and Nan Hunter, New York: Routledge.

Edelman, Lee (1994), *Homographesis: Essays in Gay Literary and Cultural Theory*, New York: Routledge.

(2004), *No Future: Queer Theory and the Death Drive*, Durham, NC: Duke University Press.

Eng, David, Judith Halberstam and José Esteban Muñoz (2005), 'What's Queer about Queer Studies Now', in special issue of *Social Text* 84/85.

Fausto-Sterling, Anne (2000), *Sexing the Body: Gender Politics and the Construction of Sexuality*, New York: Basic Books.

Ferguson, Roderick A. (2003), *Aberrations in Black: Toward a Queer of Color Critique*, Minneapolis, MN: Minnesota University Press.

Foucault, Michel (1977), *The History of Sexuality*, vol. 1, trans. Robert Hurley, New York: Vintage.

Fuss, Diana (1995), *Identification Papers*, New York: Routledge.

Garber, Marjorie (1997), *Vested Interests: Cross-Dressing and Cultural Anxiety*, New York: Routledge.

Goldberg, Jonathan (1992), *Sodometries: Renaissance Texts, Modern Sexualities*, Stanford, CA: Stanford University Press.

Gopinath, Gayatri (2005), *Impossible Desires: Queer Diasporas and South Asian Public Cultures*, Durham, NC: Duke University Press.

Halberstam, Judith (1998), *Female Masculinity*, Durham, NC: Duke University Press.

Hale, C. Jacob (1998), 'Consuming the Living, Dis(re)membering the Dead in the Butch/Ftm Borderlands', in *GLQ: A Journal of Lesbian and Gay Studies* 4:2 (April).

Halperin, David (1990), *One Hundred Years of Homosexuality and Other Essays on Greek Love*, New York: Routledge.

(1995), *Saint Foucault: Towards a Gay Hagiography*, New York: Oxford University Press.

Harper, Phillip Brian, José Esteban Muñoz and Trish Rosen (eds) (1997), 'Queer Transexions of Race, Nation, and Gender', in special issue of *Social Text* 52/53.

Hart, Lynda (1994), *Fatal Women: Lesbian Sexuality and the Mark of Aggression*, Princeton, NJ: Princeton University Press.

(1998), *Between the Body and the Flesh: Performing Sadomasochism*, New York: Columbia University Press.

Heller, Dana (ed.) (1997), *Cross-Purposes: Lesbians, Feminists, and the Limits of Alliance*, Bloomington: Indiana University Press.

Hollibaugh, Amber (2000), *My Dangerous Desires: a queer girl dreaming her way home*, Durham, NC: Duke University Press.

Hull, Gloria T., Patricia Bell Scott and Barbara Smith (eds) (1982), *All the Women Are White, All the Blacks Are Men, But Some of Us Are Brave: Black Women's Studies*, Old Westbury, NY: The Feminist Press.

Johnson, Barbara (1980), *The Critical Difference*, Baltimore: Johns Hopkins University Press.

Johnson, E. Patrick and Mae Henderson (eds) (2005), *Black Queer Studies: A Critical Anthology*, Durham, NC: Duke University Press.

Johnston, Jill (1973), *Lesbian Nation: The Feminist Solution*, New York: Simon and Schuster.

Koestenbaum, Wayne (1993/2001), *The Queen's Throat: Opera, Homosexuality, and the Mystery of Desire*, New York: Da Capo Press.

McGarry, Molly and Fred Wasserman (eds) (1998), *Becoming Visible: An Illustrated History of Lesbian and Gay Life in Twentieth-Century America*, New York: The New York Public Library, Penguin Studio.

Mercer, Kobena (1994), *Welcome to the Jungle: New Positions in Black Cultural Studies*, New York: Routledge.

Merck, Mandy, Naomi Segal and Elizabeth Wright (eds) (1998), *Coming Out of Feminism?*, Oxford: Blackwell.

Miller, D. A. (1989), *The Novel and the Police*, Berkeley, CA: University of California Press.

(1998), *Place for Us: Essay on the Broadway Musical*, Cambridge, MA: Harvard University Press.

(2005), *Jane Austen, or the Secret of Style*, Princeton, NJ: Princeton University Press.

Moon, Michael (1991), *Disseminating Whitman: Revision and Corporeality in 'Leaves of Grass'*, Cambridge, MA: Harvard University Press.

Moraga, Cherríe (1983/2000), *Loving in the War Years: lo que nunca pasó por sus labios*, Boston: South End Press.

Moraga, Cherríe and Gloria Anzaldúa (eds) (1981), *This Bridge Called My Back: Writings by Radical Women of Color*, New York: Kitchen Table/Women of Color Press.

Moraga, Cherríe and Amber Hollibaugh (1981/1983), 'What We're Rollin Around in Bed With: Sexual Silences in Feminism', in *Powers of Desire: The Politics of Sexuality*, ed. Ann Snitow, Christine Stansell and Sharon Thompson, New York: Monthly Review Press.

Nestle, Joan (2003), 'Wars and Thinking', in *Journal of Women's History* 15:3.

Prosser, Jay (1998), *Second Skins: The Body-Narratives of Transsexuality*, New York: Columbia University Press.

Quiroga, José (2001), *Tropics of Desire: Interventions from Queer Latino America*, New York: New York University Press.

Radicalesbians [Artemis March, Ellen Bedoz, Cynthia Funk, Rita Mae Brown, Lois Hart, Barbara Gladstone and others] (1970), *The Woman-Identified Woman*, Pittsburgh: KNOW Inc.

Reid-Pharr, Robert F. (2001), *Black Gay Man: Essays*, New York: New York University Press.

Rich, Adrienne (1980/2003), 'Compulsory Heterosexuality and Lesbian Existence', in *Journal of Women's History* 15:3.

Rodriguez, Juana (2002), *Queer Latinidad: Identity Practices, Discursive Spaces*, New York: New York University Press.

Roof, Judith (1991), *A Lure of Knowledge: Lesbian Sexuality and Theory*, New York: Columbia University Press.

Rubin, Gayle (1975), 'The Traffic in Women: Notes on the "Political Economy" of Sex', in *Toward an Anthropology of Women*, ed. Rayna R. Reiter, New York: Monthly Review Press.

(1984/1993), 'Thinking Sex: Notes Toward a Radical Politics of Sexuality', in *The Lesbian and Gay Studies Reader*, ed. Henry Abelove, Michèle Aina Barale and David M. Halperin, New York: Routledge.

Sedgwick, Eve Kosofsky (1985), *Between Men*, New York: Columbia University Press.

(1990), *Epistemology of the Closet*, Berkeley, CA: University of California Press.

(1993), *Tendencies*, Durham, NC: Duke University Press.

(1993), 'Queer Performativity: Henry James's New York Prefaces', in *GLQ: A Journal of Gay and Lesbian Studies* 1.

(16, January 2004), '"The L Word": Novelty in Normalcy', in *The Chronicle of Higher Education* 50:19.

Sinfield, Alan (1994), *The Wilde Century*, New York: Columbia University Press.

Solanas, Valerie (1968), *SCUM Manifesto*, London: Olympia Press.

Somerville, Siobhan B. (2000), *Queering the Color Line: Race and the Invention of Homosexuality in American Culture*, Durham, NC: Duke University Press.

Stryker, Susan and Stephen Whittle (2006), *The Transgender Studies Reader*, New York: Routledge.

Traub, Valerie (2002), *The Renaissance of Lesbianism in Early Modern England*, Cambridge and New York: Cambridge University Press.

Vermeule, Blakey (1991), 'Is There a Sedgwick School for Girls?', in *Qui Parle* 5:1 (Fall/Winter).

Warner, Michael (ed.) (1993), *Fear of a Queer Planet: Queer Politics and Social Theory*, Minneapolis: University of Minnesota Press.

Weed, Elizabeth and Naomi Schor (eds) (1997), *Feminism Meets Queer Theory (Books from differences)*, Bloomington: Indiana University Press.

Wittig, Monique (1992), *'The Straight Mind' and Other Essays*, Boston: Beacon Press.

Yingling, Thomas (1990), *Hart Crane and the Homosexual Text: New Thresholds, New Anatomies*, Chicago: University of Chicago Press.

CHAPTER 17

Feminist criticism and technologies of the body

Stacy Gillis

An understanding of the body as technologically constituted was one of the key discursive shifts in both postmodern and feminist theories in the late 1980s. Research on gender, the body and technology emerged simultaneously in a number of disciplines – from literature to sociology, from cybernetics to history – and has since proposed a number of ways in which we can and should understand the body *as* and *in* technology. While I will be drawing upon many of these debates, I am here particularly concerned with how the body is articulated in cyberspace and cybertheory: both the relationship of technology and cyberspace with the body in real life (IRL) and how this relationship has been represented in the new techno-fictions, both literary and filmic, which have emerged in the past thirty years.

The figure of the cyborg – that combination of the human and the technological – has become a symbol of the relationship between the body and technology. The cyborg also defines the contemporary cyberpunk and science-fiction text – whether it is the hardboiled console cowboy Case in William Gibson's *Neuromancer* (1984) or the hyper-sexualised Seven of Nine in *Star Trek: Voyager* (1995–2001). Its ability both to interrogate and to reify the category of the human has resulted in its appropriation by many who are eager to claim the disruptive 'postmodernity' that it contains and represents. Its apparent technological disruption of the Enlightenment body has been claimed by feminist critics: for Rosi Braidotti, the cyborg 'challenges the androcentrism of the poststructuralists' corporeal materialism' (2002: 180), while for Nina Lykke the cyborg calls into question 'the ways in which the modern scientific world-view is rooted in a long tradition that casts the non-human in the role of a mere object and exploitable resource for the human, for centuries identified with the powerful and hegemonic position of the white Western man of science, capital and industry' (1996: 24). Yet a distinction must be made between the metaphor of the cyborg – as commonly used by such theorists as Donna Haraway – and the representation of the cyborgic, which surrounds us.

Austin Booth and Mary Flanagan have aptly pointed out that 'the cyborg metaphor and its meanings have become an important cultural site of contestation' (Booth and Flanagan, 2002: 15). As the ways in which we can understand the body as and in technology are investigated, literary and filmic representations of the cyborg often become conflated with the materiality of our potentially cyborgic identities.

Technological embodiment is foregrounded by the meat/metal fusion of the cyborg, which serves to accentuate the material physicality of embodiment. While the body is the most culturally common – and the most idealised – stand-in for the real, it is produced as 'the Real' by processes of representation. N. Katherine Hayles reminds us that bodily experience references the culturally specific ways in which subjects understand and enact their bodies, as characterised by certain habits, tendencies, movements, limitations and sensitivities. '[E]mbodiment is contextual', she writes, 'enmeshed within the specifics of place, time, physiology and culture, which together compose enactment' (1999: 196). For Hayles, '[e]mbodiment never coincides exactly with "the body," however that normalized concept is understood' (1999: 196). The cyborgic continuum is not easily defined. How much technological intervention renders a human a cyborg? How much organic material might render a robot human? Where are the lines of distinction drawn between the human and the technological? Does driving a car render one cyborgic? Or does the intervention have to be more surgical, more irretrievable? For Elizabeth Grosz, when inanimate objects are touched by the body for long enough they become extensions of the body image: 'the object ceases to remain an object and becomes a medium, a vehicle for impressions and expression . . . it can be used as an instrument or tool . . . midway between the inanimate and the bodily' (1994: 81). The point of contact between the inanimate object – whether a computer keyboard or a prosthetic limb – and the body does, at some indefinable point, become a cyborgic one. The distinctions between the body and the technological become difficult to identify and categorise when one considers to what extent we are technologically embodied. Grosz argues that bodies 'can be represented or understood not as entities in themselves or simply on a linear continuum with its polar extremes occupied by male and female bodies . . . but as a field, a two-dimensional continuum in which race (and possibly even class, caste, or religion) form body specifications' (1994: 19). To this list I would add the technological as a crucial dimension of body specifications.

Since the computer revolution of the early 1980s – when Apple and Microsoft launched their respective models of the personal computer – the

cyberising of society has become a familiar subject. But while some speak of
the politics of technology as if this were a new thing, this is, of course,
patently untrue. Technology has been the primary marker of human
activity for many thousands of years. Yet the sexiness of cyberspace and
the promise that in these new spaces things could be different – this time,
we *could* forget the body – have obfuscated the lengthy history of the
relationship between the human and technology. From Jonathan Swift's
Gulliver's Travels (1726) to Mary Shelley's *Frankenstein* (1818), from Lewis
Carroll's *Through the Looking Glass* (1871) to Joseph Heller's *Catch-22*
(1961), even a cursory examination of literature reveals that the technological has been paramount in the Western literary tradition. This chapter
interrogates the cyborg and the cyberpunk tradition, a genre understood to
date from the publication of *Neuromancer* in 1984.[1] This genre – with its
hackers and cyborgs, its technological interfaces and fetishised violence –
has become synonymous with literary cyberculture. What is of particular
relevance to my argument is the way in which the cyborg and the cyborgic
often valorise Enlightenment notions of embodiment. Both representations of the cyborg and the possibilities of cyborgic identity are based
upon an account of the body as highly gendered and sexualised, physically,
intellectually and/or emotionally.

OF CYBORGS AND FEMINISM

The publication of Donna Haraway's 'A Cyborg Manifesto: Science,
Technology, and Socialist Feminism in the Late Twentieth Century'
(1985) and her subsequent *Simians, Cyborgs, and Women: The Reinvention
of Nature* (1991) are key points in accounting for a theorisation of the body
as technology through the meat-metal fusion of the cyborg. Haraway's
cyborg is a 'myth about transgressed boundaries, potent fusions, and
dangerous possibilities' (1991: 154). While her essay is primarily an investigation of socialist feminism, it is her model of the cyborg which is most
often discussed, precisely because of its transgressive and illegitimate
qualities. The cyborg, indeed, became one of the most compelling images
of the late twentieth century. Haraway uses the cyborg as a way of speaking
about the challenges that can be made to the reifying Enlightenment
politics of identity. She argues for a non-essentialist version of the relationship between sex and gender: '[t]here is nothing about being female that
naturally binds women. There is not even such a state as "being" female,
itself a highly complex category constructed in contested sexual scientific
discourses and other social practices' (1991: 155). Haraway uses the cyborg

to move beyond the essentialism debates surrounding feminism in the late 1970s and early 1980s, which emphasised the factors uniting all women, regardless of race, class and sexuality.

It is the cyborg that, for Haraway, can disrupt these debates which often 'laps[e] into boundless difference ... giving up on the confusing task of making partial, real connections' (1991: 161). The metaphor of the cyborg is so seductive because of its resistance to any hegemonic reading or account of history and ideology: '[c]yborg politics is the struggle for language and the struggle against perfect communication, against the one code that translates all meaning perfectly, the central dogma of phallogocentrism. That is why cyborg politics insist on noise and advocate pollution, rejoicing in the illegitimate effusions of animal and machine' (1991: 176). The references here to noise and resistance echo the language surrounding *écriture féminine*, and the cyborg metaphor certainly draws upon Irigarayan models of disruption (Irigaray, 1977/1985: 28–9). Haraway, however, finds it is the transgressive mixture of woman *and* technology that creates incomprehension, incoherency and the challenge to reason. Like *écriture féminine*, her cyborg feminism resists 'models of unity' (Haraway, 1991: 181), but its resistance is encoded within technology. For Haraway, the transgressive fusion of meat and metal, body and technology, human and machine in the cyborg is a powerful tool for the feminist imagination, foregrounding the artifice of gender and questioning the integrity of the Enlightenment body.

Anne Balsamo, however, wonders whether Haraway grasps how the cyborg – with all its potential for transgression – is a product of a specific historical and cultural moment (1996: 155). Similarly, Susan Bordo finds that Haraway's noisy, polluting and illegitimate cyborg is only an 'epistemological fantasy of becoming multiplicity' (1989: 144). Yet Balsamo also argues that 'cyborgs offer a particularly appropriate emblem, not only of postmodern identity, but – specifically – of woman's identity. Cyborg identity is predicated on transgressed boundaries' (1996: 155). The interrogation of the Enlightenment (male) body by the cyborg's transgressive qualities means that the cyborg, for Balsamo, should always be gendered as female. The transgression is contained within its fusion of body and technology, a fusion which allows the prime subjectivity of selfhood to coexist in the same body with the threat of otherness. The ways in which the cyborg references both self and other, the familiar and the unfamiliar, are also particularly relevant for Balsamo: '[t]hey fascinate us because they are not like us, and yet just like us. Formed through a radical disruption of other-ness, cyborg identity foregrounds the constructedness of otherness' (1996: 155). The Freudian uncanny – that which is both strange and familiar, unknown and known – is used here to articulate how a cyborg can be disruptive with its simultaneous lack and excess of meaning contained within its technological/human interface. If woman is 'an absence, outside the system of representations and autorepresentations . . . a *hole* in men's signifying economy' (Irigaray, 1974/1988: 50; emphasis in the original), then the always-female-genderedness of the cyborg complicates its interrogation of the Enlightenment body. This signifying economy uses the lack that is woman to represent the Real; in the figure of the cyborg, this is complicated by the inclusion of technology, a technology that is always grounded in the rational and material realities of science.

The figure of the cyborg has been particularly seductive for cyberfeminists who have looked to Haraway and to Sadie Plant to provide the metaphors through which to articulate new relationships between the body and technology. While Haraway argues for a celebration of how the cyborg can move us into a post-gendered world, Plant is keen to demonstrate that women and computers are already inextricably linked in a cyberfeminist celebration. For Plant, cyberfeminism is 'an insurrection on the part of the goods and material of the patriarchal world, a dispersed emergence composed of links between women, women and computers, computers and communication links, connections and connectionist nets' (1996/2000: 265). Her book *Zeros and Ones* (1997) – about Ada Lovelace, the nineteenth-century mathematician who worked with Charles Babbage on the Difference Engine, a progenitor of the computer – repeatedly emphasises her argument that women have always been intrinsically connected with cybernetic technologies. Indeed, for Plant:

the computer was always a simulation of weaving: threads of ones and zeros riding the carpets and simulating silk screens in the perpetual motions of cyberspace. It joins women on and as the interface between man and matter, identity and difference, one and zero, the actual and the virtual. An interface which is taking off on its own: no longer the voice, the gap, or the absence, the veils are already cybernetic. (1995: 63)

Women, weaving, the Web – all are part of the same nexus of activity and all offer a possibility of resistance to patriarchal discourse in Plant's work. Her rendition of 'being-woman' is largely predicated upon an account of women's historical kinship and empathy with the technological.

Plant's argument that women and feminism should find a natural home in cyberspace is embedded within an understanding of the Internet as a body-less space in which identity remains playful: 'The Internet promises women a network of lines on which to chatter, natter, work and play;

virtuality brings a fluidity to identities which once had to be fixed; and multi-media provides a tactile environment in which women artists can find their space' (1996/2000: 265). Women, through these new technologies, 'are accessing the circuits on which they were once exchanged, hacking into security controls, and discovering their own post-humanity' (Plant, 1996/2000: 265). Yet Plant cannot offer a coherent account of exactly how this resistance will take place: while arguing that women are 'accessing', 'hacking' and finding their 'own post-humanity', how this accessing and hacking is occurring and what this post-humanity means are not made evident.

Barbara Kennedy claims that cyberfeminism 'covers feminist simulations of technology, most literally through debates about power, identity and autonomy and the role of new technologies in the transformation of these characteristics... cyberfeminism defines a specific *cyborgian* consciousness – a particular way of thinking which breaks down binary and oppositional discourses' (2000: 285; emphasis in original). While it is true that recent developments in cybernetics and Internet use have substantially increased awareness of the possibilities of online gender disruption, it is debatable whether this is a new form of feminism. Postmodernism, generally, has raised questions about identity and hybridity. Moreover, debates about power, autonomy and the politics of gender have marked much feminist debate of the past century and more. Contemporary feminism is also often concerned with breaking down binary and oppositional discourses. In this context, cyberfeminism needs to interrogate its own politics and history carefully – including remembering that the relationship between women and technology has long been problematic. This interrogation should include 'disentangling cyborg feminism, gender and technology studies, cybercultural theory and e-activism' (Gillis, 2004: 179), and practitioners should remember the example of Haraway's cyborg feminism which, unlike much cyberfeminist work, provides an account of the politics which have always been at the core of feminist activity.

One of the problems with any celebration of the liberating potential of technology is that technological developments are firmly located within a capitalist structure. Our technoculture endorses identities which are located in and around certain forms of technology, an exclusionary practice. Krista Hunt points up the problems with the assumption that everyone can log in:

Access to Internet technology not only requires money to buy hardware and software, but also access to a telephone, a reliable telecommunications infrastructure, affordable connection fees, proficiency in English and tech-language, the desire to 'get connected,' technical support, the ability and desire to express oneself through text . . . many women still require 'a room of one's own' and the time to invest. (Hunt, 2001: 152)

When the revolutionary potential of technology – and particularly the personal computer and access to the Internet – is praised, the issues of accessibility are often overlooked. Globally, few have access to the supposedly liberating spaces of the World Wide Web. While these 'have nots' in the economy of cyberspace clearly may use other forms of technology – whether a quern, a loom or a shovel – there is a Western valorisation, and even fetishisation, of cybernetic technology. Economics drives both the development of new technology and access to it: 'From a critical perspective, the most salient aspect of the technologies is the issue of access and participation: knowing that barely twenty per cent of households in the world have electricity, let alone telephone-lines and modems, well may one wonder about the "democratic", let alone the "revolutionary", potential of the new electronic frontier' (Braidotti, 2002: 176). While the question of access and participation in terms of gender may have been partially redressed in the West, access to and participation in new technologies is still largely a white, Western, middle-class preserve.

READING CYBORGS

Despite its fascination with Japan and the Far East, cyberpunk, the literature of cybernetic technologies, should be understood as 'fully delineated urban fantasies of white male folklore' (Ross, 1991: 145). While Andrew Ross is here referring specifically to the pre-1990 work of William Gibson, cyberpunk film and fiction has remained mired in a particularly hardboiled account of technology, one which has a white urban masculinity as its referent. This has resulted in a representation of the cyborgic as largely white. Beth E. Kolko, Lisa Nakamura and Gilbert B. Rodman have pointed out that gender has been an overriding issue when considering the politics of identity and representation:

just as first and second-wave feminists often failed to include race and the issue of third world women in their politics, so too have many cyberfeminists elided the topic of race in cyberspace. This state of things represents the norm rather than the aberration; there is very little scholarly work that deals with how our notions of race are shaped and challenged by new technologies such as the Internet. Haraway situated the cyborg within a complex and broad matrix of identity, but scholarship has focused primarily on the gender of that cyborg rather than other elements of its identity. (2000a: 8)

While race is implicitly referenced in Haraway's argument about socialist feminism and the sexual division of labour, it is apparent that the focus on gender has overwhelmed race (and class) in the discussion of the cyborg and the relationship between the body and technology. The ways in which race is excluded not only from the debates about cyberspace but also from the social fabric of cyberspace itself are made evident by Kolko, who points out how, for example, when one is constructing an online identity in such online environments as MMPORGs (Massive Multi-Player Online Role-Playing Games), one can choose age, timezone and/or gender but not often race (Kolko, 2000: 216). In the relationship between the body and technology, representation, once more, takes precedence over identity.

Thus, as with gender, new technologies often merely reproduce cultural discourses of race. Those who have regarded cyberspace as a futurist cyber-utopia – among them Roseanne Allucquère Stone, Howard Rheingold and Michael Benedikt – regularly echo Sherry Turkle's idealistic argument that when 'identity was defined as unitary and solid it was relatively easy to recognize and censure deviation from a norm'. For Turkle, the Internet necessarily allows a 'more fluid sense of self [and] a greater capacity for acknowledging diversity' meaning that we 'do not feel compelled to rank or judge the elements of our multiplicity. We do not feel compelled to exclude what does not fit' (1996: 261). Yet while these cyber-utopians do speak to the ways in which we might consider cyberspace as a post-gendered space, they rarely speak to a post-raced space. Haraway's cyborg may have focused our attention on how technology impacts upon the gendered body but the racialised body remains in the background. Lisa Nakamura has incisively interrogated the politics of race on the Internet, pointing up the numerous ways in which race is both invisible and unsaid. Building on Kolko's work on race in online gaming environments, she argues that 'the decision to leave race out of self-description does in fact constitute a choice: in the absence of racial description all players are assumed to be white' (2002: 38). While Nakamura partly ascribes this to the typical user of the Internet – the young white middle-class male – she is also adamant that online 'alternate versions of self and race jam the ideology-machine' (2002: 49). The politics of race representation are likewise foregrounded by Claudia Springer in her discussion of the *Matrix* trilogy (1999–2003). She points out how Neo's quest to become the One, the über-hacker of the Matrix, is supported and endorsed by a series of black mentors whom he ultimately supersedes, including the cookie-baking Oracle, whose 'patiently supportive role and mystical powers place her among other similar black film characters who function to ensure a white protagonist's survival and success' (2005: 96). The futurist utopia of cyberspace has endorsed repeatedly, both in terms of online identity and in terms of representation, an understanding of the body as technologically mediated, but this body still resembles that of Enlightenment thought.

So, however it is technologically mediated, the body cannot escape embodiment: it remains enmeshed within webs of signification. For all the promise of a post-gender world, representations of the cyborg have rarely provided an account of a world in which the body is no longer a site of gender inscription. Hackers and cyborgs populate the literature of cyberpunk. Hacking is a cyborgic activity: in Gibson's *Count Zero* (1986) Bobby Newmark's metamorphosis into the hacker Count Zero, whose IRL body is always comatose as he spends all his time logged into cyberspace, demonstrates the cyborgicity of the hacker identity as does the literal way in which the crew of the Nebuchadnezzar hack into the Matrix through technological hardware inserted into their cortexes in the *Matrix* trilogy. Hacking is a locus of traditionally masculine activity, however, with its metaphors of penetration, annexation and competition.[2] Moreover, the ways in which cyberpunk draws explicitly upon the hardboiled detective fiction genre similarly serve to emphasise its masculine narrative strategies. With the lone hacker treading his way through the mean streets of cyberspace, the gender politics of *noir* are never far from cyberpunk. This complicates the representation of the female cyborg in cyberpunk. Molly Millions in Gibson's *Neuromancer* trilogy has paid for her cyborgic extensions – permanent mirrorshades and scalpel blades under her nails – through renting her body out: she worked as a prostitute, but with a cut-out chip putting her into a trance whilst her body was working. In this particular rendition of a futurist utopia for prostitution in which bodies – not identities – are prostituted, the repressed memories of what occurred during these mind-less transactions of her body do occasionally surface. Molly may be a street samurai but she is also a sex worker. The female replicants in Ridley Scott's *Blade Runner* (1982) are similarly contained by their female flesh – Pris is a 'basic pleasure model' whose violent attempt to sustain her own pleasure when she clasps Rick Deckard between her thighs in an abortive attempt at masturbation is punished by a death scene which emphasises how close *le petit mort* of orgasm is to death. As Andreas Huyssen has pointed out, as soon as 'the machine came to be perceived as a demonic, inexplicable threat and as the harbinger of chaos and destruction . . . woman, nature, machine had become a mesh of signification which all had one thing in common: otherness' (1986: 70).

From the figure of the robot Maria in Fritz Lang's *Metropolis* (1926) to Trinity in the *Matrix* trilogy, the female cyborg is overtly sexualised and usually destroyed. In that cyberpunk draws upon *noir*, this sexualisation of the female cyborg should be understood in terms of the *femme fatale* and the long tradition of containing those who challenge the tropes of traditional femininity.

In drawing upon the *noir* tradition, cyberpunk, however, has another – albeit not often acknowledged – origin in the Gothic. The social deviance and disruption in the Gothic fictions of the eighteenth century can be read as a (feminised) counterpart to the rationality of the Enlightenment, a disruption which continues in current fictions: 'Gothic signifies a writing of excess ... In the twentieth century, in diverse and ambiguous ways, Gothic figures have continued to shadow the progress of modernity with counter-narratives displaying the underside of enlightenment and humanist values' (Botting, 1996: 1–2). If cyberpunk draws upon the technological to render its account of the (female) body as cyborgic, then Gothic tropes can undermine this. Hardboiled detective fiction and cyberpunk are sustained by a rational masculinity which resists irrationality. Reason, activity and power are located within the body of the (male) hacker, in contrast with the dangers of the female body. The rational masculinity which is foregrounded in cyberpunk and its predecessor, detective fiction, is threatened by the presence of the Gothicised female body, haunting its boundaries, both corporeally and textually (Gillis, 2007b). Not surprisingly, it is often the female authors of cyberpunk who explore its Gothic overtones, playing up its transgressive qualities and not always locating these within the figure of the cyborg. While it is the masculinist strand of cyberpunk which is commercially more successful, such female authors as Pat Cadigan often subvert the gender politics of cyberpunk in novels like *Synners* (1991).[3] A particularly powerful interrogation of the relationship between the body and technology can be found in Shelley Jackson's hypertext novel *Patchwork Girl* (1995). A time-travelling cybergic *flâneuse*, the Patchwork Girl is the female monster in Mary Shelley's *Frankenstein* (1818). Torn apart by Victor Frankenstein, who is horrified by the sight of the monstrous female body, in *Patchwork Girl* the monster is (re)assembled by Mary Shelley: 'Like the female monster's body, the body of this hypertext is also seamed and ruptured, comprised of disparate parts with extensive links between them' (Hayles, 2000: 23). In returning to the origins of science fiction in the Gothic *Frankenstein*, Jackson locates the female body in a narrative which, through the nature of hypertext, writes itself anew each time it is read.

TECHNOLOGICAL MEDIATION

The study of technology and the body does, of course, move beyond the language of representation. While the cyborg offers one way of thinking through the technologically mediated body, there is also the question of what kind of bodies exist in cyberspace. Roseanne Stone argues that the synchronous communication possibilities of the Internet pose new problems: 'not simply problems of accountability (i.e., who did it) but of warrantability (i.e., did a body/subject do it) . . . that is, is there a physical body involved in this interaction anywhere?' (1995: 87). Early on in the life of the Internet, a 'rape' took place online in a MOO.[4] A group of individuals who were largely known to each other through their textual avatars (including Mr Bungle and Starslinger) formed an online community. Mr Bungle hacked control of others' identities and forced avatars to perform sex acts on himself and on other members of the community. The members of the community who had been textually violated and who had watched it occurring used the term rape to describe the unstoppable experience of watching an online textual identity perform these acts on the screen. This experience – by no means unique in cyberspace – raises the question of how we are to understand the relationship not only between the body and technology, but between identity, subjectivity and technology. Dianne Currier draws upon Gilles Deleuze and Felix Guattari's notion of assemblage to argue for a recognition of the existence of the body in cyberspace as 'not simply a technologically generated information space or place, but as a series of assemblages comprised of elements of the technical, social, discursive, material, and immaterial' (2002: 536). For Currier, mapping such assemblages is vital to understanding how 'discourses and practices of femininity and masculinity intersect with those of technology and technological artifacts' (2002: 536–7). Since technology is the site of power, mapping and reading the ways in which the body is mediated by technology – whether the washing machine, the telephone or the computer – is essential to the feminist project.

To map the entire Internet could only be possible within a Borgesian universe: it would now be impossible for us to grasp the sheer magnitude of material available through Web browsers to the general surfer. Yet even a brief saunter through the Web indicates that women do dominate our cyberspace, albeit through the proliferation of sex sites. This is particularly telling given that women's engagement with technology in literature has been dominated by the masculine hardboiled version of femininity, with its sexualised *femme fatale*. While women do write cyberpunk and science fiction, imagining how gender might be – or might have been – reconfigured through these new technologies, this literature has not entered the mainstream market. Dominated by a masculinist cyberpunk tradition which stretches from *Neuromancer* to *The Matrix*, the politics of the literary marketplace provide more evidence of the traditional models of gender. This is not to say, however, that the transgressive potential of the cyborg has not provided a challenge to Enlightenment politics and histories:

> We might expect, then, that computer intelligence and robotics would embrace binary splits and emphasize the dominance of reason and logic over the irrational. However, because the blurred boundaries between mind and machine, body and machine, and human and nonhuman are the very legacy of cybernetics, automated machines, in fact, provide new ground upon which to argue that gender and its representations are technological productions. (Halberstam, 1991: 439–40)

Understanding gender – both in terms of identity and representation – as technological provides one escape route from the reification of the Enlightenment body. We can then begin to assemble a reading of how certain accounts of woman and femininity are constructed and contained by particular readings of the technological. As Haraway argues, 'we are all chimeras, theorized and fabricated hybrids of machine and organism; in short, we are cyborgs. The cyborg is our ontology; it gives us our politics' (1991: 150). While the figure and the metaphor of the cyborg can be deeply problematic, it reminds us that in order to think critically about technology we must always return to the human.

NOTES

1. While female authors of science fiction, such as Octavia Butler, Pat Cadigan and James Tiptree, Jr [Alice Sheldon], have been at times categorised as writing cyberpunk, the genre is largely populated by commercially successful male authors: William Gibson, Neal Stephenson and Richard Morgan.
2. For an ethnographic study of hacking, see Rasmussen and Håpnes (1991); for a reading of the hacker in culture, see Ross (1990); and, for a reading of the hacker in science fiction, see Fernbach (2000).
3. See note 1. Many of these female authors have female protagonists, going some way towards counteracting the masculine interface with technology.
4. A MOO is an Object-Oriented MUD (Multi-User Domain). A virtual environment on the Internet, MOOs allows users to build objects, rooms and places. For more on the rape in LambdaMOO, see Dibbell (1993).

BIBLIOGRAPHY

Balsamo, Anne (1996), *Technologies of the Gendered Body: Reading Cyborg Women*, Durham, NC: Duke University Press.

Booth, Austin and Mary Flanagan (2002), 'Introduction', in Flanagan and Booth (2002).

Bordo, Susan (1989), 'Feminism, Postmodernism, and Gender-Scepticism', in *Feminism/Postmodernism*, ed. Linda J. Nicholson, London: Routledge.

Botting, Fred (1996), *Gothic*, London: Routledge.

Braidotti, Rosi (2002), *Metamorphoses: Towards a Materialist Theory of Being*, Cambridge: Polity.

Currier, Dianne (2002), 'Assembling Bodies in Cyberspace: Technologies, Bodies, and Sexual Difference', in Flanagan and Booth (2002).

Dibbell, Julian (1993), 'A Rape in Cyberspace; or How an Evil Clown, a Haitian Trickster Spirit, Two Wizards, and a Cast of Dozens Turned a Database into a Society', in *Village Voice* 38:15.

Fernbach, Amanda (2000), 'The Fetishization of Masculinity in Science Fiction: The Cyborg and the Console Cowboy', in *Science Fiction Studies* 27:2

Flanagan, Mary and Austin Booth (eds) (2002), *Reload: Rethinking Women + Cyberculture*, Cambridge, MA: MIT Press

Gibson, William (1984), *Neuromancer*, London: Gollancz.

(1986), *Count Zero*, London: Gollancz.

Gillis, Stacy (2007a), 'Neither Cyborg Nor Goddess: The (Im)Possibilities of Cyberfeminism', in *Third Wave Feminism: A Critical Exploration*, ed. Stacy Gillis, Gillian Howie and Rebecca Munford, Basingstoke: Palgrave.

(2007b), 'The (Post)Feminist Politics of Cyberpunk', in *Gothic Studies* 9.

Grosz, Elizabeth (1994), *Volatile Bodies: Towards a Corporeal Feminism*, Bloomington: Indiana University Press.

Halberstam, Judith (1991), 'Automating Gender: Postmodern Feminism in the Age of the Intelligent Machine', in *Feminist Review* 17:3.

Haraway, Donna (1985), 'A Manifesto for Cyborgs: Science, Technology, and Socialist Feminism in the 1980s', in *Socialist Review* 80.

(1991), *Simians, Cyborgs, and Women: The Reinvention of Nature*, New York: Routledge.

Hawthorne, Susan and Renate Klein (1999), 'CyberFeminism', in *CyberFeminism: Connectivity, Critique and Creativity*, ed. Susan Hawthorne and Renate Klein, Melbourne: Spinifex.

Hayles, N. Katherine (1999), *How We Became Posthuman: Virtual Bodies in Cybernetics, Literature, and Informatics*, Chicago: University of Chicago Press.

(2000), 'Flickering Connectivities in Shelley Jackson's *Patchwork Girl*: The Importance of Media-Specific Analysis', in *Postmodern Culture* 10:2.

Hunt, Krista (2001), 'On the Edge of Connection: Global Feminism and the Politics of the Internet', in *Feminism(s) on the Edge of the Millennium:*

Rethinking Foundations and Future Debates, ed. Krista Hunt and Christine Saulnier, Toronto: Inanna Press.

Huyssen, Andreas (1986), *After the Great Divide: Modernism, Mass Culture and Post-Modernism*, Bloomington: Indiana University Press.

Irigaray, Luce (1974/1988), *Speculum of the Other Woman*, trans. Gillian C. Gill, Ithaca, NY: Cornell University Press.

(1977/1985), *This Sex Which Is Not One*, trans. Catherine Porter and Carolyn Burke, Ithaca, NY: Cornell University Press.

Kennedy, Barbara (2000), 'Introduction', in *The Cybercultures Reader*, ed. David Bell and Barbara Kennedy, London: Routledge.

Kolko, Beth E. (2000), 'Erasing @race', in Kolko, Nakamura and Rodman (2000b).

Kolko, Beth E., Lisa Nakamura and Gilbert B. Rodman (2000a), 'Introduction', in Kolko, Nakamura and Rodman (2000b).

(eds) (2000b), *Race in Cyberspace*, London: Routledge.

Lykke, Nina (1996), 'Introduction', in *Between Monsters, Goddesses and Cyborgs: Feminist Confrontations with Science, Medicine and Cyberspace*, ed. Nina Lykke and Rosi Braidotti, London: Zed Books.

Nakamura, Lisa (2002), *Cybertypes: Race, Ethnicity, and Identity on the Internet*, London: Routledge.

Plant, Sadie (1995), 'The Future Looms: Weaving Women and Cybernetics', in *Body and Society* 1.

(1996/2000), 'On the Matrix: Cyberfeminist Simulations', in *The Gendered Cyborg: A Reader*, ed. Fiona Hovenden et al., London: Routledge.

(1997), *Zeros and Ones: Digital Women and the New Technoculture*, London: Fourth Estate.

Rasmussen, Bente and Tove Håpnes (1991), 'Excluding Women from the Technology of the Future? A Case Study of the Culture of Computer Science', in *Futures* 23.10.

Ross, Andrew (1990), 'Hacking Away at the Counterculture', in *Postmodern Culture* 1:1.

(1991), *Strange Weather: Culture, Science and Technology in the Age of Limits*, London: Verso.

Springer, Claudia (2005), 'Playing It Cool in *The Matrix*', in *The Matrix Trilogy: Cyberpunk Reloaded*, ed. Stacy Gillis, London: Wallflower.

Stone, Roseanne Allucquère (1995), *The War of Desire and Technology at the Close of the Mechanical Age*, Cambridge, MA: MIT Press.

Turkle, Sherry (1996), *Life on the Screen: Identity in the Age of the Internet*, London: Weidenfeld and Nicolson.

Wolmark, Jenny (1999), *Cybersexualities: A Reader in Feminist Theory, Cyborgs and Cyberspace*, Edinburgh: Edinburgh University Press.

Postscript: flaming feminism?

Susan Gubar

The chapters contained in this volume ask us to consider decades of published scholarship that has analysed the inequities set in place by male monopolies over Western culture, excavated the diverse aesthetic achievements of literary women and linked gender biases to a host of racial, sexual, ethnic and national ideologies of subjugation. Given the weight and reach of this extensive enquiry, is it time to devise a new ceremony appropriate to the novel situation we find ourselves in? For surely an appreciation of women's centrality in literature and in critical responses to literature has gained ground among all but the most antediluvian or recondite of cultural historians. Taking a cue from Virginia Woolf's *Three Guineas*, finely elucidated in these pages by Jane Goldman, let us consider the ritual of destroying a phrase that just might have become obsolete, the words 'feminist literary criticism'. Does the rubric have any meaning or future usefulness now that women writers participate so actively in the literary marketplace as well as the scholarly marketplace of ideas that we call the humanities? Since literary critics with every conceivable methodological approach and in every conceivable area of study employ gender as a category of analysis, should we type the phrase 'feminist literary criticism' in a large font, print it out, and then solemnly apply a match, while exulting at how quickly it burns? What a light dances over the world of letters now populated by literary men and women, academic women and men working together for the same causes!

The chapters of *A History of Feminist Literary Criticism* prove not only how much feminist literary historians and theorists have achieved over the past five or so decades but also how long their lineage is. To begin with, Carolyn Dinshaw, Helen Wilcox and Susan Manly consider medieval, Renaissance, seventeenth- and eighteenth-century literary history by describing the harmful effects of misogynist representations of women in societies where 'there was keen awareness of the masculine domination of textual tradition', as Carolyn Dinshaw puts it. Yet struggling within and against such images, Helen Wilcox shows, imaginative women writers even in the earlier periods of literary history often functioned 'as feminist critics themselves in their discourses on the nature of their work and of women's authorship in general'. Indeed, according to Susan Manly, it was by recognising 'the power of textual representations of women' that Mary Wollstonecraft managed to target the prominent aesthetic and educational theorists of her own day and thereby become the founding figure in feminist literary criticism. Her equally influential successors, Virginia Woolf and Simone de Beauvoir, continued to emphasise a panoply of material impediments to the full flowering of women's creativity, as Jane Goldman explains about *A Room of One's Own*. Woolf and Beauvoir also continued to stress the harmful effects of prevailing mythologies that, as Elizabeth Fallaize points out about *The Second Sex*, identify women with the body and with nature in such a manner that 'men are able to maintain themselves in the master/subject position'.

If Part I of *A History of Feminist Literary Criticism* explains why the term 'feminist literary criticism' had to come into being, Part II illuminates how its practitioners grappled with many complexly related tasks. Mary Eagleton and Helen Carr describe early efforts to examine male-authored images of women that contributed to female alterity or otherness, and at the same time they map the subsequent turn towards re-evaluating female authors' achievements in fiction and poetry, which had previously been deemed minor and thus relegated to the margins of the canon or neglected altogether. Just as Linda Anderson describes the challenges personal and autobiographical feminist criticism pose to normative academic discourse, Arlene R. Keizer surveys the critical and theoretical contestations of African American feminists from The Combahee River Collective to bell hooks and Toni Morrison, who also profoundly affected the rise of so-called whiteness studies. The contributions of lesbian scholars, Caroline Gonda demonstrates, began early and outside traditional academic discourse with such pioneers as Jeannette H. Foster and Barbara Grier and poets like Judy Grahn, although massive anthologies of lesbian literature and meta-critical surveys of the field of lesbian studies quickly proliferated. From Stephen Heath and Paul Smith to Peter Murphy, Calvin Thomas explains, men in criticism have made important contributions to feminism, especially when they helped to illuminate the social construction of masculinity in work that led to the emergence of masculinity studies and queer theory.

With the term 'feminist literary criticism' ramifying in so many different directions, does the incursion of poststructuralism – explored in the last part of *A History of Feminist Literary Criticism* – definitely prove that such an umbrella term has become obsolete, that it should be torched, the air cleared? That women and men are working together for the same cause is a postulate informing Claire Colebrook's chapter on such theorists as Jacques Derrida, Michel Foucault and Luce Irigaray. For she believes that the poststructuralists' repudiation of 'the philosophical ideal of pure truth or presence' laid the groundwork not only for deepening the understanding of the socially and discursively constructed performance of gender, but also for comprehending the dynamics of gender performativity through literary representations. Analyses of sexual difference and the sexed body, which, as Madelon Sprengnether shows, owe much to the multivalent meditations of Sigmund Freud, surfaced most lyrically in the so-called French feminism of Hélène Cixous, Luce Irigaray and Julia Kristeva. Their highly metaphorical and densely philosophical texts have been 'marketed in English as representative of a feminism distinctly French'; however, Judith Still shows why each of these writers has to be understood as quite distinctive in her approach to sexual as well as maternal difference and to the relationship between writing and the body.

In the concluding chapters of this volume, readers can trace the multiplication of a plurality of feminist literary criticisms. The promotion of French and poststructuralist feminism began before the rise of postcolonial studies, but surely contributed to it, as did the speculations of African American theorists on the black diaspora. Chris Weedon explains that Western feminist thinking 'runs the risk of masking the very real differences between First and Third World geographical locations'. Yet in a host of disciplines – she lists 'literary studies, cultural studies, history, development studies, anthropology and social sciences' – globalisation focuses the attention of feminists on the ongoing mechanisms of imperial domination at work in the world today. Subjects in all of these locations have also been 'queered' by scholars and activists who have populated women's studies, lesbian studies and the newly emerged field of queer theory. According to Heather Love, feminism 'deeply influenced the methodology and commitments of queer scholarship', as criticism about gender and sex began to be complemented by scholarship attentive to multiple sexualities. Finally, Stacy Gillis traces why and how cyberfeminists have begun to deal with 'the technologised body', increasingly embodied in new and varied ways.

With so much dispersal, will the centre hold? More to the point, *should* the label 'feminist literary criticism' continue to hold such disparate intellectual endeavours and political allegiances together? In *Three Guineas*, Woolf claimed to have 'cremated the corpse' of the word 'feminism' when it became 'an old word, a vicious and corrupt word that has done much harm in its day and is now obsolete' (Woolf, 1938/1966: 101). She meant, I suspect, that in a world of sexual equality women would no longer have to insist on defending their rights or decrying their wrongs, but could instead join with men in dedicating their combined efforts to combating those forces of tyranny and injustice so threatening to the wellbeing of humanity. Yet, after turning some twenty pages, the reader of *Three Guineas* will find Woolf ruefully returning to her ambition 'to burn a certain corrupt word', here admitting that her 'boast it seems had an element of brag in it' (1938/1966: 120). The same could be said, I believe, for those who might speculate that 'feminist literary criticism' has accomplished what needed to be done, that it can now be incinerated as so much outmoded debris.

Each methodological stage of feminist literary criticism enumerated by the authors in this volume will be wanted by scholars seeking to clarify aspects of literary history still in need of exploration. Images of women harmful to the health and welfare of both women and men continue to proliferate, of course, but we have also not fully understood what the terms 'woman' and 'man' mean in a host of representational contexts in the past. Many women writers have been recovered, yet much work is needed to bring to light more lost poets and novelists, as well as female playwrights, essayists, biographers, autobiographers, diarists, travel- and science-writers and women shaping genres and media in popular culture. As ethnicity studies, along with postcolonialism, increasingly inflect feminist inquiry, many Asian, Hispanic, Caribbean, African and Eastern European literary women will begin to be excavated and interpreted not only in terms of their linguistic and national traditions but also in terms of international and comparative influences. Just as important, feminists were at the critical vanguard in the development of poststructuralism, African American studies, queer theory, postcolonial and cultural and technology studies; however, the feminists positioned in all these areas, as well as their successors, need to sustain their work at making the methodologies of these fields sensitive to and nuanced about the problems and possibilities that women face.

A perusal of the pages of this volume proves that certain scholars and thinkers made particularly valuable and visible contributions to the evolution of feminist approaches to representation and creativity. The naming of prominent academic stars always leaves certain deserving people out or overvalues some over and against others; however, I suspect that many readers would agree that in the first stages of critique and recovery Adrienne Rich, Alice Walker, Elaine Showalter and Gloria Anzaldúa played vanguard roles; that in the second stage of ramification Luce Irigaray,

Gayatri Spivak and Eve Sedgwick took on celebrity status; and that the prominence of poststructuralism in feminism is largely owing to the writings of Judith Butler. To these names, many would add the names of women particularly significant for readers in the United Kingdom: Angela Carter, Germaine Greer and Juliet Mitchell, for example. But none of these extraordinary thinkers on either side of the Atlantic could have written without numerous others labouring at their multiple tasks. The prominence and intellectual currency of these writers inside the academy prove that within institutions of higher education feminism has managed to ignite a major transformation of departments and programmes, courses and conferences and conversations throughout the humanities.

Yet just as Woolf knew that the word 'feminism' had not, alas, become antiquated in her lifetime, I believe that it – and its critical offshoots – have not become obsolete in ours, for the gains inside the academy have not been matched by comparable changes outside it. A few salient statistics may be useful to explain the basis for my view. In the United States, a rape occurs every six minutes. Of women in Columbia, 44% have experienced abuse by a spouse or a partner. One in three women in Portugal and Germany has had to cope with domestic violence. In the Bahamas, the ratio of women to men (aged fifteen to twenty-four) who contract HIV is seven to one. In Afghanistan, one in fifteen mothers dies during pregnancy and birth. The national age of consent for sexual activity in Japan is thirteen. In Guatemala and Argentina, women receive 59% of what men are paid for the same work. As of 2005, women in the United Kingdom in full-time employment earned 79% of that earned by men, and ethnic minority women had an employment rate of 42%. In Brazil, 9% of parliamentarians are women. Homosexuality is punishable by death in Yemen, the United Arab Emirates, Saudi Arabia, Iran, Sudan and Mauritania. In Panama, the ratio of women to men receiving higher education is one to seven. To educators especially, the fact that about two-thirds of the world's illiterate are women remains distressing.[1]

Like feminists in other contexts, feminist literary critics know that what Woolf called the 'tyranny of the patriarchal state' has not withered away in the many native lands we currently inhabit, and we therefore need to continue to use our words to set fire to the old hypocrisies. During a period of perpetual warfare that encourages attitudes that feminists often contest and that feels very much like a backlash, it is appropriate – for those of us who care about the incandescent and pacific artistry of literature – to look back and summarise what was achieved yesterday, in part so as to find ways of sustaining our blazing up tomorrow. I hope that the chapters in *A History of Feminist Literary Criticism* will promote renewed efforts to further the future intellectual history of feminism, as new generations of thinkers address the burning issues that still need to be broached. Just as Virginia Woolf did, feminists of the future might seek to infuse aesthetic matters (usually deemed marginal to major historical perplexities and possibilities) with a hard gem-like flame more purposeful and political than the one Walter Pater called for (Pater, 1873/1980: 189). We need to apply rags, petrol and matches not to feminism or feminist criticism but to enduring inequities, for we have not yet done with the pedagogic light feminists and feminist critics shed inside and outside the academy.

NOTE

1. These statistics are quoted from the web sites of the United Nations and various health organisations.

BIBLIOGRAPHY

Pater, Walter (1873/1980), *The Renaissance: Studies in Art and Poetry*, Berkeley: University of California Press.
Woolf, Virginia (1938/1966), *Three Guineas*, New York: Harcourt.

Index

Note: book and article titles are in italics; * indicates a character treated as a subject.

CPSIA information can be obtained at www.ICGtesting.com
Printed in the USA
LVOW132343091012

302206LV00005B/1/P